T0184276

Lecture Notes in Computer Science 14458

Founding Editors

Gerhard Goos
Juris Hartmanis

The series Lecture Notes in Computer Science (LNCS), including its subseries Lecture Notes in Artificial Intelligence (LNAI) and Lecture Notes in Bioinformatics (LNBI), has established itself as a medium for the publication of new developments in computer science and information technology research, teaching, and education.

LNCS enjoys close cooperation with the computer science R & D community, the series counts many renowned academics among its volume editors and paper authors, and collaborates with prestigious societies. Its mission is to serve this international community by providing an invaluable service, mainly focused on the publication of conference and workshop proceedings and postproceedings. LNCS commenced publication in 1973.

Dion H. Goh · Shu-Jiun Chen ·
Suppawong Tuarob
Editors

Leveraging Generative Intelligence in Digital Libraries: Towards Human-Machine Collaboration

25th International Conference on Asia-Pacific Digital Libraries, ICADL 2023
Taipei, Taiwan, December 4–7, 2023
Proceedings, Part II

 Springer

Editors
Dion H. Goh ⓘ
Nanyang Technological University
Singapore, Singapore

Shu-Jiun Chen ⓘ
Academia Sinica
Taipei, Taiwan

Suppawong Tuarob ⓘ
Mahidol University
Tambon Salaya, Amphoe Phutthamonthon,
Thailand

ISSN 0302-9743   ISSN 1611-3349 (electronic)
Lecture Notes in Computer Science
ISBN 978-981-99-8087-1   ISBN 978-981-99-8088-8 (eBook)
https://doi.org/10.1007/978-981-99-8088-8

Preface

Welcome to the proceedings of the of the 25th International Conference on Asia-Pacific Digital Libraries (ICADL 2023; https://icadl.net/icadl2023/). Since its inception in 1998 in Hong Kong, the ICADL series has become one of the major digital libraries conferences, along with the Joint Conference on Digital Libraries (JCDL) and the Theory and Practice of Digital Libraries (TPDL) conferences, where researchers and practitioners meet, network, and share knowledge and best practices.

This year's edition of the conference was held in Taipei, Taiwan from December 4 to December 7, 2023. As more countries around the world emerge from the COVID-19 pandemic, the conference was organized as an in-person event, but also featured online presentations for participants who were not able to travel to Taipei. ICADL 2023 was co-located with the 11th Asia-Pacific Conference on Library Information Education and Practice (A-LIEP 2023; https://a-liep.org/) as well as the annual meeting of the Asia-Pacific chapter of iSchools (AP iSchools; https://ischools.org/). These events were collectively known as the "2023 International Forum on Data, Information, and Knowledge for Resilient and Trustworthy Digital Societies" (https://ifdik2023.conf.tw/site/page.aspx?pid=901&sid=1521&lang=en).

In recognition of the growth and popularity of generative artificial intelligence (GAI), the theme of ICADL 2023 was "Leveraging Generative Intelligence in Digital Libraries: Towards Human-Machine Collaboration". In a relatively short span of time, GAI applications such as ChatGPT and Midjourney have captured the public's imagination with their potential for content generation. Being repositories of knowledge, digital libraries and their stakeholders may be positively or negatively impacted by GAI. Consequently, this conference aimed to explore the role of GAI in digital libraries and welcomed papers in this regard.

In response to the conference call, 85 papers from 21 countries were submitted to ICADL 2023. The review process was double-blind. Each submission was reviewed by at least three Program Committee (PC) members. Based on the reviews and recommendation from the PC, 15 full papers, 17 short papers, 2 practice papers and 12 poster papers were selected for inclusion in the proceedings. These papers covered a diverse range of topics, reflecting the interdisciplinary nature of the field of digital libraries. These topics include information retrieval, knowledge extraction and discovery, cultural and scholarly data, information seeking and use, digital archives and data management, design and evaluation of information environments, and applications of GAI in digital libraries.

We would like to thank all those who contributed to ICADL 2023. This conference would not have been possible without the effort and teamwork of many individuals across the globe. We thank the members of the Program Committee for their time, effort and expertise in reviewing the submissions. The Conference Chair, Hao-Ren Ke, worked tirelessly to bring this conference to fruition. Thanks also to the Publicity Chairs, Songphan Choemprayong, Adam Jatowt, Chern Li Liew, Akira Maeda, Maciej Ogrodniczuk and Sue Yeon Syn, as well as the Web Chair, Shun-Hong Sie. In addition, we are grateful to Adam Jatowt, Emi Ishita and Shigeo Sugimoto who have provided leadership and support during the planning and implementation phases of this conference.

Finally, we would like to thank all the authors, presenters, and participants of ICADL 2023. This conference is made possible by your support and contributions.

December 2023

Dion H. Goh
Shu-Jiun Chen
Suppawong Tuarob

Organization

Conference Co-chairs

Shu-Hsien Tseng   National Central Library, Taiwan
Hao-Ren Ke   National Taiwan Normal University, Taiwan

Program Committee Co-chairs

Dion H. Goh   Nanyang Technological University, Singapore
Shu-Jiun Chen   Academia Sinica, Taiwan
Suppawong Tuarob   Mahidol University, Thailand

Publicity Co-chairs

Songphan Choemprayong   Chulalongkorn University, Thailand
Adam Jatowt   University of Innsbruck, Austria
Chern Li Liew   Victoria University of Wellington, New Zealand
Akira Maeda   Ritsumeikan University, Japan
Maciej Ogrodniczuk   Institute of Computer Science, Polish Academy of Sciences, Poland
Sue Yeon Syn   Catholic University of America, USA

Web Chair

Shun-Hong Sie   National Taiwan Normal University, Taiwan

Program Committee

Trond Aalberg   Norwegian University of Science and Technology, Norway
Biligsaikhan Batjargal   Ritsumeikan University, Japan
Chih-Ming Chen   National Chengchi University, Taiwan
Kun-Hung Cheng   National Chung Hsing University, Taiwan
Songphan Choemprayong   Chulalongkorn University, Thailand

Chiranthi Wijesundara   University of Colombo, Sri Lanka
Dan Wu   Wuhan University, China
Zhiwu Xie   University of California, Riverside, USA
Marcia Zeng   Kent State University, USA
Maja Žumer   University of Ljubljana, Slovenia

Additional Reviewers

Banerjee, Bipasha   Li, Da
Bernard, Guillaume   Mibayashi, Ryota
Day, Min-Yuh   Mohd Pozi, Muhammad Syafiq
Husnain, Mujtaba   Wang, Yuanyuan
Iqbal Kajla, Nadeem   Wu, Qian
Kahu, Sampanna

Contents – Part II

Scholarly Information Processing

Knowledge Extraction

Contents – Part I

Social Media Analytics

Information Retrieval

Information Seeking and Use

Design and Evaluation

Development of the Polyglot Asian Medicine Knowledge Graph System

Christopher S. G. Khoo[1]([✉]), Michael Stanley-Baker[1], Faizah Binte Zakaria[2], Jinju Chen[3], Shaun Q. R. Ang[1], and Bo Huang[1]

[1] Nanyang Technological University, Singapore, Singapore
chriskhoo@pmail.ntu.edu.sg, msb@ntu.edu.sg, {sang034,
BHUANG014}@e.ntu.edu.sg
[2] National University of Singapore, Singapore, Singapore
fzakaria@nus.edu.sg
[3] Nanjing University, Nanjing, China
dg1814001@smail.nju.edu.cn

Abstract. The Polyglot Asian Medicine system hosts a research database of Asian traditional and herbal medicines, represented as a knowledge graph and implemented in a Neo4j graph database system. The current coverage of the database is mainly traditional Chinese medicines with some Malay and Indonesian data, with plans to extend to other Southeast Asian communities. The knowledge graph currently links the medicine names in the original and English languages, to alternate names and scientific names, to plant/animal parts they are made from, to literary and historical sources they were mentioned in, to geographic areas they were associated with, and to external database records. A novel graph visualization interface supports user searching, browsing and visual analysis. This is an example of representing a digital humanities research dataset as a knowledge graph for reference and research purposes. The paper describes how the knowledge graph was derived based on a dataset comprising over 25 Microsoft Excel spreadsheets, and how the spreadsheet data were processed and mapped to the graph database using upload scripts in the Neo4j Cypher graph query language. The advantages of using a knowledge graph system to support user browsing and analysis using a graph visualization interface are illustrated. The paper describes issues encountered, solutions adopted, and lessons learned that can be applied to other digital humanities data.

Keywords: Knowledge Graph · Graph Database · Graph Visualization · Traditional Chinese Medicine · Herbal Medicine · Digital Humanities

1 Introduction

The Polyglot Asian Medicine knowledge graph system (accessible at https://kgraph.sg/polyglot/) hosts a research database of Asian traditional and herbal medicines, represented as a knowledge graph and implemented in a Neo4j graph database management system. A graph visualization interface supports user searching, browsing and visual

D. H. Goh et al. (Eds.): ICADL 2023, LNCS 14458, pp. 3–11, 2023.
https://doi.org/10.1007/978-981-99-8088-8_1

analysis. The coverage of the knowledge graph currently focuses on traditional Chinese medicines, with some Malay, Bau (Sarawak), and Abui (Indonesian ethnic group) data. There are, however, plans to expand the knowledge graph to more Southeast Asian countries and ethnic communities through collaborations with researchers in the region. The knowledge graph currently links medicine names in the original and English languages to alternate names and scientific names, to plant/animal parts they are made from, to literary and historical sources they were mentioned in, to geographic areas they were associated with, to recorded medical uses, and to external database records with more information on them. There are plans to link the medicines to pharmacological information later.

This is an example of applying knowledge graph technologies to a digital humanities research dataset, with potential extension to pharmacological data. This paper describes how the knowledge graph was derived from the researchers' dataset comprising over 25 Microsoft Excel spreadsheets (later converted to Google Sheets), and how the spreadsheet data were mapped to the knowledge graph in the graph database, using upload scripts in the Neo4j Cypher graph query language. We discuss our solutions to issues encountered, and lessons learned that can be applied to other digital humanities datasets. We also show how the knowledge graph can be visualized for browsing and visual analysis, as well as presented in a text interface.

There are a few knowledge graph systems that have been implemented for digital humanities (especially digital heritage) data. The focus of these projects was often on the ontology design and the automatic extraction of information from text to populate the ontology. Examples are the *biografiasampo.fi* knowledge graph of 13,000 historical persons in Finland [1], the Canton Revolutionary History Knowledge Graph representing historical information of the Canton Revolution in China [2], the Universal Type Digital Humanities Research Platform on Chinese Ancient Books in the National Central Library of Taiwan, and the Digital Humanities Research Platform for Biographies of Malaysian Personalities.

2 Knowledge Graph Technologies Used

Knowledge graph is often equated with ontology, semantic network, semantic web, linked data and Resource Description Framework (RDF), though each term emphasizes different aspects of knowledge representation. Ehrlinger and Wöß [3] and Bergman [4] have provided extensive surveys of knowledge graph definitions. However, we propose an alternative definition that distinguishes *knowledge graph* from *ontology* and emphasizes its support for human information seeking and information use. We propose that the focus of a knowledge graph is less on logical reasoning, but more on connecting things in a graph (network) representation. The growth of graph databases has stimulated interest in these aspects of knowledge graphs. We informally characterize a knowledge graph as a network of nodes connected by directed links, where nodes represent resources (ideas, concepts and entities) and links represent semantic relations between them. The nodes are assigned meaning by labeling them with classes from a taxonomy, and assigning them properties. The links are also labeled with relationship types and may be assigned properties as well.

For our knowledge graph implementation, we adopted the Neo4j graph database management system[1]—a popular graph database software based on the *labeled property graph* model. *Labeled property graph* can be viewed as a light-weight alternative to RDF/OWL2.[2] Barrasa [5] and Feeney [6] have compared the two models. A major difference is that in a labeled property graph, the links (relations) can be assigned properties. In an RDF/OWL2 ontology, links with properties have to be represented as an intermediate node linked to the source and target nodes. A labeled property graph, as implemented in a Neo4j database, is schema-free (or schema-less) as the database does not store a schema specifying mandatory properties for each node type as well as a datatype for each property. Nor does it store domain-range and cardinality restrictions[3] commonly found in RDF/OWL2 ontologies. Thus, a node or link can have any property (i.e., attribute-value pair). This makes it easier to represent digital humanities datasets that include data from multiple sources and in multiple languages, stored in many spreadsheets, and are continually expanded with new types of data. It makes it possible for the knowledge graph to evolve with changing conceptualizations and ideas for analysis and application. However, some structure and style guide need to be imposed on the data, outside of the graph database system.

The Polyglot Asian Medicine knowledge graph system has the following system architecture:

1. *a Neo4j graph database* storing the knowledge graph, and performing search and analytic operations on it;
2. *a Web API* serving as a middleware system, performing additional data processing and mediating the interaction between the graph database and the Web interface;
3. *a Web interface* with a graph (network) visualization function.

The primary data storage is Google Sheets, which are used for data entry. Google Sheet has a *publish-to-csv* function that dynamically converts a spreadsheet to a CSV file at a specified URL. Upload scripts (in Neo4j's Cypher graph query language) can then be submitted to the Neo4j database to retrieve the CSV file (from the specified URL) to process and map to the knowledge graph. The graph database is thus used only for searching and analysis, and not for data entry.

3   Designing the Knowledge Graph

The Polyglot Asian Medicine data were culled from twenty-six dictionaries and botanical surveys. Malay plant data were manually transcribed into spreadsheets, whereas Chinese dictionary data were harvested (with permission) from the Zhongyi Shijia (中醫世家) website in 2015 [7]. Textual provenance data (i.e., books and documents where the medicine name first appeared in the Chinese tradition) was augmented through bibliographic research. Botanical identifications of the plants were reviewed and validated by

---

[1] https://neo4j.com/.

[2] https://www.w3.org/TR/rdf11-concepts/; https://www.w3.org/TR/owl2-primer/.

[3] However, Neo4j recently introduced *node property existence constraints* in the enterprise version of the software (see https://neo4j.com/docs/cypher-manual/current/constraints/), which allows the developer to specify mandatory node properties.

the Medicinal Plant Names Services (MPNS) department of Kew Gardens. The botanical names were augmented with historical synonyms.

The dataset was originally stored in over 25 Microsoft Excel spreadsheets. We considered converting the spreadsheets to a relational database to assure the referential integrity of the links (i.e., check that the links refer to existing nodes) and also to impose some property constraints. As some of the spreadsheets have complex structures, conversion to a relational database in third normal form would necessitate decomposing each spreadsheet into multiple tables, each table representing entities of a particular type. We decided that this would disrupt the researchers' mental model of the dataset, and make data entry more difficult and error-prone (even with the use of data views and data-entry forms). We have found that digital humanities researchers are comfortable with spreadsheets, and it is more natural to enter and store related information in the same spreadsheet. So, a significant decision was made to work with the researchers' spreadsheets, with minor adjustments. The spreadsheets were converted to Google Sheets to support collaborative data entry as well as direct upload to the graph database on Neo4j's AuraDB cloud database service. This section describes the issues encountered with processing the data and mapping them to nodes and links in the graph database.

Identifying Entities and Entity Types. The first step in designing a knowledge graph is to decide on the entity types (or classes) and entity instances to represent as nodes in the graph. Some entity types are obvious, for example *drug* (represented by the drug name) and geographic *region*. However, as the data includes historical information, the same drug may have different names in different historical periods and in different regions. These alternative drug names may be associated with different properties, for example different geographic regions and different recorded sources (provenance). Thus, it was decided to represent the *Main_Drug* and *Alternate_Drug_Name* as different nodes and different node types. This is useful for linking a drug used in one community and language, with a similar drug found in another community/language.

Some drug node properties have associated properties themselves. For example, a drug's provenance (ancient book or manuscript that recorded the drug) will have attributes such as *author, year* (or year range) of authorship, *libraries/archives* holding it, etc. The *author* property may have associated properties of *name, year range*, etc. Thus, the provenance source and its author are represented as separate nodes.

A second reason for representing a property as a separate node is if it can function as a useful intermediate node for linking other entities. Thus, *scientific names* are represented as separate nodes so they can serve to link different drug names (possibly from different communities/languages) that are associated with the same scientific name.

Thus, the reason for representing a particular property as a node may be structural (e.g., it has associated properties), conceptual (conforming to the conceptualization of the researcher), or pragmatic (for the purpose of browsing and exploring links, and for analyzing relationship paths).

Determining Link Structure in a Spreadsheet. Table 1 lists, as example, some of column headers of the *Main Drug* spreadsheet, with presumed entity types highlighted in bold print, and their associate properties in light print. This illustrates that several entity types may be recorded in the same spreadsheet, with their associated properties. There is usually an implied link from the first entity type (*Main_Drug*) to the other seven entity types. The data may have a hierarchical structure—for example, *Provenance* has a link to *Author* (i.e., *Provenance_Author*). Thus, each row in the spreadsheet represents a small sub-graph of the knowledge graph.

Table 2 shows sample data from the *Main Drug* spreadsheet, focusing on the *Main_Drug* and links to four entity types. The upload script that maps the spreadsheet data to the knowledge graph (in the graph database) specifies a link type for each of the four entity types.

An interesting feature in the spreadsheet is *Data_Source* (in italics), which indicates the data source for all the data in the particular row of the spreadsheet. In our implementation, the *Data_Source* property is stored as a link property, for all the links derived from the row of data.

Another feature is that the relation between a *Main_Drug* and the other entity types is not 1:1 but many:many. Table 2 shows that a *Main Drug* may occupy a few rows with different *Data_Sources* and multiple instances of the other four entity types. For example, the third drug in Table 2 棉花壳 is associated with two *Scientific Names* (i.e., two *scientific_name* links), taken from the same *Data Source* (stored as link property). For data entry convenience, the researcher may even enter multiple entity instances in the same spreadsheet cell with a punctuation separator. For example, in Table 2 row 1, two regions are specified: "Liaoning;Hebei". In row 3, two plant parts are specified: "Root;Rhizome". In these cases, a string processing function (*split*) is used to separate the multiple entity instances to create separate nodes for them.

A related issue is that two *Data_Sources* may provide the same *Scientific Name* for a *Main Drug* (not illustrated in Table 2). In this case, only one *scientific_name* link is created, but its *Data_Source* property will have multiple values (either specified in a list structure or concatenated into a string with a punctuation separator).

Table 1. Column headers in the Main Drug spreadsheet, indicating entity types (in bold print) and associated properties (in light print)

Main_Drug_ID, Main_Drug_Name
Data_Source_ID [relation property]
Scientific_Name_ID, Scientific_Name
Organism_Type
Provenance_ID, Provenance_Title, Provenance_Dates, **Provenance_Author**
Pharmaceutical_Name
Common_English_Names
Plant_Parts_Chinese, Plant_Parts_English
Regions_Chinese, Regions_English

When an entity (e.g., Scientific_Name *Gossypium arboreum L.*) appears multiple times in the spreadsheet, its properties need be listed only once. This is because each entity is represented by a unique node in the knowledge graph. Thus, the spreadsheet

Table 2. Sample spreadsheet data for Main Drug and linked entities

Main_ Drug	Data_ Source	Scientific_ Name	Provenance	Plant_ Parts	Regions
扁豆衣	中华本草	Lablab purpureus subsp. purpureus	安徽药材		Liaoning; Hebei
扁豆衣	中药大辞典		安徽药材	Seed Coat	
银线草根	中药大辞典		安徽药材	Root; Rhizome	
棉花壳	中华本草	**Gossypium arboreum L.**	百草镜		Gansu; Xinjiang
棉花壳	中华本草	**Gossypium herbaceum L.**	百草镜		Gansu; Xinjiang
铁棒锤茎叶	中药大辞典	Aconitum pendulum N.Busch	北方常用中草药手册	Stem Leaf	
铁棒锤茎叶	中华本草	Aconitum flavum Hand.-Mazz.	北方常用中草药手册		South Shaanxi; South Gansu
瓦楞子	中华本草	Sapharca inflata (Reeve)	本草备要		Coast of China; Liaoning
瓦楞子	中华本草	Scapharca subcrenata (Lischke)	本草备要		Coast of China; Liaoning
瓦楞子	中药大辞典		本草备要		Zhejiang; Jiangsu

contains many blank cells for properties of entities that appear on multiple rows, and the upload script needs to check that a property value cell is not blank (i.e., null) before adding the property to the node. A related issue is when a property is listed multiple times (in multiple rows) for an entity. Then it has to be determined whether the property is multi-valued (to be stored in a list) or single-valued (implying that only the first or last value need be retained), so that the upload script can be written to handle it appropriately. In the case of multi-valued properties, the script has to check that a property value does not already exist in the node or link, before adding the property value.

Spreadsheet Errors to Lookout for. As the data entry is not done by data specialists, and the data may be contributed by multiple persons or aggregated from multiple sources, various unexpected errors may be present in the spreadsheets:

- Cell values with leading or trailing blanks: a *trim* function should always be applied to remove spaces from the beginning and end of each value;
- Cells that look blank but contain 1 or more spaces, which may lead the database system to create node properties (especially the ID property) with value " " or even "" (empty string): we issue a Cypher command to delete all "blank" nodes of various types after data upload;

- Cells with multiple values ending with the separator (e.g., *"value1;value2;"*): the semicolon separator at the end will cause the script to assume there is an empty string after the semicolon after "splitting", resulting in a blank node being created.

4   Interface Design and Knowledge Graph Visualization

A Web interface was developed to take advantage of the network structure of the knowledge graph. Figure 1 shows the interface displaying one *Main_Drug* node with related entity nodes (accessible at: https://kgraph.sg/polyglot/?drug=CDN00011). The main center panel displays the properties of the *Main_Drug*, with related (linked) entity nodes displayed in tabbed panels on the right. In Fig. 1, a list of *Alternate_Drug_Names* for the Main_Drug are shown on the right panel.

A graph visualization of the *Main_Drug* node and linked nodes are shown on the graph display canvas. Users can double-click or right-click on a node to display neighbor nodes (i.e., linked nodes), thereby browsing the knowledge graph by traversing links. On the tabbed panels on the right, users can navigate in the same way by clicking on the "Focus on this in main panel" button, which will display the entity on the main center panel, with linked nodes on the right tabbed panels.

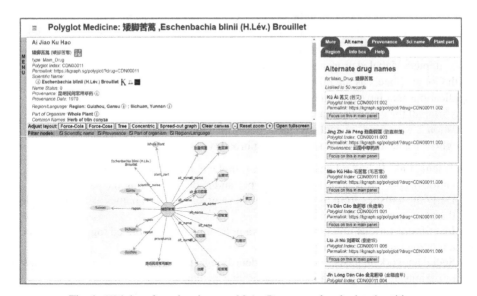

Fig. 1. Web interface showing one *Main_Drug* record and related entities

An advantage of the graph visualization is its capability to show how two or more entities of interest are related. Figure 2 shows a graph that is derived from the graph of Fig. 1 by double-clicking on the scientific name. It shows two *Main_Drug* nodes with the same scientific name, as well as two *Alternate_Drug_Names* (highlighted in dark pink) with different *Provenance* sources. This is one kind of visual analysis: eye-balling a graph visualization to gain insights on relationships and relation structure.

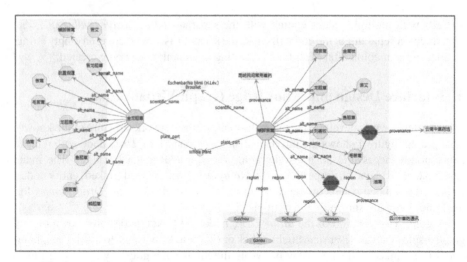

Fig. 2. Relations between two *Main_Drug* nodes having the same *Scientific_Name*

5 Conclusion

We have shared lessons learned in applying knowledge graph technologies to a digital humanities research dataset, to develop a Web application to support browsing, reference and research. We have found that the flexibility of the knowledge graph technologies adopted—labeled property graph, graph database and graph visualization—together with Google Sheets as the primary data store, can meet the needs of digital humanities applications that have evolving datasets and changing conceptualization.

After all the effort to create a "full-stack" knowledge graph application, an obvious question is what kinds of analysis can be performed on the knowledge graph to gain new insights? We have identified the following broad types of analysis:

1. Tracing links to find related nodes, for example: tracing paths between two drugs (or entities), specifying allowed relation types and node types along the path;
2. Deriving statistics from tracing links, for example: scientific names associated with the most number of drugs;
3. Identifying various link patterns, for example: three entities linked together to form a relation triangle (triadic closure);
4. Social network analysis, for example: identifying sub-clusters/sub-networks of drugs or regions, linked by certain relations or intermediate nodes.

References

1. Hyvönen, E., Rantala, H.: Knowledge-based relation discovery in cultural heritage knowledge graphs. In: Digital Humanities in Nordic Countries Proceedings of the Digital Humanities in the Nordic Countries 4th Conference. CEUR-WS.org (2019)
2. Wu, J., Jiang, Y., Chen, X., Guo, L., Wei, X., Yang, X.: "The Canton Canon" Digital Library based on knowledge graph. In: 10th International Conference on Educational and Information Technology (ICEIT), pp. 171–179. IEEE (2021)

3. Ehrlinger, L., Wöß, W.: Towards a definition of knowledge graphs. In: SEMANTICS 2016: Posters and Demos Track, Leipzig, Germany, 13–14 September 2016 (2016)
4. Bergman, M.K.: A common sense view of knowledge graphs [blog post]. Adaptive Information, Adaptive Innovation, Adaptive Infrastructure Blog, 1 July 2019
5. Barrasa, J.: RDF triple stores vs. labeled property graphs: What's the difference? [Blog post]. Neo4j blog, 18 August 2017
6. Feeney, K.: Graph fundamentals—Part 2: Labelled property graphs [blog post]. Medium.com, 26 September 2019
7. 王刚 [Wang Gang]. 中医世家 [Zhongyi shijia] (2006). https://www.zysj.com.cn/

Understanding iPusnas User Experience Among Students, Workers, and Housewives

Aditia[1], Rahmi[2(✉)] ⓘ, and Harry Susianto[3]

[1] Undergraduate Program in Library Science, Faculty of Humanities, Universitas Indonesia, Depok 16424, Indonesia

[2] Department of Library and Information Science, Faculty of Humanities, Universitas Indonesia, Depok 16424, Indonesia
rahmi.ami@ui.ac.id

[3] Faculty of Psychology, Universitas Indonesia, Depok, Indonesia

Abstract. iPusnas, a mobile library application owned by the National Library of Indonesia, allows users to borrow digital books accessible through mobile devices freely. However, the application has received unfavorable reviews on the digital marketplace. This research examines iPusnas' user experience by assessing factors such as effectiveness, efficiency, satisfaction, and subjective user experience. The study targets end-users composed of students, workers, and housewives. A mixed-method strategy is used in this study, incorporating usability testing, the System Usability Scale (SUS), and the User Experience Questionnaire (UEQ) as data-gathering techniques. Findings suggest a minor yet significant variation in effectiveness. There are no considerable differences across groups regarding efficiency and satisfaction. However, students demonstrated low satisfaction levels, while workers and housewives rated their satisfaction as adequate. The UEQ data shows that the app scores below average in the Attractiveness and Efficiency categories, while its Perspicuity score is poor. The study concludes by discussing these findings' implications, suggestions, and potential limitations.

Keywords: Digital Library · User Experience · Mobile Library Application · Usability Testing · System Usability Scale (SUS) · User Experience Questionnaire (UEQ) · End-user Group

1 Background

According to the Central Statistics Agency of Indonesia [1], approximately two-thirds of the Indonesian population, or around 180 million individuals, owned mobile phones, and 82%, or 224 million individuals, were internet users by 2021. The National Library of Indonesia's (Perpusnas) digital library app, iPusnas, was developed to cater to the reading and literacy requirements of these internet-connected mobile phone users. Users can access digital books for free, share their reading collections, and interact with other users through this application, available on Android, iOS, and computers.

D. H. Goh et al. (Eds.): ICADL 2023, LNCS 14458, pp. 12–29, 2023.
https://doi.org/10.1007/978-981-99-8088-8_2

Previous research using the Performance, Information, Economy, Control, Efficiency, and Services (PIECES) framework by Maulana [25] and the Technology Acceptance Model (TAM) by Prastiwi & Jumino [32] has assessed iPusnas' effectiveness and determined it to be both effective and satisfying. However, these studies did not specifically explore user experience on iPusnas, and their conclusions diverged from user reviews on digital app marketplaces. For instance, as of February 2023, iPusnas had been downloaded over a million times, rated by 27 thousand users, and scored 3.7 out of 5 on Google Play and 2.7 out of 5 on the App Store. These ratings suggest that the app's performance is suboptimal.

Genc-Nayebi & Abran [9] suggest that user ratings generally align with expert evaluations, implying that users' complaints are valid. User reviews have also highlighted several issues with iPusnas, including an unappealing display, login difficulties, issues downloading books, and app crashes. Moreover, book recommendations on the homepage do not always align with users' preferences, and the reader assistance feature is inconsistently available across all collections. Several factors such as user satisfaction, user interface, reliability, and user experience significantly influence the use of digital library applications, as noted by Kiran & Singh [19], Matusiak [24], Ming et al. [27], Rafique et al. [33, 34], Ye et al. [45], and Zhao et al. [48]. As such, further investigation is necessary to assess iPusnas' user experience and address these challenges.

Usability testing is a common method for evaluating an application's user experience and has been employed to examine different applications and websites. Examples include the iPekalonganKota library application [7], the University of Toronto Scarborough Library website [10], the E-Dunhuang Cultural Heritage Library website [14], and the Chongqing University digital library application [44]. However, usability testing primarily focuses on effectiveness, efficiency, and user satisfaction [16]. Therefore, to delve into more subjective elements of user experience, such as emotions, perceptions, and user preferences, additional measurements, like the User Experience Questionnaire (UEQ), are required [22, 41].

Following the approach of Febrianti & Adhy [7] and Kous et al. [20], this study concentrates on the end-user group. This approach is chosen because iPusnas is meant for all Indonesians, and every library user seeks a user-friendly, efficient, and satisfactory digital library system [31]. To adequately represent the end-user group, this study's participants consist of three main categories: students, workers, and housewives.

This research aims to evaluate and compare iPusnas users' experience, divided into students, workers, and housewives, using usability testing, System Usability Scale (SUS), and UEQ methods. The research seeks to answer: 1) What are the effectiveness, efficiency, satisfaction, and subjective user experience of iPusnas? and 2) Are there significant differences in effectiveness, efficiency, and satisfaction between the groups? This research evaluates iPusnas' effectiveness and efficiency via usability testing and user satisfaction through SUS. It also measures subjective user experience, including aspects of Attraction, Perspicuity, Dependability, Stimulation, and Novelty, using UEQ. The study further analyzes participant responses during usability testing and participant answers during interviews.

The study's findings are expected to elucidate the effectiveness, efficiency, satisfaction, and subjective experiences of iPusnas users and determine if significant differences exist among the user groups. The research also evaluates user responses during usability testing and user interviews. This paper will discuss the study's findings in various sections, beginning with a literature review, followed by methodology, results, discussion, and conclusions.

2 Literature Review

2.1 iPusnas

iPusnas is an application managed by the National Library of Indonesia, serving as both a digital library and a social platform that allows users to exchange information. The app is accessible via Android, iOS, and desktop computers. A standout feature of iPusnas is its provision of various digital books from diverse genres, which users can borrow—up to five books at a time, each for a five-day period, free of charge [17].

In addition, iPusnas hosts other features such as eReaders, ePustaka, feeds, and bookshelves. The eReader is a built-in digital book-reading tool with features including a table of contents, bookmarks, search functionality, theme and font customization options, and note-taking. ePustaka is a feature that curates specific collections from various institutions or publishers. The feed feature showcases other users' activities, fostering interaction among users. Lastly, the bookshelf feature exhibits books currently borrowed, those on a user's wish list, and those previously borrowed and returned [17].

2.2 User Experience and Usability

User experience, as defined by Hassan & Galal-Edeen [13], encompasses all user interactions with a product, starting from their initial feelings towards it, progressing to their understanding of its functionalities, and on to meet their needs, expectations, and goals in various usage scenarios. Important aspects to consider include the characteristics of the user (such as abilities, background, and age), user motivation, the product's characteristics (including hedonic and pragmatic aspects), the product's image, advertising, and comparable user experiences.

User experience is often used interchangeably with usability, and the two are frequently intertwined. Usability refers to the extent to which users can use a system, product, or service to accomplish their objectives effectively, efficiently, and satisfactorily within a specific usage context [16]. Hassan & Galal-Edeen [13] suggest that user experience can be viewed as an extension of usability, as it encompasses additional elements such as the product's aesthetic qualities, the stimulation it provides, and the user's emotional connection to the product.

2.3 Usability Testing

Usability testing is a method used to assess the user-friendliness of a design, product, or service, incorporating users as a source of data via observed interactions and interviews [12]. Such tests typically aim to gauge user ease of use, effectiveness, efficiency, accessibility, and satisfaction by having participants complete a predefined set of tasks or scenarios. During these tests, participants are often encouraged to follow a think-aloud protocol, a technique where participants verbalize their goals and thoughts as they inter-act with a product [12]. This method facilitates a better understanding for moderators and observers of participants' expectations and reactions to their experiences.

While usability testing is a common method for evaluating digital libraries, many studies involve a single, homogenous group of participants, often students. Examples include tests conducted on the University of Toronto Scarborough Library website [10], the E-Dunhuang cultural heritage library website [14], and the Chongqing University digital library application [44]. These evaluations, confined to homogenous groups, mainly reflect similar needs and interests and are less capable of exploring the needs of groups with diverse characteristics [20]. Thus, it is crucial to conduct usability tests involving various participant groups.

Kous et al. [20] performed usability tests to assess academic library websites across five distinct end-user groups: students, college students, retirees, researchers, and work-ers. The results demonstrated variations in ratings between the groups, particularly regarding effectiveness and efficiency. Febrianti & Adhy [7] also conducted a usability study evaluating the iPekalongan Kota digital library application across different user groups. The study included junior high school students, high school students, univer-sity students, workers, and housewives and discovered differences in perceptions among these groups.

2.4 User Experience Questionnaire (UEQ)

The User Experience Questionnaire (UEQ) is a tool created by Andreas Hinderks, Martin Schrepp, and Jörg Thomaschewski. This questionnaire is split into six facets: Attrac-tiveness, Perspicuity, Efficiency, Dependability, Stimulation, and Novelty. It includes 26 items, each featuring a seven-point answer scale. Research studies by Kuhar & Merčun [21] and Maricar et al. [23] have employed the UEQ to assess digital libraries. An Indonesian version of the UEQ has been adapted by Santoso et al. [36].

The adaptation process by Santoso et al. [36] involved translating the questionnaire from English to Indonesian and then back to English, with each translation handled independently by two individuals. The adapted version was then tested on 213 respon-dents to assess the user experience of the Student-Centered E-Learning Environment (SCELE). The test results displayed relatively consistent results, with Cronbach's Alpha coefficients of 0.81 for Attraction, 0.78 for Perspicuity, 0.74 for Efficiency, 0.58 for Dependability, 0.64 for Stimulation, and 0.72 for Novelty. According to Santoso et al. [36], the lower Dependability score could be attributed to the lesser importance of this feature in the user experience of the learning platform or potential issues with item interpretation on that particular scale.

2.5 System Usability Scale (SUS)

The System Usability Scale (SUS) is a standardized tool frequently used to assess a product's usability, encompassing effectiveness, efficiency, and satisfaction in its usage context, as Zarour & Alharbi [47] stated. Developed by John Brooke in 1996, the SUS questionnaire was devised as a rapid method for understanding user perceptions regarding the utility of a product or system [5]. The SUS questionnaire comprises ten items with a five-point Likert scale for responses. Sauro & Lewis [37] and Bangor et al. [2] have expanded subjective judgments and score gradations for SUS. In the realm of Library and Information Science, SUS has been used to gauge user views and usability in several digital libraries such as the Saudi Commission for Health Specialties (SCFHS) [49], Universitas Indonesia Libraries [30, 50], National Library of Turkey [15], and the digital library of Depok City [35].

Sharfina & Santoso [39] translated SUS into Indonesian, carrying out the adaptation in two stages. Initially, two translators, possessing distinct understandings of SUS, translated it from English to Indonesian. Post deliberation and consensus on the translated results, a bilingual native speaker of English and Indonesian translated the text back into English to validate the content's alignment with the original version. Experts reviewed the final translation to ensure consistency between the original and translated versions. Sharfina & Santoso [39] tested the Indonesian version of SUS on 108 respondents in evaluating SCELE, yielding consistent results with a Cronbach's Alpha coefficient value of 0.84.

3   Methodology

This study employs a hybrid methodology, which is a technique that integrates both qualitative and quantitative strategies [6]. A qualitative approach was used to conduct usability testing, while the quantitative approach involved a survey utilizing the System Usability Scale (SUS) and User Experience Questionnaire (UEQ) as tools for data collection. The fusion of usability testing and surveys enhances the reliability of the data procured [46] in evaluating the user experience with iPusnas.

The target population for this study comprises individuals who reside or work in the Jabodetabek region, selected for the ease of conducting the testing process. The study categorized participants into three groups: students, workers, and housewives, with each group having five members, summing up to 15 participants. The selection process and determination of participant numbers were based on recommendations by Febrianti & Adhy [7] and Kous et al. [20], who stressed the necessity of including end-users in the study to grasp the desires and needs intrinsic to each user demographic. Furthermore, having five individuals in each group is the minimal recommended number for usability testing, as it is believed to identify 80% of user experience issues [11, 29]. Students were included due to their need for reading materials for school assignments or general reading pursuits. Workers were selected as they often required reading materials to aid their tasks or professional roles. Lastly, housewives were chosen due to their need for reading resources for child development or enhancing knowledge of household needs like cooking.

The research team disseminated questionnaires via the SurveyMonkey platform to recruit participants to social media and instant messaging applications. This questionnaire also served as a preliminary screening tool for prospective participants. Titled "Research Evaluation of Digital Book Reading Application Evaluation," the questionnaire was circulated from March 8 to April 14, 2023. The chosen title aimed to deter

Table 1. The task in *usability testing*

No.	Task Instructions
1	Sign up for a new iPusnas account using an email address
2	Log into iPusnas using the account details provided by the researcher
3	Search for the book titled "In Cold Blood" and proceed to borrow it
4	Open the book you borrowed, navigate to the eighth page (the first page), and read the opening paragraph
5	Apply the bookmark feature on the eighth page and alter the scrolling method (transition) to advance to the subsequent page
6	Write a review of the book you have read with the comment, "Pretty good book."
7	Access the iPusnas feeds page and start following one of the users featured on the iPusnas feeds homepage
8	Search for the "iDonasi" ePustaka and borrow or queue one of its books
9	Verify the list of borrowed books, queued books, and your book borrowing history
10	Navigate to profile details and update the profile description with today's date

participants from exploring the iPusnas application ahead of the test. The question-naire contained queries concerning the participant's readiness to partake in the test, prior experience with the iPusnas application, alignment of their schedules with the test schedule, and contact details. Participants were chosen via convenience sampling based on participant availability and researcher convenience [6].

This study involves three stages. The initial stage is usability testing, where partici-pants are asked to perform ten tasks to assess the effectiveness and efficiency of iPusnas (refer to Table 1 and Fig. 1). During this phase, participants are instructed to follow the think-aloud protocol. The second phase entails completing the UEQ and SUS question-naires to measure various aspects and user satisfaction, following the UEQ handbook's guidelines [38]. The final stage involves an interview to gather additional feedback on the iPusnas usage experience, including any difficulties encountered by the participants.

The research focuses on four primary aspects: effectiveness, efficiency, satisfaction, and subjective user experience. Effectiveness is gauged based on the number of tasks completed by participants [7, 20], while efficiency is measured by the time taken by participants to complete their tasks [7, 20]. Satisfaction is determined based on the results from the SUS questionnaire completion [2, 20, 37], and subjective user experience is assessed via the results from the UEQ completion.

$$Effectiveness = \frac{(S + (P \times 0.5))}{N}$$

Description:

S = The total number of tasks completed successfully.
P = Total number of half-completed tasks.
N = Total number of tasks performed.

$$Efficiency = \frac{Tb}{Tk} = \frac{\sum_{j=1}^{R} \sum_{i=1}^{N} n_{ij} t_{ij}}{\sum_{j=1}^{R} \sum_{i=1}^{N} t_{ij}}$$

Description:

Tb = The amount of time spent completing each task.
Tk = The total amount of time required to complete all tasks.
R = Total number of participants.
N = Total number of tasks.
n_{ij} = The results of task i by participant j; If the user completes the task successfully, then nij = 1, if half completed, then nij = 0.5, if not completed, nij = 0.
t_{ij} = Total time spent by participant j on task i. If the task is not completed, time is counted until the participant leaves the task.

$$Satisfaction = 2.5 \times [\sum (a_x - 1) + \sum (5 - b_y)]$$

Description:

a_x = Participant responses for SUS items with an odd number x.
b_y = Participant response for SUS item with even number y.

In this study, every test was conducted separately under a controlled environment. Both a researcher and a research aide oversaw the testing procedure. The researcher, acting as the moderator, was in charge of running the test and communicating with the participants. They handed out written tasks as detailed in Table 1 and relayed them orally to the participants. There were no set time limits for these tasks; they were deemed finished either when the participants completed the instructions or chose to stop. Throughout the testing and interview sessions, the research assistant, who is studying Library Science, monitored the proceedings and took note of the participants' comments.

The testing was conducted in a secluded, distraction-free room, employing two mobile devices: one device was used to capture the participant's facial expressions and voices, while the other was used for testing. The device chosen for testing was the Xiaomi Redmi Note 10, equipped with Android 12, a 6.43-inch screen, and 4 GB RAM. The iPusnas app version 1.5.4 was utilized for the test. After each test session, all application data was purged and reset.

Before the commencement of the test, the moderator requested that the participants fill out a consent form and assured them of the privacy of their data. The test was explained as a means to evaluate the performance of the iPusnas application, not to assess individual capabilities. As a token of gratitude, participants received rewards for their involvement. The entire testing process, including the time to welcome the participants, averaged about 30 min per participant. Testing was conducted from March 17, 2023, to April 15, 2023.

The gathered data was subsequently analyzed both quantitatively and qualitatively. SPSS version 25 was employed to provide a quantitative data description and ascertain significant variations between groups. The Kruskal-Wallis H method and pairwise comparisons were used to identify significant discrepancies in effectiveness, efficiency, and satisfaction between the groups. To provide an outline of the UEQ results, an Excel sheet

Fig. 1. Sample screenshots from the test

from the UEQ website (https://www.ueq-online.org/) was utilized. Qualitative data were analyzed by reviewing and coding user comments collected through the think-aloud protocol and interview responses. Similar remarks and responses were coded as KDJ, as depicted in Table 3.

4 Result

4.1 Demographic Data

In this research, 15 individuals participated, of which 67% were females and 33% were males, ranging in age from 14 to 55 years (refer to Table 2). The participants hailed from three different cities: Depok (60%), Bogor (20%), and Jakarta (20%). Around 26% of the participants reported having experience with iPusnas, while 74% had never used it. However, those who had previously used iPusnas only did so occasionally, not regularly.

4.2 Quantitative Result

Effectiveness. An analysis among groups indicated that the Workers group had the highest task completion rate at 97% (48.5/50). The Students group accomplished 92%

Table 2. Demographic characteristics data in each group

Attribute/Group name	Students		Workers		Housewives	
	n	%	n	%	n	%
Gender						
Male	2	40	3	60	–	–
Female	3	60	2	40	5	100
Age						
11–20 years old	2	40	–	–	–	–
21–30 years old	3	60	5	100	2	40
31–40 years old	–	–	–	–	2	40
41–50 years old	–	–	–	–	–	–
51–60 years old	–	–	–	–	1	20
Domicile						
Jakarta	–	–	3	60	–	–
Bogor	2	40	–	–	1	20
Depok	3	60	2	40	4	80
Tangerang	–	–	–	–	–	–
Bekasi	–	–	–	–	–	–
Experience using iPusnas						
Yes	2	40	–	–	2	40
No	3	60	5	100	3	60

(46/50) of tasks, while the Housewives group achieved a 74% (37/50) success rate. As per the standards Kous et al. [20] set, the iPusnas application did not meet the minimum effectiveness benchmark of 75% for the Housewives group. Figure 2 visually represents the degree of task accomplishment per group with assistance from a moderator. For instance, of the 92% successful tasks in the Students group, 8% (4/50) were achieved with moderator guidance.

The Kruskal Wallis H test showed minor significant variances in efficiency between the groups ($\chi^2(4) = 5.886, p = 0.053$), with a mean rank of 7.90 for the Students group, 11.40 for the Worker group, and 4.70 for the Housewives group. The pairwise comparison test revealed a significant difference between the Housewives and the Workers group ($p = 0.030$).

Efficiency. Figure 3 illustrates the mean time taken to complete tasks for each group. The line graph shows the average task completion time for all groups combined. The Workers group had the quickest average task completion time (54.67 ± 10.34 s), followed by the Students group (64.03 ± 21.867 s) and then the Housewives group (70.53 ± 24.36 s). Despite taking more than average time on some tasks (such as tasks three and five), the Students group explored the task without a moderator's assistance. The Kruskal Wallis

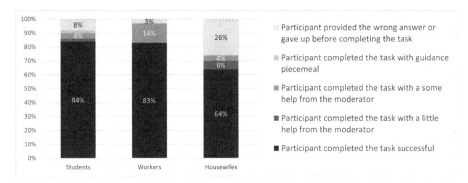

Fig. 2. Task completion relationship with the help from the moderator

H test found no significant difference in efficiency between the groups ($\chi^2(4) = 5.228$, $p = 0.073$), with a mean score of 7.80 for the Students group, 11.30 for the Worker group, and 4.90 for the Housewife group. The pairwise comparison test also revealed no significant efficiency differences between the groups.

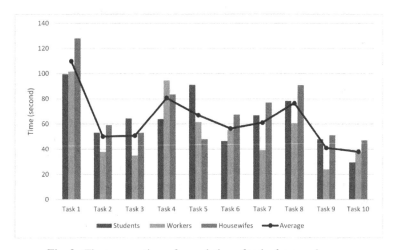

Fig. 3. The average time of completion of tasks from each group

Satisfaction. As depicted in Fig. 4, the satisfaction levels of each group, as measured by the SUS, are as follows: Students scored 51, Workers scored 55, and Housewives scored 57. According to the interpretations by Sauro and Lewis [37] and Bangor et al. [2], the Students' group evaluated their satisfaction with using iPusnas as grade F, indicating poor satisfaction. Meanwhile, the Workers and Housewives groups evaluated their satisfaction with iPusnas as grade D, signifying acceptable satisfaction levels. The Kruskal-Wallis H test found no significant differences in satisfaction among the groups ($\chi^2(4) = 0.228$, $p = 0.886$), with mean scores of 7.20 for the Students group, 8.70 for the Worker group and

8.10 for the Housewife group. The pairwise comparison test also indicated no significant differences in satisfaction among the groups.

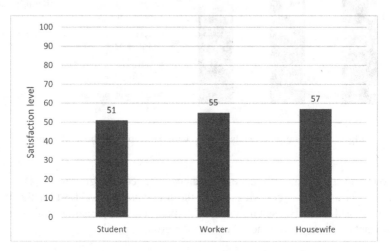

Fig. 4. The level of satisfaction in each group

UEQ. Figure 5 displays the results of the UEQ evaluation. The aspect of Attractiveness received an average score of 1.11, a Perspicuity score of 0.52, an Efficiency score of 1.03, a Dependability score of 1.40, a Stimulation score of 1.35, and a Novelty score of 0.80. Schrepp [38] suggests a score above 0.8 indicates a positive evaluation. All dimensions except for Perspicuity received a positive review. However, according to the UEQ benchmark, the aspects of Attractiveness and Efficiency fall into the below-average category, while the Perspicuity aspect is classified as poor. All UEQ scales in this study produced results consistent with Cronbach's Alpha values: 0.90 for Attractiveness, 0.92 for Perspicuity, 0.89 for Efficiency, 0.77 for Dependability, 0.87 for Stimulation, and 0.94 for Novelty.

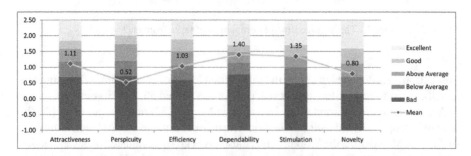

Fig. 5. UEQ Results and Benchmarks

4.3 Qualitative Findings

Table 3 shows the findings from the analysis of participants' feedback during usability tests and their interview responses, categorized by how often they occurred. The topic most frequently discussed was buttons, as reflected by KDJ1 (47%), KDJ2 (33%), KDJ4 (33%), and KDJ8 (20%). Next in frequency was the subject of registration instructions, highlighted by KDJ3 (33%). However, the latest version of the app (1.6.0) has addressed this by incorporating a registration button. Participants also brought up issues like a repetitive interface and some unrelated features (KDJ5, 33%), the absence of an instructional guide or a description of the app's functions (KDJ6, 33%), and security worries during the sign-up phase (KDJ7, 27%).

Regarding the buttons, especially those labeled as KDJ3, KDJ4, and KDJ8, students made the most comments. Workers, on the other hand, frequently mentioned Button KDJ1 and also expressed unhappiness with the repetitive nature of the interface. Meanwhile, during usability tests and interviews, housewives voiced concerns about the lack of a user guide or explanatory material for Button KDJ6.

Table 3. Participant Interview Comments and Answers

Code	Comments	Students	Workers	Housewives	Total	%
		n	*n*	*n*	*n*	
KDJ1	Icons do not accurately represent the features they denote	3	3	1	7	47
KDJ2	The buttons lack labels	3	1	1	5	33
KDJ3	There are no instructions for the registration process	1	3	1	5	33
KDJ4	The button arrangement is difficult to locate and identify	1	2	2	5	33
KDJ5	The interface appears monotonous, and some features seem less relevant	0	3	2	5	33
KDJ6	There is no user manual or clarification of the features	1	1	3	5	33
KDJ7	The registration process lacks security measures	2	1	1	4	27
KDJ8	The color of the button does not contrast well with the background	3	0	0	3	20

5 Discussion

5.1 Main Findings

This research gauges the user experience of iPusnas through usability testing, the System Usability Scale (SUS), and the User Experience Questionnaire (UEQ), specifically focusing on users' effectiveness, efficiency, satisfaction, and subjective user experience. Interestingly, 74% of the 15 participants had never used iPusnas before, contrasting Kous et al.'s [20] study, where most participants were already familiar with the tested product. The goal was to reduce potential bias from participants with previous exposure to the product [3, 43].

The research discovered minor differences in effectiveness across all groups and significant differences between the Workers and Housewives groups. These findings align with Kous et al.'s [20] study, which identified significant effectiveness variances. However, while Kous et al.'s research reported significant differences in efficiency, this study did not. Also, Kous et al. found that the Students group showed the highest success rate (effectiveness) and quickest average task completion time (efficiency). In contrast, this research and Febrianti & Adhy's [7] study identified the Worker group as the top performer.

The Students group in this research and Febrianti & Adhy's [7] study scored the lowest satisfaction levels, differing from Kous et al.'s research, which found the Senior group to be the least satisfied. Interestingly, despite sharing similar characteristics with the Senior group, the Housewives group in this study and Febrianti & Adhy's [7] research exhibited the highest satisfaction levels. Despite their performance metrics, similar to the Senior group, this indicated the lowest effectiveness and efficiency. However, this study aligns with Kous et al.'s [20] research finding no significant difference in satisfaction.

According to Sauro and Lewis [37] and Bangor et al. [2], the satisfaction level of the Students group indicates that iPusnas falls into a subpar category, earning a grade of F. Additionally, the UEQ results reveal that iPusnas' Perspicuity aspect is considered poor, while the Attractiveness and Efficiency aspects are below average. These findings contrast with Maulana's [25] study, which suggests that iPusnas offers a satisfactory user experience based on the PIECES framework. This study's results also diverge from Prastiwi & Jumino's [32] research, which reported high satisfaction levels using the Technology Acceptance Model (TAM).

Analyzing feedback from usability testing and interview responses produced findings similar to Febrianti & Adhy's [7] study. Problems related to button design and functionality discussed in KDJ1, KDJ2, KDJ4, and KDJ8 were also present in that study. Participants found it challenging to locate some of the iPusnas buttons due to the absence of descriptive labels, a hidden button location in the lower right corner, and a lack of contrasting colors. In addition, this study and Febrianti & Adhy's [7] research noted the lack of immediate email confirmation upon successful account registration (KDJ7). The divergence with Febrianti & Adhy's [7] research relates to feedback about the monotonous interface, several less relevant features (KDJ5), and the lack of a user manual or explanation of features (KDJ6).

5.2 Research Implication

Digital library applications like iPusnas are created to foster remote interactions between libraries and their patrons [27]. Crucial to promoting literacy is the ease of access and abundant reading resources such as books [26, 28, 40]. However, if a library application is deemed unreliable or unsatisfactory, users might hesitate to use it [27, 33, 34, 45, 48]. Users might desert digital libraries that offer a poor user experience [18, 24]. The National Library of Indonesia, which is accountable for iPusnas, must endeavor to enhance user performance and satisfaction to boost literacy.

iPusnas and similar applications are viewed as a library extension to promote inclusivity. However, many digital libraries overlook accessibility [4]. This research also discovered that the housewives' group's effectiveness did not meet standards and required assistance with iPusnas. Moving forward, the National Library of Indonesia should ensure iPusnas can be accessed by all demographic groups.

Poor user experience can tarnish a brand image [8]. Twum et al. [42] suggested that a library's brand image correlates with service quality and user loyalty. A low-quality user experience in digital library applications indicates subpar service quality, which could tarnish the library's brand image. The damaged brand could undermine the library's trust and reputation, leading to users leaving due to diminished loyalty.

5.3 Recommendation

This study's findings have led to the following recommendations for the development of iPusnas:

1. Adding Labels to Buttons. iPusnas primarily uses icons for its buttons. It is crucial to understand that users can perceive these icons differently. For instance, some participants mistook the review button icon for a comment button. Also, a few participants spent more time identifying the button, and some abandoned tasks related to providing reviews. Therefore, labeling these buttons for clarity is necessary, enabling iPusnas users to quickly and easily comprehend them.
2. Adopting Standard Colors. Certain buttons in iPusnas do not have a clear contrast with the background color, requiring users to concentrate more to locate these buttons. iPusnas should adhere to the Web Content Accessibility Guidelines (WCAG) in choosing colors to ensure that users' accessibility needs are met.
3. Providing a Guide and Explanation for First-Time Use. The participants in this study spent a considerable amount of time exploring the application when performing tasks. This is because no instructions or guides were provided for first-time app use. While the app does have an onboarding page, it does not offer any explanation about iPusnas features. Onboarding pages are the initial pages when a user first accesses the application. The researchers recommend that iPusnas fully utilize the onboarding page to explain the features available in iPusnas thoroughly.

5.4 Limitations and Recommendations

This study does come with a few limitations. Chief among these is the limited participant count (15 participants grouped into three categories) and the participants' concentration in Depok, Jakarta, and Bogor, making applying these results universally challenging. The concentration on the age group 21–30 in the Workers' group further hampers the generalizability. Regardless of these restrictions, the study can still offer suggestions for enhancing any digital library application grounded in the observed findings.

The short data collection timeline and resource constraints posed significant hurdles to recruiting a more diverse participant pool. This limitation led to the inclusion of participants with prior experience with iPusnas, even though the study initially targeted participants without any prior experience with the application. Another issue encountered was releasing an iPusnas application update during data collection. The National Library rolled out version 1.6.0 on March 22, 2023, while data gathering commenced on March 17, 2023. This study was based on the prior version, so its findings may not fully reflect the user experience with the latest version of iPusnas.

The study paves the way for future investigations. It can serve as a valuable reference in library and information science related to user experience and digital libraries. Future studies could gather data from a larger and more diverse set of participants, including retirees, traders, researchers, and community groups from the most remote, isolated, and underdeveloped areas (*daerah Terdepan, Terpencil, dan Tertinggal* - 3T). The effectiveness of the recommendations provided by this study can also be a topic of interest in upcoming research. Other fields, such as computer science, might explore digital library application evaluations using different techniques, such as heuristic evaluations.

6   Conclusion

This research assesses iPusnas user experiences via usability testing, System Usability Scale (SUS), and User Experience Questionnaire (UEQ). It gauges the effectiveness, efficiency, satisfaction, and subjective experiences of end users, specifically students, workers, and housewives. The study reveals that the effectiveness rates for the Students, Workers, and Housewife groups are 92%, 97%, and 74%, respectively. The average task completion time (efficiency) is 64 s for Students, 54 s for Workers, and 70 s for Housewives. The satisfaction scores are 51 for Students, 55 for Workers, and 57 for Housewives. UEQ-based subjective experience metrics show scores of 1.11 for Attractiveness, 0.52 for Perspicuity, 1.03 for Efficiency, 1.40 for Dependability, 1.35 for Stimulation, and 0.80 for Novelty.

The study uncovers a minor but notable difference in effectiveness, with a significant difference between the Housewives and Workers groups. No significant differences were found in efficiency and satisfaction across all groups. The effectiveness of the Housewives group falls short of the minimum usability threshold. The Student group's satisfaction indicates an unsatisfactory iPusnas experience (bad category), while the Workers and Housewives groups show a satisfactory experience (OK category). UEQ results reveal positive evaluations for all aspects except Perspicuity. However, compared to the UEQ benchmark, the Attractiveness and Efficiency aspects are below average, with the Perspicuity aspect falling into the poor category. Based on these findings, this study advocate including button labels, adjusting color contrast, and providing a user guide upon first use.

Acknowledgments. The authors are grateful to the anonymous reviewers for their constructive feedback, which significantly improved the manuscript. This work was generously supported by a grant from the Universitas Indonesia, grant number NKB-1202/UN2.RST/HKP.05.00/2022. Any opinions, findings, and conclusions described here are the authors and do not necessarily reflect those of the sponsors.

References

1. Badan Pusat Statistik: Indonesian telecommunications statistics 2021 (2021). https://www.bps.go.id/publication/2022/09/07/bcc820e694c537ed3ec131b9/statistik-telekomunikasi-indonesia-2021.html
2. Bangor, A., Kortum, P., Miller, J.: Determining what individual SUS scores mean: adding an adjective rating scale. J. Usability Stud. **4**(3), 114–123 (2009)
3. Berkman, A.E.: General interaction expertise: an approach for sampling in usability testing of consumer products. Hum.-Comput. Interact. Interact. Des. Usability, 397–406,(2007). https://doi.org/10.1007/978-3-540-73105-4_44
4. Beyene, W.M.: Realizing inclusive digital library environments: opportunities and challenges. Res. Adv. Technol. Digit. Libr., 3–14 (2016). https://doi.org/10.1007/978-3-319-43997-6_1
5. Brooke, J.: SUS: a retrospective. J. Usability Stud. **8**(2), 29–40 (2013)
6. Creswell, J.W., David Creswell, J.: Research Design: Qualitative, Quantitative, and Mixed Methods Approaches, 5th edn. SAGE, Los Angeles (2018)
7. Febrianti, S.A., Adhy, S.: Usability evaluation of iPekalonganKota with different end-user groups using usability testing and USE questionnaire methods. In: 2021 5th International Conference on Informatics and Computational Sciences (ICICoS), 2021-Novem, pp. 104–109 (2021). https://doi.org/10.1109/ICICoS53627.2021.9651841
8. Garzotto, F., Sorce, F., Bolchini, D., Yang, T.: Empirical investigation of web design attributes affecting brand perception. In: Proceedings of the 6th Nordic Conference on Human-Computer Interaction: Extending Boundaries, pp. 188–197 (2010). https://doi.org/10.1145/1868914.1868939
9. Genc-Nayebi, N., Abran, A.: A measurement design for the comparison of expert usability evaluation and mobile app user reviews. In: CEUR Workshop Proceedings (2018)
10. Guay, S., Rudin, L., Reynolds, S.: Testing, testing: a usability case study at University of Toronto Scarborough Library. Libr. Manag. **40**(1–2), 88–97 (2019). https://doi.org/10.1108/LM-10-2017-0107
11. Hartson, R., Pyla, P.: The UX Book: Agile UX Design for Quality User Experience, 2nd edn. Elsevier, Amsterdam (2019)
12. Hass, C.: A practical guide to usability testing. Consum. Inform. Digit. Health, 107–124 (2019). https://doi.org/10.1007/978-3-319-96906-0_6
13. Hassan, H.M., Galal-Edeen, G.H.: From usability to user experience. In: 2017 International Conference on Intelligent Informatics and Biomedical Sciences (ICIIBMS), pp. 216–222 (2017). https://doi.org/10.1109/ICIIBMS.2017.8279761
14. Hu, X.: Usability evaluation of E-Dunhuang cultural heritage digital library. Data Inf. Manage. **2**(2), 57–69 (2018). https://doi.org/10.2478/dim-2018-0008
15. Inal, Y.: University students' heuristic usability inspection of the National Library of Turkey website. Aslib J. Inf. Manag. **70**(1), 66–77 (2018). https://doi.org/10.1108/AJIM-09-2017-0216
16. International Organization for Standardization: Ergonomics of human-system interaction - Part 11: Usability: Definitions and concepts (ISO 9241-211:2018) (2018). https://www.iso.org/standard/63500.html

17. iPusnas: How to use (n.d.). https://ipusnas.id/en/howto.html. Accessed 27 Feb 2023
18. Jiang, T., Luo, G., Wang, Z., Yu, W.: Research into influencing factors in user experiences of university mobile libraries based on mobile learning mode. Library Hi Tech (2022). https:// doi.org/10.1108/LHT-11-2021-0423
19. Kiran, K., Singh, D.: Exploring user experiences with digital library services: a focus group approach. Digit. Libr. Univ. Ubiquit. Access Inf. **5362**, 285–293 (2008). https://doi.org/10. 1007/978-3-540-89533-6_29
20. Kous, K., Pušnik, M., Heričko, M., Polančič, G.: Usability evaluation of a library website with different end-user groups. J. Librariansh. Inf. Sci. **52**(1), 75–90 (2020). https://doi.org/ 10.1177/0961000618773133
21. Kuhar, M., Merčun, T.: Exploring user experience in digital libraries through questionnaire and eye-tracking data. Libr. Inf. Sci. Res. **44**(3), 101175 (2022). https://doi.org/10.1016/J. LISR.2022.101175
22. Kushendriawan, M.A., Santoso, H.B., Putra, P.O.H., Schrepp, M.: Evaluating user experience of a mobile health application 'Halodoc' using user experience questionnaire and usability testing. Jurnal Sistem Informasi **17**(1), 58–71 (2021). https://doi.org/10.21609/jsi.v17i1.1063
23. Maricar, M.A., Pramana, D., Putri, D.R.: Evaluation of the use of SLiMS in E-Library using user experience questions (EUQ). Jurnal Teknologi Informasi dan Ilmu Komputer **8**(2), 319 (2021). https://doi.org/10.25126/jtiik.2021824443
24. Matusiak, K.K.: Perceptions of usability and usefulness of digital libraries. Int. J. Hum. Arts Comput. **6**(1–2), 133–147 (2012). https://doi.org/10.3366/ijhac.2012.0044
25. Maulana, Y.I.: Evaluation of the level of satisfaction of users of the national digital library (iPusnas) using the PIECES framework. Bianglala Informatika **6**(1) (2018). https://doi.org/ 10.31294/bi.v6i1.5904
26. Merga, M.K., Mat Roni, S.: The influence of access to e-readers, computers and mobile phones on children's book reading frequency. Comput. Educ. **109**, 187–196 (2017). https:// doi.org/10.1016/J.COMPEDU.2017.02.016
27. Ming, J., Chen, R., Tu, R.: Factors influencing user behavior intention to use mobile library application: a theoretical and empirical research based on grounded theory. Data Inf. Manage. **5**(1), 131–146 (2021). https://doi.org/10.2478/dim-2020-0037
28. Nassimbeni, M., Desmond, C.: Availability of books as a factor in reading, teaching and learning behaviour in twenty disadvantaged primary schools in South Africa. S. Afr. J. Libr. Inf. Sci. **77**(2) (2011). https://doi.org/10.7553/77-2-52
29. Nielsen, J.: Why you only need to test with 5 users. Nielsen Norman Group, March 18 2000. https://www.nngroup.com/articles/why-you-only-need-to-test-with-5-users/
30. Nuriman, M.L., Mayesti, N.: Evaluation of the usability of Universitas Indonesia websites using a usability scale system. Baca Jurnal Dokumentasi Dan Informasi **41**(2), 253 (2020). https://doi.org/10.14203/j.baca.v41i2.622
31. Okhovati, M., Karami, F., Khajouei, R.: Exploring the usability of the central library websites of medical sciences universities. J. Librariansh. Inf. Sci. **49**(3), 246–255 (2017). https://doi. org/10.1177/0961000616650932
32. Prastiwi, M.A., Jumino, J.: Efektivitas aplikasi iPusnas sebagai sarana temu balik informasi elektronik Perpustakaan Nasional Republik Indonesia. Jurnal Ilmu Perpustakaan **7**(4) (2018)
33. Rafique, H., Almagrabi, A.O., Shamim, A., Anwar, F., Bashir, A.K.: Investigating the acceptance of mobile library applications with an extended Technology Acceptance Model (TAM). Comput. Educ. **145**, 103732 (2020). https://doi.org/10.1016/j.compedu.2019.103732
34. Rafique, H., Anwer, F., Shamim, A., Minaei-Bidgoli, B., Qureshi, M.A., Sham-shirband, S.: Factors affecting acceptance of mobile library applications: structural equation model. Libri **68**(2), 99–112 (2018). https://doi.org/10.1515/libri-2017-0041

35. Ratnawati, S., et al.: Evaluation of digital library's usability using the system usability scale method of (a case study). In: 2020 8th International Conference on Cyber and IT Service Management (CITSM), pp. 1–5 (2020). https://doi.org/10.1109/CITSM50537.2020.9268801

36. Santoso, H.B., Schrepp, M., Yugo Kartono Isal, R., Utomo, A.Y., Priyogi, B.: Measuring user experience of the student-centered e-learning environment. J. Educ. Online **13**(1), 1–79 (2016)

37. Sauro, J., Lewis, J.R.: Quantifying the User Experience: Practical Statistics for User Research, 2nd edn. Elsevier, Amsterdam (2016)

38. Schrepp, M.: User Experience Questionnaire Handbook, vol. 9 (2023). www.ueq-online.org

39. Sharfina, Z., Santoso, H.B.: An Indonesian adaptation of the system usability scale (SUS). In: 2016 International Conference on Advanced Computer Science and Information Systems (ICACSIS), pp. 145–148 (2016). https://doi.org/10.1109/ICACSIS.2016.7872776

40. Sikora, J., Evans, M.D.R., Kelley, J.: Scholarly culture: how books in adolescence enhance adult literacy, numeracy and technology skills in 31 societies. Soc. Sci. Res. **77**, 1–15 (2019). https://doi.org/10.1016/j.ssresearch.2018.10.003

41. Sunardi, Julian, I., Murad, D.F., Riva'i, R.Y.: Combining UEQ and eye-tracking method as usability evaluation for mobile apps. In: 2021 3rd International Conference on Cybernetics and Intelligent System (ICORIS), pp. 1–6 (2021). https://doi.org/10.1109/ICORIS52787.2021.9649529

42. Twum, K.K., Yalley, A.A., Agyapong, G.K.-Q., Ofori, D.: The influence of public university library service quality and library brand image on user loyalty. Int. Rev. Publ. Nonprofit Market. **18**(2), 207–227 (2021). https://doi.org/10.1007/s12208-020-00269-w

43. Walper, D., Kassau, J., Methfessel, P., Pronold, T., Einhäuser, W.: Optimizing user interfaces in food Production: gaze tracking is more sensitive for A-B-testing than behavioral data alone. In: Eye Tracking Research and Applications Symposium (ETRA), 6 February 2020. https://doi.org/10.1145/3379156.3391351

44. Wei, Q., Chang, Z., Cheng, Q.: Usability study of the mobile library app: an example from Chongqing University. Library Hi Tech **33**(3), 340–355 (2015). https://doi.org/10.1108/LHT-05-2015-0047

45. Ye, P., Liu, L., Gao, L., Mei, Q.: Influence of information and service quality on users' continuous use of mobile libraries in China. J. Cases Inf. Technol. **22**(1), 57–71 (2022). https://doi.org/10.4018/JCIT.2020010104

46. Zaphiris, P., Dellaporta, A., Mohamedally, D.: User needs analysis and evaluation of portals. Portals, 52–62 (2018). https://doi.org/10.29085/9781856049832.007

47. Zarour, M., Alharbi, M.: User experience framework that combines aspects, dimensions, and measurement methods. Cogent Eng. **4**(1), 1421006 (2017). https://doi.org/10.1080/23311916.2017.1421006

48. Zhao, Y., Deng, S., Zhou, R.: Understanding mobile library apps continuance usage in China: a theoretical framework and empirical study. Libri **65**(3) (2015). https://doi.org/10.1515/libri-2014-0148

49. Jamal, A., et al.: Usability analysis of a health sciences digital library by medical residents: cross-sectional survey. JMIR Formative Res. **5**(6), e23293 (2021). https://doi.org/10.2196/23293

50. Prasetya, Y., Rahmi, R.: Pilot study on user experience analysis of universitas Indonesia library website. Tik Ilmeu Jurnal Ilmu Perpustakaan dan Informasi **7**(1), 105–116 (2023)

Personalized Treasure Hunt Game
for Proactive Museum Appreciation
by Analyzing Guide App Operation Log

Jinsong Yu[1], Shio Takidaira[2], Tsukasa Sawaura[3], Yoshiyuki Shoji[1,4(✉)] [iD],
Takehiro Yamamoto[5], Yusuke Yamamoto[6], Hiroaki Ohshima[5], Kenro Aihara[7],
and Noriko Kando[8]

[1] Aoyama Gakuin University, Sagamihara, Kanagawa 252-5258, Japan
yu@sw.it.aoyama.ac.jp
[2] Dai Nippon Printing Co., Ltd., Shinjuku, Tokyo 162-0062, Japan
takidaira@sw.it.aoyama.ac.jp
[3] COLOPL, Inc., Shibuya, Tokyo 150-6032, Japan
sawaura@sw.it.aoyama.ac.jp
[4] Shizuoka University, Hamamatsu, Shizuoka 432-8011, Japan
shojiy@inf.shizuoka.ac.jp
[5] University of Hyogo, Kobe, Hyogo 651-2197, Japan
t.yamamoto@sis.u-hyogo.ac.jp, ohshima@ai.u-hyogo.ac.jp
[6] Nagoya City University, Nagoya, Aichi 467-8501, Japan
yusuke_yamamoto@acm.org
[7] Tokyo Metropolitan University, Hachioji, Tokyo 192-0397, Japan
kenro.aihara@tmu.ac.jp
[8] National Institute of Informatics, Chiyoda, Tokyo 101-0003, Japan
kando@nii.ac.jp

Abstract. This paper proposes a method for enhancing museum visits by turning them into a personalized treasure hunt game. This approach uses gamification to augment visitor experiences, explicitly addressing the issue of retaining information during casual museum visits. This is achieved by creating quizzes customized to each visitor's interests and providing unique perspectives for appreciating exhibits. These quizzes, developed through analyzing museum guide logs and individual visitor preferences, encourage visitors to explore exhibits, thereby intensifying their engagement proactively. The game entails visitors identifying specific exhibits, guided by hints like images and maps, and inputting the exhibit IDs to win in-game rewards. Field studies employing actual data from the National Museum of Ethnology in Japan evaluated this approach's efficacy. Experimental results suggest that visitors are more likely to remember exhibit details connected to quiz answers, even two weeks after their visit. Participants also enjoyed the impromptu exploration encouraged by the treasure hunt game.

Keywords: Gamification · Museum Guide · Personalization

1   Introduction

Visiting museums and viewing their exhibits is one of humankind's most critical intellectual activities. For example, many international travel tours include museum visits as part of the course to experience the region's culture. Many educational institutions also include museum studies as part of their curricula.

Despite visiting museums being recommended for learning purposes, not all visitors necessarily approach them with a clear objective. Specifically, visitors who arrive at museums for tours or extracurricular activities without particular motivation tend to wander through the venue passively, simply following the set route. Yenawine *et al.* [21] report a phenomenon where such passive museum experiences do not result in lasting knowledge or memories for the visitors.

In a case study, Housen *et al.* conducted tours with curatorial explanations at the Museum of Modern Art, New York, investigating visitor satisfaction and the knowledge that remained in memory. Their findings suggest that, while increasing the amount of information presented through additional explanations can raise satisfaction levels, it may not necessarily lead to knowledge acquisition if the experience remains passive.

Such phenomena, where passive observation does not lead to learning, have been pointed out in museum studies to emphasize the importance of active and autonomous experiences. For instance, Folk [6] argues that "Free Choice Learning" is crucial in museum learning contexts. The concept of Free Choice Learning posits that learners do not merely follow a predetermined route but learn by actively choosing what they are interested in.

For additional examples, Hein *et al.* [9] proposes a learning model based on Constructivism, stating that visitors build knowledge internally rather than through information from exhibits. Furthermore, Bain *et al.*, within the concept of "Object-Centered Learning," argues that there is greater value in personally interpreting exhibits and connecting them to daily life than merely looking at external knowledge presented through exhibits or explanatory text [13].

Indeed, an energetic and proactive appreciation is pivotal to ensuring that a museum experience is both meaningful and educational. However, catalyzing such autonomous engagement can often present a challenge. As such, numerous initiatives have been undertaken to facilitate proactive appreciation.

One traditional approach is the implementation of orienteering games, often embodied as stamp collecting, within the museum. In these games, museum curators prepare a list of selected exhibits. They then generate stamp sheets that provide hints about these exhibits and distribute them among the participants. Guided by these hints, participants then embark on an exploratory journey through the museum, seeking out the designated exhibits.

Stamp Collection Screen   **Quiz and Hints Screen**

Fig. 1. Screenshots of the treasure hunt game in the museum (Some parts are over-written for translation). Player finds four treasures (designated exhibits) to collect four stamps, aiming to complete with as few hints used as possible. The Quiz and Hint screen shows information about the treasure. Photos, exhibit locations, tags, and descriptions are displayed, but initially, they are blurred or hidden.

Such museum experiences utilizing orienteering aim to promote active observation by encouraging visitors to seek out items based on hints provided, turning the game into a springboard for autonomous engagement. Furthermore, curators often design much orienteering along a consistent theme.

In recent years, gamification that includes puzzle-solving has been increasingly adopted as an advanced mechanism to enhance museum experiences. For instance, institutions such as the Tokyo National Museum and the Louvre Museum offer game-like experiences. Participants of these games navigate through the museum while solving puzzles and searching for exhibits, utilizing tools like smartphones or puzzle sheets. Through these interactive game experiences, participants can develop an interest in and deepen their understanding of the exhibits.

While these game-based experiences can stimulate proactive appreciation, they also entail substantial costs for creation. In the case of orienteering, experts need to identify exhibits that align with a particular concept and decide which exhibits the participants should visit. Similarly, for puzzle games, specialists in riddles or quizzes must design the game according to the exhibits they want to showcase and the messages they want to convey. As a result, it is challenging to offer multiple orientation or puzzle games simultaneously within a single museum.

Consider an individual visiting a museum, without pre-established interests, as part of a school activity. They may opt for a museum guide device's orienteering function, potentially gaining knowledge about the rally's themes and featured exhibits. However, this knowledge might not align with their personal interests, reducing the chance of it being used in the future. Engaging with a topic related to their interests makes them more likely to recall the related exhibit, indicating effective knowledge acquisition from the visit.

In this study, we propose a method that dynamically generates a personalized treasure hunt game by analyzing the behavior logs of a museum guide device. Figure 1 shows an example of an actual gameplay screen. A stamp card screen appears when a player launches the game feature on the museum guide. Players hunt for four exhibits to collect four stamps. After tapping the button under the first stamp field, a quiz screen is generated dynamically by analyzing the visitor's operation log. The quiz screen includes a request for the treasure, *i.e.*, exhibit to be found, as well as hints in the form of images, maps, tags, and descriptions, which are initially obscured. Hidden hints can be revealed in a step-by-step manner. The player can get a stamp when they find the correct exhibit and inputs its ID. If incorrect, two hints are revealed. The player aims to collect all four stamps with as few hints as possible.

The main novelty of our method is its ability to be personalized by connecting the game with the museum guide. Visitors at the museum often use the guide app to read detailed information about exhibits or to check the location of their favorite exhibits. These actions are reflected in the operation logs, strongly indicating their interests. It encompasses not only an individual's conscious interests but also latent interests and unconscious actions. Our method analyzes these logs and extracts common tags from the exhibits they viewed frequently. Then, while retaining these tags, they seek out an unseen exhibit as "treasure".

We implemented a prototype of a treasure hunt game that can actually be used at a museum and conducted a subject experiment on-site. We evaluated how the game experience was perceived and analyzed whether the exhibits they found were remembered two weeks later. During this process, we altered part of the generated quizzes for experimental purposes, allowing us to verify the effects of personalization and the impact of raising awareness of one's interests.

2   Related Work

This study aims to enhance museum experiences through personalized treasure hunts. This section introduces prior research on learning support through treasure hunts, gamification in museums, and personalization, and discusses the positioning and novelty of our study.

2.1   Treasure Hunt Game in Education

Treasure hunt games have been used since ancient times for education, mainly for young children. In recent years, research has been progressing on computer applications to facilitate the educational benefits of these games. For instance, Farella *et al.* [7] argue for the effectiveness of treasure hunt games on mobile devices when the game design is conducted by teachers themselves. Kohen-Vacs *et al.* [11] have enabled a digital-supported treasure hunt game outside the school using the location information of mobile devices.

Relevant to our research, Ng *et al.* [12] have realized a treasure hunt game using mobile devices in museums. Their study reports that gamification increases the learning effect compared to traditional guides. Ceipidor et al. [2] have also realized a treasure hunt game in museums using QR codes. Cesário [3] propose advanced gamification at the maritime museum that fits the museum's theme.

The novelty of our work lies in its ability to personalize the treasure hunt by integrating it with a museum guide. The museum guide is well-suited to estimating the user's latent interests from queries input by the user and the exhibits they viewed in detail. Additionally, although not utilized in this experiment, unconscious actions derived from scroll and acceleration sensors and the exhibits viewed from beacons or location information can also be detected. Using these to provide tailored treasure hunts must help individuals' learning.

2.2   Gamification in Museum

Gamification in museums has long been a focus of attention, especially research on mobile device learning support. Yatani et al. [20] propose learning with PDAs in museums. In their study, the device is intended to help multiple people solve questions collaboratively to better understand the exhibit content. Ueda et al. [18] also propose a system that encourages independent appreciation of each exhibit by generating a three-choice quiz for each museum exhibit. Our research similarly aims to aid learning in museums through gamification. To this end, the technical challenge in this study is to make such gamification dynamically generable and tailored to the individual.

In recent years, with the development of mobile technology, research on gamification using Augmented Reality (AR) has also been active [4,5]. Methods for estimating visitor location and enabling interaction with exhibits using Wi-Fi, beacons, infrared communication, etc. are also being investigated [15]. As an example of research that combines location information within a museum with gamification, Rubino et al. [16] propose a viewing method based on storytelling.

The guide app used in our research also can estimate location using beacons and read text using a camera, but at this time, it is not being utilized for games. Based on these studies, enabling richer input and output based on location could improve the gaming experience and make learning more meaningful.

2.3   Personalization of Museum Experience

Personalizing museum experiences and promoting individualized learning have been actively pursued in recent years. Wang et al. [19]propose a project that allows visitors to design their own viewing plans at the museum by connecting the local museum to the web. In their project, visitors can examine exhibits on a web application in advance, input exhibits of interest, and navigate a course tailored to them on a PDA.

Shoji et al. [17] propose a method of personalizing not the museum experience itself, but its souvenirs, to help secure personal memories when reviewing them later. In their research, they analyze the logs of museum guide devices, estimate the exhibits the visitor may have been interested in, and print them on postcards.

As a study that personalizes the way each exhibit is viewed, Keil *et al.* [10] propose a method of displaying exhibits of interest in various ways using AR technology. By pointing a tablet device at the exhibit, additional explanations are added, or a synthesized narrative video is played. In the context of personalizing museum experiences, Pujol *et al.* [14] have researched personalized storytelling in various museums. Our study applies such personalization in conjunction with gamification. The goal is not just to show a simple route, but to actively encourage searching, to firmly anchor personal interests in memory.

In research related to this study, Camps-Ortueta *et al.* [1] propose a method of making games enjoyable by personalizing the gaming experience itself. Their research also discusses that educational games are fundamentally dull and the fun found in regular games is limited during learning sessions. In our study, only the exhibits targeted in the game are subject to personalization. Still, in the future, the number of stamps collected, game rules, and difficulty levels should also be personalized.

3 Personalized Treasure Hunt Game Generation

This section explains the mechanism of the application for supporting users' proactive museum appreciation. As our method is closely linked to the actual guide terminal, we use the implemented prototype as an example in the explanation. Our application operates on an iPad and can search and view detailed information for over 4,000 exhibits in a the National Museum of Ethnology, Japan.

3.1 System Overview

This section describes an outline and overall picture of the system. This application consists of front-end and back-end components. The front end aids viewing exhibits by facilitating search and presenting detailed information. During this, the user's activity logs are collected. On the server side, the received logs are analyzed, and quizzes personalized to each individual are generated. The front end is implemented as an iOS app in Swift. The back end is implemented in Python, and the screens are displayed using Vue.js, a JavaScript framework. Our system's screen transition is shown in Fig. 2.

The "Recommended Exhibits" screen is initially presented when launching the guide app, where various exhibits are randomly arranged. From this list view, which also includes search results, users often tap on various exhibits to view their detailed information. The application continually logs the extent to which the detail screens of each exhibit are viewed.

Next, when "Treasure Hunt Game" is selected from the main menu, the built-in browser within iOS is launched. The operation logs are sent to the server, where they are analyzed, and a quiz tailored to the user is generated. When the user starts the game, a stamp sheet without any stamps is displayed. On this screen, users can view the game instructions. By pressing the "Question 1"

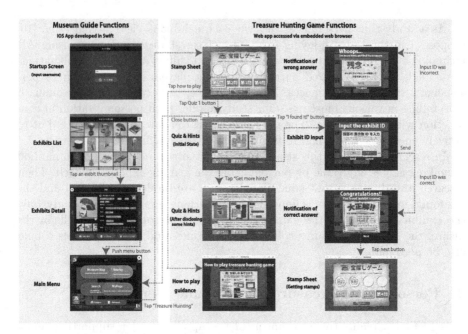

Fig. 2. Screen transition of actual gameplay on the app. Player access both the guide screen and game screen to find exhibits in the museum. They can get a stamp when they input the correct exhibit.

button under the stamp, users can navigate to the detail screen of the treasure hunt target.

The detail screen displays instructions and four hints about the treasure the user should find. The instruction includes personal interests and viewpoints. For example, "You were paying close attention to pots. While noticing the different materials used in different regions, please find the following pot in the Africa area."

The hints are a photo, a map, tags, and a description. Initially, these hints are blurred and hard to see (top image in Fig. 3). The photo is pixelated and low resolution. The map is not narrowed down, so the search range covers the entire museum. No tags are displayed. The description is also blurred and unreadable.

By tapping the "Get More Hints" button, users can gradually reduce the blur on any hints, as shown in Fig. 3. Each hint can be clarified in four stages, and since there are four items, users can get hints up to 12 times in total. When the hint button is pressed, the image's resolution gradually improves, and in the end, the original resolution of the exhibition image can be seen. The map also gradually narrows the search range, eventually narrowing to about 10 m. The number of tags gradually increases. The text gradually becomes readable as the blur is removed word by word.

Initial State

Hint button has
never been tapped.

Photo resolution: 4px x 4px
Area: 100m x 100m
Tags: 0 percent showed
Description: unreadable

Intermediate

Disclosured 8 hints
of 12

Photo resolution: 10px x 10px
Area: 40m x 40m
Tags: 60 percent showed
Description: Some terms can
be clearly read.
Rest part is blurry
but barely
readable.

Final State

Disclosured all hints
Photo resolution: Same to
original
Area: 10m x 10m
Tags: all tags are showed
Description: Completely clear

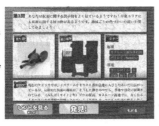

Fig. 3. Screenshots of hints to be disclosed in stages. Each time a player presses the "Get More Hints" button, photo, map, tags, and description are displayed more clearly, step by step. The player can press the button 12 times.

Table 1. Questionnaire results on usability. The average score of eight participants (from 1 to 5), and the standard deviation of each participant's score.

Evaluation	AVG	SD
Amusingness	4.3	0.5
Usability	3.1	1.3
Design	3.9	0.7
Serendipity	3.9	1.0
Interests Expended	3.8	0.5
Fit Interests	3.9	0.7
Difficulty	3.4	1.4
Cost	3.5	0.9
Quality of Hints	2.6	1.1
Photo Usefulness	4.4	0.6
Map Usefulness	2.5	2.0
Tag Usefulness	4.1	0.7
Description Usefulness	3.5	0.9

Table 2. The number of players who remembered the treasure exhibits two weeks later (out of 8). Each player solved one question from each of the four types of quizzes. They were asked about recall, recognition, and whether they liked the quiz.

method	# Recall	# Recognition	# Favorite
Quality Only	8	7	4
Quality+ViewPoint	7	8	1
Interest Only	7	7	2
Interest+ViewPoint	5	6	1
Average	6.75	7.00	–

Using these gradually revealed hints as clues, the player searches for exhibits on the guide or on-site at the museum. Pressing the "I Found it!" button at the bottom of the treasure hunt target's detail screen displays a dialog where they can input the exhibit ID. The exhibit ID is a unique 8-letter string given to each exhibit, composed of a Roman character and seven digits, such as "H0123456'. This ID can be seen on-site exhibit signage and on the exhibit detail screen within the guide app.

If the player inputs the correct ID, they can view detailed information about that exhibit and receive a stamp on their sheet as a reward. At this point, the number of times the player presses the "Get More Hints" button before finding the treasure is recorded. If an incorrect ID is entered, two levels of hints are forcibly disclosed. Players need to find the treasure with as few mistakes and as few hints as possible.

3.2 Estimate Player's Interest from Operating Log

The system generates a personalized quiz when a player opens a new Quiz and Hints screen for the first time. The system estimates their interests from the uploaded log. It counts the tags on the exhibits they have viewed in detail.

An individual's interests are expressed as a set of multiple tags. For example, pairs like "Art, Dance" or several tags like "Hunting, Religion, Ceremony, Wooden Products" represent individual interests. These combinations of tags are scored based on their count and how many times they appear in the log. The system treats several top tag sets as the player's interests.

3.3 Ranking Treasure Candidates by Generating Quizzes with Templates

Next, the system seeks out exhibits that align with the player's estimated interests, and that the player has not yet seen, to present them as treasures. The system extracts all exhibits tagged with the tag sets of the player's interests. The system removes exhibits from the extracted ones the player has seen before, and those displayed physically close to those already seen. This encourages the player to walk around and see more related exhibits while searching.

These exhibits are candidates for treasures, and the system generates multiple quizzes using templates. Depending on the metadata and type of exhibit, some templates may be applicable while others may not. Therefore, we prepared multiple quiz templates in advance and manually scored them for quiz-like characteristics. Then, the system applies the templates for all treasure candidates and presents the quiz with the highest score.

Our prepared templates are basically in the form of "Let's look for [treasure category] in the [display area]". To this template, we add a part that expresses interest, such as "It seems you are interested in [one interest tag]," and a feature that provides a viewpoint, such as "Let's search while paying attention to [viewpoint name]".

In the ethnographic museum we used for this case, each exhibit is tagged with multiple OCM (Outline of Cultural Materials) tags, which indicate what the exhibit has been used for, and OWC (Outline of World Cultures) tags, which indicate where the exhibit has been used. These tags are valuable resources for generating personalized quizzes and providing hints to guide the players' treasure hunt.

Only certain tags can be used as [treasure category] or [interest]. For example, tags that indicate a type, such as "534: MUSICAL INSTRUMENTS", can be used, but abstract tags like "805: ORDERING OF TIME" are unsuitable for quizzes. Therefore, we manually prepared templates for each tag that is easy to search for as a noun. Moreover, for abstract tags that appear frequently, we have prepared a template for each tag, like "Let's look for exhibits related to [abstract topic]".

Similarly, the template corresponding to the viewpoint differs depending on the tag. For example, drawing attention to "differences in color by region" When drawing attention to "differences in shape by use", the target exhibit can only be a tool, and only if their usages are different. To address such situations, we prepared many templates for specific combinations of OCM included in a candidate's interest tags and OCM. For instance, if the interested OCM is 222, 223, 224, or 227, and the OCM of the treasure starts with 28, a template that creates a quiz sentence focusing on "differences in materials by use" can be applied.

Such a rule and the combination of actual sentence patterns are generally considered more specific when there are fewer applicable candidates for the template. Therefore, scores were manually assigned to the templates in order of strict conditions. The system applies the templates to the candidates, and selects the candidate that fits the template with the highest score as the treasure for the player to seek.

3.4 Design to Facilitate Gamification

We've designed and improved the reward system to make this treasure hunt game enjoyable. Firstly, we have designed the game interface, using the metaphor of treasure hunt and stamp collecting. In line with the theme of the treasure hunt, we gave it a look of a parchment on a wooden desk. Additionally, we have added a metallic texture to each component.

Next, we designed the gaming experience always to display progress and stages. Generally, in gamification, it is said to be crucial for the progress and achievements to be visualized [8]. Therefore, we adopted a format in which hints for the quiz are gradually disclosed. A stamp is collected on the sheet when the player finishes a quiz. This way, they can check how far their learning has progressed.

In addition, stamps served not merely as a visualization of progress, but also as rewards that users were delighted to obtain. The appearance of the stamps resembles the stamp traditionally used in Japan on high-scoring test papers (*i.e.*, ⬤). Furthermore, the design of the stamps became increasingly elaborate as users accumulated more of them. The screen effects at the moment of stamp acquisition were also striking, with a glowing ring pressing the stamp and a shaking screen effect.

Moreover, we provided a clear objective for the game. By specifying the number of hints used and ensuring hints are forcibly disclosed upon failure, we created gameplay aimed at completing the game with as few hints as possible. To facilitate this, the system recorded the number of hints disclosed so far in completing the treasure hunt, allowing for future review. This process may allow for more vital impressions of exhibits by recognizing failures that caused additional hint disclosure. It is also likely to stimulate the incentive for revisits by inciting an ambition to attempt the game with fewer disclosed hints in subsequent attempts.

4   Evaluation

A prototype system was implemented and field-tested in an actual museum to verify the efficacy of the proposed application. This experiment was conducted on-site at an actual museum, using images and metadata of its exhibits, under the collaboration of the museum authorities.

4.1   Evaluation Task

We had participants play the treasure hunt game on-site at the museum and later investigated whether they remembered the exhibits they searched for and those they saw along the way. The participants consisted of eight university students.

Initially, participants received an operation explanation for the museum guide app, and freely appreciated the exhibits at the museum site for 30 min. After that, we gathered the participants and generated a treasure hunt game based on each person's log up to that point. They then started playing the treasure hunt, moving around the exhibition hall until they collected four stamps. After they finished collecting all stamps, they returned to the preparation room and answered a questionnaire regarding the usability evaluation.

Specifically, the questions first asked if the participant was personally interested in the museum itself, the cultural anthropology that was the subject of the experiment, and puzzle-solving games. On a five-point scale, they were then asked to provide an overall rating for fun, usability, design, *etc.*. Similarly, they were asked to rate whether the image, map, tags, and description were useful in the quiz. Lastly, they were asked to give free-form answers on points such as what they liked, what quizzes they enjoyed, what they disliked, what they would like to see improved, and any other comments.

In addition, all participants were asked two weeks later what exhibits they remembered. For the memory survey, participants were first asked to write on paper what exhibits were answers to the quiz and quiz sentences they remembered, to confirm their recall ability. Next, in a recognition task, seen and unseen exhibits were mixed and presented to see if they could correctly discriminate.

4.2   Compared Methods

Four methods were compared within the participants to measure the effect of the interest in the exhibits themselves, personalization, and showing the viewpoint on memory consolidation. In the game, players need to search for four exhibits. During the experiment, these four exhibits were split into two that would be interesting for anyone and two that were tailored to the individual. Then, for each, they searched with and without a given viewpoint. To prevent order effects, the sequence of questions is randomized for each individual.

4.3   Experimental Result

This section verifies whether the proposed system was accepted and whether it affected memory consolidation. Firstly, as an evaluation of whether gamification was accepted, Table 1 shows the results of a usability survey immediately after the actual experiment. The results showed that while the fun of the treasure hunt game itself was highly rated, usability was not rated as highly. It was found that the quality of the hints was particularly low-rated. Also, map-based hints seem unhelpful.

Next, to measure whether gamification helped learning, Table 2 shows the degree of memory retention after two weeks. Searching for exhibits in a treasure hunt leads to stronger memories than just viewing them. Personalization and showing viewpoints have limited effects, but searching for catchy exhibits helped memorization.

5   Discussion

Firstly, the results of the usability evaluation are discussed. Nearly all participants expressed that they found the treasure hunt game enjoyable. Especially noteworthy were comments relating to enjoyment, which suggested that gradually revealing hints and walking around the location, while examining all possible candidates, was considered fun.

Regarding usability, the overall evaluation was not high. Among the freely written comments related to usability, the first notable issue was dissatisfaction with the guide app itself, used as a platform for the treasure hunt game. Specifically, participants pointed out the inconvenience of having to search for each exhibit in the guide while in front of it, even if they thought they had the correct keyword in the search function, and the exhibit did not appear. This suggests a need for a feature that allows finding "the exhibit in front of you" without keyword searching, potentially using a beacon or AR technologies.

Additionally, numerous comments were observed about integrating the guide app and the treasure hunt system. Specifically, even though the ID was displayed in the guide, the need to manually note it and then re-enter it was identified as one reason for the low rating. Also mentioned was the difficulty in reading and inputting the small exhibit ID displayed at the museum site. The exhibit IDs at the site are often written small at the bottom right of the description plate in a dimly lit venue, which might not have been suitable for users to input.

Improvements such as recognizing the location using beacon technology or image recognition, and considering the exhibit found if the user is in front of it or takes a picture of it, could be considered for these input-related issues.

Regarding the effectiveness of hints, some participants found the map-based hints unhelpful. This is generally because museums organize their exhibit spaces according to specific themes. Once a tag is visible, it is possible to predict the exact location of an exhibit more accurately than using a map. Therefore, when operating such a system, it is crucial to consider the granularity of hints and devise ways to ensure that tags related to regions are not revealed before the map.

The difficulty of the treasure hunt showed variability among individuals (which was expected, as two of the quiz questions were tailored to the individuals), and the average rating was not high. Comments regarding the quiz quality were largely positive, such as "Indeed, it accurately captured my interests". There were also opinions like "It's recognizable even without hints", "The photo doesn't resemble the actual object", and "The regional name tag narrows down the target too much".

Feedback was also received regarding the appreciation experience itself through the treasure hunt game. Comments about the effort required. Such as, the museum is too large, so after collecting logs for 30 min, solving four quiz questions was tiring, and they got tired because they had to move to an area they had already visited.

To operate such gamification in the museum, estimating interest in advance through preliminary questions or personalizing the game based on logs collected during gameplay might be beneficial. Additionally, considerations should be made for adjusting the number of stamps to collect or considering the proximity of the exhibits for the treasure hunt.

Next, the impact of the treasure hunt game on the retention of the target exhibits in memory is discussed. Overall, it was found that the exhibits targeted in the treasure hunt left a strong impression, with 84% of the participants able to recall those exhibits. Prompting participants to search for exhibits using hints might increase the possibility of those exhibits remaining in memory.

Next, we will focus on the order effects for analysis. In this experiment, the order was changed depending on the person, so the order effects should not appear between the methods. However, it is conceivable that the memory consolidation effect of the treasure hunt may decrease with familiarity. We counted how many exhibits the subjects remembered in the treasure hunt, which they solved in different orders. Seven participants could recall the answers to the first, second, and third questions, and six participants could recall the answer to the fourth question (out of eight participants). Completing four consecutive treasure hunts requires walking around the museum for an hour. Therefore, the degree of memory retention may decrease because participants get tired and accustomed to the game.

Next, we verified the effects of personalization and explicit presentation of viewpoints. Overall, they tended not to remember when asked to find exhibits considering personal interests compared to when they were asked to find manually selected exhibits. One potential reason could be the difference in the effect on memory between the intrinsic interest of the exhibit and the alignment with personal interest. The exhibits selected manually were exciting and surprising (for example, food samples not typically found in museums, cute animal statues, etc.).

On the other hand, the personalized treasures were similar to the exhibits that the participants had repeatedly seen in the early stages. They might have struggled to recall exhibits that felt repetitive or lacked novelty. Furthermore, many personalized treasures were understated, reflecting the nature of many museum exhibits. Therefore, it's essential to consider the inherent charm of the exhibits when designing the treasure hunt.

Next, we analyze the effect of highlighting a viewpoint suggested. Many participants in the interview survey reported not noticing the guidance about these critical viewpoints. Our game's rules focus on finding the target exhibits with as few clues as possible, causing participants to concentrate solely on the hints and ignore the given directives. This issue suggests a flaw in game design: the structure that encourages productive viewing is not synchronized with the reward system. To fix this, it might be necessary to adopt a system where rewards are granted only when they view the exhibit with attention to the highlighted viewpoint (*e.g.*, they must take pictures of different parts of the treasure and the exhibits they have seen to get a stamp).

Lastly, we discuss the importance of difficulty level. In the interviews, most participants mentioned the difficulty of the quiz. For example, one participant stated that the exhibit was difficult to find and remained in their memory because it was displayed in a different area than they had imagined. Another participant mentioned that they could not remember the exhibit because they accidentally found the correct exhibit in one try with a tag search, without even looking at the actual object. To make it an enjoyable and educational game, it would be necessary to keep it easy enough for anyone to clear, yet challenging enough to be memorable.

6   Conclusion

In this study, we proposed a method to enable proactive museum appreciation by gamifying museums with a personalized treasure hunt format. We implemented a prototype that integrates with an actual museum guide app, analyzes individual logs, and generates quizzes. The experimental results showed that such a game experience was enjoyable for users, and the exhibits they sought remained in their memory more than those they simply viewed.

However, the effect of personalization was limited, and there was a tendency for eye-catching exhibits sought out simply to be more easily remembered. Room for improvement was found in the method of presenting desired viewpoints and in how hints are provided. Future modifications are being planned to make the treasure hunt more practical, including adjustments to the difficulty level and selecting catchy exhibits.

Acknowledgements. This work was supported by JSPS KAKENHI Grants Number 21H03775, 21H03774, and 22H03905. The research was also supported by ROIS NII Open Collaborative Research 2023 (Grant Number 22S1001).

References

1. Camps-Ortueta, I., González-Calero, P.A., Quiroga, M.A., Gómez-Martín, P.P.: Measuring preferences in game mechanics: towards personalized chocolate-covered broccoli. In: van der Spek, E., Göbel, S., Do, E.Y.-L., Clua, E., Baalsrud Hauge, J. (eds.) ICEC-JCSG 2019. LNCS, vol. 11863, pp. 15–27. Springer, Cham (2019). https://doi.org/10.1007/978-3-030-34644-7_2

2. Ceipidor, U.B., Medaglia, C.M., Perrone, A., De Marsico, M., Di Romano, G.: A museum mobile game for children using QR-codes. In: Proceedings of the 8th International Conference on Interaction Design and Children, pp. 282–283 (2009)
3. Cesário, V., Radeta, M., Matos, S., Nisi, V.: The ocean game: assessing children's engagement and learning in a museum setting using a treasure-hunt game. In: Extended Abstracts Publication of the Annual Symposium on Computer-Human Interaction in Play, p. 99–109 (2017). https://doi.org/10.1145/3130859.3131435
4. Damala, A., Cubaud, P., Bationo, A., Houlier, P., Marchal, I.: Bridging the gap between the digital and the physical: design and evaluation of a mobile augmented reality guide for the museum visit. In: Proceedings of the 3rd International Conference on Digital Interactive Media in Entertainment and Arts, pp. 120–127 (2008)
5. Damala, A., Marchal, I., Houlier, P.: Merging augmented reality based features in mobile multimedia museum guides. In: Anticipating the Future of the Cultural Past, CIPA Conference 2007, 1–6 October 2007, pp. 259–264 (2007)
6. Falk, J.H., Dierking, L.D.: Learning from Museums. Rowman & Littlefield, Lanham (2018)
7. Farella, M., Taibi, D., Arrigo, M., Todaro, G., Fulantelli, G., Chiazzese, G.: An augmented reality mobile learning experience based on treasure hunt serious game. In: ECEL 2021 20th European Conference on e-Learning, pp. 148–154. Academic Conferences International Limited (2021)
8. Hamari, J., Koivisto, J., Sarsa, H.: Does gamification work?-a literature review of empirical studies on gamification. In: 2014 47th Hawaii International Conference on System Sciences, pp. 3025–3034. IEEE (2014)
9. Hein, G.E.: Learning in the Museum. Routledge, London (2002)
10. Keil, J., et al.: A digital look at physical museum exhibits: designing personalized stories with handheld augmented reality in museums. In: 2013 Digital Heritage International Congress (DigitalHeritage), vol. 2, pp. 685–688. IEEE (2013)
11. Kohen-Vacs, D., Ronen, M., Cohen, S.: Mobile treasure hunt games for outdoor learning. Bull. IEEE Tech. Committee Learn. Technol. 14(4), 24–26 (2012)
12. Ng, K.H., Huang, H., O'malley, C.: Treasure codes: augmenting learning from physical museum exhibits through treasure hunting. Pers. Ubiquit. Comput. 22, 739–750 (2018)
13. Paris, S.G.: Perspectives on Object-Centered Learning in Museums. Routledge, London (2002)
14. Pujol, L., Roussou, M., Poulou, S., Balet, O., Vayanou, M., Ioannidis, Y.: Personalizing interactive digital storytelling in archaeological museums: the chess project. In: 40th Annual Conference of Computer Applications and Quantitative Methods in Archaeology, pp. 93–100. Amsterdam University Press (2012)
15. Raptis, D., Tselios, N., Avouris, N.: Context-based design of mobile applications for museums: a survey of existing practices. In: Proceedings of the 7th International Conference on Human Computer Interaction with Mobile Devices and Services, pp. 153–160 (2005)
16. Rubino, I., Barberis, C., Xhembulla, J., Malnati, G.: Integrating a location-based mobile game in the museum visit: evaluating visitors' behaviour and learning. J. Comput. Cult. Herit. (JOCCH) 8(3), 1–18 (2015)
17. Shoji, Y., et al.: Museum experience into a souvenir: generating memorable postcards from guide device behavior log. In: 2021 ACM/IEEE Joint Conference on Digital Libraries (JCDL), pp. 120–129 (2021). https://doi.org/10.1109/JCDL52503.2021.00024

18. Ueta, M., et al.: Quiz generation on the electronic guide application for improving learning experience in the museum. In: BIRDS+ WEPIR@ CHIIR, pp. 96–104 (2021)
19. Wang, Y., et al.: Cultivating personalized museum tours online and on-site. Interdisc. Sci. Rev. **34**(2–3), 139–153 (2009)
20. Yatani, K., Onuma, M., Sugimoto, M., Kusunoki, F.: Musex: a system for supporting children's collaborative learning in a museum with PDAs. Syst. Comput. Jpn. **35**(14), 54–63 (2004)
21. Yenawine, P.: Visual Thinking Strategies: Using Art to Deepen Learning Across School Disciplines. Harvard Education Press, Cambridge (2013)

Creating Digital LAM Content for Schools: Modelling User Involvement in Multi-organisational Context

Riitta Peltonen[1]([⊠]) and Marko Nieminen[2]

[1] The National Library of Finland, University of Helsinki, Unioninkatu 36, Helsinki, Finland
riitta.peltonen@helsinki.fi
[2] Department of Computer Science, Aalto University, Konemiehentie 2, Espoo, Finland
marko.nieminen@aalto.fi

Abstract. Public services are usually created in a network of organisations, meta-organisations that consist multiple actors with variety of capacities. Managing work in meta-organisations face unique challenges due to multiple stakeholders with different understandings of the tasks. Management of the work requires shared base understanding of contributions needed from multiple stakeholders and for many tasks, this is not yet properly understood and modelled. User-centred design, even it supports well multi-disciplinary development of systems and services with multiple actors and can be applied to ascertain a balanced outcome from the design work, is one of these areas that lacks this understanding and requires further modelling. Typically, user-centred design responsibilities are set in a public organisation who creates the digital service platform. Through our case on creating digital library, archive, and museum (LAM) content service for schools, we study how user centred design activities happen outside the platform provider organisation. More specifically, we study how the content creation organisations can utilise the expertise of a teacher and identify how this expertise can be incorporated in content creation organisations. Based on our findings we form a tentative model for user involvement in meta-organisations (UIMO) which aims to formulate a structure for the user-centred design responsibilities in networked environment.

Keywords: Human-centred design · user involvement · inclusive design · design networks · meta-organisations · Public Value Management

1 Introduction

User-centred design is acknowledged as a recommendable approach for digital product and service creation with an emphasis of involving stakeholders, especially end users, in the design process [1]. Similar thoughts have been raised for creating public services under the term co-production [2, 3]. In Finland, public administration has provided official guidance for including user-centred design activities in online service design and development [4].

D. H. Goh et al. (Eds.): ICADL 2023, LNCS 14458, pp. 46–61, 2023.
https://doi.org/10.1007/978-981-99-8088-8_4

The Public Value Management doctrine emphasises that public services are produced in a networked environments and that it is important to pay attention to managing the division of work between organisations [2, 3]. With networked environment we refer here a network of independent public organisations producing common services in coalition i.e., in meta-organisation. However, there is not much attention to the division of work and tasks between organisations in the network. Public sector has received criticism that its guidance focuses only on requiring user-centred design in platform acquisition and procurement [5], but not in the content creation stage.

Libraries, archives and museums (LAM) organisations know how to use cultural heritage materials to support learning [6, 7, pp. 91–133, 8]. However, they have received criticism about not listening to the needs of schools and not connecting the content to the national curriculum [9]. The user-centred design approach can address this through the inclusion of teachers, the end-users of the service.

In this paper, we use the Finna Classroom service pilot as a case study. We address both types of criticism that the digital public service production as well as the LAM organisations have received. We pay attention to including user-centred design activities outside the actual platform creation, including the content design phase.

As the outcome, we form a tentative model for organizing user involvement in a national level meta-organisation for producing cultural heritage content for education. We present our experiences from the practical case of creating Finna Classroom and emphasise activities that do not typically take place on the platform development side but in the participating content specialist organisations.

The Finna service is an example of public digital service produced in a network of libraries, archives and museums. At the time of the study 2019, the Finna Classroom was a new type of educational LAM content service for schools that broadened the contributions of the national Finna.fi digital library. The platforms parts of the Finna Classroom are created by one organisation and the content comes from multiple organisations.

Our approach aims at making it easy for participating content producer organisations to involve a teacher in the design process. We examine how the digital service development projects utilised the opportunity to include the teacher in the process. We aim to understand what human-centred design activities should happen outside platform creation.

Based on the previous framing, the main research question for this paper is: *How to model and coordinate digital LAM content creation in a user-centred multi-stakeholder (meta-organisation) project?*

2 Conceptual Background

2.1 User-Centred Content Creation

Public service development emphasises the need for co-production [10–13]. Co-production can refer to a range of activities [10]. We focus only to the participative co-production i.e., to empowering users to participate in the design of future services.

Principles and processes of user-centred design appear in ISO-9241–210 [1]. There are several aligned design processes, too: Contextual design [14–16], Goal-Directed

Design [17–21], Scenario-based Design [22], Lauesen's User Interface Design [23] and the Usability Engineering Lifecycle [24]. Following the principles of user-centred design [25], all models start from researching users, analysing the data, and compressing the results into visualisations [14, 17, 18, 22–24]. Mayhew [24, p. 5] distinguishes between processes that are meant for a clearly defined starting point and processes that are meant for innovating new products. The ones for clear starting point utilize lighter user research. ISO 9241–210 [1] acknowledges this variability; projects can start from different levels and user-centred design activities can be applied in project-specific manner. All models include iterative UI design, an implementation phase [14, 17, 18, 22–24], and evaluation with users. In their process models, Mayhew [24, pp. 1–16] and Lauesen [23, pp. 44–45] explicitly mention taking the product into production and with feedback gathering and usability testing. However, the processes are typically made for digital product creation, and they don't acknowledge e.g., that there is more generic concept creation for content platform and then each content provided through it can be its own information product created separately.

The need to include customised content for different users according to their needs is typical in content creation processes. Also, writing and structuring content consistently is a similarly important process requirement, as well as content assessment, where one determines how the users will benefit from the specific content. Examples include Kostur [26] and Carliner [27] in the field of information design, Kwahk et al. [28] in health and medical information, and Blythe [29] in university online course content.

Carliner [27] proposes using an information design model that contains three levels: physical (ability to find information), cognitive (intellectual), and affective (emotional). Carliner's [27] framework contains information product specific business and user need research, setting requirements based on research data, designing the information product against those requirements, and evaluating the created product with the users. If you would apply ISO 9241–210 [1] purely to content creation, this would be in line with the recommendations of the standard.

2.2 The Impact of the Networked Nature of a Meta-organisation for Design Activities

The networked nature of service production has been acknowledged on the private and public side for already over a decade [30, pp. 93–117, 32, 33, 2, 3]. User-centred design processes and participative methods have been suggested as tools for organisations to coordinate their work [31]. However, regarding the user-centred design processes, all models seem to assume that the design work is done inside one organisation, which includes stakeholders in its design process and gives them the opportunity to affect it.

The specific focus of this paper is on meta-organisation. Meta-organisation is a network of organisations lacking the formal authority that would arise from employment contracts [32]. For meta-organisation it is critical to pay attention how individual organisations work together and how they divide and allocate tasks between organisations [32, 33]. Also, The Public Value Management (PVM) doctrine acknowledges the governance of public services and the need to manage the networked nature of public service creation [2, 3].

PVM's stance on efficiency is to check on a continuous basis that the activities fit the purpose and, with regard to its stance on accountability, to negotiate the goal setting and responsibilities within the network of stakeholders [3]. The principles of human-centred design (user research and testing) support checking that the activities are fit for the purpose.

This does not seem to be visible in the current discussion: how to apply human-centred design processes to public digital service development in meta-organisations?

3 Context of the Study, Data and Methods

3.1 Context of the Study: Creating LAM Content for Education

Our research environment, the Finna service, is a shared digital interface for Finnish LAM organisations [34]. The Finna coalition (of member organisations) fits into the description of a meta-organisation: the participants for the development of the platform and its content come from several separate organisations. The Finna team of the National Library of Finland (NLF) does the platform development, but the content comes from all LAM organisations. They are separate organisations with separate management, bound together only by signed agreements with NLF that define the outlines of their responsibilities [34]. The final outcome is not a result of the work of only one organisation, but all of them. The Finna coalition is a significantly sized meta-organisation, since practically all Finnish libraries, archives and museums are prospective partners through the Finna coalition [34, 35]. The Finna service was first launched in 2012 and at the time of the study in 2019 it already had over 300 libraries, archives and museums delivering content through the platform [34, 36].

The website and service Finna.fi is the national search interface for all the materials provided by the Finna member organisations. The Finna service interface is directly integrated into the collection systems of the Finnish LAM organisations. A user can directly search the scattered books, articles, images, documents etc. based on their meta-information. At the time of the study 2019 The Finna Classroom service was a new type of service addition to the Finna service family: the produced content offering for schools was built on top of Finna.fi content. It offers a national interface for Finnish LAM organisations to deliver curated and produced content for schools, and for schools it offers ready-made LAM content packages that are attached to the national curriculum.

3.2 Process and Participants

The starting point of the research was the beginning of the content creation pilot when focus of the work moved to the content provider organisations. Before the study phase, Finna team had formed the assumption that the Finna.fi website does not currently properly fulfil the needs of teachers and schools. Their work had started from user research and included co-innovation workshops with content-producing LAM organisations. Based on this, the project narrowed down to the Finna Classroom service concept and decision to pilot it with a small number of LAM content providers was made. Basically, the concept idea was created by following principles of user-centred design and co-creation on platform activities side and thus following current theory and recommendations.

The participating LAM organisations were Finna content provider organisations. Finna team recruited participating content production LAM organisations with two methods. First, the idea of the pilot/experiment was introduced in events targeting Finna customer organisations. Second, the Finna service directly invited handpicked customer organisations to participate. The aim was to cover libraries, archives, and museums, to select organisations that are likely to have materials of interest to schools at the national level. Still, there was the intent to select organisations of different sizes and with a different focus in their collections. Additionally, the intent was to include organisations covering minority cultures. In the end, there were seven content creator organisations: 1 library, 2 archives, and 4 museums. The library and two of the museums were bigger including the number of staff. The two archives and two museums were small with focused collections having also smaller staff. One of the bigger museums had a staff member with teacher training and the library curator had pedagogical education, but he worked with university students. With the selected organisations, the pilot was focused on cultural heritage content.

The User Involved into the Pilot was a Teacher. In the context of schools, the users would be pupils and teachers. We assumed that, in practice, the teacher is the gatekeeper who has the biggest impact on making the decision on how and which parts of the materials will be used. Since the pupils are minors, working with them would require additional consent agreements with their parents. We concluded that as the first step, we would involve teachers in content creation. Involving pupils would be an advanced step and can be taken after the first stage has progressed sufficiently. Our aim was to lower the threshold of involving a teacher in the content design activities and observe how content creation organisations would utilise the opportunity to interact with the teacher, map the activities to existing user-centred design and gather understanding weather it would matter were the UX work would have been done. For the duration of the study, Finna team hired a history teacher to be available for contact.

Information exchange and collaboration points between the teacher and the organisations are visualised in Fig. 1. The NLF Finna team agreed with each pilot organisation that they would curate a material packet from their own materials for schools. Possibly, they could also ideate readymade pedagogical ideas on how to utilise the material in education. Should the pilot organisations not create the pedagogical ideas, the teacher would be there for that task.

The Finna team had separate 1.5–2 h long kick-off meetings with each of the pilot organisations. In the meetings, they were introduced to the details of the Finna Classroom service and they were given a short introduction on how to curate materials in the Finna.fi website. They were able to ideate with the history teacher about the part of the curriculum the materials would fit, what focus in the materials would bring value for education, and what type of material is acceptable to children. This part became the place for organisations to perform the initial user research in the form of interviewing the teacher.

During the content creation phase, the pilot organisations could contact the history teacher anytime to ask for further consultation. There were two variations of this. 1) The organisations created both the curated material package and utilisation ideas themselves and asked the opinion of the teacher. At the end, the teacher did an informal review of the material set. 2) The organisations curated the material package themselves, but the teacher created the utilisation ideas. First, the organisations curated the material package and asked for teacher's opinions. In the end, the teacher did an informal review of the materials and created utilisation ideas. When needed, the teacher asked for opinions and clarifications.

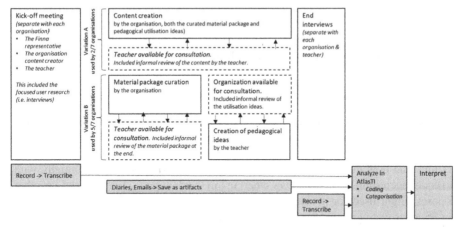

Fig. 1. Data points of information exchange and collaboration, data collection methods and analysis

3.3 Methods

The data collection methods were a selection of qualitative data collection methods. The kick-off meetings were recorded and the free discussions between the pilot organisation and the teacher were transcribed. The pilot organisations were asked to keep a diary on topics or situations where they wanted to consult the teacher. Two of the pilot organisations returned the diary sheet. Emails between the pilot organisations and the teacher were saved for analysis purposes. Both diaries and the emails were anonymised.

After the pilot, the teacher and six out of seven content creators were interviewed. The duration of the interviews varied between 15–30 min. The interviews were recorded and transcribed, and as part of the transcribing process, the identifiers of organisations and names were anonymised. The interviews with the pilot organisations were half-structured with pre-set themes. However, the discussion was free, and it allowed exploring emerging themes as well. Initially, there were five pre-set main themes: selecting the topics of the material packets to be created, creating the content for the material packets, creating readymade pedagogical utilisation ideas, using the Finna.fi website as a curation tool, and general feelings after the pilot. The underlying subtheme related to most of the main themes was: in which parts did they use the opportunity to contact the teacher? During the third interview, arising from the content, a subtheme emerged; was the nature of the materials such that it risked creating a distorted or too stereotypical image of the past if handled wrong? This was systematically included in the rest of the interviews. The interview with the teacher was also half structured to allow interesting subthemes to emerge. The main theme was only how the work proceeded with each of the organisations.

The data analysis methods followed the five-step process that Renner and Taylor-Powell [37] describe for analysing qualitative data: 1) Get to know one's data by reading through /listening to it several times. 2) Focus the analysis, 3) Categorise information, recognise the themes and patterns and organise them into coherent categories that can be pre-set or emergent, 4) Identify patterns and connections within and between categories, and 5) Interpret findings. The transcribed recordings of the kick-off meetings and the interviews and the emails were analysed with Atlas.ti software.

4   Results

The research was focused to the parts of the material that involve the teacher in the content design. These include relevant parts of the transcripts of the kick-off meetings, emails between the pilot organisations and the teacher, and parts of the end interviews that illustrate how the interaction worked out. The material was tagged initially with 140 codes according to *small themes* emerging in the dialogue. 71 codes used for other purposes. Eight used for profiling organisations. 56 that were analysed in this study. The 56 codes were grouped further into 15 slightly larger categories (later referred to as *subcategories*) and even further three larger categories (later referred as *categories* that all emerged from the materials.

The first category was the information that is useful to all organisations regardless of the topics of their collections (later referred as *General information*). The second category was information that was relevant only in the context of the collections of the organisation (later referred as *Unique dialogue*). The third category was that *Materials might have features that make contact with the teacher even more important* (e.g., such a feature could be that they are about minorities).

The General information was information that could be useful to any organisation producing materials packets for history teaching. Capturing this type of information during the pilot helped Finna team to create general instructions for all the future content-producing organisations. It consisted of four smaller subcategories:

1. Information about national curriculum
2. Practical realities related to teachers' work and how it affects what they want from extra materials
3. Instructions to consider when adding information into a material packet
4. Points to consider when selecting individual materials for a material package.

Timing wise it was practical to collect during creation of the first content products (i.e. during the pilot). It would have not mattered which organisation gathers that information, as long it was gathered a cross the first content production creations and distributed to every content producer org, but the platform provider organisation's orchestrator type of role fit for this.

The Unique dialogue category meant unique interaction topics between the teacher and the organisations that made sense only in the context of the collections of the pilot organisations, i.e., information that cannot be translated into instructions relevant to all organisations. This needed to be done separately by each content provider org.

Even though the discussion was collection-specific, the purpose behind the discussion topics had similarities between organisations. There were three different purposes that emerged from the discussion, and they reflected the phase the content creation was in. The first *purpose* behind the unique dialogue was the *initial finding of the context of use of the information product, related usage needs and limitations*. The second was the *informal review of the curated material package* and the third was about *creating the pedagogical utilisation ideas*.

The initial finding of the context of use of the information product, related usage needs and limitations was information product specific business and user need research. This purpose further split into six different narrower information topics to seek out:

1. List topics in order to recognise which interests the teacher (initial narrowing down of topics)
2. Identifying the connection (of the initially narrowed down topics) to the curriculum and finding an interesting angle to complement typical schoolbooks
3. How teachers would use the materials related to a particular topic in teaching, including possible cross-subject usage
4. Which topic or subtopic would especially benefit from extra materials (in addition to schoolbooks)
5. Delimiting criteria for the materials
6. Materials unsuitable for children/school

All the organisations first looked for help in selecting the most interesting collection topics by listing their existing collection themes to quickly identify which interested the teacher. The teacher discussed with all, how the interesting collection topics connect to the national curriculum. With 3/7 organisations, the teacher also discussed how they could in practice utilise the materials in teaching; one organisation representative who had very recently studied the pedagogy of teaching history themselves mentioned that they had considered this while selecting the materials for the package. With 4/7 organisations, there was also discussion about the potential usage of the materials for cross-subjects: e.g., same set of materials could be useful for all history, Finnish, and art education. These two topics were combined into one subcategory: How teachers would use the materials related to a particular topic in teaching, including possible cross-subject usage. Also, 4/7 organisations spontaneously found topics about which the teacher mentioned that it would be *"really good to have extra materials related to it in addition to schoolbooks"*.

Going through these information topics helped all the organisations to direct their content creation work to topics potentially bringing the most value for schools. Once the most interesting themes were identified, 5/7 organisations used the opportunity to discuss with the teacher what criteria to use in narrowing down the amount of materials. The museum with the content creator who had recent pedagogical studies mentioned using their training in narrowing down the materials.

2/7 organisations had worries that certain types of materials might be unsuitable for children for different reasons (e.g., funeral pictures or propaganda-type material, or the content being just text e.g., letters). Concerning all these worries, the answer was that the ages of the children need to be considered, but as the materials can be very interesting especially for teaching high school aged children, it was much better to ask and not just leave the material unused just in case.

All the organisations looked help to find most interesting collection parts, but discussing how well the topics of the collections matched with the curriculum topics brought in clear differences in the more detailed focus of the discussion. 2/7 organisations had collections that were easy to connect with a topic from the national curriculum already on the heading level, e.g., a collection related to a particular war. These topics are frequently spotlighted at schools and schoolbooks have lots of material related to them. Discussion with these topics were related to finding a particular subtopic that is not covered well in the schoolbooks, but which would bring additional value for the teaching. Not many organisations had these types of topics in their collections. Much more common was that the organisation had collections that on the topic level were not mentioned in the curriculum, but in discussions with the teacher, it was identified that some of the collections are directly connected to a curriculum topic. These topics could very well be subtopics that are not that well covered by the schoolbooks and could bring additional value for the teacher. With these types of themes, the dialogue between the teacher and the organisations focused on recognising the connections to the curriculum and identifying the additional angle that they could bring into the teaching.

Lightweight user evaluation was used by all the organisations. The curation work, writing introductions and adding additional information to the materials was rather straightforward for the organisations once they received rough guidelines on what was expected from them. This did not require contact with the teacher. The unique interaction found in this phase was at the end of the phase when requesting a review of the created materials. The teacher reviewed all the created material packages. Additional materials to the package were proposed for 3/7 organisations originating from the organisation's own materials or via shifting materials from one package to another to make them more versatile for schools. One of the three organisations were such that they had their own pedagogically trained staff member and others were such that the organisation didn't have one available. This dialogue with the teacher could be seen as informal user evaluation of the content.

Creating readymade pedagogical ideas brought out the biggest differences between organisations, the third purpose of having a dialogue with the teacher with how to utilise the packet as part of the teaching. Only 2/7 organisations created the ideas themselves. The two organisations that made the pedagogical utilisation ideas themselves were the ones with content creators that had pedagogical training themselves, and for them this combined with the content creation phase.

Some of the Materials Contained Features that Created a Risk. At this stage, it was possible to identify additional profiling features from the material: features that created a risk that, if used carelessly, instead of deepening learning, they could create a distorted picture of the past. In summary they were:

1. Materials related to a minority (e.g., indigenous people) or an otherwise defined group of people (e.g., working class)
2. Materials that were historical propaganda material (e.g., war time materials meant for influencing home front attitudes)

3. The collections of the organisation were rather small, or they had digitised only small portion of their collections

Three organisations had material that was related to a minority or an otherwise defined group of people. In two of these cases, there was a worry that, if not approached properly, the material could create a distorted picture of this group and emphasise stereotypies, but if used with care they could enrich the education and e.g., make the minorities visible. Similarly, in two of the cases, the material was historical propaganda material, exactly the type of material that brings opportunities to teach source criticism and skills to interpret such materials, but if used carelessly they can create a distorted image of the past. These risky cases overlapped somewhat.

Altogether 4/7 organisations (three of these were smaller organisations, one bigger with their own pedagogical staff) had this type of risky material and half of them felt (all smaller organisations) that it helped a lot that there was the possibility to discuss the image created by the material package with the teacher. Even further, they felt that creating readymade pedagogical utilisation ideas together with the teacher helped to guide the usage into a good direction. Two of the organisations mentioned themselves that either their collections are rather small or that they have digitised only a small portion of their collections. One of them consciously compensated for this and themselves additionally used other available materials in the Finna.fi service from another organisation to create a more varied packet. The teacher also proposed for the three organisations to add a few available materials from other organisations into their material packages to make them more versatile.

By its nature this information was also general and useful to all the content creation organisations in form of check list of typical risk factors. Preconisation of it benefitted from pilot phase where findings were extracted.

5   Discussion

In this chapter, we initiate the formulation of the tentative model for organising user involvement in the creation of digital LAM content service for schools.

Based on the current ISO standard [1], existing process models (Contextual design [14–16], Goal-Directed Design [17–21], Scenario-based Design [22], Lauesen's User Interface Design [23] and the Usability Engineering Lifecycle [24]) and Finnish recommendations for Design and Development of Public Online Service [4] we take as the starting point that platform development of a new digital service and implementation should follow user-centred design processes. The process can roughly be simplified to five phases: Research, Innovate & Problem scope, Design & Testing, Implementation and Follow-up. User involvement should happen at least in Research and Design & Testing phases. This is visualised in Fig. 2 bottom layer. This was not focus of this research, even though the earlier phases in Finna Classroom work had followed this. This matches also the traditional view what user-centred design activities should include when not counting the nature of meta-organisation and networked nature of the work in it.

Carliner's [27] framework suggest that also on information product design phase there should happen user-centred design activities that can be simplified to three phases

Research, Information product design and evaluation and Deliver. Similarly to platform creation, user involvement should happen at least in Research and Evaluation phases.

Based on our findings in these user-centred design activities happened unique dialog that made sense only in the context of the collections of the individual content provider. This would suggest that these activities need to be done by the individual content provider organisations individually and cannot be combined to any general user-centred design activities done. e.g. by platform provider organisation. However, our findings also suggest that at this point very light research with just one end user made difference. In our opinion, this suggests that if in the platform concepting phase has been done wider user research, per information products it is enough to do just light additional user involvement. In content services new information products are created continuous basis, so also these activities should be done continuous basis by the particular content provider organisation who happens to be creating new information product for the platform.

Our findings brought two clear differences compared to Carliner's [27] framework. The first difference was that there was also general information, useful to all content provider organisation, to be found during the pilot phase. For identifying this information, it was useful that one researcher was following initial user research done by the first content creator organisations and extracted general information that could be translated to general instructions and checklists for all the organisations. Based on this we would suggest that, when creating a new content service, a pilot content production phase is useful where platform developer follows initial user research done by the content provider orgs and extracts general information and forms general content guidelines for information products.

The second difference was that related to creating education LAM content for schools. Based on our findings for most LAM organisations (the ones without their own pedagogical resource) the work in practice was divided in two phases: the curation of the material package and creating additional pedagogical utilisation ideas. The latter required pedagogical expertise and in practise heavier involvement from the teacher.

Our pilot set-up was such that the user-centred design was "prototyped" by hiring a teacher for the duration of the pilot to be available contact. Our assumption was that once that it was recognised in more detail where and how it would be important to include teachers into the process, it would be possible to create more sophisticated process proposals that could be based on volunteer participation. Including a teacher whose role is to entirely write the utilisation ideas and hand them to the organisations to publish with their material packets turns into a lot more than just lightweight volunteer participation in a user-centred design process. A specific task requires adequate resourcing. So based on this study we cannot recommend one particular method for teacher involvement for this phase.

However, we do not recommend take the easiest approach and focus only curating material packages. Since among general findings one of the things that came up on dialog between the teacher and the content providers, teacher in general wished for pointers how and from which angle to approach the materials. Additionally concerning topics with a risk of accidental misuse, the readymade utilisation ideas are useful for guiding teachers to use them correctly. So we believe that this is important step, even based on this study we can not recommend exact methodology, we still have made it visible in the tentative user involvement model.

The adaptation of Carliner's framework as described is visualised in the Fig. 2 in the middle layer. We recommend using pilot phase where in the initial user research phase there is also included cross topic studies to capture also available general information. But after the pilot phase, each content provider org should independently do light user involvement when they are creating information products. We also recommend separating creation of teacher expertise requiring extra materials into separate phase where heavier user involvement is used.

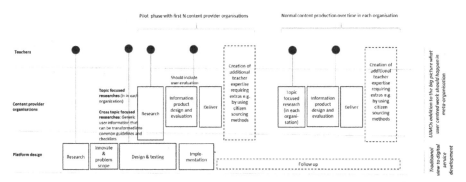

Fig. 2. Integrated process model of The User Involvement in Meta-organisations (UIMO) for educational content service creation.

5.1 Reliability and Limitations

The tentative UIMO model was created in the context of Finland level meta-organisation, Finland specific cultural heritage content and Finland specific curriculum. We would expect that it could be applicable similarly on national level context in other countries as well. However, it is likely that our study does not capture the complexity of international meta-organisations. For example, on producing the Europeana website there are at least the platform provider organisation (continent level aggregator), country level aggregators and then the individual content provider organisations in each country [38].

It is likely, that the specifically resourced history teacher in the project, lowered the threshold to contact the user. For our particular pilot this characteristic was desirable, but it introduces two limitations. First, the results best reflect content produced for history teaching. Second, based on this study alone, we cannot recommend any exact methods to be used to enable teacher participation, especially when it comes to tasks taking more time and effort from the teacher, e.g., the creation of pedagogical materials.

Another minor limitation in this study relates to the non-neutral researcher (being a member of the NLF Finna team). It is not likely that this created a major impact, the focus was on the interaction between the content-producing organisations and the teacher.

5.2 Proposals for Future Work

It would be interesting to enhance the proposed model regarding the creation of pedagogical ideas for curated material packages. Crowdsourcing could be a one direction.
Reasons like, organisations do not have the knowledge to solve the problem internally or
that the crowd is large and some members are motivated to solve the problem, add propa-
bility of an organisation to use citizen-sourcing [39]. Nam [40] lists two citizen-sourcing
methods, contests and collaborative websites as sourcing strategies for collecting professional knowledge. Another approach would be experimenting on e.g. on municipality
level wider co-operation between city museums and local schools and allow local teachers to use bit of their working time to contribute their working time for this type of work.
Osborne [41] has remarked that there are fundamental differences between private and
public services that need to be taken into consideration when applying service-dominant
logic to public services. One of the differences he lists is that a user can receive two public services that, in a joint offering, define what the final experience will be. In this case
the experience of a student depends on how well the two education services provided
by the school and the LAMs work together. Furthermore, other public services could
have common interests: teacher training, for instance, could potentially utilise this type
of educational material service and, at the same time, contribute to it.

It would be interesting to verify further the applicability of the model in cultural
heritage domain: applicability in other countries, applicability when producing content
for other target audiences than education and, perhaps even, study the applicability of
the model outside cultural heritage domain such as health care.

6 Conclusions and Recommendations

In this article, we have analysed the process of co-creation, in which the first Finna
Classroom content entities were produced. To support content creator libraries, archives
and museums we integrated a representative of the user, a teacher, into a project producing
first content packages to the Finna Classroom service pilot. Along observing their co-
operation, we examined the research question: *How to model and coordinate digital
LAM content creation in a user-centred multi-stakeholder project?*

Our outcome of this process is a tentative UIMO model for User Involvement in
Meta-Organisations, see Fig. 2. The foundation of the model presents the traditional
view of user-centred design activities taking place in digital service development. Our
findings identify additional activities that should happen in the content provider LAM
organisations during the content creation phases and thus add complementary structure
to the traditional view of the user-centred design when considering responsibilities in
meta-organisation. Our UIMO model emphasises the role of the follow-up phase that
has been weak in traditional development process models. This emphasis may serve
to reveal new dependencies for consideration in future development of digital LAM
platforms and content creation.

In preparing for the creation of content for digital services, we recommend careful
identification of participant-specific responsibilities and tasks, and careful coordination
and alignment of the tasks with the overall process. Also a pilot phase is of importance: collaborative exploration of cross-content topics to generate findings on general

observations of needs of the schools that can be translated into general instructions and checklists. Furthermore, according to principles of user-centred design, prior to making new content available to the public, we advice each actor and organisation doing content production to perform lightweight user testing per each information product they create.

References

1. ISO 9241–210, Ergonomics of human-system interaction – Part 210: Human-centered design for interactive systems. International Standard Organisation, Geneve (2019)
2. O' Flynn, J.: From new public management to public value: paradigmatic change and managerial implications. Austr. J. Publ. Administr. **66**(3), 353 (2007)
3. Stoker, G.: Public value management: a new narrative for networked governance? Am. Rev. Publ. Administr. **36**(1), 41–57 (2006)
4. JUHTA: JHS 190 Design and Development of Public Online Service (In Finnish: JHS 190 Julkisen verkkopalvelun suunnittelu ja kehittäminen), 13 6 2014,https://www.suomidigi.fi/sites/default/files/2020-07/JHS190_0.doc. Accessed 31 Jan 2021
5. Kautonen, H., Nieminen, M.: A critical look at the prerequisites of user-centred ICT procurements in the public sector (In Finnish: Julkisten ICT-hankintojen käyttäjäkeskeisyyden edellytysten kriittinen tarkastelu.), Hallinnon Tutkimus, vol. 38, no. 3, pp. 155–173 (2019)
6. Savenije, G.M., De Bruijn, P.: Historical empathy in a museum: uniting contextualisation and emotional engagement. Int. J. Herit. Stud. **23**(9), 832–845 (2017)
7. Talboys, G.K.: Using Museums as an Educational Resource. An Intoductory Handbook for Studens and Teachers. 2nd. ed. Taylor & Francis Group, New York (2016)
8. Arnold, D.: Using museum objects to stimulate student interest in Australian curriculum. Hist. Ethos **20**(2), 11–17 (2012)
9. Marcus, A.S., Levine, T.H., Grenier, R.S.: How secondary history teachers use and think about museums: current practices and untapped promise for promoting historical understanding. Theor. Res. Soc. Educ. **40**(1), 66–97 (2012)
10. Osborne, S.P., Strokosch, K.: It takes two to tango? Understanding the co-production of public services by integrating the services management and public administration perspectives. Br. J. Manage. **24**(1), S31–S47 (2013)
11. Osborne, S.P., Radnor, Z., Nasi, G.: A new theory for public service management? Toward a (Public) service-dominant approach. Am. Rev. Publ. Administr. **43**(2), 135–158 (2013)
12. Radnor, Z., Osborne, S.P., Kinder, T., Mutton, J.: Operationalizing co-production in public services delivery: the contribution of service blueprinting. Publ. Manage. Rev.: Co-product. Publ. Serv. **16**(3), 402–423 (2014)
13. Pestoff, V.: Citizens and co-production of welfare services: childcare in eight European countries. Publ. Manage. Rev.: Co-product.: Third Sect. Delivery Publ. Serv. **8**(4), 503–519 (2006)
14. Holtzblatt, K., Beyer, H.: Contextual Design Defining Customer-Centred Systems. Morgan Kaufmann Publishers, San Francisco (1998)
15. Beyer, H., Holtzblatt, K., Baker, L.: An agile customer-centered method: rapid contextual design. In: Zannier, C., Erdogmus, H., Lindstrom, L. (eds.) Extreme Programming and Agile Methods - XP/Agile Universe 2004. Lecture Notes in Computer Science, vol. 3134, pp. 50–59. Springer, Heidelberg (2004). https://doi.org/10.1007/978-3-540-27777-4_6
16. Holtzblatt, K., Beyer, H.: Contextual Design. Design for Life. Elsevier, Cambridge (2017)
17. Cooper, A.: About Face: The Essentials of User Interface Design. Hungry Minds Inc, New York (1995)

18. Cooper, A., Reinmann, R.: About Face 2.0: The Essentials of Interaction Design. Wiley Publishing Inc, Indianapolis (2003)
19. Cooper, A.,Reinmann, R., Cronin, D.: About Face 3: The Essentials of Interaction Design. 3rd rev. ed. Wiley Publishing Inc, Indianapolis (2007)
20. Goodwin, K.: Designing for the Digital Age. How to Create Human-Centered Products and Services. Wiley Publishing Inc, Indianapolis (2009)
21. Cooper, A., Cronin, D., Noessel, C., Reimann, R.: About Face: The Essentials of Interaction Design. Wiley Publishing Inc, Indianapolis (2014)
22. Carroll, J., Rosson, M.: Usability Engineering: Scenario-Based Development of Human Computer Interaction. Morgan Kaufmann Publishers Inc, San Francisco (2003)
23. Lauesen, S.: User Interface Design. A Software Engineering Perspective. Pearson Education Limited, Harlow (2005)
24. Mayhew, D.: The Usability Engineering Lifecycle: A Practitioner's Handbook for User Interface Design. Morgan Kaufmann Publishers, San Francisco (1999)
25. Gould, J., Lewis, C.: Designing for usability: key principles and what designers think. Commun. ACM **28**(3), 300–311 (1985)
26. Kostur, P.: Incorporating usability into content management (2006)
27. Carliner, S.: Physical, cognitive, and affective: a three-part framework for information design. Tech. Commun. **47**(4), 561–576 (2000)
28. Kwahk, J., Smith-Jackson, T.L., Williges, R.C.: From user-centered design to senior-centered design: designing internet health information portals. Proc. Hum. Factors Ergon. Soc. Ann. Meet. **45**(6), 580–584 (2001)
29. Blythe, S.: Designing online courses: user-centered practices. Comput. Compos. **18**(4), 329–346 (2001)
30. Prahalad, C., Ramaswamy, V.: The Future of Competition Co-creating Unique Value with Customers. Harward Business School Press, Boston (2004)
31. Virtanen, P., Stenvall, J.: The evolution of public services from co-production to cocreation and beyond new public management's unfinished trajectory? Int. J. Leaders. Publ. Serv. **10**(2), 91–107 (2014)
32. Gulati, R., Puranam, P., Tushman, M.: Meta-organization design: rethinking design in interorganizational and community contexts. Strateg. Manag. J. **33**(6), 571–586 (2012)
33. Vale, J.: Individual intellectual capital versus collective intellectual capital in a meta-organization. J. Intellect. Capital **17**(2), 279–297 (2016)
34. Hormia-Poutiainen, K., Kautonen, H., Lassila, A.: The Finnish national digital library: a national service is developed in collaboration with a network of libraries, archives and museums. Insights: UKSG J. **26**(1), 60–65 (2013)
35. Kautonen, H.: Evaluating digital library's service concept and pre-launch implementation. In: Proceedings of the 5th International Conference of Applied Human Factors and Ergonomics AHFE 2014, Krakov, Poland (2014)
36. Täppinen, T., Kulmala, H., Champagne, E., Honkanen, V.: FINNA usage and trends 2018 (in Finnish: FINNA Käyttö ja trendit 2018). Wunder, Helsinki (2019)
37. Renner, M., Taylor-Powell, E.: Analyzing qualitative data. In: Programme Development & Evaluation, pp. 1–10. University of Wisconsin-Extension Cooperative Extension, Madison (2003)
38. Europeana, About. https://www.europeana.eu/en/about-us. Accessed 10 Sep 2023

39. Afuah, A., Tucci, C.: Crowdsourcing as a solution to distant search. Acad. Manage. Acad. Manag. Rev. **37**(3), 355–375 (2012)

40. Nam, T.: Suggesting frameworks of citizen-sourcing via government 2.0. Gov. Inf. Quart. **29**(1), 12–20 (2012)

41. Osborne, S.P.: From public service-dominant logic to public service logic: are public service organizations capable of co-production and value co-creation? Publ. Manag. Rev. **20**(2), 225–231 (2018)

Using Information System Success Model to Explore Graduate Students' Satisfaction and Individual Impact Toward the Use of National Digital Library of Theses and Dissertations in Taiwan

Wei-Hsiang Hung[2,1] , Yi-Shan Hsieh[2] , Chin-Cheng Lin[2] , Bing-Yi Chen[2] ,
and Hao-Ren Ke[2(✉)]

[1] National Central Library, Taipei, Taiwan
[2] Graduate Institute of Library and Information Studies, National Taiwan Normal University,
Taipei, Taiwan
{weldon,kelly9310,jimmy3357,antonello,calvenke}@ntnu.edu.tw

Abstract. The National Digital Library of Theses and Dissertations in Taiwan (NDLTD hereafter) is the largest and most comprehensive information system for academic theses and dissertations in Taiwan. It serves as a vital resource for numerous graduate students who seek to access and utilize relevant information during their research endeavors. By searching and browsing past research studies, students can further develop their own research topics. Moreover, upon completion of their studies, students can share their findings online with other researchers. Despite the extensive usage of NDLTD, there has been a lack of investigation into user satisfaction and its individual impact. Therefore, this study aims to explore the satisfaction levels and individual effects experienced by graduate students when using this system based on the Information System Success Model. This research seeks to provide insights into graduate students' usage of the system and can serve as a reference for future system optimization and enhancements.

Keywords: National Library · Theses and Dissertations System · Information System Success Model

1 Introduction

The thesis and dissertation of doctoral and master's students hold paramount importance as academic publications. Libraries around the world are committed to establishing relevant systems for hosting and providing access to these academic works, aiming to offer scholarly services and support. In Taiwan, the National Central Library (NCL hereafter) has established and maintains the largest and most comprehensive system, NDLTD (https://ndltd.ncl.edu.tw), for doctoral and master's theses and dissertations. NDLTD is a free online service system available to the general public, which is legally designated as the repository system according to the Degree Conferral Act of Taiwan. It has become a widely used online system among many graduate students as well as other researchers. The primary objective of NDLTD is to collect theses and dissertations from universities and colleges in Taiwan, actively providing knowledge enhancement and value-added services to support academic research and reveal the research achievements of Taiwanese graduate students (National Central Library, n.d.). Since its inception in 2010 until December 2022, NDLTD has attracted over 500 million visitors (National Central Library, 2023), with more than 4.9 billion searches conducted, averaging around 400 million annual browsing and retrieval activities and over 30 million monthly searches by researchers. Considering the significant usage and demand for NDLTD, previous satisfaction surveys conducted annually by the NCL solely focused on the overall satisfaction, without delving into the satisfaction regarding system quality and information quality.

DeLone and McLean (1992) synthesized over 180 articles published between 1981 and 1987 and proposed the Information System Success Model (ISSM hereafter), which consists of six major indicators: System Quality, Information Quality, Use, User Satisfaction, Individual Impact, and Organization Impact (Fig. 1). Research has confirmed that quality indicators have an impact on information system use and user satisfaction, and there is a mutual influence between information system use and user satisfaction. Furthermore, information system use and user satisfaction directly or indirectly influence individuals and organizations (Chou, 2014; Hsieh & Su, 2015). This study adopts ISSM proposed by DeLone and McLean. Four indicators, quality, system quality, user satisfaction, and individual impact, are utilized to investigate the system satisfaction and its impact on individuals regarding the use of NDLTD.

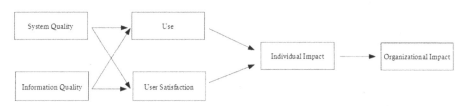

Fig. 1. ISSM (Delone & McLean, 1992)

2   Research Method

Considering the specific purpose of NDLTD and the aim of this study to explore user satisfaction and its effects on individuals, four indicators of ISSM were selected for measurement. These indicators are as follows:

1. Information Quality: evaluating the data quality of NDLTD, the measurement items include precision, accuracy, currency, completeness, and relevance/usefulness.
2. System Quality: assessing the system quality of NDLTD, the measurement items include ease of use, ease of learning, reliability, adaptability, and response time.

3. User Satisfaction: evaluating the satisfaction level of users with the use of NDLTD. The measurement items include user information satisfaction, user satisfaction, and overall satisfaction.
4. Individual Impact: assessing the impact on individuals after using NDLTD. The measurement items include ability to identify solutions, time to decision, time taken to complete a task, and improve personal productivity.

This study assumes that user satisfaction is influenced by both information quality and system quality. Furthermore, it posits that user satisfaction has an impact on individuals. Based on the above indicators and the objectives of this study, the research model (Fig. 2) and the research hypotheses are proposed as follows:

Fig. 2. Model of the research

H1: Information quality has a positive impact on User satisfaction.
H2: System quality has a positive impact on User satisfaction.
H3: User satisfaction has a positive impact on Individual impact.
In this study, the responses of the enrolled graduate students in Taiwan were assessed by a set of questionnaire items containing 21 items in information quality, system quality, user satisfaction and individual impact. Data was gathered from 119 students using an online questionnaire distributed through Facebook.

3   Findings

Students' reactions and responses toward the use of NDLTD are summarized in following aspects: information quality, system quality, user satisfaction and individual impact. Tables 1, 2, 3 and 4 summarizes the research findings.

This study employed multiple regression analysis to validate the overall statistical results of ISSM. Through SPSS analysis (as shown in Table 5), the VIF values between the groups ranged from 1.000 to 1.782, all of which were less than 10, indicating that the collinearity effect is within an acceptable range.

The results of hypothesis testing in this study (Fig. 3) are as follows:

H1: "Information Quality" has a positive impact on "User Satisfaction" ($b = 0.513$, $p < 0.001$). This validation result aligns with the findings of DeLone & McLean (1992, 2003), indicating that Information quality has a positive influence on "User Satisfaction". Therefore, improving information quality has a positive effect on user usage behavior.

H2: "System Quality" does not have a positive impact on "User Satisfaction" ($b = 0.067$, $p > 0.05$). One possible reason could be that, despite NDLTD's system quality

Table 1. Summarize of Information Quality Aspect.

Questions	Strongly Disagree → Strongly Agree					Mean	SD
	1	2	3	4	5		
	Number of respondents						
The information of NDLTD is precise	1	8	26	63	21	3.8	0.8
The information of NDLTD is accurate	1	0	21	56	41	4.1	0.8
The information of NDLTD is current	5	13	46	37	18	3.4	1.0
The information of NDLTD is complete	5	7	31	52	24	3.7	1.0
The information of NDLTD is relevant	3	10	28	50	28	3.8	1.0

Table 2. Summarize of System Quality Aspect.

Questions	Strongly Disagree → Strongly Agree					Mean	SD
	1	2	3	4	5		
	Number of respondents						
The interface of NDLTD is easy to use	10	14	34	41	20	3.4	1.2
The use of NDLTD is ease of learning	3	10	29	54	23	3.7	1.0
The function of NDLTD is complete	7	22	26	45	19	3.4	1.1
The response time of NDLTD is quick	12	23	31	34	19	3.2	1.2
The stability of NDLTD is reliable	9	16	32	39	23	3.4	1.2

possibly not meeting students' expectations, they still choose to use it because of its unique features and alignment with their specific usage needs.

H3: "User Satisfaction" has a positive impact on "Individual Impact" ($b = 0.681$, $p < 0.001$). This result is consistent with previous similar studies, demonstrating that "User Satisfaction" positively affects "Individual Impact". Thus, enhancing "User Satisfaction" with the system leads to a positive impact on individual outcomes.

Table 3. Summarize of User Satisfaction Aspect.

Questions	Never Used	Strongly Disagree → Strongly Agree					Mean	SD
	0	1	2	3	4	5		
	Number of respondents							
I am satisfied with the search function of NDLTD	1	6	15	29	49	19	3.5	1.1
I am satisfied with the download function of NDLTD	7	9	25	22	44	12	3.2	1.2
I am satisfied with the related information link function of NDLTD	16	5	9	31	43	15	3.5	1.0
I am satisfied with the reference format function of NDLTD	33	6	9	25	33	13	3.4	1.1
I am satisfied with the bibliography collection function of NDLTD	48	5	10	23	24	9	3.3	1.1
Overall, I am very satisfied with NDLTD	0	3	10	40	51	15	3.6	0.9

Table 4. Summarize Individual Impact Aspect.

Questions	Never Used	Strongly Disagree → Strongly Agree					Mean	SD
	0	1	2	3	4	5		
	Number of respondents							
Using NDLTD helps me understand research trends	5	18	29	47	20	5	3.5	1.1
Using NDLTD assists me in solving research problems	3	11	27	60	18	3	3.7	0.9
Using NDLTD saves my time in deciding research topic	9	22	45	29	14	9	3.1	1.1
Using NDLTD is beneficial for writing my thesis/dissertation	3	5	14	63	34	3	4.0	0.9
Using NDLTD contributes to my research growth	4	6	17	70	22	4	3.8	0.9

Table 5. Multiple Regression Analysis.

Independent variable	Dependent variable	
	User satisfaction	Individual impact
Information quality	0.513***	
System quality	0.067	
User satisfaction		0.681***
R2	0.289	0.272
Adj-R2	0.277	0.266
F value	23.565	43.762
Significance	0.000	0.000
VIF	1.782	1.000

*** $p < 0.001$; ** $p < 0.01$; * $p < 0.05$.

Fig. 3. Multiple Regression Path Diagram

4   Conclusion

This study aims to evaluate the responses of enrolled graduate students toward the use of NDLTD. Participants provided overall satisfaction scores for information quality, system quality, user satisfaction, and individual impact, with ratings ranging from 3.41 to 3.76. The research hypotheses were validated through regression analysis. Through regression analysis, the research hypotheses were validated, indicating a significant influence of "information quality" on "user satisfaction," subsequently impacting individuals positively. However, the relationship between "system quality" and "user satisfaction" was found to be non-significant. This may be due to the uniqueness of NDLTD, which necessitates users to use it or other reasons that require further investigation.

According to the above research findings, it is highly recommended that NDLTD should implement a diverse range of strategies to guarantee the delivery of clear, accurate, current and pertinent information, as it has been demonstrate to have a considerable impact on user satisfaction. The study is preliminary. In the future, ongoing data collection and evaluation is needed. It is hope that NDLTD could play the role as a pivotal resource supporting both research and personal growth for graduate students.

References

Chou, S.: Extending the technology acceptance model and the information systems success model to explore user satisfaction with the signature verification system [Unpublished master's thesis]. Chung Hua University, Taiwan (2014)

DeLone, W.H., McLean, E.R.: Information systems success: the quest for the dependent variable. Inf. Syst. Res. **3**(1), 60–95 (1992)

DeLone, W.H., McLean, E.R.: The DeLone and McLean model of information systems success: a ten-year update. J. Manag. Inf. Syst. **19**(4), 9–30 (2003)

Hsieh, P., Su, Y.: A study exploring critical success factors in the electronic medical record information system for medical information staff: the extension of a successful model system. J. Med. Health Inf. Manage. **13**(2), 19–39 (2015)

National Central Library. (n.d.). About us. National Central Library (Taiwan).https://etds.ncl.edu.tw/cgi-bin/gs32/gsweb.cgi/ccd=5zJATV/aboutnclcdr

Digital Archives and Data Management

Emerging Trends in Content Management Systems (CMSs) for Library Websites: A Study of Selected Academic Libraries in the Philippines

Marvin Factor[1]([✉]) [iD], April Manabat[2,3] [iD], Josephine Maghari[1] [iD], and Yugosto Balbas[1] [iD]

[1] De La Salle University, 2401 Taft Avenue, 1004 Malate Manila, Philippines
{marvin.factor,josephine.maghari,yugosto.balbas}@dlsu.edu.ph
[2] Nazarbayev University, 53 Kabanbay Batyr, Nur-Sultan, Kazakhstan
april.manabat@nu.edu.kz
[3] Polytechnic University of the Philippines, A. Mabini Campus, Anonas Street, Sta., Mesa, 1016 Manila, Philippines
armanabat@pup.edu.ph

Abstract. The COVID-19 pandemic has accelerated the adoption of technology in academic institutions, including libraries, to support research, learning, and information dissemination. Content management systems (CMSs) have emerged as valuable tools for libraries to efficiently create and manage content-rich websites without extensive programming knowledge. This study focuses on the assessment of CMSs used by the top four Philippine universities based on the 2020 QS Asia University Rankings. By analyzing the libraries' websites and CMS functionalities, the researchers explored how these systems facilitate research, learning, and information sharing during the pandemic. The study also investigated the challenges and advantages associated with CMSs for library website management. Findings revealed that WordPress and Drupal were the CMSs employed, with Adobe Muse, Microsoft ASP.Net, and Springshare serving as additional platforms. While these CMSs enhance communication with library patrons due to their customizability and user-friendliness, only one library has a dedicated guide for navigating library services in the "new normal". Recognizing their websites as primary communication channels, all four libraries have leveraged their CMSs to ensure easy access to collection and service information for their patrons.

Keywords: Content Management System (CMS) · Academic libraries · Library websites · Philippines

1 Introduction

The upturn of the pandemic has forced many educational institutions to suddenly embrace and accept the use of various available technologies to ensure continuity in delivering educational services. Libraries, as the informational arm of any educational institution, are also using various technologies to deliver efficient and effective library services to their patrons even during challenging times. Having a library website has become their main communication channel in connecting to their clients. Hence, managing such websites should not be taken lightly.

Though it might sound a little technical for some, website management has become a little bit handy for many libraries with the use of content management systems. Content Management System (CMS) facilitates the creation and modification of digital content, including files, images, electronic documents, audio files, and many more, in real-time or as needed. It is designed to enable the deployment and publishing of any kind of website [15]. It is also a software application used to create, customize, and manage information and enables libraries to quickly build, deploy, and maintain content-rich websites without the knowledge of programming languages [21].

Since CMSs do not require much knowledge of programming languages, many libraries saw the potential of CMS to help them manage their websites. For instance, Ohio State University (OSU) felt the need for a CMS after determining that they needed an easy-to-use website management system that allows content providers to have undivided attention to content and have others work on the technicalities of the platform [2]. This further allows the libraries to come up with a professional-looking website that includes consistency in the design and layout as well as its maintenance in a more manageable, less challenging manner. As time goes by, the use of CMS for website management in academic libraries has noticeably increased [6]. From the traditional use of websites to convey basic information such as library hours and policies, more libraries have found their websites as their main communication tool and include more information and complexities in their websites which later realized basic website authoring functionalities and features as inadequate to their needs, thus, thought of CMSs to help manage their website (p. 42). This indeed signifies the benefits of using CMSs in managing library websites as more and more libraries become more visible online.

This study focuses on the assessment of the content management systems (CMSs) of the academic libraries of the top four (4) Philippine universities based on the 2020 QS Asia University Rankings for Higher Education Institutions (HEIs). Using the evaluation criteria from related literature, the researchers examined and assessed the academic libraries' websites and identified what CMSs they were using, the various functions and features, and how they helped in research, learning, and information dissemination, especially in this time of the pandemic. In addition, this study aims to identify the challenges and opportunities of using CMS for library website management.

2 Related Literature

2.1 Websites for Communication and Its Management in Libraries

As more and more industries, organizations, and even individuals become visible online, many are seeing the value of websites as their main communication channels which has been evident in several studies. In a study conducted by Micik & Kunesova [19], they argued that accessibility and visibility of career websites as a primary communication channel, companies should consider website optimization strategies to attract generation Y (aka millennials) potential employees. They also noted that for career websites to serve their purpose, they should include all relevant information, be user-friendly, and attractive. In another study, Garcia, Duran & Maia [11] also noted the importance of websites as a main digital communication channel for Portuguese small and mid-sized enterprises (SMEs) and that corporate websites should have e-commerce functionalities to be considered mature enough.

Given that websites play an important role as a digital communication channel, the need to provide more comprehensive and compelling website content is now considered by many companies and organizations. More focus is given to website content creation with little knowledge of website development or programming language. Thus, the use of web content management systems (CMSs) has come into play. Content Management System (CMS) helps in creating and managing content without much knowledge of the technicalities of hypertext markup language (HTML) [11]. CMSs can also be of great use not just for information dissemination but also for digital marketing. This has also been evident in libraries where CMSs are used for the said purpose [6, 12, 13, 23, 24, 27]. Through the utilization of CMSs as an added tool for website management, they were able to provide more robust and comprehensive library websites.

User experience should also be considered in website management and the use of CMSs can help enhance that. In a related study, Tjong [26] identified the success of using CMS in institutions to improve learning quality by conducting an evaluation of user satisfaction at Bina Nusantara University. Her study focuses on critical success factors from user perception. The study revealed that the CMS Binusmaya 2.0 still must undergo many improvements to meet user satisfaction as expressed in the answers to open questions by SMEs. This also includes many features that need to be added and their usage is not efficient so often have to make SME do repetitive work.

The websites are the primary source of information for a library. They help in communicating with the users who cannot frequently visit the library due to several reasons. Library website is a communication tool between the services of the library and their users in the digital world [10]. Libraries should take advantage of the Web site by using creative and unique ways to communicate the library's purpose and vision during times of constant change and competition [16]. It is essential in the sense that it helps in the development of long-term relationships with patrons. Without a website, a library may find it difficult to prove its significance to its potential users in modern times [17]. The implementation of CMS dramatically changes the role of the web services staff and requires training for the librarians and staff who are now empowered to provide the content [7].

2.2 Content Management Systems for Library Website Management

The need to adopt a CMS is, mainly, to find an answer to the challenge of managing, modifying, and updating a large volume of information. The need to use the same content on different media with different characteristics requires suitable systems of collection and management. In addition, it makes personalization very easy to reach, with the advantage of communicating in different ways, depending on the target. The adoption of CMSs to manage academic libraries' websites is increasing, but not all CMSs are created equal. A library's website is its virtual "branch" and is vitally important to the functioning of the library. The management of such an important component of the library should not be left to chance [6]. The use of CMSs in managing library websites has been evident in several studies. Comeaux and Schmetzke [5] reviewed the academic library websites of the fifty-six campuses offering ALA-accredited graduate degrees (generally larger universities) and used tools and examined page code to determine on their own if the libraries used CMSs, as opposed to polling librarians at those institutions to ask them to self-identify if they used CMSs. They identified nineteen out of fifty-six (34%) sites using CMSs. The authors offered this caveat, "It is very possible that more sites use CMSs than could be readily identified. This is particularly true for 'home-grown' systems, which are unlikely to leave any readily discernible source code" (p. 43). With the different methodologies and population groups in these studies, it was not possible to draw conclusions regarding CMS adoption rates within academic libraries over time using these results. In a similar study, Connell [6] surveyed academic library web managers from four-year institutions to discover whether they had adopted CMSs, which tools they were using, and their satisfaction with their website management system. Other issues, such as institutional control over library website management were raised.

The survey results showed that CMS satisfaction levels vary by tool and that many libraries do not have input into the selection of their CMS because the determination was made at an institutional level. Moreover, the study conducted by Rafiq, Ashiq, Rehman & Yousaf [22] examined the quality of library websites of QS world's top-ranked medical libraries' services, resources, information dissemination tools, and training opportunities for library users. The study also revealed that the most famous five dissemination tools were Facebook, Twitter, Instagram, YouTube, and LinkedIn.

2.3 Challenges of Using CMS

While the abovementioned literature shows that CMS permits the creation costs of information and knowledge to be minimized, maximizing their value in a number of ways, there are also challenges in using it that should also be considered. One challenge is that the process of selecting and implementing a CMS is not a fully technical one. The selection must be tied to the goals and strategy of the library and parent organization, must meet specific local requirements for functionality, and must include revision of the content management environment, meaning new roles for the people involved with the website. Another challenge was and continues to be a lack of a turn-key library CMS. Several libraries that did a systematic requirements-gathering process generally found that the readily available CMSs did not meet their requirements, and they ended up writing their own applications [28]. Building a CMS is not a project to take lightly, so only a select few libraries with dedicated in-house programming staff are able to take on such an endeavor. The sharing of the requirements of these in-house library-specific CMSs is valuable for other libraries in identifying their own requirements [2]. These challenges of using CMS will help other academic libraries in choosing suitable CMSs for their libraries.

3 Methodology

This study employed a descriptive approach to assess the content management systems (CMSs) of the academic libraries of the top four (4) Philippine universities based on the 2020 QS Asia University Rankings for Higher Education Institutions (HEIs). The researchers made use of Web Content Analysis and adopted the evaluation criteria from Krouska, Virvou, & Troussas [15] and the library website survey from Pathak, Pal, & Rai [20] studies with some modifications such as the inclusion of the dedicated page for COVID-19 information, social media accounts, chat box, etc. The study made use of, the heuristic evaluation, a usability inspection method for computer software that helps to identify usability problems in the user interface design [25]. It specifically involves evaluators examining the interface and judging its compliance with recognized usability principles. Furthermore, the researchers also employed the cognitive walkthrough method which is a usability inspection method used to identify issues in interactive systems, focusing on how easy it is for new users to accomplish tasks with the system [18]. Through heuristic evaluation and cognitive walkthrough, this study showed different ways to help library users learn to navigate and find different resources and acquire information through their library websites. To identify the CMSs used by academic libraries, the researchers used Wappalyzer [1], Builtwith [4], and WhatCMS [9] website applications.

4   Results and Discussion

4.1   Profile of Academic Libraries

The academic libraries were identified based on the top four (4) Philippine universities on the 2020 QS Asia University Rankings HEIs. All academic libraries studied were located in the National Capital Region, Philippines. Academic libraries A and B are located in Quezon City, while academic libraries C and D are located in the City of Manila. In terms of population, Library D serves a very large population with a range of 35,000–39,999 enrolled students followed by Library A with a range of 20,000–24,999 enrollees. The two other libraries, Library B and C have almost the same range of 10,000–14,999 enrolled students. All academic libraries support the courses and programs offered leading to officially recognized higher education degrees such as bachelor's degrees, master's degrees, and doctorate degrees in several areas of study. In addition, Libraries B, C, and D, are formally affiliated with the Christian-Catholic institution, except with Library A which is run by a non-sectarian institution.

4.2   CMS Profile of Libraries

All four academic libraries use CMS as tools such as WordPress, Drupal, Adobe Muse, Microsoft ASP.Net, and Springshare for website management and as software support for web-based applications as shown in Table 1. WordPress is the most used CMS. These libraries found their CMS a useful tool for communicating with their library patrons as it is customizable and easy to use. Although information related to their services, collections, and policies was already included on their websites, only one library has a dedicated library guide on making use of the library and its services in the new normal. To provide virtual synchronous reference services, all libraries were using chats to communicate with their patrons. To widen their reach, all libraries strengthen their online library presence on various social media platforms such as Facebook, Instagram, and Twitter.

All libraries have a new book display, a web-OPAC facility, checking and borrowing books online, and a library webpage. They also offer services such as online book reservations, updating the library webpage, and maintaining it with the help of library personnel. Additionally, they provide lists of print journals, e-journals, e-books, online databases, and information on library rules and borrowing rules. Most libraries have archives for new books, while consortium memberships and librarian information are common. Library B lacks some services like archives for new books, online book reservations, and a subscribed bibliographic online database. Library D uses a combination of CMS platforms and does not have certain services like archives for new books, online book reservations, and a link to the institutional repository. Additionally, information about library staff is missing for Library A and Library D. Each library is a member of different consortia, with varying numbers of e-journals provided by each consortium. Library A has additional features like a dedicated webpage/guide for COVID-19 pandemic-related information and presence on multiple social media platforms. Library C has a chat box for user interactions.

Table 1. Academic Library CMSs website survey.

Library & Miscellaneous Services	Library A	Library B	Library C	Library D
CMS	WordPress	Drupal	WordPress	WordPress
Additional CMS	Not Found	Not Found	Springshare	Adobe Muse, Microsoft ASP.Net
New Books Display	Yes	Yes	Yes	Yes
Archives – New Books Display				
New issue Arrivals	Yes	Not Found	Yes	Yes
Web-OPAC Facility	Yes	Yes	Yes	Yes
Online Book Reservation	Yes	Yes	Yes	Not Found
Checking and Borrowing Books Online	Yes	Yes	Yes	Yes
Library Website	Yes	Yes	Yes	Yes
Frequency-Updating Library Webpage	Yes	Yes	Yes	Yes
Library Web Page Maintained By	Library Personnel	Library Personnel	Library Personnel	Library Personnel

(*continued*)

Table 1. (*continued*)

Library & Miscellaneous Services	Library A	Library B	Library C	Library D
List of Print Journals	Yes	Yes	Yes	Yes
List of Print Journals Holdings	Yes	Yes	Yes	Yes
List of e-Journals (A–Z)	Yes	Yes	Yes	Yes
List of e-Journals with Archives	Yes	Yes	Yes	Yes
List of e-Journals with Links	Yes	Yes	Yes	Yes
List of Subscribed Full-Text Online Databases	Yes	Yes	Yes	Yes
List of Subscribed Bibliographic Online Databases	Yes	Not Found	Yes	Not Found
List of Free e-Journals (respective discipline)	Yes	Yes	Yes	Yes
List of e-Books	Yes	Yes	Yes	Yes
Link to Institutional Repository	Yes	Not Found	Yes	Yes
Current Awareness Services (CAS)	Yes	Yes	Yes	Yes
Selective Dissemination of Information (SDI)	Yes	Yes	Yes	Yes
Library Rules	Yes	Yes	Yes	Yes
Borrowing Rules	Yes	Yes	Yes	Yes
Section-Wise Information	Yes	Yes	Yes	Yes
No. of Library Staff	Not Found	5 Admin Staff 17 Librarian 32 Library Staff 6 It Staff	Not Found	26 Supports Staff 3 Library Administrators 30 Librarians

(*continued*)

Table 1. (*continued*)

Library & Miscellaneous Services	Library A	Library B	Library C	Library D
List of Library Staff	Yes	Yes	Not Found	Yes
Consortium Membership	Yes	Yes	Yes	Yes
Name of Consortium	Wiley Online Library – Consortium of Engineering Libraries-Philippines (CELPh) Wiley Online Library – South Manila Educational Consortium (SMEC) ASEAN University Network Inter-Library Online (AUNILO) Inter-University Consortium (IUC) Esc Philippines	Wiley Online Library – Consortium of Engineering Libraries-Philippines (CELPh) Wiley Online Library – South Manila Educational Consortium (SMEC) Inter-University Consortium (IUC) Esc Philippines	Wiley Online Library – Consortium of Engineering Libraries-Philippines (CELPh) Wiley Online Library – South Manila Educational Consortium (SMEC) ASEAN University Network Inter-Library Online (AUNILO) De La Salle Philippines (DLSP) Libraries South Manila Educational Consortium (SMEC) Inter-University Consortium (IUC)	Wiley Online Library – Consortium of Engineering Libraries-Philippines (CELPh) Wiley Online Library – South Manila Educational Consortium (SMEC)
No. of e-Journals by Consortium	5+	4+	7	2+
Librarian Information	Yes	Yes	Not Found	Not Found

(*continued*)

Table 1. (*continued*)

Library & Miscellaneous Services	Library A	Library B	Library C	Library D
Webpage/ Guide for COVID-19 Pandemic-Related Information[a]	Yes	Not Found	Not Found	Not Found
Social Media Accounts[a]	Facebook, Twitter, Instagram	Facebook, Twitter, Instagram	Facebook, Twitter	Facebook, Twitter, Instagram
Library Chatbox[a]	Yes	Not Found	Yes	Yes

[a] Additional items added

Library Websites During the Pandemic

The library websites serve as the main communication channel for users during the pandemic. Most libraries redirect their users to their library websites in addition to their social media platforms to properly communicate their services and programs with their users especially during the crisis as many libraries decided to temporarily close their physical doors. During the COVID-19 pandemic, academic library websites witnessed several trends in their CMS. One of the most significant shifts was a heightened emphasis on virtual services and remote access. Libraries rapidly expanded their digital collections necessitating seamless integration of resources into their CMS. It also prioritized clear communication regarding closures, safety protocols, and virtual services through prominently featured announcements and dedicated COVID-19 information pages. Implementation of chatbots to provide assistants 24/7 was also a notable trend to answer pandemic-related queries. That is why it is indeed imperative for libraries to have a robust library website alongside other communication channels to provide relevant information during the pandemic. Thus, examining the library website features of these four (4) libraries to provide such information was considered. The study revealed that only one library has a dedicated page or library guide for COVID-19 pandemic-related information such as useful links, relevant policies, and services useful for the users. In addition, all libraries provided additional information to their social media platforms found on their websites as they believe that the library should be where the users are. Moreover, these libraries would also like to be in touch with their clients and provide at least synchronous and instant communication with them. Hence, incorporating ways how to start a chat message platform with clients. There is no doubt that websites serve as a primary tool to communicate with library users. Thus, finding ways to enhance user experience on the use of library websites should be considered by librarians. With CMS, library website management becomes even easier for libraries and librarians. With little to no knowledge of programming languages, library websites can still look relevant, professional, and presentable especially to end users.

5 Conclusion

During the COVID-19 pandemic, libraries have relied on their CMSs to effectively communicate with their clients remotely. With physical library doors temporarily closed to flatten the curve, CMSs have played a crucial role in providing essential information to meet research and scholarly needs, ensuring the continuity of the learning process. While libraries employ different CMSs based on their specific requirements, they have all leveraged the full potential of their chosen platforms. Some libraries have even invested in proprietary CMSs to ensure the delivery of information in a proper and easily understandable manner. However, despite the convenience and ease CMSs offer in managing websites, some libraries still find them insufficient and develop their own methods to manage their CMSs and websites. Recognizing that their websites, along with social media platforms, serve as the primary channels of communication, all four libraries have utilized CMSs to their fullest extent, enabling patrons to access information about collections and services with just a simple click.

References

1. Apps – Wappalyzer. https://www.wappalyzer.com/apps/. Accessed 7 Apr 2023
2. Black, E.: Selecting a web content management system for an academic library website. Inf. Technol. Libr. **30**(4), 185–189 (2011)
3. Benevolo, C., Negri, S.: Evaluation of content management systems (CMS): a supply analysis. Electron. J. Inf. Syst. Eval. **10**(1), 9–22 (2007)
4. BuiltWith Homepage. https://builtwith.com/. Accessed 7 Apr 2023
5. Comeaux, D., Schmetzke, A.: Accessibility of academic library web sites in North America: current status and trends (2002–2012). Library Hi Tech **31**(1), 8–33 (2013)
6. Connell, R.: Content management systems: trends in academic libraries. Inf. Technol. Libr. **32**(2), 42–55 (2013)
7. Coombs, K.: Navigating content management. Libr. J. **133**(24) (2008)
8. Das, S.: A systematic study of integrated marketing communication and content management system for millennial consumers. In: Innovations in Digital Branding and Content Marketing, pp. 91–112 (2021)
9. Detect which CMS a site is using - What CMS? https://whatcms.org/. Accessed 7 Apr 2023
10. Devi, K., Verma, M.: Content evaluation and the design trends of National Institutes of National Institutes of Technology (NITS) library websites of India: an evaluative study. J. Indian Libr. Assoc. **53**, 2–3 (2017)
11. García-García, M., Carrillo-Durán, M., Maia, J.: The maturity of corporate websites as a digital communication channel in Portuguese SMEs' process of adopting e-commerce. Sustainability **13**(21), 11972 (2021)
12. Goans, D., Leach, G., Vogel, T.: Beyond HTML: developing and re-imagining library web guides in a content management system. Library Hi Tech **24,** 29–53 (2006)
13. Islam, M.N., Islam, M.S., Sagorika, S.: Content management system (CMS): application of Joomla to website development in Libraries and Information Centers. In: Vision 2021: The Role of Libraries for Building Digital Bangladesh, pp. 83–116. Library Association of Bangladesh, Bangladesh (2021)
14. Kane, D., Hegarty, N.: New website, new opportunities: enforcing standards compliance within a content management system. Library Hi Tech **25**(2), 276 (2007)

15. Krouska, A., Troussas, C., Virvou, M.: Comparing LMS and CMS platforms supporting social e-learning in higher education. In: 8th International Conference on Information, Intelligence, Systems & Applications (IISA), pp. 1–6. Information, Intelligence, Systems & Applications (IISA), Cyprus (2017)

16. Kuchi, T.: Communicating mission: an analysis of academic library websites. J. Acad. Librariansh. **32**(2), 148–154 (2006)

17. Kumar, V.: Qualities of a library website: evaluating library websites of new IITs. Int. J. Inf. Dissem. Technol. **4**(4), 283–288 (2014)

18. Mahatody, T., Sagar, M., Kolski, C.: State of the art on the cognitive walkthrough method, its variants and evolutions. Int. J. Hum. Comput. Interact. **26**(8), 741–785 (2010)

19. Mičík, M., Kunešová, H.: Using an eye tracker to optimise career websites as a communication channel with Generation Y. Econ. Res.-Ekonomska Istraživanja **34**(1), 66–89 (2021)

20. Pathak, S.K., Pal, M., Rai, V.: Proper content management to the library website: evaluation of all IIT's library websites. In: International-CALIBER 2008, pp. 353–359 (2008)

21. Patnaik, R., Mishra, M.K.: Role of content management software (CMS) in libraries for information dissemination. In: 4th International Symposium on Emerging Trends and Technologies in Libraries and Information Services, Emerging Trends and Technologies in Libraries and Information Services (ETTLIS), pp. 117–121. 2015 4th International Symposium, Kazakhstan (2015)

22. Rafiq, S., Ashiq, M., Ur Rehman, S., Yousaf, F.: A content analysis of the websites of the world's top 50 universities in medicine. Sci. Technol. Libr. **40**, 260–281 (2021)

23. Rogers, C.R.: Social media, libraries, and Web 2.0: how American libraries are using new tools for public relations and to attract new users. South Carolina State Documents Depository, pp. 1–7 (2009)

24. Sivankalai, S.: Academic libraries' content management trends. Libr. Philos. Pract. (e-Journal) **8**(19), 1–13 (2021)

25. Tan, W.S., Liu, D., Bishu, R.: Web evaluation: heuristic evaluation vs. user testing Int. J. Ind. Ergonomics **39**(4), 621–627 (2009)

26. Tjong, Y.: Successful measurement of Content Management System implementation. In: 2016 International Conference on Information Management and Technology (ICIMTech), pp. 311–314, Indonesia (2016)

27. Trivedi, M.: Blogging for libraries and librarians. Libr. Philos. Pract. **11**(1), 1–4 (2016)

28. Wiggins, R., Remley, J., Klingler, T.: Building a local CMS at Kent State. Library Hi Tech **24**(1), 69–101 (2006)

29. Yu, H.: Content and Workflow Management for Library Websites: Case Studies. Ed. IGI Global, Pennsylvania (2005)

The Pivotal Role of Preprint Platforms in Disseminating COVID-19 Research: A Global Investigation of Country-Level Activities

Hiroyuki Tsunoda[1]([✉]) [iD], Yuan Sun[2], Masaki Nishizawa[2], Xiaomin Liu[3],
Kou Amano[2] [iD], and Rie Kominami[1] [iD]

[1] Tsurumi University, Yokohama, Kanagawa 2308501, Japan
tsunoda-h@tsurumi-u.ac.jp
[2] National Institute of Informatics, Tokyo 1018430, Japan
[3] National Science Library, Chinese Academy of Sciences, Beijing 100190, China

Abstract. Researchers initiated immediate research on COVID-19 following the declaration of the pandemic, but the traditional cycle of scientific information distribution was ill-equipped to share rapid outputs. Preprints provided a platform for immediate sharing of outputs, leading many COVID-19 studies in medical biology and clinical medicine to be submitted in this format. Preprints were collected from bioRxiv and medRxiv, and metadata of published preprints were collected from PubMed. We investigated the number of published preprints submitted by country and metadata for the peer review period for COVID-19 and non-COVID-19 preprints. Our research found preprints from 128 countries. Submissions peaked in May 2020, five months following the declaration of the pandemic. Using the Mann-Whitney U test, we found the peer review period for COVID-19 published preprints was significantly shorter than for non-COVID-19 preprints. The research suggests many countries have an in-built system that facilitates swift and continuous responses to crises in the scientific community.

Keywords: Preprints · COVID-19 · Peer Review · Bibliometrics

1 Introduction

Wuhan, China, reported its first case of coronavirus disease 2019 (COVID-19) in early December 2019. By January 30, 2020, WHO had declared a global pandemic, and in response, research institutions in various countries quickly initiated research on the disease. These studies were posted in preprints [1–3]. Preprints, i.e., papers published before journal submission, allow researchers to share their results immediately [4]. Amid the global disruption, various preprint hosting sites emerged, including bioRxiv (operated by Cold Spring Harbor Laboratory [CSHL]) and medRxiv (operated by CSHL, Yale University, and BMJ). Intensive research began on and about COVID-19 and its sequela. This was pivotal as patients with COVID-19 required up-to-date medical care. Results from preclinical and clinical studies through preprints enabled the swift sharing of COVID-19 research results with the community [5]. However, issues arose. Scientists posted

D. H. Goh et al. (Eds.): ICADL 2023, LNCS 14458, pp. 82–89, 2023.
https://doi.org/10.1007/978-981-99-8088-8_7

manuscripts on preprint servers before they were peer-reviewed. These servers subsequently became flooded with submissions, causing bioRxiv and medRxiv to quickly enhance their usual screening procedures [6]. Since preprints are not peer-reviewed, problems arose with the quality of the research. Nevertheless, many peer-reviewed journals eventually published these sufficiently high-quality preprints [7]. Indeed, there are often very few changes between the preprints and the published article [5]. Preprints allow peers to post comments, which can be beneficial when polishing the paper [8]. Consequently, preprints submitted to a journal have shorter peer review periods, and new scholarly information is distributed more quickly [9, 10]. In part, publications represent a corresponding level of scientific and technological advancements at the global and regional scale [11]. Therefore, in this paper, we analyzed the metadata of these preprints by using the first author, who has the most important responsibility for the study [12], and their country. We defined the country of the preprint as the location of the institution to which the first author was affiliated. During the COVID-19 pandemic, the role of preprints in disseminating science was clarified, as well as their significant impact on scientific communication [13, 14]. COVID-19 is a trending topic as the disease is unprecedented in the scientific community. Hence, this study will identify the situation in preprints as it relates to their publishing on popular topics such as COVID-19.

2 Methods

This study defined preprints as a manuscript submitted to bioRxiv and medRxiv. These two platforms were chosen as they focus on COVID-19 research and development and archive many basic and clinical research preprints in the medical field. We defined a "published preprint" as a preprint manuscript that was subsequently submitted to a journal and underwent peer review. Data was collected from bioRxiv and medRxiv, and metadata of published preprints were obtained from PubMed using an Application Programming Interface (API). References published in PubMed were assigned a subject heading symbol by the NLM (United States National Library of Medicine); the PubMed subject heading unique code for COVID-19 is D000086382. We used the PubMed subject heading to identify the subject of the published preprints as COVID-19. We defined the peer review period as the number of days from the submission date to the journal to the date of acceptance. The country attributed to each published preprint was determined based on the location of the first author's affiliated institution. A full counting method was used to count the number of countries.

3 Results

Figure 1 shows the number of submissions on COVID-19 published preprints. Submissions began in January 2020, when the WHO declared a pandemic, and peaked at over 700 in May 2020. Since then, the number of submissions has decreased, but it remained above 300 from 2020 to the first half of 2021. The peer review period for journals usually requires several months from submission to acceptance. Therefore, preprints are not published in journals immediately after submission to the archive. The reason for the decrease from the second half of 2021 to 2022 is thought to be due to the peer review of journals.

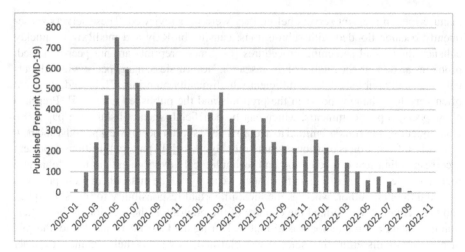

Fig. 1. Published Preprints on COVID-19 (2020–2022).

There were 64,675 preprints submitted to preprint platforms and published in journals from January 1, 2020, to December 31, 2022. The first author of the COVID-19 publication preprints belonged to 128 countries. Table 1 shows the top 15 countries with the largest published preprints.

Table 1. Top 15 Countries of Published Preprint on COVID-19 (2020–2022).

Country	Published Preprints	Peak (Date)
USA	2,774	232 (May 2020)
UK	1,226	89 (May 2020)
China	550	103 (March 2020)
Germany	450	38 (June 2020)
Canada	372	23 (November 2020)
France	287	34 (May 2020)
Italy	279	36 (May 2020)
Japan	243	18 (May 2020)
India	239	17 (April 2020)
Spain	236	25 (May 2020)
Brazil	204	21 (June 2020)
Australia	184	14 (June 2020)
Switzerland	176	14 (May 2020)
Netherlands	151	11 (May 2020)
Israel	118	14 (May 2020)

These preprints were analyzed in the country of affiliation of the paper's first author. Figure 2 shows the number of preprints in the top 15 countries, and Fig. 3 shows their peak months. More than 100 published preprints were first published in the archives. In many countries, the peak of preprint submissions occurred after May 2020. China and India experienced their peaks before May 2020, with China reaching its peak in March 2020 and India in April 2020.

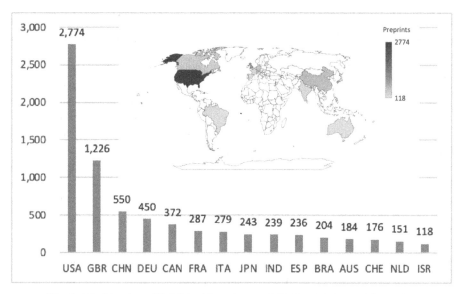

Fig. 2. The Number of Published Preprints on COVID-19 in Top 15 Countries.

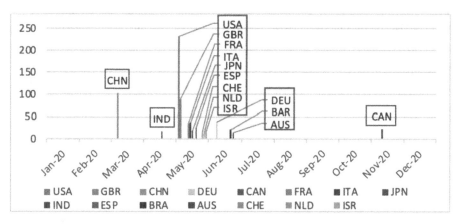

Fig. 3. Peak of Published Preprints on COVID-19 in Top 15 Countries.

We analyzed significant differences in peer-review time between COVID-19 and non-COVID-19 preprints for countries with four or more published preprints. Seventy-four countries had four or more COVID-19 published preprints and non-COVID-19 published preprints. The peer review period for COVID-19 published preprints in 58 countries was shorter than that for non-COVID-19 published preprints, of which 29 countries were significantly shorter by the Mann-Whitney U test. Conversely, COVID-19 published preprints took longer to be peer-reviewed in 16 countries and significantly more in 4 countries. The peer review period in the top 15 countries was shorter for COVID-19 than for non-COVID-19. Table 2 shows the difference in the peer-review period for COVID-19 and non-COVID-19 published preprints.

Table 2. The Number of Days for Published Preprint on COVID-19 (2020–2022).

Country	COVID-19	non-COVID-19	Difference	Country	COVID-19	non-COVID-19	Difference	
IRQ	49.0	160.0	−111.0	CAN	107.0	135.0	-28.0	**
GEO	27.0	131.0	-104.0	HKG	100.0	127.0	-27.0	
SVN	74.0	134.0	-60.0	NLD	113.0	139.0	-26.0	**
TUR	66.0	126.0	-60.0	IRL	85.0	110.0	-25.0	
SWE	77.5	137.0	-59.5	PRT	100.0	124.5	-24.5	*
HUN	62.0	120.5	-58.5	BGD	106.5	130.5	-24.0	
KEN	85.0	139.0	-54.0	IND	93.0	116.0	-23.0	**
SGP	94.0	147.0	-53.0	CZE	102.5	124.5	-22.0	
ZAF	71.5	124.0	-52.5	AUS	105.0	126.0	-21.0	**
IRN	98.0	149.5	-51.5	DNK	109.0	130.0	-21.0	**
PER	55.5	106.0	-50.5	ISR	110.5	130.0	-19.5	**
ITA	70.5	120.0	-49.5	TWN	96.0	115.0	-19.0	*
AUT	90.0	139.0	-49.0	BRA	99.0	117.5	-18.5	
CHE	97.0	146.0	-49.0	ARG	104.5	120.0	-15.5	
EGY	64.0	113.0	-49.0	OMN	82.5	97.0	-14.5	
FIN	80.0	128.5	-48.5	PHL	95.0	109.5	-14.5	
BEL	87.0	134.0	-47.0	THA	73.0	86.0	-13.0	
VNM	71.0	116.0	-45.0	IDN	97.0	107.0	-10.0	
FRA	93.0	136.0	-43.0	MEX	112.0	119.5	-7.5	
DEU	94.0	136.0	-42.0	ARE	104.0	106.0	-2.0	
CYP	114.5	154.5	-40.0	LKA	110.0	112.0	-2.0	
LBN	70.0	110.0	-40.0	SAU	92.0	92.0	0.0	
CHN	79.0	118.0	-39.0	ROU	111.5	107.0	4.5	
JPN	87.0	126.0	-39.0	URY	102.5	93.0	9.5	
USA	98.0	136.0	-38.0	MYS	89.0	78.0	11.0	
ECU	72.5	109.5	-37.0	ETH	170.0	147.0	23.0	
GBR	101.0	138.0	-37.0	NZL	142.0	108.5	33.5	**
COL	103.0	139.0	-36.0	ISL	203.0	169.0	34.0	
ESP	88.0	124.0	-36.0	KWT	99.5	64.5	35.0	
POL	79.0	114.0	-35.0	LUX	170.0	124.5	45.5	
NGA	106.5	140.0	-33.5	PAK	128.0	82.5	45.5	
QAT	67.0	99.0	-32.0	JOR	109.0	59.0	50.0	

(*continued*)

Table 2. (*continued*)

Country	COVID-19	non-COVID-19	Difference	Country	COVID-19	non-COVID-19	Difference	
UGA	83.0	115.0	-32.0	EST	179.5	112	67.5	
KOR	91.5	123.0	-31.5	CHL	172.0	92.0	80.0	*
RUS	83.0	112.5	-29.5	ZMB	206.0	124.0	82.0	
NOR	101.0	130.0	-29.0	CUB	168.0	85.0	83.0	*
GRC	87.5	116.0	-28.5	NPL	188.0	98.5	89.5	*

[Note: * is $p < 5\%$ significant, ** is $p < 1\%$ significant]

In the scatter diagram on Fig. 4, red circles are significant and blue circles are not significant.

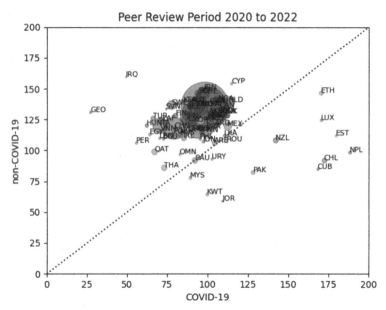

Fig. 4. Peer Review Period for Published Preprints on COVID-19 and non-COVID-19 (2020–2022). (Color figure online)

4 Discussion and Conclusion

Our study shows that preprint platforms played a vital role in disseminating research on COVID-19, originating from 128 different countries. The rapid increase and subsequent peak of published papers indicated the scientific community's prompt response to the pandemic. These platforms facilitated critical academic exchange in a public health emergency. The decrease in the number of published papers over time might reflect the disease's prevalence at any given time, suggesting a transition from emergency to routine research. Preprints played a significant role in keeping up with the rapidly changing strains of COVID-19. For example, the Alpha strain first appeared in the United Kingdom in September 2020, the Beta strain in South Africa in May 2020, the Gamma strain in Brazil in November 2020, and the Delta strain in India in October 2020. From the initial discovery of these new variants to their confirmation, there has been an increase in the number of published papers, indicating that researchers from around the globe are continuously tracking virus mutations and conducting clinical and mechanistic research. It is evident that there are fewer basic research papers (6,622) compared to clinical papers (20,197) based on the statistics from the bioRxiv and medRxiv preprint platforms. As the emergency stabilizes, the number of papers may also decline, a characteristic feature of clinical papers. The transformation of COVID-19 research papers from preprints to journal publications meant the peer-review time for most articles was shorter than for non-COVID-19 articles. This suggests journals published research trends and supported academic research with their brand influence and mature information dissemination channels. This helped disseminate research updates that benefited scholars worldwide. The COVID-19 outbreak has not only raised awareness of preprint platforms in multiple countries, but it has provided a new platform for academic exchange. Our results indicate a pivotal role of preprints in disseminating timely research during a public health crisis. However, further studies are needed to investigate the sustainability of this trend as the pandemic subsides and the relationship between preprints and journal publications evolves.

Acknowledgments. This work was supported by JSPS KAKENHI Grant Numbers JP19K12707, JP20K12569, JP22K12737, and ROIS NII Open Collaborative Research 2023 (23FS01).

References

1. Guterman, E.L., Braunstein, L.Z.: Preprints during the COVID-19 pandemic: public health emergencies and medical literature. J. Hosp. Med. **15**(10), 634–636 (2020)
2. Oikonomidi, T., Boutron, I., Pierre, O., Cabanac, G., Ravaud, P.: COVID-19 NMA consortium.: changes in evidence for studies assessing interventions for COVID-19 reported in preprints: Meta-research study. BMC Med. **18**(1), 402 (2020)
3. Vlasschaert, C., Topf, J.M., Hiremath, S.: Proliferation of papers and preprints during the coronavirus disease 2019 pandemic: progress or problems with peer review? Adv. Chronic Kidney Dis. **27**(5), 418–426 (2020)
4. Hoy, M.B.: Rise of the Rxivs: how preprint servers are changing the publishing process. Med. Ref. Serv. Q. **39**(1), 84–89 (2020)
5. Brierley, L., et al.: Tracking changes between preprint posting and journal publication during a pandemic. PLoS Biol. **20**(2), e3001285 (2022)
6. Kwon, D.: How swamped preprint servers are blocking bad coronavirus research. Nature **581**(7807), 130 (2020)
7. Nelson, L., Ye, H., Schwenn, A., Lee, S., Arabi, S., Hutchins, B.I.: Robustness of evidence reported in preprints during peer review. Lancet Glob. Health **10**(11), e1684–e1687 (2022)
8. Malički, M., Costello, J., Alperin, J.P., Maggio, L.A.: Analysis of single comments left for bioRxiv preprints till September 2019. Biochem. Med. **31**(2), 020201 (2021)
9. Tsunoda, H., Sun, Y., Nishizawa, M., Liu, X., Amano, K.: The influence of bioRχiv on PLOS ONE's peer-review and acceptance time. Proc. Assoc. Inf. Sci. Technol. **57**(1), e398 (2020)

10. Tsunoda, H., Sun, Y., Nishizawa, M., Liu, X., Amano, K.: How preprint affects the publishing process: duration of the peer review process between bioRxiv and journal papers. Proc. Assoc. Inf. Sci. Technol. **59**(1), 505–509 (2022)
11. Wang, P., Tian, D.: Bibliometric analysis of global scientific research on COVID-19. J. Biosaf. Biosecur. **3**(1), 4–9 (2021)
12. Riesenberg, D., Lundberg, G.D.: The order of authorship: who's on first? JAMA **264**(14), 1857 (1990)
13. Fraser, N., et al.: The evolving role of preprints in the dissemination of COVID-19 research and their impact on the science communication landscape. PLoS Biol. **19**(4), e3000959 (2021)
14. Tsunoda, H., Sun, Y., Nishizawa, M., Liu, X., Amano, K. Kominami, R.: Role of preprints in scholarly communication on COVID-19: a quantitative sur-vey of medRxiv and bioRxiv. In: Proceedings of the ISSI 2023 (in press)

The Semantic Mapping of RiC-CM to CIDOC-CRM

Lina Bountouri[ID], Matthew Damigos[ID], Markella Drakiou[ID],
Manolis Gergatsoulis[✉][ID], and Eleftherios Kalogeros[ID]

Laboratory on Digital Libraries and Electronic Publishing, Department of Archives,
Library Science and Museology, Ionian University, Corfu, Greece
{mgdamigos,manolis,kalogero}@ionio.gr

Abstract. This paper investigates the semantic closeness between the
Records in Contexts - Conceptual Model (RiC-CM) and the CIDOC Conceptual Reference Model (CIDOC-CRM). The research aims to establish
a bridge between these two conceptual models, enabling interoperability
and seamless integration of data. In this context, we define a mapping of
(1) the main RiC-CM entities (focusing on the record-related entities) to
CIDOC-CRM entities, (2) the main RiC-CM attributes to CIDOC-CRM
(paths of) properties and entities, and (3) the (mainly, record-related)
relations of RiC-CM to CIDOC-CRM (paths of) properties and entities.
With this research, we achieve a deeper understanding of the semantic
relationship between the two models.

Keywords: Archival Conceptual Models · RiC-CM · CIDOC-CRM ·
Semantic Mappings · Ontologies

1 Introduction

In a world where data silos have been broken for years, conceptual models and
ontologies are used for information integration, and promoting interoperability between data of related domains. In the cultural heritage field, CIDOC-Conceptual Reference Model (CIDOC-CRM) [8] and Europeana Data Model
(EDM) [12] are widely used for integrating heterogeneous data and enabling
effective data sharing. In the context of archives, recently, a similar conceptual
model, called the Records in Contexts Conceptual Model (RiC-CM) [16], was
proposed for this purpose. RiC-CM is a new, high-level conceptual model for
the definition of archives, records and other related entities, which is gradually
implemented by archival organizations, along with the corresponding ontology
(RiC-O) [2]. CIDOC-CRM is widely acknowledged as a suitable framework for
modeling the interconnectedness and mappings between diverse cultural heritage
sources. Works in this direction include VRA [14] and Dublin Core mappings [17]
to CIDOC-CRM.

Archives are part of cultural heritage information [7]. Integrating this type of
data with other cultural heritage information, mainly to support effective analysis of information and its further enrichment, is a practical need; e.g., enriching

D. H. Goh et al. (Eds.): ICADL 2023, LNCS 14458, pp. 90–99, 2023.
https://doi.org/10.1007/978-981-99-8088-8_8

information related to architectural styles [5] with associated archives. Although RiC-CM focuses on modeling data related specifically to archival records, it cannot be employed for integrating other types of cultural heritage information. CIDOC-CRM, however, can be leveraged for this purpose. The ICA also acknowledges [2] the necessity for mappings between certain entities or properties of RiC-O and other models such as CIDOC-CRM, IFLA-LRM, PREMIS, etc. This highlights the importance of establishing connections and relationships between different cultural heritage data models for enhanced interoperability.

In this paper, we study the semantic closeness between RiC-CM and CIDOC CRM, by defining the semantic mappings between them. The main objective is to facilitate the interoperability and integration of data that are modeled on RiC-CM through its transformation and/or translation to CIDOC-CRM data. The main contribution of this work is the mapping of the main RiC-CM entities (focusing on the record-related entities) to CIDOC-CRM entities, (presented in Sect. 4.1), and the mapping of the (mainly, record-related) relations of RiC-CM to CIDOC-CRM (paths of) properties and entities (presented in Sect. 4.2). Besides, we present the main ideas for the mapping of RiC-CM attributes to CIDOC-CRM (paths of) properties and proper entities (see Sect. 4.3).

2   Related Work

The need of semantic mappings between archival metadata, and CIDOC-CRM is discussed in [6], where a mapping from the Encoded Archival Description (EAD) to CIDOC-CRM is presented. This mapping has been defined in the context of integrating archival metadata to wider cultural heritage resources, implementing CIDOC-CRM as their data model and integrator. This research work defines the three main conceptual views of the archive: the archive as a physical, information and linguistic object. EAD expresses these conceptual views of the archive, together with their related metadata and relations.

A related work is also presented in ICON Project [1]. ICON Project made use of CIDOC-CRM for the integration of archival resources with other cultural heritage information, defining and using mappings from EAD, EAC-CPF and EAG to CIDOC-CRM. Similarly, in [6], an archive is represented both as a physical and linguistic object, mapped to the related CIDOC-CRM entities E71 Human-Made Thing and E33 Linguistic Object.

EPISA (Entity and Property Inference for Semantic Archives) [4] created a new description model for archives and promoted the semiautomatic creation of metadata. The primary objective of the project was to connect the national Portuguese archives with the global network of semantic linked data. As a result of this effort, the ArchOnto [3,18] model was defined. ArchOnto data model integrates five ontologies that cover various aspects of the archival domain: CIDOC-CRM (base ontology), N-ary, DataObject, ISAD Ontology, and Link2DataObject. In the context of this project, mapping description rules from ISAD(G) to CIDOC-CRM were defined [19].

It is worth noting that the RiC-CM is a relatively new conceptual model, and in this respect, there are not many research works up to recently that define mappings from or to this model. In the bibliography, there is one implementation of related mappings in a tool called RiC-O Converter [10]. RiC-O Converter is an open-source command-line tool, employed to convert EAD finding aids and EAC-CPF authority records to RDF files conforming to Records in Contexts ontology (RiC-O). As a result, mappings between EAD and EAC to RiC-O have been defined and implemented. Using them, the tool converts EAD and EAC to RDF/XML containing instances of RiC-O entities and properties.

3   Conceptual Models for Archives and Cultural Heritage

RiC-CM [13] is the first officially released conceptual model in the archives world. It encompasses and replaces the essential archival standards, published by the International Council on Archives (ICA), which are ISAD(G), ISAAR(CPF), ISDF and ISDIAH. The critical difference between the RiC-CM and these four standards is that RiC-CM does not model a finding aid (which is the archival description tool), but it models all the related to the archival description entities, their attributes and relations. Through this radical swift in the archival description methodology, switching from data structure models to ontologies, the ICA believes that RiC-CM will be employed as a cross-domain archival domain model to provide integrated access [16]. On the other hand, CIDOC-CRM [8] is a core ontology of the cultural heritage domain, intending to provide a common and extensible semantic framework to which information can be mapped, facilitating the information integration of cultural heritage information. CIDOC-CRM can help implementers to formulate the requirements for information systems, serving as a guide for conceptual modeling [9]. CIDOC-CRM expresses semantics as a sequence of path(s) of the form entity-property-entity. It is an event-based model and its main concepts are the temporal entities. As a consequence, the presence of CIDOC-CRM entities, such as actors, dates, places, and objects, implies their participation to an event or an activity [11].

4   The Mapping of RiC-CM to CIDOC-CRM

In this section, we show that a single CIDOC-CRM entity is not sufficient to map each RiC-CM entity (not even an attribute). Multiple CIDOC-CRM entities might be required to properly represent different perspectives of a RiC-CM entity. These entities are typically related to each other through a set of properties (and potentially other entities). To describe such type of expressions, we use the concept of path (expression), which is a sequence of CIDOC-CRM entities related to each other through properties of CIDOC-CRM; i.e., $E_1 \rightarrow P_1 \rightarrow E_2 \rightarrow P_2 \cdots \rightarrow P_{n-1} \rightarrow E_n$, where $E_1, \ldots, E_n$ are CIDOC-CRM entities and $P_1, \ldots, P_{n-1}$ are properties connecting the corresponding entities. To express multiple paths starting from the same entity, we use branches (borrowed by $XPath$ [20]), denoted as $E[B_1] \ldots [B_n]$, where E is an entity and $B_1, \ldots, B_n$ are paths. If we want to use a property of a property, we also use branching notation; e.g., $P[S \rightarrow E]$, where P is a property with property of property S and E

is an entity (in CIDOC-CRM this is always the entity E55 Type). In addition, there are cases where we want to set a constant value V for all the instances of a certain entity; e.g., the type (i.e., entity E55 Type) should be RiC-A38 Scope and content for all the instances of the entity. In such a case, we use the notation $E(V)$, where E is a CIDOC-CRM entity and V represents a constant value that is applied over all the instances; e.g., E55 Type (RiC-A38 Scope and content).

The path E22 Human-Made Object → P128 carries → E73 Information Object, for example, represents instances where a human-made object instance is carried by an information object instance. Similarly, the path expression E73 Information Object→P3 has note[P3.1 has type→ E55 Type(RiC-A03 Authenticity Note)]→E62 String describes instances of information object that have notes of type RiC-A03 Authenticity Note, which are given by string values.

4.1   Mapping the Main RiC-CM Entities

The core archival entities as defined by RiC-CM are [13]: RiC-E02 Record Resource and RiC-E06 Instantiation, RiC-E07 Agent and RiC-E14 Event.

RiC-E02 Record Resource and RiC-E06 Instantiation: A RiC-E02 Record Resource entity includes instances of one of the following entities: RiC-E03 Record Set, RiC-E04 Record or RiC-E05 Record Part. These entities represent archival resources, such as instances of an archive or a set of records (for example, an instance of RiC-E03 Record Set), or of an archival unit (for example, an instance of RiC-E04 Record or RiC-E05 Record Part). RiC-E06 Instantiation entity is introduced in RiC-CM [13] to distinguish the content information from the representation of each RiC-E02 Record Resource (and its subentities) on one or more carriers (similarly to the FRBR model [15]). RiC-E06 Instantiation is mandatory to properly define instances of RiC-E04 Record or RiC-E05 Record Part. More specifically, it defines that their information content is inscribed on a carrier in a persistent, recoverable form. It is worth noting that the archival resources that the aforementioned entities represent (an archive, a set of records, their respective parts, such as a manuscript or a DVD, and their instantiations) are not one-dimension resources. They are resources with multiple semantic aspects, which are expressed through the archival description. In detail, as defined in [6], the main semantic aspects of an archival resource are:

- an archival resource is a **physical object** that acts as evidence for the functions/activities of the person or of the corporate body that produced it, and
- an archival resource is an **information object** that includes information in different **languages**.

According to this analysis, the RiC-CM entities RiC-E02 Record Resource, RiC-E03 Record Set, RiC-E04 Record, RiC-E05 Record Part and RiC-E06 Instantiation are all mapped to the following CIDOC-CRM entities:

- E22 Human-Made Object to define that an archival resource is a physical object,

- E73 Information Object to define that an archival resource is an information carrier,
- E33 Linguistic Object to define that the information included in an archival resource are expressed in one ore more languages.

To express the relationships between the various aspects of an archival resource, the following CIDOC-CRM path is defined: E22 Human-Made Object→ P128 carries → E73 Information Object→ P67 refers to → E33 Linguistic Object. This path declares that an archival resource is a physical object that has been created by human activity (E22 Human-Made Object) that carries (P128 carries) information, which is immaterial and can be carried by any physical medium (E73 Information Object). The information carried by the archival resource can be expressed in one or more languages (P76 refers to → E33 Linguistic Object).

RiC-E07 Agent: RiC-CM entity RiC-E07 Agent defines entity that act or performs an activities (RiC-E15 Activity), which results in the generation of an archival resource. This entity includes instances of other entities, such as [16]:

- RiC-E08 Person, which defines instances of physical persons,
- RiC-E09 Group, which defines instances of families or corporate bodies (sub-entities RiC-E10 Family and RiC-E11 Corporate Body),
- RiC-E12 Position, which defines instances of an intersection of person and group, and
- RiC-E13 Mechanism, which is a newly introduced in the archival world entity, allowing the description of human technological proxies.

Given these definitions, the instances of the RiC-E07 Agent entity can be mapped:

a) to instances of the CIDOC-CRM E39 Actor, in case they represent instances of corporate bodies, persons, and families, included in the sub-entities of RiC-E07 Agent (RiC-E08 Person, RiC-E09 Group, RiC-E10 Family and RiC-E11 Corporate Body). In CIDOC-CRM, instances of the entity E39 Actor comprise people, either individually or in groups, who have the potential to perform intentional actions of kinds for which someone may be held responsible [8];
b) to instances of the CIDOC-CRM E71 Human-Made Thing entity, when the sub-entity RiC-E13 Mechanism of RiC-E07 Agent is used. Note that the CIDOC-CRM E71 Human-Made Thing defines human-made physical things, which are characterized by relative stability, similarly to the RiC-E13 Mechanism entity [8].

RiC-E14 Event: According to RiC-CM [13], the entity RiC-E14 Event defines an event as something that happens in time and space. A particular event may occur at a specific moment in time, or it may occur over a long period of time. A sub-entity of RiC-E14 Event is the RiC-E15 Activity, which defines purposeful human activity. Both RiC-CM and CIDOC-CRM are event-orientated conceptual models. This facilitates the definition of the semantic mapping of the event-related entities between the two models. For example, both RiC-CM and CIDOC-CRM entities, such as RiC-E07 Agent/E39 Actor, often participate to an event or an activity, in order to define the creation or modification of a resource. The semantic mapping of RiC-CM to CIDOC-CRM maps the RiC-CM entity RiC-E14 Event to the CIDOC-CRM Entity E5 Event and the RiC-CM entity RiC-E15 Activity to the CIDOC-CRM Entity E7 Activity.

4.2   Mapping the Relations of the Main RiC-CM Entities

In this section, we present the mapping of (the most important) RiC-CM relations to CIDOC-CRM (mainly the relations having as domain or range the entity RiC-E02 Record Resource and its subentities, and the entity RiC-E06 Instantiation). The main idea is to map the domain (resp. the range) of the RiC-CM relation to the corresponding CIDOC-CRM entities and then map the RiC-CM relation ether to a CIDOC-CRM property or to a CIDOC-CRM path, leading from the CIDOC-CRM entity corresponding to the RiC-CM relation's domain to the CIDOC-CRM entity corresponding to the RiC-CM relation's range.

The mapping of the relations of RiC-CM appears in Table 1. The table consists of four columns. In the first column appears the RiC-CM relations code and name, in the second and the third column appear the IDs of the RiC-CM Entities corresponding to the domain and range (respectively) of the RiC-CM relation. Finally, in the last column of the table, we present the CIDOC-CRM property or the CIDOC-CRM path, connecting the CIDOC-CRM Entities (appearing in bold) corresponding the domain and range of the RiC-CM relation.

To facilitate the presentation, we group the mapping as follows:
Relations between Instances of the Entity RiC-E02 Record Resource and/or its Subentities: RiC-R010 is original of, RiC-R011 is draft of, and RiC-R012 has copy are all mapped to P130 shows features of property of CIDOC-CRM. To distinguish between them, we denote the type of similarity using the property of property P130.1 kind of similarity and assigning as instance of the target entity E55 Type the name of the corresponding RiC-CM relation.

Concerning the RiC-CM relation RiC-R013 has reply, the main idea behind its mapping to the CIDOC-CRM is that the instance of the RiC-E02 Record Resource (domain) motivates (as a reply) the production (E12 Production) of the new instance of the RiC-E02 Record Resource. Finally, the next three RiC-CM relations of this group, namely RiC-R024 includes or included, RiC-R003 has or had constituent, and RiC-R004 has or had component, express structural relations and thus they are mapped to the P46 is composed property of CIDOC-CRM.
Relations between Instances of the Entity RiC-E02 Record Resource or its Subentities to RiC-E07 Agent: RiC-R027 has creator relates instances of RiC-E02 and RiC-E06 with instances of RiC-E07 Agent). To map this relation to CIDOC-CRM, we use the following CIDOC-CRM path: P108i was produced by → E12 Production → P14 carried out by [P14.1 in the role of (RiC-R027i is creator of)]. The main idea is that, in CIDOC-CRM, we relate a human-made Object to an agent that took part in its creation, by referring to the production event (instance of E12 Production) that has as a result the creation of this human-made Object.

The mapping of the relation RiC-R039 is or was holder of is easier as the property CIDOC-CRM P49i is former or current keeper of has similar scope note.

Relating Record Resources to their Subjects: Concerning the relations RiC-R019 has or had subject, RiC-R020 has or had main subject, and RiC-R021 describes or described, we map all of them to the P67 refers to property of CIDOC-CRM. The distinction between them is achieved through the P67.1 has type property of property and the corresponding instance of the CIDOC-CRM entity E55 Type.

Relating Record Resources to their Instantiations: To map RiC-R025 has instantiation to CIDOC-CRM, we employ the P130 shows features of property and specialize it through P130.1 kind of similarity to denote that the similarity refers to the instantiation of a Record Resource. Finally, RiC-R004 has or had component is mapped to P46 is composed of property as it expresses structural information.

Expressing Ownership and Intellectual Property: RiC-R037 is or was owner of and RiC-R040 is or was holder of intellectual property rights of relations are mapped to P51i is former or current owner of and P105i has right on properties, respectively.

Notice that, in this paper (as well as in Table 1), we do not present the mapping of the inverse relations. However, this mapping can be easily implied. The main idea is to start from the path entity corresponding to the relation's range and replace the CIDOC-CRM properties by their inverse properties.

4.3   Mapping the Attributes of the Main RiC-CM Entities

In this section, we present an overview of the mapping of the attributes of RiC-CM record-related entities to CIDOC-CRM paths. RiC-CM attributes describe characteristics of the entities [16] and are distinguished from them in that entities mainly model information that is central to the purpose of archival records.

The concept of attribute is not defined in CIDOC-CRM. To model RiC-CM attributes in CIDOC-CRM we use paths. Taking into consideration the mapping between CIDOC-CRM and RiC-CM entities (see Sect. 4.1), each attribute A of an entity E is mapped to a path in CIDOC-CRM, such as the first entity in the path is one of the CIDOC-CRM entities that E maps to.

Following the aforementioned approach, the attribute RiC-A22 Identifier, is mapped to the CIDOC-CRM path: E22 Human-Made Object → P1 is identified by → E42 Identifier. Similarly, the RiC-A28 Name also refers to identification patterns and is mapped to the CIDOC-CRM path E22 Human-Made Object → P1 is identified by → E41 Appellation. The majority of attributes are mapped to notes through paths that use the CIDOC-CRM property P3 has note. For example, the attribute RiC-A03 Authenticity Note applying to the entities RiC-E03, RiC-E04, RiC-E05,RiC-E06 is mapped to the path E73 Information Object→P3 has note[P3.1 has type→ E55 Type(RiC-A03 Authenticity Note)]→E62 String.

Table 1. Mapping the RiC-CM relations to CIDOC-CRM.

RiC-CM Relation	Domain ID	Range ID	CIDOC-CRM property/path
Relations between instances of the entity RiC-E02 Record Resource and/or its subentities			
RiC-R010 is original of	RiC-E04	RiC-E04	E22 Human-Made Object→P130 shows features of [P130.1 kind of similarity→ E55 Type (RiC-R010i has original)]→E22 Human-Made Object
RiC-R011 is draft of	RiC-E04	RiC-E04	E22 Human-Made Object→P130 shows features of [P130.1 kind of similarity→ E55 Type (RiC-R011 is draft of)]→E22 Human-Made Object
RiC-R012 has copy	RiC-E02	RiC-E02	E22 Human-Made Object→P130 shows features of [P130.1 kind of similarity→ E55 Type (RiC-R012 has copy)]→E22 Human-Made Object
RiC-R013 has reply	RiC-E02	RiC-E02	E22 Human-Made Object→P17i motivated→E12 Production→ P108 has produced→E22 Human-Made Object→P2 has type→ E55 Type (RiC-R013i is reply to)
RiC-R024 includes or included	RiC-E03	RiC-E03, RiC-E04	E22 Human-Made Object→P46 is composed of→E22 Human-Made Object
RiC-R003 has or had constituent	RiC-E04	RiC-E05	E22 Human-Made Object→P46 is composed of→E22 Human-Made Object
RiC-R004 has or had component	RiC-E06	RiC-E06	E22 Human-Made Object→P46 is composed of→E22 Human-Made Object
Relations between instances of the entity RiC-E02 Record Resource or its subentities to RiC-E07 Agent			
RiC-R027 has creator	RiC-E02, RiC-E06	RiC-E07	E22 Human-Made Object→P108i was produced by→E12 Production→ P14 carried out by [P14.1 in the role of (RiC-R027i is creator of)]→E39 Actor
RiC-R039 is or was holder of	RiC-E07	RiC-E02, RiC-E06	E39 Actor→P49i is former or current keeper of→E22 Human-Made Object
Relating Record Resources to their subjects			
RiC-R019 has or had subject	RiC-E02	RiC-E01	E73 Information Object→P67 refers to [P67.1 has type→ E55 Type (RiC19i is or was subject of)]→E1 CRM Entity
RiC-R020 has or had main subject	RiC-E02	RiC-E01	E73 Information Object→P67 refers to [P67.1 has type→ E55 Type (RiC20i is or was main subject of)]→E1 CRM Entity
RiC-R021 describes or described	RiC-E02	RiC-E01	E73 Information Object→P67 refers to [P67.1 has type→ E55 Type (RiC-R021 describes or described)]→E1 CRM Entity
Relating Record Resources to their Instantiations			
RiC-R025 has instantiation	RiC-E02	RiC-E06	E22 Human-Made Object→P130 shows features of [P130.1 kind of similarity→ E55 Type (RiC-R025i is instantiation of)]→E22 Human-Made Object
RiC-R004 has or had component	RiC-E06	RiC-E06	E22 Human-Made Object→P46 is composed of→E22 Human-Made Object
Expressing ownership and intellectual property			
RiC-R037 is or was owner of	RiC-E08, RiC-E09, RiC-E12	RiC-E01	E39 Actor→P51i is former or current owner of→E22 Human-Made Object
RiC-R040 is or was holder of intellectual property rights of	RiC-E08, RiC-E09, RiC-E12	RiC-E02, RiC-E06	E39 Actor→P105i has right on→E22 Human-Made Object

5   Conclusion

In this paper, we defined the mapping of the main RiC-CM entities to their corresponding CIDOC-CRM entities. We mapped the main relations of the RiC-E02 Record Resource entity and its subentities to CIDOC-CRM (path of) properties and entities. We also presented an initial mapping of the attributes of the RiC-E02 Record Resource entity to CIDOC-CRM paths.

For future work we plan to complete the mapping of relations for all RiC-CM entities to CIDOC-CRM. Additionally, we will focus on mapping the RiC-O (RiC Ontology) that is based on RiC-CM to CIDOC-CRM.

References

1. ICON Project: content integration in Portuguese national archives using CIDOC-CRM. Zenodo (2019). https://doi.org/10.5281/zenodo.2594705
2. International council on archives records in contexts ontology (ICA RiC-O) version 0.2 (2021). https://www.ica.org/standards/RiC/RiC-O_v0-2.html. Accessed 07 June 2023
3. ArchOnto specification (2023). https://purl.org/episa/archonto. Accessed 07 June 2023
4. The EPISA project – entity and property inference for semantic archives (2023). https://episa.inesctec.pt/. Accessed 07 June 2023
5. Agathos, M., Kalogeros, E., Gergatsoulis, M., Papaioannou, G.: Documenting architectural styles using CIDOC CRM. In: Tseng, Y.H., Katsurai, M., Nguyen, H.N. (eds.) ICADL 2022. LNCS, vol. 13636, pp. 345–359. Springer, Cham (2022). https://doi.org/10.1007/978-3-031-21756-2_27
6. Bountouri, L., Gergatsoulis, M.: The semantic mapping of archival metadata to the CIDOC CRM ontology. J. Arch. Organ. **9**(3–4), 174–207 (2011)
7. Bountouri, L.: Archives in the Digital Age: Standards, Policies and Tools. Chandos Publishing (2017)
8. CIDOC CRM Special Interest Group: Classes & Properties Declarations of CIDOC-CRM version: 7.1.2 (2022). https://www.cidoc-crm.org/html/cidoc_crm_v7.1.2.html
9. CIDOC CRM Special Interest Group: The CIDOC Conceptual Reference Model (CRM) (2023). https://www.cidoc-crm.org/
10. Clavaud, F., Francart, T., Charbonnier, P.: RiC-O converter: a software to convert EAC-CPF and EAD 2002 XML files to RDF datasets conforming to records in contexts ontology. J. Comput. Cultural Heritage (2023). https://doi.org/10.1145/3583592
11. Doerr, M.: The CIDOC CRM: an ontological approach to semantic interoperability of metadata. AI Mag. **24**, 75–92 (2003)
12. Doerr, M., Gradmann, S., Hennicke, S., Isaac, A., Meghini, C., Van de Sompel, H.: The Europeana data model (EDM). In: World Library and Information Congress: 76th IFLA General Conference and Assembly, vol. 10, p. 15 (2010)
13. EGAD - Expert Group on Archival Description: Records in Contexts - Conceptual Model (2023). https://www.ica.org/en/records-in-contexts-conceptual-model
14. Gaitanou, P., Gergatsoulis, M.: Defining a semantic mapping of VRA Core 4.0 to the CIDOC conceptual reference model. Int. J. Metadata Semant. Ontol. **7**(2), 140–156 (2012)

15. IFLA: Functional Requirements for Bibliographic Records (2009). https://cdn.ifla.
    org/wp-content/uploads/2019/05/assets/cataloguing/frbr/frbr_2008.pdf
16. International Council on Archives: Records in Contexts Conceptual Model. Tech-
    nical report (2021), consultation draft v0.2
17. Kakali, C., et al.: Integrating Dublin core metadata for cultural heritage collections
    using ontologies. In: Proceedings of the 2007 International Conference on Dublin
    Core and Metadata Applications, DC 2007, Singapore, 27–31 August 2007, pp.
    128–139 (2007)
18. Koch, I., Ribeiro, C., Teixeira Lopes, C.: ArchOnto, a CIDOC-CRM-based linked
    data model for the Portuguese archives. In: Hall, M., Merčun, T., Risse, T.,
    Duchateau, F. (eds.) TPDL 2020. LNCS, vol. 12246, pp. 133–146. Springer, Cham
    (2020). https://doi.org/10.1007/978-3-030-54956-5_10
19. Melo, D., Rodrigues, I.P., Varagnolo, D.: A strategy for archives metadata rep-
    resentation on CIDOC-CRM and knowledge discovery. Semant. Web 14, 553–584
    (2023)
20. W3C: XML Path Language (XPath) 2.0 (2007). http://www.w3.org/TR/xpath20/

Automatically Detecting References from the Scholarly Literature to Records in Archives

Tokinori Suzuki[1]([✉]) [iD], Douglas W. Oard[2] [iD], Emi Ishita[1] [iD], and Yoichi Tomiura[1]

[1] Kyushu University, Fukuoka, Japan
`tokinori@inf.kyushu-u.ac.jp`
[2] University of Maryland, College Park, MD, USA

Abstract. Scholars use references in books and articles to materials found in archives as one way of finding those materials, but present systems for archival access do not exploit that information. To change that, the first step is to find archival references in the scholarly literature; that is the focus of this paper. Several classifier designs are compared using a few thousand manually annotated footnotes and endnotes assembled from a large set of open access papers on history. The results indicate that fairly high recall and precision can be achieved.

Keywords: Archival references · Classification · Test collection

1 Introduction

Scholars refer to existing materials to support claims in their scholarly work. Citation to books, journal articles, and conference papers can be detected by automated systems and used as a basis for search or bibliometrics (e.g., using citation databases such as Google Scholar, Web of Science, or Scopus). However, there are no comparable databases for citation to the rare, and often unique, unpublished materials in archival repositories. Our goal in this paper is to begin to change that by automating the process of detecting scholarly citation to materials in an archive. We call such citations Archival References (AR).

Our work is motivated by the task of discovering archival content. A recent survey of users of 12 U.S. archival aggregators (e.g., ArchiveGrid, or the Online Archive of California) found that there were a broad range of users for such search services [26]. One limitation of archival aggregation, however, is that it presently relies on sharing metadata that is manually constructed by individual repositories. In the long run, we aim to augment that with descriptions mined from the written text that authors use to cite the archival resources on which they have relied. To do that at scale, we must first automate the process of finding citations that contain archival references. That is our focus in this paper.

Prior studies suggest that that very substantial numbers of archival references exist to be found [3,18,22]. As an example, Bronstad [3] manually coded citations

D. H. Goh et al. (Eds.): ICADL 2023, LNCS 14458, pp. 100–107, 2023.
https://doi.org/10.1007/978-981-99-8088-8_9

Table 1. Examples of citations containing archival references. "Strict" citations contain only archival references; "About" citations also include other accompanying text.

Strict	About	Citation
✓		Roosevelt to Secretary of War, June 3, 1939, Roosevelt Papers, O.F. 268, Box 10; unsigned memorandum, Jan. 6, 1940, ibid., Box 11.
	✓	Wheeler, D., and R. García-Herrera, 2008: Ships' logbooks in climatological research: Reflections and prospects. Ann. New York Acad. Sci., 1146, 1–15, doi:10.1196/annals.1446.006. Several archive sources have been used in the preparation of this paper, including the following: Logbook of HMS Richmond. The U.K. National Archives. ADM/51/3949

in 136 books on history, finding 895 (averaging 6.6 per book) citing archival repositories. HathiTrust, for example, includes more than 6.5 million open access publications, so we would expect to find millions more archival references there.

As the examples in Table 1 illustrate, archival references differ in important ways from references to published content. Most obviously, conventions used to cite unpublished materials differ from those used to cite published materials [1,25]. The elements of an archival reference (e.g., repository name, box and folder) are different from the elements for published sources (e.g., journal name, volume and pages). It is also common for archival references to include free-form explanatory text within the same footnote or endnote [7].

In this paper, we aim to begin the process of assembling large collections of archival references by building systems capable of automatically detecting them at large scale. To do this, we have collected documents, automatically detected footnotes and endnotes, annotated some of those "citations" for use in training and evaluation, and compared several classifiers. Our results indicate that automatically detecting archival references is tractable, with levels of recall and precision that we expect would be useful in practical applications.

2   Related Work

Studies of scholars who make use of archival repositories indicate that references in the scholarly literature are among the most useful ways of initially finding the repositories in which they will look. For example, Tibbo reported in 2003 that 98% of historians followed leads found in published literature [24], and Marsh, et al. found in 2023 that of anthropologists 73% did so [16]. There is thus good reason to believe that archival references could be useful as a basis for search. While expert scholars may already know where to look for what they need, search tools that mimic that expert behavior could be useful to novices and itinerant users, who comprise the majority of users in the survey mentioned above [26].

Researchers interested in information behavior and in the use of archives have long looked to citations as a source of evidence, but such studies have almost invariably relied on manual coding of relatively small sets of such references [4, 8,10–13,17,18,22,23]. In recent years, rule-based techniques have been applied to detect archival references [2,3], but we are not aware of any cases in which trained classifiers that rely on supervised machine learning have yet been built.

3   Methods

Here we describe how we assemble documents, find citations in those documents, and decide which citations contain archival references.

3.1   Crawling Documents and Extracting Citations

Our first challenge is to find documents that might include citations that contain archival references. Since we know that historians cite archival sources, we chose to focus on papers in history. We therefore crawled papers with a discipline label of History and a rights label of Open Access by using the public Semantic Scholar API.[1] That API requires one or more query terms. To get a set of query terms, we collected the abstracts of the 2,000 most highly cited papers from Scopus that were published in 2021 with a discipline label of Arts and Humanities. We collected terms in those abstracts sorted in the order of their frequency. Then we issued those terms one at a time to Semantic Scholar, and retrieved PDF files. After repeating this process for some number of keywords, we merged the resulting sets of PDF files. Most of our experiments were run on the 1,204 unique documents that resulted from using the most frequent 5 keywords (the KW5 document set), but we also conducted some experiments with the roughly 13,000 unique documents from using the most frequent 14 keywords (KW14).

We then parsed the documents using GROBID [15], an open-source toolkit for text extraction from academic papers. In the KW5 document set, GROBID found at least one footnote or reference (i.e., at least one citation) in 690 documents. In KW14, GROBID found at least one citation in 5,067 documents.

3.2   Detecting Archival References

For this paper, we built three types of classifiers to detect archival references.

Rule-Based (RB) Classifier. Our RB classifier has a single rule: IF a citation includes any of the strings "Box", "Folder", "Series", "Fond", "Container", "Index", "index", "Manuscript", "manuscript", "Collection", "collection", "Library", "library", "Archive", or "archive" THEN it contains an archival reference. Regular expression matching is done without tokenization, lowercasing, or stemming. This is similar to an approach used by Bronstad [3] to search

---

[1] https://www.semanticscholar.org/product/api.

the full text of papers for mentions of repositories. We selected our terms after examining the results from Subset 1 (described below).

Repository Name (RN) Classifier. Our RN classifier looked for one of 25,000 U.S. repository names from the RepoData list [9]. However, across all our experiments RN found only one match that had not also matched a RB classifier term. We did use RN to guide sampling, but we omit RN results for space.

Support Vector Machine (SVM) Classifiers. We experimented with three SVM variants. All using radial basis function kernels, which we found to be better than linear kernels in early experiments. In "SVMterm" the features are frequencies of terms found in citations. Specifically, we tokenized every citation on whitespace or punctuation and removed stopwords. Our tokenizer does not split URLs, so URLs are processed as single term. For our other SVMs, we tokenized each citation using NLTK, used a lookup table to select the pretrained GloVe embedding for each term [20], and then performed mean pooling to create a single embedding per citation. We experimented with both 50 (SVM50) and 300 dimensions (SVM300). We report results for SVM300, which were better than SVM50 with larger training sets. For each SVM we swept C from 1 to 100 by 5 and used the value (20) that gave the best results. We set the gamma for the radial basis function to the inverse of the number of feature set dimensions (e.g., 1/300 for SVM300).

3.3   Sampling Citations for Annotation

We drew five samples from KW5 and one from KW14. One approach ("by document") was to randomly order the documents and then sample citations in their order of occurrence. The other ("by citation") was to randomly order all citations regardless of their source document, and then sample some number of citations from the head of that list. Subsets are numbered in order of their creation. Focusing first on the 59,261 documents in KW5, random selection for Subsets 1 and 6 found 45 archival references among 3,500 sampled citations, a prevalence of 1.3%. This skewed distribution would make it expensive to find enough positive examples for supervised learning, so we turned to system-guided sampling. We merged positive classification results from our RB and RN classifiers to create Subset 2, annotating the first 600 citations (randomized by document). We then trained SVM50 on Subset 2 and used it to guide our draw of Subset 3, manually annotating all 760 citations (randomized by document). To create Subset 4, we first randomly selected and annotated 1,000 of the 59,261 citations (randomized by citation) and then added 259 citations that RB or RN classified as archival references. GROBID found 346,529 citations in the KW14 document set. We randomly sampled 20,000 of those and ran four classifiers on that sample: RB, RN, SVM300, and a BERT classifier (that did not perform well, the description of which we omit for space reasons). We merged and deduplicated positive results from those classifiers, resulting in 880 citations. We call that Subset 5.

3.4 Annotation Criteria and Annotation Process

Our annotation goal was to label whether extracted citations are archival references using two criteria: "Strict" if it included one or more archival references, with no other text; or "About" if it included one or more archival references together with explanatory text. Table 1 shows examples. The first has two archival references, and nothing else, satisfying our Strict criterion. The second has one archival reference and some explanatory text, satisfying our About criterion.

Annotation was done by two annotators. Annotator A1, the first author of this paper (a computer scientist) annotated Subsets 1 through 4 and Subset 6. Before performing any annotation, he examined the citation practice in 207 pages of endnotes from three published books in history [5,21,27] and from one journal article in history [19]. A1's initial annotations of Subsets 1 and 2 were reviewed by the second author of this paper (an iSchool faculty member). A1 reannotated subsets 1 and 2 and then annotated subsets 3, 4, and 6. For time reasons, Subsets 3 and 4 were annotated only by the Strict criterion. Annotation requires some degree of interpretation, so additional research was conducted using Google when necessary (e.g., to see if some unfamiliar word might be a repository name).

Subset 5 was assessed by annotator A2, a Library Science Ph.D. student studying archives. We trained A2 in three phases. First, we demonstrated how to judge whether a citation is an archival reference (by either criterion) using 50 examples from Subset 4. Then A2 annotated 50 more citations from KW14 with the same criteria prevalence. The first three authors then met with A2 to discuss their annotations, and then A2 coded 120 more citations from KW14 We computed Cohen's Kappa [6] between A1 and A2 on those 120 citations as 0.80 (substantial agreement, according to Landis and Koch [14]). Finally, A2 annotated the 880 citations in Subset 5. All our annotations are on GitHub.[2]

4 Results

As measures of effectiveness we report Precision (P), Recall (R) and F_1. Table 2 shows results with Strict+About training. We used two approaches to choosing training and test data. In one, we used separate training and test sets. Because of distributional differences between the training and test sets, this yields conservative estimates for the Recall and Precision that could be obtained in practice with more careful attention to that factor. To avoid distributional differences, we also experimented with training and testing on same subset(s), using five-fold cross-validation. Cross-validation yields somewhat optimistic estimates for Recall and Precision, since that approach eliminates systematic differences in the decisions made by different annotators, and it entirely removes all differences between the distributional characteristics of the training and test sets. Considering results from the two approaches together thus allows us to characterize the range of Precision, Recall and F_1 values that we might expect to see in practice.

Focusing first on the Eval S+A block in Table 2, we see that detecting archival references is not hard. The RB classifier achieves excellent Recall with no training at all, although its Precision is quite poor. Among SVMs, SVM300 does best in every case by F_1. It seems that distributional differences are adversely affecting Recall and Precision when the training and test sets differ (although 95% confidence intervals are about ±0.2 on the low-prevalence Subset 6 test set). From the Eval: S and Eval: A blocks of Table 2, we see that a classifier with both S and A annotations for training is much better at finding S than A.

As Table 3 shows, removing A from training doesn't help to find more S. Compare, for example, Recall in the second set of experiments in both Tables 2 and 3, both of which were trained and tested on Subset 5. There, training with S+A correctly found more S annotations than did training with only S.

Table 2. Results for classifiers trained with both Strict (S) and About (A) annotations as positive examples. P = Precision, R = Recall, best F_1 bold. Train or test, with number of positive S and A annotations (after removal of any training citations from the test set). Top block: detecting all citations containing archival references; subsequent blocks: same classifiers evaluated only on citations with S or A annotations.

| | Train: 1+2 (114S, 22A) | | | Train: 5 (243S, 18A) | | | Train: 5 (243S, 18A) | | |
| | Test: Cross-Validation | | | Test: Cross-Validation | | | Test: 6 (7S, 21A) | | |
Eval: S+A	P	R	F_1	P	R	F_1	P	R	F_1
RB	0.24	1.00	0.39	0.30	1.00	0.47	0.22	0.65	0.33
SVMterm	0.99	0.68	0.80	0.92	0.74	0.82	0.30	0.50	0.38
SVM300	0.94	0.79	**0.85**	0.86	0.81	**0.83**	0.50	0.50	**0.50**
Eval: S	P	R	F_1	P	R	F_1	P	R	F_1
RB	0.20	1.00	0.33	0.28	1.00	0.44	0.11	0.86	0.19
SVMterm	0.92	0.75	0.82	0.91	0.78	**0.83**	0.17	0.64	**0.27**
SVM300	0.86	0.80	**0.83**	0.81	0.81	0.81	0.16	0.64	0.25
Eval: A	P	R	F_1	P	R	F_1	P	R	F_1
RB	0.03	1.00	0.06	0.02	1.00	0.04	0.11	0.50	0.18
SVMterm	0.06	0.31	0.10	0.03	0.56	0.05	0.15	0.50	0.23
SVM300	0.08	0.45	**0.14**	0.05	0.72	**0.08**	0.34	0.45	**0.39**

Table 3. Results for detecting Strict (S) annotations by classifiers trained on only Strict annotations as positive examples. Notation as in Table 2.

| | Train: 1+3+4 (110S) | | | Train: 5 (243S) | | | Train: 5 (243S) | | | Train:1+3 (54S) | | |
| | Test:Cross-Validation | | | Test:Cross-Validation | | | Test: 6 (7S) | | | Test: 4 (56S) | | |
Eval: S	P	R	F_1	P	R	F_1	P	R	F_1	P	R	F_1
RB	0.31	0.71	0.43	0.29	1.00	0.45	0.11	1.00	0.20	0.28	0.63	**0.38**
SVMterm	0.69	0.35	0.46	0.91	0.72	**0.80**	0.20	0.64	0.30	0.06	0.95	0.11
SVM300	0.82	0.58	**0.68**	0.87	0.75	**0.80**	0.36	0.57	**0.44**	0.07	0.95	0.13

---

[2] https://github.com/tokinori8/archive-citation-collection.

5   Conclusion and Future Work

We have shown that archival references can be detected fairly reliably, with F_1 values between 0.5 and 0.83, depending on how well the training and test sets are matched. We have also developed and shared collections that can be used to train and evaluate such systems. Annotator agreement indicates that our Strict and About criteria for characterizing archival references are well defined and replicable. Most archival references satisfy our Strict criterion, and unsurprisingly it is Strict classification decisions where we do best. Experiments with separate training and test sets point to potential challenges from systematic differences in prevalence that result from sampling differences. This work is thus a starting point from which second-generation collections might be built with even better control over prevalence matching between training and test sets, and more robust classification results might be achieved using classifier ensembles. Given our promising results for this archival reference detection task, our next step will be to develop algorithms to segment individual archival references, and then to extract specific elements (e.g., repository name or container).

Acknowledgments. This work was supported by JSPS KAKENHI Grant Number JP23KK0005.

References

1. American Psychological Association, et al.: Publication Manual of the American Psychological Association. American Psychological Association (2022)
2. Borrego, Á.: Measuring the impact of digital heritage collections using Google Scholar. Inf. Technol. Libr. **39**(2) (2020)
3. Bronstad, K.: References to archival materials in scholarly history monographs. Qual. Quant. Methods Libr. **6**(2), 247–254 (2019)
4. Brubaker, J.: Primary materials used by Illinois state history researchers. Ill. Libr. **85**(3), 4–8 (2005)
5. Carlson, E.: Joe Rochefort's War: The Odyssey of the Codebreaker Who Outwitted Yamamoto at Midway. The Naval Institute Press (2013)
6. Cohen, J.: A coefficient of agreement for nominal scales. Educ. Psychol. Measur. **20**(1), 37–46 (1960)
7. David-Fox, M., Holquist, P., Martin, A.M.: Citing the archival revolution. Kritika Explor. Russ. Eurasian Hist. **8**(2), 227–230 (2007)
8. Elliott, C.A.: Citation patterns and documentation for the history of science: some methodological considerations. Am. Arch. **44**(2), 131–142 (1981)
9. Goldman, B., Tansey, E.M., Ray, W.: US archival repository location data (2022). https://osf.io/cft8r/. Accessed 17 Jan 2023
10. Heinzkill, R.: Characteristics of references in selected scholarly English literary journals. Libr. Q. **50**(3), 352–365 (1980)
11. Hitchcock, E.R.: Materials used in the research of state history: a citation analysis of the 1986 Tennessee Historical Quarterly. Collect. Build. **10**(1/2), 52–54 (1990)
12. Hurt, J.A.: Characteristics of Kansas history sources: a citation analysis of the Kansas Historical Quarterly. Ph.D. thesis, Emporia Kansas State College (1975)

13. Jones, C., Chapman, M., Woods, P.C.: The characteristics of the literature used by historians. J. Librariansh. **4**(3), 137–156 (1972)
14. Landis, J.R., Koch, G.G.: The measurement of observer agreement for categorical data. Biometrics **33**(1), 159–174 (1977)
15. Lopez, P., et al.: GROBID: generation of bibliographic data. Open source software (2023). https://github.com/kermitt2/grobid. Accessed 6 Feb 2023
16. Marsh, D.E., St. Andre, S., Wagner, T., Bell, J.A.: Attitudes and uses of archival materials among science-based anthropologists. Archival Sci. 1–25 (2023)
17. McAnally, A.M.: Characteristics of materials used in research in United States history. Ph.D. thesis, University of Chicago (1951)
18. Miller, F.: Use, appraisal, and research: a case study of social history. Am. Arch. **49**(4), 371–392 (1986)
19. Neufeld, M.J., Charles, J.B.: Practicing for space underwater: inventing neutral buoyancy training, 1963–1968. Endeavour **39**(3–4), 147–159 (2015)
20. Pennington, J., Socher, R., Manning, C.D.: GloVe: global vectors for word representation. In: Proceedings of the 2014 Conference on Empirical Methods in Natural Language Processing (EMNLP), pp. 1532–1543 (2014)
21. Prange, G.W.: At Dawn We Slept. The Untold Story of Pearl Harbor. Penguin Books (1991)
22. Sherriff, G.: Information use in history research: a citation analysis of master's level theses. Portal Libr. Acad. **10**(2), 165–183 (2010)
23. Sinn, D.: The use context of digital archival collections: mapping with historical research topics and the content of digital archival collections. Preserv. Digit. Technol. Cult. **42**(2), 73–86 (2013)
24. Tibbo, H.: Primarily history in America: how U.S. historians search for primary materials at the dawn of the digital age. Am. Archivist **66**(1), 9–50 (2003)
25. University of Chicago Press Editorial Staff: The Chicago Manual of Style. University of Chicago Press (2017)
26. Weber, C.S., et al.: Summary of research: findings from the building a national finding aid network project. Technical report, OCLC (2023). https://doi.org/10.25333/7a4c-0r03
27. Yokoi, K.: Global Evolution of the Aircraft Industry and Military Air Power. Nihon Keizai Hyoronsha Ltd. (2016). (in Japanese)

Unveiling Archive Users: Understanding Their Characteristics and Motivations

Luana Ponte[ID], Inês Koch[✉][ID], and Carla Teixeira Lopes[ID]

Faculty of Engineering of the University of Porto and INESC TEC,
Rua Dr. Roberto Frias, 4200-465 Porto, Portugal
up201805965@up.pt, ines.koch@inesctec.pt, ctl@fe.up.pt

Abstract. An institution must understand its users to provide quality services, and archives are no exception. Over the years, archives have adapted to the technological world, and their users have also changed. To understand archive users' characteristics and motivations, we conducted a study in the context of the Portuguese Archives. For this purpose, we analysed a survey and complemented this analysis with information gathered in interviews with archivists. Based on the most frequent reasons for visiting the archives, we defined six main archival profiles (genealogical research, historical research, legal purposes, academic work, institutional purposes and publication purposes), later characterised using the results of the previous analysis. For each profile, we created a persona for a more visual and realistic representation of users.

Keywords: Archives · Archive users · User profiles · Personas

1 Introduction

Archival institutions have experienced changes over the years taking advantage of new technologies. Digital archives are also an example of archives evolution. They promote easy access to archival materials via the Internet. However, since not all archival users have technological skills, it becomes crucial to know their motivations, their challenges when visiting the archives, and how they behave when searching for information.

Users tend to be diverse, having different characteristics, motivations, and skills. To ensure their information needs are met, it is necessary to consider their different profiles. This study aims to understand the users of archives and identify their characteristics, motivations and difficulties in the search process. We focus on the case of the Portuguese archives. To collect user views on this matter, we have analyzed the data of a survey run at an institutional level. We have also interviewed professionals from several Portuguese archives to complement user views with professional ones. In the end, we create personas based on the most frequent reasons for visiting the archive.

ⓒ The Author(s), under exclusive license to Springer Nature Singapore Pte Ltd. 2023
D. H. Goh et al. (Eds.): ICADL 2023, LNCS 14458, pp. 108–122, 2023.
https://doi.org/10.1007/978-981-99-8088-8_10

2 Archives and Their Users

Public archives are repositories of national history housing materials from the public and private sectors [1]. Archives aim to gather, organise, and preserve national historical interest available to society.

Archive users cover various profiles, from general users to teachers, students, genealogists, or even historians [10]. In other words, users seek information from archival materials [3]. Since the 1980s, user studies have collected information about users and their use of archival materials [9]. The focus of user studies has changed over time, with the development of technologies and the changing research trends being factors that have influenced these changes. The research topics of archival user studies can be divided into three categories, which may or not be related — information needs, information seeking, and information use [9].

To study archival users, researchers have used various methods. Several user studies have continuously used reference question analysis. This method analyses the questions asked through correspondence collected by letter, fax, or email to identify user needs. Duff and Johnson [4] analysed reference questions posed by email to archivists to understand how archival users seek information. Conway created a method that focuses on understanding the researchers who visit the archives. His main goal was to show how archivists can benefit from comprehensive user studies programs and how they can build one [3]. Burke et al. [2] studied the needs of end-users of language archives by having a team of linguists and information scientists interview language archive managers and end-users.

More recently, Web analytics has become a research method in user studies. This method has also started to be used in archives, as it allows "measuring users' actions, understanding some aspects of users' behaviour and initiating a continuous programme of improvement of online services" in archival environments. Repositories can dramatically improve access, increase usage, and heighten user satisfaction by interpreting Web analytics data in light of repository goals and other information concerning use (such as usability studies) [8,9].

When studying users, it is convenient to communicate profiles efficiently in various contexts. Personas are helpful for this purpose. Tu et al. [11] created personas from the definition of user profiles. Personas are fictional characters representing similar users' user characteristics [5,11]. Personas combine different aspects of real people, such as name, occupation, age, gender, or level of education.

3 Methodology

The Portuguese Archive Network comprises two national archives, the National Archives of the Torre Tombo (ANTT) and the Portuguese Centre of Photography (CPF), sixteen district archives, and the Overseas Historical Archive. This network is managed by the General Directorate of Books, Archives and Libraries (DGLAB), which is responsible for protecting, conserving, and ensuring access to significant documentary heritage [7]. DGLAB has been adopting systems that allow users to carry out online activities that would be done in a presential environment. Archives provide services such as information requests, searches, consultation in person, reproduction, certification, and registration. These services are available online via the electronic counter, through the CRAV[1] (Real Consultation in a Virtual Environment), or in person at any DGLAB archive [7]. In addition, users can also search for information online. DigitArq[2] is a system that allows the user to access online a set of services only available in person at the Archives. It is possible to consult the institution's catalogue, view scanned documents, request digital reproductions, reserve documents for on-site reading, request certificates or obtain information.

To better understand archive users, we conducted a study in the context of Portuguese Archives, organised in four steps, as shown in Fig. 1.

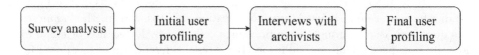

Fig. 1. Stages followed for the definition of DGLAB's archive user profiles

3.1   Survey Analysis

In the first stage, we analysed the DGLAB satisfaction survey[3], which aims to assess the performance of DGLAB services and determine the priority interventions the institution should make to improve its services. The survey is available on the ANTT website[4] throughout the year. For our analysis, we considered the answers from 2015 to 2022, focusing on the questions potentially useful for our goals: inquiries related to demographic characteristics and users' educational backgrounds. After analysing the survey, we began cross-referencing the data between the reasons for visiting the archive — genealogical research, historical research, legal purposes, academic work, institutional purposes and publication purposes — with the demographic data.

3.2   Initial User Profiling

We defined the initial profiles with the findings derived from the crossed-data analysis. To make the visualisation of the profiles more appealing and realistic, we transformed them into personas and gave each one a name and an image taken from a stock image website.

---

[1] Website CRAV—Available at: https://crav.arquivos.pt/login.
[2] Website DigitArq—Available at: https://digitarq.arquivos.pt/.
[3] Available at: https://www.surveymonkey.com/r/X8MMNBJ.
[4] https://antt.dglab.gov.pt/sondagem-aos-clientes/.

3.3   Interviews with Archivists

Next, based on these profiles, we interviewed National and District Archives archivists to complement the users' information with the professionals' viewpoint. Besides allowing the contraposition of users' and archivists' perspectives, interviews also allowed us to gather information about users' motivations for accessing archives and their difficulties while searching for information. The archivists' answers are based on users visiting the archives personally. We conducted these interviews online to allow reaching more archivists from many regions. The archivists who were not available for the interviews could answer the interview questions offline through an online form.

3.4   Final User Profiling

Finally, the final profiles were defined based on the results of the DGLAB satisfaction survey and the answers given during the interviews by the archivists.

Since the interviews revealed significant information and archivists expressed themselves differently, it became imperative to develop a method for standardising and summarising the responses. Standardisation was applied to gender, frequency (visit or help), motivations or difficulties in finding information.

Regarding gender, users were assumed to be "*male*" or "*female*" based on expressions said by archivists, such as "*more men*" or "*more women*". In the absence of gender predominance, it would be considered "*no distinction*".

Regarding the frequency of visits and help requests, we created a scale with the options "*Very infrequent*", "*Infrequent*", "*Frequent*" and "*Very frequent*". To standardise each response it was considered the synonyms of these expressions and the quantifiers added to the casual expressions mentioned by the archivists, such as "*very*", "*a lot*", "*some*", "*rare*", among others.

Mainly for motivations, synonymous expressions were taken into account, such as "*college work*" was equivalent to "*academic work*", so it is only necessary to use one expression.

When the archivists referred to providing guidance to the user on how, where, and what to search for, this was taken as "*guidance*" representing the initial assistance that many users need. Responses mentioning the difficulty of reading older documents were defined as "*palaeography*", suggesting a lack of palaeographic knowledge among users. Difficulties in using and accessing DigitArq and CRAV were defined as "*DigitArq*" and "*CRAV*" respectively. Less common responses such as "*form filling*" were maintained and not standardised. Some answers were not standardised, as they varied more between archives. They have only been summarised to express what the archivist mentioned briefly.

In assigning the characteristics to each persona, the most frequent response corresponding to each file is assigned, as in the surveys. However, as the demographic data is crossed in both sources of information, it is normal that ambiguity arises when the most frequent values are different in both sources. Figure 2 presents the decisions made to attribute demographic characteristics when ambiguity arises. When the mode of response is identical in the surveys and the interviews, the data are attributed. When the mode is not identical, it is checked if the second most frequent answer in the interviews is equivalent to the mode in the surveys. Otherwise, it may be necessary to analyse the data annually to check the most frequent answers each year and assign the most frequent value that appears more often.

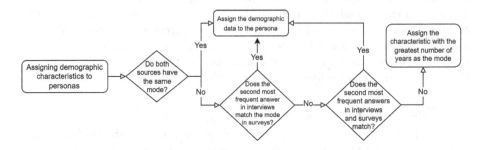

Fig. 2. Demographic data assignment flowchart

Research data from this study is available in the INESC TEC research data repository [6].

4   Survey Analysis and Initial Profiling

We gathered 4661 responses from the satisfaction survey between 2015 and 2022. Each answer refers to the last interaction the respondent had with the archive. Among the respondents, 2692 (57.8%) are male and 1969 (42.2%) are female.

The users' age ranges frequency is the `Total` column of Table 2. The age ranges shown in the table were defined by DGLAB. The age with the highest number of users is between 48–52, the mode in three reasons for visiting the archive.

The majority of the respondents, that is, 1539 (33.6%), have a Bachelor's degree, followed by high school education with 855 (18.7%) users, postgraduate with 828 (17.9%) users, 796 (17.4%) users with Master's degree, 515 (11.2%) users with a PhD and 53 (1.2%) users with elementary education.

The vast majority of users, 3324 (71.3%), visited the archive online, while only 1337 (28.7%) users visited it in person.

Most users (2668 users, 57.2%) responding to the survey have visited the archive for the first time. The distribution of users per frequency of visits is shown in Table 1. Of those who did not visit the archive for the first time, 517 (11.1%) users often visit the archive at least once every six months.

Regarding the users' motivations, the survey includes six predefined options. The most frequent reason for visiting is Genealogical research, with 2234 users (47.9%), followed by Historical research, with 914 users (19.6%), Legal purposes, with 845 users (18.1%), Academic work, with 242 users (5.21%), Institutional purposes, with 79 users (1.7%) and, finally, Publication purposes, with 62 users (1.3%).

Table 1. Frequency of visits to the archive

Frequency of visits to the archive	Frequency
First time visiting the archive	**2668 (57.2%)**
At least once every 15 days	249 (5.3%)
At least once every 6 months	517 (11.1%)
At least once a year	409 (8.8%)
At least once a month	405 (8.7%)
Almost every day or at least once a week	413 (8.9%)

There is also an option for users to mention "other" reasons. Only 285 users (6.1%) selected this option, answering mainly that they intended to obtain birth or baptismal certificates. We excluded this reason from Table 2 for its low expressiveness. However, it will be counted and included in the total percentages.

Table 2. User's characteristics frequency by reason for visiting the archive

	Genealogical	Historical	Legal	Academic	Institutional	Publication	Total
Male	60.3%	63.8%	52.8%	44.6%	51.9%	53.2%	57.8%
Female	39.7%	36.2%	47.2%	55.4%	48.1%	46.8%	42.2%
18-22	2.2%	1.9%	0.4%	9.9%	1.3%	1.6%	2.1%
23-27	4.2%	6.0%	3.3%	12.0%	1.3%	1.6%	4.6%
28-32	7.0%	8.8%	7.2%	**15.3%**	6.3%	3.2%	7.6%
33-37	9.3%	9.6%	8.3%	13.6%	7.6%	11.3%	9.3%
38-42	10.2%	12.0%	11.4%	13.6%	**17.7%**	11.3%	11.0%
43-47	11.2%	10.1%	14.0%	7.4%	12.7%	**21.0%**	11.5%
48-52	**12.8%**	**12.3%**	**15.5%**	9.5%	10.1%	6.5%	**12.6%**
53-57	12.1%	10.9%	10.4%	7.9%	15.2%	11.3%	11.6%
58-62	12.4%	10.2%	11.4%	5.0%	15.2%	12.9%	11.6%
63-67	8.5%	7.3%	8.5%	3.7%	5.1%	12.9%	8.0%
68-72	6.2%	6.5%	6.5%	1.7%	2.5%	4.8%	6.2%
73-77	2.9%	3.1%	1.8%	0.0%	5.1%	1.6%	2.7%
78-82	0.8%	1.0%	0.8%	0.4%	0.0%	0.0%	0.9%
over 83	0.2%	0.4%	0.6%	0.0%	0.0%	0.0%	0.4%
Primary	1.2%	0.7%	1.7%	0.4%	0.0%	0.0%	1.2%
High school	20.2%	11.4%	23.2%	5.0%	23.4%	8.1%	18.7%
Bachelor	**34.7%**	23.8%	**43.6%**	20.5%	**41.6%**	**27.4%**	**33.6%**
Postgrad	22.8%	10.8%	15.9%	7.1%	15.6%	17.7%	17.9%
Master	15.0%	26.0%	12.0%	**35.1%**	16.9%	21.0%	17.4%
PhD	6.1%	**27.4%**	3.5%	31.8%	2.6%	25.8%	11.2%

We also analysed the characteristics of the users accessing the archives for each main reason. Table 2 presents gender, age-range and educational background frequency by reason. As seen in the table, the male gender is the most common, the ages are mostly between 40 and 60, and the most common academic qualification is a university degree.

Table 2 shows the cross-referencing of the reasons for visiting as defined by DGLAB and the demographic characteristics — gender, age, and education. The values in bold per column are the most frequent for each dimension. The initial profiles were defined based on the mode of each of these dimensions, e.g., the persona of the Genealogical research motive is characterised by a male (60.3%), aged between 48 and 52 years old (12.8%) and has a Bachelor's degree (34.7%).

5   Interviews with the Archivists and Final Profiling

For this study, we contacted all National and District Archives of Portugal and the Overseas Historical Archive. The interviews were conducted with DGLAB archivists selected by the corresponding archive. We obtained in total 12 answers out of 18 — 10 interviews and two answers on the form. The 12 archives included in the study are: ANTT, CPF, and the District Archives of Beja (ADB), Bragança (ADBR), Évora (ADE), Faro (ADF), Guarda (ADG), Leiria (ADL), Porto (ADP), Santarém (ADS), Viana do Castelo (ADVC) and Vila Real (ADVR). The interviews were semi-structured and guided by a script available in our research dataset. These interviews were conducted during April and June 2023. All the questions in the script were asked for all the reasons for the visit, i.e. six times.

During the interviews, a particular situation arose about one of the archives, the Portuguese Centre of Photography (CPF). This is due to the fact that the CPF is an archive that gathers mainly photographic documents, meaning it differs from the other district and national archives, comprising a greater diversity of document types. According to the CPF archivist, there are only four main reasons for visiting: Exhibition Purposes, Publication Purposes, Research (although it was not mentioned, it is implied that it is Historical Research) and Academic Work. Given the nature of this archive, it was expected that the reasons for visiting it would differ. Thus, only the first reason pointed out by the archivist will not feature in the data analysis of this study, given its specificity.

Table 3. User's characteristics frequency by reason for visiting the archive – Interviews

	Genealogical	Historical	Legal	Academic	Institutional	Publication
Male	67%	33%	17%	25%	8%	33%
Female	0%	17%	17%	8%	25%	8%
No distinction	25%	50%	58%	67%	0%	33%
Very infrequent	17%	33%	0%	33%	33%	33%
Infrequent	58%	8%	25%	8%	33%	33%
Frequent	17%	33%	25%	42%	8%	8%
Very frequent	0%	17%	25%	0%	0%	0%

The results of the interviews will be presented below by reason of visit. For each reason, the most frequent answers of the archivists are presented, starting with their characteristics and moving on to their motivations and doubts when interacting with the archive.

Table 3 presents, in percentage, the results obtained in the interviews alluding to the gender and frequency of visit of each profile. Table 4 presents the most frequent motivations mentioned during the interviews, by archive and by profile. The data are distributed by profile and by the archives that mention the respective motivations. The column "% by profile" represents the number of archives, in percentage, that said the motivation presented in the column "motivations" by profile. The column "% by motivation" represents, in rate, the number of archives that mentioned the motivation regardless of the profile.

Table 4. Main motivations for visiting archives

Motivation	Profiles	Archives	% by profile	% by motivation
Academic activities	Historical research	ANTT; ADG; ADVR; ADB; ADBR	42%	67%
	Academic work	ADG; ADVR; ADB; CPF; ADBR; ADVC	50%	
	Publication purposes	ADG; ADB; ADP	25%	
Acquisition of nationality	Legal purposes	ADP; ADVC; ADG; ADVR; ADBR	42%	58%
	Genealogical research	ANTT	8%	
	Institutional purposes	ADE	8%	
Certificates	Legal purposes	ADP; ADBR	17%	25%
	Institutional purposes	ADP; ADB; ADBR	25%	
Dissertation/Thesis writing	Historical research	ADP; ADVC; ADBR; CPF	33%	42%
	Academic work	ADP; ADE; ADVC	25%	
	Publication Purposes	ADE	8%	
Family tree	Genealogical research	ADP; ANTT; ADVC; ADG; ADVR;ADE; ADBR; ADF	67%	67%
Habilitation of heirs	Legal purposes	ADVC; ADB; ADE; ADBR	33%	33%
	Institutional purposes	ADVC; ADB	17%	
Personal research	Historical research	ADB; CPF	17%	25%
	Publication purposes	ADG	8%	
Property registration	Legal purposes	ADVR; ADBR	17%	17%
Research activities	Historical research	ANTT; ADG; ADE	25%	33%
	Academic work	ANTT; ADB	17%	
Scientific publications	Historical research	ADP; ADVR; ADBR	25%	42%
	Academic work	ADP	8%	
	Publication purposes	ADE; ADB; ADVR; ADBR	33%	

5.1   Genealogical Research

This profile (Fig. 3) is mainly represented by male individuals (8 statements). A single age, rather than an age range, was assigned for the final profiling to make the personas more realistic. So the age assigned to the persona in this profile was 50 years old. The most frequent age range mentioned is between 40 and 50 years (3 statements). Four archivists said they have many visits from retired users over 60. This profile's most common academic qualification is a *Bachelor's degree* (4 statements) and *higher education* (4 statements).

It is rare for this profile to visit the physical archive (7 responses) since much documentation is digitised and accessible online through DigitArq.

The motivations are based on constructing the family tree (8 statements). Some users do genealogy services for others (2 statements) — professional genealogists.

Users often ask archivists for help (7 mentions as "frequent"), mainly based on research guidance (9 mentions), for instance, how to start the family tree, what, how, and where to search. The way documents are written can also become a constraint. The need for knowledge of palaeography makes it easier for users to read the oldest manuscripts (7 statements).

Archivists considered that age and education were the most significant factors influencing the ISB of this profile. Older users are better at reading older documents but find it more difficult to access CRAV and DigitArq; retired researchers and professors have more advanced research habits than other users, and professional genealogists are more demanding.

The unique characteristic of these users is their curiosity (2 responses), and they have an affective connection with their motivations (1 mention).

5.2 Historical Research

This profile (Fig. 3) has no predominance of gender (6 statements) based on the interview responses. The most frequent exact age range is 30 to 40 (mentioned 3 times). The academic qualification most often cited is a *Bachelor's degree* (7 mentions).

The most common answers regarding the frequency of archive visits are "*very infrequent*" (4 mentions) and "*frequent*" (4 mentions). Since they are considered seasonal users, the archivists can interpret their frequency of visits differently.

All archivists stated that the primary motivations for this profile are gathering information for academic and research purposes, such as writing theses or publishing scientific articles.

It is rare for this user to ask for help (4 statements as "*very infrequent*" and 4 statements as "*infrequent*"). Their doubts and difficulties are mainly related to the need for guidance (6 mentions) and the use of DigitArq (2 mentions). Two archivists also mentioned a lack of palaeography knowledge, which makes it difficult for users to read older documents.

Four archivists mentioned that educational background and age could influence these users' behaviour. Archivists stated that although some users have higher academic qualifications, they still need help or know how to read older documents. Regarding age, archivists mentioned that older users define their search better than younger ones. Other archives revealed that younger users are more autonomous and demanding. They are also considered specialised and knowledgeable about the documentation present in the archive.

5.3 Legal Purposes

This is also a profile (Fig. 3) with no gender majority (7 statements). The age range that stands out is between 40 and 50 years old (4 mentions). However, archivists mentioned that this profile is very diverse. Most users have only a *high school education* (5 statements) and *Bachelor's degree* (6 mentions).

The frequency of visits is ambiguous. The exact number of archives mentioned that it is infrequent, frequent, or very frequent (3 mentions for each answer) for users to visit the physical archive. According to the interviewees, these users

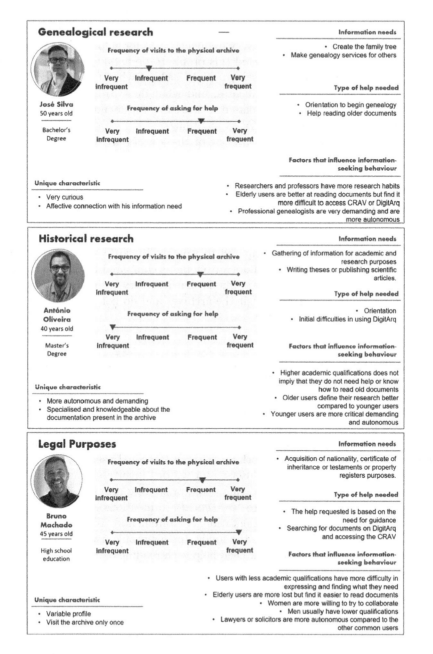

Fig. 3. Genealogical research, Historical research, and Legal Purposes Personas

often visit the archive once to resolve their legal issues and do not return. For the archivists, this could be a situation that is assumed to be either frequent, in the sense that different people show up regularly, or infrequent because users do not return.

Their motivations concern the acquisition of nationality (5 statements), habilitation of heirs (4 statements), or property registers purposes (2 statements).

It is a profile that frequently or very frequently asks for help (each answer with four statements). Archivists reported this profile to be highly dependent. Users request support for guidance (6 statements), such as what type of documents to search for, how to obtain certificates, and what data to fill in to request a certificate. Some doubts are also related to searching for documents on DigitArq (3 statements) and accessing CRAV (3 mentions).

The factors influencing the behaviour of these users are education (3 mentions), age (3 statements), gender (1 statement), and job occupation (1 statement). Users with less academic qualifications need help to express and find what they need in the archive. Regarding age, elderly users are, on the one hand, more lost, but on the other hand, find it easier to read documents. Regarding gender, archivists mentioned that women are more willing to try collaborating in the sense of accepting the help provided than men. One archive said that men usually have lower qualifications compared to women. Regarding profession, users who are lawyers or solicitors are more autonomous compared to the other users.

A unique characteristic of this profile is that it is very variable, and they are not everyday users. Often, they visit the archives and do not return.

5.4   Academic Work

This profile (Fig. 4) has no gender predominance (8 mentions). The most frequently mentioned age range is 20 to 30 (5 mentions). The most common academic qualification is a *Bachelor's degree* (8 statements), and the second most frequent is *Master's degree* (5 answers).

This profile visits the archive frequently (5 mentions as "*frequent*"). However, some archivists reported that this frequency of visits might only be regular while users are doing some academic work or research (seasonal users).

Most archivists revealed that users' motivations involve gathering information for writing dissertations, academic work, or writing articles.

Help requests in this profile are "*infrequent*" (5 mentions). Users need assistance with their initial search orientation (7 statements), including where to start the search and how to locate the fonds. In this profile, two archivists mentioned that users of academic work need help with reading older documents, i.e., palaeographic knowledge.

The factors influencing information-seeking behaviour are work purpose, gender, and age. The work purpose affects the user's motivation to perform the search. Regarding gender, one archive mentioned that female users conduct more well-defined searches when compared to men, which leads the latter to need more guidance. Finally, regarding age, younger users are more critical, demanding, and autonomous compared to older ones.

Their unique characteristics are that they can easily consult DigitArq fonds and are comfortable with information technology. They are also more confident in their research, autonomous, and demanding.

5.5   Institutional Purposes

Seven archives mentioned that the main users of this profile (Fig. 4) are institutions, such as conservatories, consulates, city halls, universities, and cultural and local associations. There is no gender, age, or academic qualification assigned. It is a profile that very infrequently (4 answers out of 9) visits the physical archives, as most users make their requests through the CRAV system, email, or phone.

As stated by the archivists, motivations vary according to the type of institution. Courts use archives to request records when a legal case has been reopened, and consequently, they may require files or other types of documents and information. Notarial offices use archives to obtain information for deeds, probate proceedings, or to authenticate documents. Institutions such as law firms request statutes and visit the archive for citizenship certificates for other individuals. Other institutions visit the archive for recreational activities or exhibitions.

These users rarely ask for help (7 *"infrequent"* answers). They seek help filling out forms, searching DigitArq, and requesting services through the CRAV. Archivists mentioned that this profile has clear ideas of what they want. They often request the information search service, i.e. users ask the archive to search for a certain document.

There is no record of factors influencing the behaviour of these users. They usually represent a service and have very specific needs, close to the motivations for legal purposes.

5.6   Publication Purposes

This is a motive (Fig. 4) more frequent in male users (5 mentions) with a *Bachelor's degree* (4 statements) between 40 and 50 years old (3 mentions).

This profile visits the archive infrequently (4 statements as *"infrequent"*). The motivations of these users can be both academic and non-academic. Users seek information in the archive for their articles, dissertations, or other publications.

It is *"very infrequent"* (7 mentions) for these users to ask for help. Four archivists did not point out any doubt that is considered standard among these users. One of the archives mentioned that their doubts refer to obtaining authorisation to use documents from the archive for their publications. There is no record of responses regarding factors that may influence the behaviour of these users in the archive. Concerning the unique characteristics of these profiles, archivists mentioned that these users are very strict with the information they seek and are also very autonomous, as they have their search and need for information well defined.

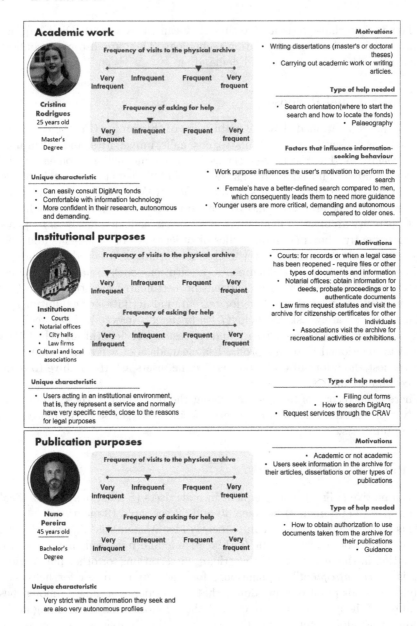

Fig. 4. Academic Work, Institutional Purposes and Publication Purposes Personas

6   Conclusions

This work allowed us to define the users of DGLAB's archives by collecting information through two different methods — surveys and interviews with the archivists, which provided information about users' characteristics and research motivations, as well as the help they often request.

The two stages of data collection were essential, not only to confirm the validity of the users' characteristics but also to obtain new information not present in the survey regarding their motivation to visit the archive and what are their difficulties.

The profiles, except for academic work and institutional purposes, have aspects in common. They are represented by male gender, aged between 40 and 50. With the exception of legal purposes, all profiles have a degree. The academic work profile is the youngest and the only one with female representation. The institutional purposes profile is the most peculiar one since the users of this profile are institutions.

Research motivations vary by profile, yet historical research and academic work profiles are quite similar. The most common questions among the profiles are the need for guidance, i.e. how to start and do research, and also help in reading old documents (palaeography). Access to CRAV and DigitArq are also some common challenges among the profiles.

The next step of this study will be carried out in the in-person archives. The aim is to observe and analyse the behaviour of the different profiles in the archival environment. Through the Think Aloud method, it will be possible to observe how users seek information in the archive by verbalising their actions. This way, it will be possible to validate the users' motivations and challenges directly.

Acknowledgements. Special thanks to Dr José Furtado for his help in the initial phase of this study and for providing the data from the satisfaction surveys. Thanks, also, to all the DGLAB archivists for their willingness to participate in this study. This work is financed by National Funds through the Portuguese funding agency, FCT – Fundação para a Ciência e a Tecnologia within project DSAIPA/DS/0023/2018. Inês Koch is also financed by National Funds through the Portuguese funding agency, FCT, within the research grant 2020.08755.BD.

References

1. Blais, G., Enns, D.: From Paper Archives to People Archives: Public Programming in the Management of Archives. Archivaria (1990). https://archivaria.ca/index.php/archivaria/article/view/11723
2. Burke, M., Zavalina, O.L., Chelliah, S.L., Phillips, M.E.: User needs in language archives: findings from interviews with language archive managers, depositors, and end-users. University of Hawaii Press (2022). http://hdl.handle.net/10125/74669
3. Conway, P.: Facts and frameworks: an approach to studying the users of archives. Am. Arch. **49**(4), 393–407 (1986). https://doi.org/10.17723/aarc.49.4.p21825jp21403087
4. Duff, W., Johnson, C.: A virtual expression of need: an analysis of e-mail reference questions. Am. Arch. **64**(1), 43–60 (2001). https://www.jstor.org/stable/40294158
5. Grudin, J., Pruitt, J.: Personas, Participatory Design and Product Development: An Infrastructure for Engagement (2002). https://ojs.ruc.dk/index.php/pdc/article/view/249

6. Ponte, L., Koch, I., Teixeira Lopes, C.: Analysis of the interviews with DGLAB archivists and DGLAB satisfaction survey. Dataset, INESC TEC (2023). https://doi.org/10.25747/P54W-E587

7. DGLAB: Arquivos da Direção-Geral do Livro dos Arquivos e das Bibliotecas: Regulamento de serviços em linha e presenciais (2022)

8. Prom, C.J.: Using web analytics to improve online access to archival resources. Am. Arch. **74**(1), 158–184 (2011). https://www.jstor.org/stable/23079005

9. Rhee, H.L.: Reflections on archival user studies. Ref. User Serv. Q. **54**(4), 29–42 (2015). https://www.jstor.org/stable/refuseserq.54.4.29

10. Saurombe, N., Ngulube, P.: Perceptions of user studies as a foundation for public programming activities by archivists from east and southern Africa. ESARBICA J. **35**, 30–46 (2016). eISSN: 0376-4753. https://www.ajol.info/index.php/esarjo/article/view/152446

11. Tu, N., Dong, X., Rau, P.L.P., Zhang, T.: Using cluster analysis in Persona development. In: 2010 8th International Conference on Supply Chain Management and Information, pp. 1–5 (2010). https://ieeexplore.ieee.org/document/5681684

The Openness of Digital Archives in Japanese Universities and Its Opportunities

Widiatmoko Adi Putranto[1]([⊠]) [iD], Regina Dwi Shalsa Mayzana[2] [iD], and Emi Ishita[1] [iD]

[1] Department of Library Science, Kyushu University, Fukuoka, Japan
putranto.widiatmoko.761@s.kyushu-u.ac.jp,
ishita.emi.982@m.kyushu-u.ac.jp
[2] Archives and Records Management Study Program, Universitas Gadjah Mada, Yogyakarta, Indonesia
regina.d.s@mail.ugm.ac.id

Abstract. This study aims to examine the presence and openness of digital archives among Japanese national universities based on nine survey items, including the existence of digital archives, openness levels, organization and presentation of information, and availability of English information. The authors annotated 86 library websites and found that digital archives at Japanese university libraries are relatively extensive in quantity, yet they tend to be accessible only in Japanese. More than half (57%) of the national university libraries make their digital archives available online, with the combined features of open-compliant licenses and restricted policies. From the analysis of the collected data, it is evident that there are possibilities to enhance more inclusive accessibility for diverse user groups while widening global engagement to support the Japanese university internationalization agenda by improving the online presentation and organization and the extent of the openness qualities of the digital archives. Making collections available online, which is currently the case, does not always automatically make them open, but unlocks the first step of the process to pursue further opportunities to exploit the potential of digitization projects.

Keywords: digital archives · Japanese universities · digital libraries · open access

1 Introduction

There has been a growing trend among Japanese institutions to digitize cultural materials. The National Diet Library, a Japanese national library, together with the National Archives of Japan and the Agency of Cultural Affairs, has been conducting ongoing digitization of cultural materials they possess, as well as initiating open access to various extents [1]. Similarly, most Japanese universities have been working on digitizing their cultural heritage materials, including some of the most distinguished resources known as rare books and special collections. These collections are heterogeneous and unique, and they may carry knowledge that is not available anywhere because of their

D. H. Goh et al. (Eds.): ICADL 2023, LNCS 14458, pp. 123–138, 2023.
https://doi.org/10.1007/978-981-99-8088-8_11

limited number. They often contain heritage materials that are culturally and histori-cally significant [2]. Rare books and special collections also provide an opportunity to distinguish the identity of academic libraries among the increasingly homogeneous elec-tronic resources [3]. According to Sugimoto [1], in Japan, digital collections of cultural materials or resources are often known as "digital archives." Therefore, this study uses the terms "digital collections" and "digital archives" interchangeably to describe such collections.

While digitization has helped preserve original materials and provide digital access for users, it is certainly not the end goal. Instead, there are further opportunities and challenges to ensure that digital resources at Japanese universities reach their maxi-mum potential by making them more discoverable and allowing them to reach a wider audience. Digital archives naturally eliminate travel constraints. Further, access to cul-tural heritage can be provided inexpensively through digital libraries in order to develop a democratic and ideal information society [1, 4]. Owing to the potential benefits of discovering Japan-related resources, the Japanese government also encourages diverse institutions to open their data for research, social, and economic benefits [5]. In this regard, "opening" data refers to the notions of open data and open access, which pro-pose that data should be freely available and accessed online by the public without barriers [6]. Being open is not just about creating online digital archives. This means having essential features that ensure that collections are available to the public via online platforms or application programming interfaces (API) [7], as well as accessibility to reuse and remix [8]. When open data are useful, they become open knowledge [9]. To disseminate digital resources, websites are currently one of the most convenient and effective platforms [10]. However, multiple issues in the form of policy, infrastructure, legal rights, ethics, and privacy may challenge institutions in considering opening their digital resources [7, 11–13]. While many studies have used the World Wide Web Con-sortium (W3C) Web Accessibility Initiative reference to discuss accessibility for people with disabilities, this study explores the opportunities for web accessibility in terms of the language and cultural constraints of digital archives.

One opportunity to open data to a wider audience is through international outreach. Japan has been pursuing internationalization initiatives for its universities through the Top Global University Project [14]. The government pushes internationalization through Japanese universities by providing English programs, collaborating with various global universities, inviting more international scholars, or even opening a chance for for-eigners to work [14–16]. However, Japanese universities face numerous challenges in internationalizing their institutions because of issues such as funding and quality assess-ment [15, 17]. If the provision of a foreign language on websites is argued to enhance the process of internationalization [18], offering open access to English information in digital archives will allow resources and knowledge of Japanese culture and materials to be available for diverse international audiences seeking to learn more about Japan for education, research, business, creativity, or even collaboration. Japanese university libraries will have the opportunity to be "content publishers and distributors" of reliable resources and knowledge about Japanese culture and materials [12]. With more and wider audiences visiting Japanese university libraries online, there may be an opportunity to advance Japan's visibility and relevance in global academic communities.

Based on this background, this study examines the openness of digital archives at Japanese universities. A web survey of special digitized collections of cultural heritage content on Japanese university library websites was conducted to explore the extent to which digital archives were available and accessible online. This includes examining and identifying (1) the openness of digital archives, (2) key issues in the accessibility of digital archives, and (3) opportunities to unlock the greatest potential of digital archives at Japanese universities. The findings are used as a basis for exploring opportunities that may arise as a result of improving the quality and openness of digital archives at Japanese universities. Once digital archives are made available online, it is imperative to further explore how open and accessible they are, especially for international and non-Japanese users. It is also essential to identify the features that contribute to improving and limiting accessibility in order to propose possible approaches to democratizing spaces of development towards more plural communities of users.

2 Literature Review

Several studies have examined digital archives in Japanese institutions, including the development of the diversity of Japanese digital archives across different levels of cultural institutions and portals [1, 5, 19–21]. Nearly two decades ago, Miyata [22] discussed the issues and expectations of digital archives in Japanese museums, noting general and practical issues regarding the long-term storage of materials, technical issues in building digital archive systems, and administrative issues. In contrast, the present study attempts to depict the state of digital cultural materials maintained by university libraries. Finally, Koga [23], in a study of the policy, practices, and projects of Japanese digital archives and libraries, found that extensive infrastructure, such as plans and budgets, is more important for the sustainability of digital archives in the long term than issue-oriented strategies. This study attempts to complement Koga's conceptual findings by offering a hands-on approach to improving digital archives.

Furthermore, a more technical approach to improving the ease of access to online information can be taken by examining how information is presented and organized online. Inoue et al. [24] examine the typographic layouts of Japanese websites by discussing the concept of web comfortability, or "pleasantness on the website," which aims to satisfy the user by providing a stressless use of the website. This validates the significance of one of the survey items in the present study, namely the presentation and organization of information online. Yeo et al. [25] conducted a study on designing an interactive digital archive of Japanese historical architecture. This study is also concerned with the difference in information availability between Japanese and English websites. Marcus and Krishnamhurti [26] found that cultural dimensions affect the patterns of similarity and differences in website designs. Another study on a similar topic was conducted by Yamakawa [27], who wrote a thesis about the comparison of cross-cultural web designs between the United States and Japan and how mistranslation of the website may cause misunderstanding among users.

3   Method

3.1   Sample

According to the latest official report on higher education in Japan issued by the Ministry of Education, Culture, Sports, Science and Technology, there were 1,224 higher education institutions in Japan as of 2011, including 780 universities, 387 junior colleges, and 57 colleges of technology [28]. Among the 780 universities, 86 were national universities. This study used all 86 Japanese national university library websites as a sample. National universities were considered ideal for the sample of this study because they play an important role as benchmarks for higher education institutions in Japan. National universities in Japan have also been established in every prefecture; therefore, there is a high probability that they will hold collections of local materials. Being government-funded institutions, opening digital archives is important for these universities, as they are expected to be transparent and disseminate resources for the benefit of the public.

3.2   Survey Items

Nine survey items were developed to examine the openness of digital archives. The items were formulated based on a combination of several references. The first is the OpenGLAM principles for the openness of cultural data summarized by Roued-Cunliffe [13], which include releasing metadata on artifacts, not applying new digital copyright to works in the public domain, being clear about the reuse of published data, using machine-readable open file formats, and engaging with the public about open content. The second is the accessibility principle of the Web Accessibility Initiative, which involves perceivable information and user interfaces, operable user interfaces and navigation, understandable information and user interfaces, robust content, and reliable interpretation [29]. Finally, openness levels are based on the categories of GLAM digitization and Open Access (OA) implementation [30].

Based on these references, this study developed three categories, divided into nine survey items, to examine the openness of digital archives on library websites. As shown in Table 1, each survey item has a different option for identifying the sample. The survey was conducted in two phases. The first phase aimed to identify the presence of digital archives of cultural materials on library websites by examining three survey items: (1) the existence of archives, (2) how visible the location of the archives was on library websites, and (3) the availability of information about digital archives in the English and Japanese versions of library websites. Two authors annotated the surveys. Both authors are native non-Japanese speakers and use machine translation to assist with the examination of websites with no English information.

Table 1. Outline of Survey Items

Phase	Category	Survey Items	Options
1 (Sample size: 86)	Existence of digital archives	Availability of digital archives	Available Not Available
		Visibility of digital archives	A – Available on library homepage B – Available under submenu(s) C – Available but require further browsing than submenus, and eventually be directed to Japanese pages D – Only available through Japanese pages 0 – Not Available
		Availability of information about digital archives in English and Japanese websites	1 – Identical with no substantial differences 2 – Similar with few information missing 3 – Contrast with significant features only available in Japanese 0 – Not Available
2 (Sample size: 62)	Information organization	Openness level of digital archives	Full Adoption In Transition Restricted No Collections Online
		Presentation of digital archives	A – both content and metadata are available B – either the metadata or the contents are unavailable C – no collections online
		Organization of digital archives	Grouped based on Theme (TG) Highlighted Collections (HC) Grouped based on Media (CM) Unstructured Search Box (SB) Not Available

(*continued*)

Table 1. (*continued*)

Phase	Category	Survey Items	Options
	Availability of English information	On digital archives homepage	Available Partially Available Not Available
		On digital archives' metadata	
		On digital archives' policies	

The data obtained in Phase 1 on the number of Japanese universities with digital archives on library websites served as a sample for Phase 2. Phase 2 focuses on the openness of digital archives by examining two main survey items: information organization and information provision in English. The item of information organization is further divided into three sub-items, namely (4) openness level, (5) presentation of archives, and (6) organization of archives, whereas the item of information provision in English consists of the following sub-items: (7) English information on the archives, (8) English information on the archives' metadata, and (9) English information on the archives' policies. For survey items (7), (8), and (9), based on an examination of the content, we identified the provision of English information with three options: A for available, PA for partially available, or NA for not available. By partially available, we mean that information on the webpages is presented in a combination of English and Japanese, not in two types of complete information, each in Japanese and English.

For survey item (4), we used the OpenGLAM criteria [30], as shown in Table 2.

Table 2. Categories of Digitization and OA Implementation

Category	Description
Restricted	Digital archives are subject to blanket IPR claims or opaque text-based policies prohibiting most reuse
In transition	Digital archives either permit reuse under licenses that release some rights but retain others or are released on a collection-by-collection basis under open compliant statements
Full adoption	Digital archives are released under open-compliant statements as a matter of policy
No archives online	Due to technical, financial, legal, and/or access barriers associated with digital archives management

Two annotators coded all the survey items. To obtain reliable results, Cohen's kappa [31] was used to measure intercoder agreement before the actual coding. Annotator A trained Annotator B prior to each phase. We used five institutions for both Phases 1 and

2 as examples during training. Subsequently, both annotators conducted coding independently, and the results were calculated using Cohen's kappa intercoder agreement. Three rounds of annotation were performed for Phase 1, with samples consisting of five, ten, and ten institutions. One round of annotation was performed with samples from 10 institutions in Phase 2. We obtained substantial agreement with scores of 0.9, 0.4, and 0.8, respectively, for each round of Phase 1 and 0.78 for Phase 2. We did not compute kappa for survey item (6) because the labels had no limitations. Finally, each annotator coded the remaining samples independently by dividing them evenly for each phase, consisting of 56 and 47 samples, respectively. Each annotator also added a note to each sample in case of unusual or notable findings. Annotator A met with Annotator B to analyze a few difficult cases and then adjudicate the results of the analysis for each item.

4 Results

4.1 Existence of Digital Archives

Table 3 shows the availability of digital archives, where 57.0% of university libraries have collections and the rest 43.0% do not have digital archives available. Of the total 43.0% of universities with no available collections, 17.4% of university libraries declare that they hold rare books and special collections in physical formats, whereas the other 26.6% do not provide any information about them. In line with research done by Tokizane [20], which shows that the trend of online access to digital archives is thriving among diverse cultural institutions, our survey shows that the number of digital archives in Japanese national university libraries can be categorized as high.

Table 3. Availability of digital archives on library websites

Availability of Digital Collections		Number			
Available (A)		49	57.0%		
Not Available (NA)		37	43.0%		
	NA, but declared			15	17.4%
	NA			22	26.6%
Total		**86**	**100%**		

4.2 Visibility of Digital Archives

As shown in Table 4, only 17.4% of university libraries make their digital archives links or information about rare books and special collections easily accessible right from their English website homepages. 9.3% of libraries provide information in English, but once users access it, they will be directed to the Japanese page. Meanwhile, 37.2% of links or information about them are only available from Japanese websites. This indicates that finding digital archives on English websites is challenging.

Table 4. Visibility of digital archives on the English version of library websites

Visibility of Digital Archives Information	Number	
A – Available on library homepage	15	17.4%
B – Available under submenu(s)	9	10.5%
C – Available but require further browsing than submenus, and eventually be directed to Japanese pages	8	9.3%
D – Only available through Japanese pages	32	37.2%
0 – Not Available	22	25.6%
Total	**86**	**100%**

4.3 Availability of Information About Digital Archives on English and Japanese Websites

Table 5 shows that 33.7% of the library websites present information on digital archives both in Japanese and English, while 31.4% of the websites show Japanese-only information. Nevertheless, in 3.5% of websites with Japanese and English information and in 5% of Japanese-only websites, the machine translation does not fully work, which means that it can be interpreted as only providing Japanese information. For example, information about digital archives on library #31, #67, and #68 websites is unable to be translated because the text was presented as pictures. Moreover, the machine translator could not translate the digital archive metadata in libraries #65 and #71, while 25.6% of libraries do not mention any information about digital archives. Our survey shows that there is little information about digital archives on the English version of the library websites. This leads us to check the Japanese versions of the library websites to see if there is also little information on digital archives.

We found differences between English and Japanese websites. Table 6 shows that 55.8% of English websites had a very contrasting amount of information compared to Japanese websites. They miss several essential features, including access to digital archives, information about digital archives, policies about digital archives, types of rare books, and special collections available on Japanese websites. An interesting example is

Table 5. Availability of information on digital archives on library websites

Availability of Information about Digital Archives	Number	
Japanese and English	29	33.7%
Japanese and English, *machine translation does not work*	3	3.5%
Japanese	27	31.4%
Japanese, *machine translation does not work*	5	5.8%
Not Available in either English or Japanese	22	25.6%
Total	**86**	**100%**

Library #57. Although the English website provides access to essential features of digital archives, the types of digital archives become much more diverse when switching to the Japanese page. In fact, there are only 10.5% of library websites that provide identical information on the English and Japanese pages. Even the appearance and design of the websites did not change. It is important to point out that some cases show that the design of websites between English and Japanese homepages can also be completely different.

Table 6. Information gap between English and Japanese library websites

Information Gap between English and Japanese Pages	Number	
1 – Identical with no substantial differences	9	10.5%
2 – Similar with few information missing	7	8.1%
3 – Contrast with significant features only available in Japanese	48	55.8%
0 – Not Available	22	25.6%
Total	**86**	**100%**

4.4 Openness of Digital Archives

Despite the fact that 49 (57%) Japanese university websites provided online access to digital archives, as shown in Table 3 previously, their levels of openness varied. As shown in Table 7, 59.2% of libraries apply a restricted policy where digital archives are limited to research and education purposes only or prior application is needed to reuse the materials. The next largest category of openness is In Transition, which applies to digital archives in 32.6% of libraries. This means that while some archives fall under an open-compliant policy or license, others retain some rights and are restricted to reuse. Finally, there are only 8.2% of digital archives that fall under the category of Full Adoption, meaning that universities have made all available digital archives have a clear open-compliant statement policy or license, indicating that they can be freely used without any prior applications needed.

Table 7. Openness levels of Digital Archives

Openness Levels of Digital Archives		Number	
Available	Full Adoption	4	8.2%
	In Transition	16	32.7%
	Restricted	29	59.1%
Total		**49**	**100%**

4.5 Online Presentation of Digital Archives

Once digitized, the digital surrogates of the collections consist of both content and meta-data. While some digital archives are available and can be browsed online, others are not. Table 8 shows the findings of survey (5), where only 24.5% of the library websites provided visual access to high-resolution content of their digital archives through different APIs. Among the rest of 75.5% of them, it is a combination of some of the digital archives being presented with both high-resolution content and metadata; some were presented as thumbnails in JPEG or PDF format that needed to be downloaded to be visible, and some others were only listed.

Table 8. Online presentation of Digital Archives information

Online Presentation of Digital Archives Information	Number	
A – Both content and metadata are available	12	24.5%
B – Either the metadata or the contents are unavailable	37	75.5%
Total	**49**	**100%**

4.6 Organization of Digital Archives

Library websites present their digital archives or declare their rare books and special collections based on several categories. As shown in Table 9, most library websites have introduced digital archives based on this theme. Even library websites without digital archives declare that they have few books, and special collections often provide this information. Some digital archive portals also equip users with search boxes. Eight institutions provide "pick-up archives," which are groups of highlighted archives that may assist new users who have no specific purpose for exploring. The two institutions declare that they have rare books and special collections without mentioning any specific themes or details. One institution presented its archives without any theme or grouping structure and instead listed all of their archives in PDF format.

Table 9. Organization of Digital Archives

Organization of Digital Archives	Number
Grouped based on Theme (TG)	59
Highlighted Collections (HC)	8
Grouped based on Media (CM)	2
Unstructured	1
Search Box (SB)	27
Not Available	24
Total	**121**

4.7 Availability of English Information on the Digital Archives

The availability of English digital archive information is limited, as shown in Table 10. We found that English information on digital archive homepages, metadata, and policies was mostly unavailable. Only 9.3% of digital archive homepages provided English information, while 27.9% of others only had English partially, and 62.8% did not have English information at all. Examples of partially available information can be found on library websites #2 and #10. Although the digital archives of metadata field names and a few descriptions, such as copyright, are in English, other information, such as notes, types, or publishers, is still in Japanese.

Table 10. English Information on Digital Archives

English	Available		Partially Available		Not Available		Total	
Homepage	8	9.3%	24	27.9%	54	62.8%	**86**	**100%**
Metadata	0	0%	30	34.9%	56	65.1%	**86**	**100%**
Policy	6	7%	7	8.1%	73	84.9%	**86**	**100%**

5 Discussion

5.1 Improving Presentation of Archives Online

Web Interface. Cyr and Smith [32] noted that pleasant designs and usability features are likely to provide users with a better experience and encourage them to revisit sites. However, based on the findings from survey number (4), we found that a number of archives in 75.5% of institutions with digital archives were only listed in pdf or JPEG format on the websites, and the contents were only visible once they were downloaded. In addition to being ineffective, this might create inconveniences for users compared with websites that provide visual access to the content of their digital archives. Collections of diverse materials also require visual discovery options and flexible access to information systems [33, cited in 34].

Harris and Weller [35] noted that building pleasant interactions and outreach is significant in developing connections and collaborations between special collections and users. However, as identified in survey number (2), there are only 15 libraries that put digital archive links or information rights on their homepages. Berger [36] argues that special collections should be placed on the homepage for accessibility and outreach to users. This finding also suggests that institutions value their special collections highly.

Our findings also show that the majority of digital archives can only be accessed from or are available on the Japanese version of the websites. Wada [26] explained that the design and aesthetic standards of Japanese websites are often different from those of Western websites. Japanese websites tend to appear cluttered with a large amount of cramped information [37]. In addition, 19 libraries provide each type of digital archive, which is completely different from designed websites. Thus, improving the website design and putting the link to the digital archives in more accessible positions on both Japanese and English websites might improve the accessibility of the archives and eventually their discoverability and exposure to a wider audience.

Curating Archives. Many libraries manage an extensive number of archives, and although this provides users with many choices, it may overwhelm them. Scholars or users with specific purposes and needs may already know what they want to discover, and the large number of resources available online is beneficial to them. Nevertheless, the democratization of cultural heritage through open access means that these archives are no longer exclusively available for scholars, research, and educational purposes, but also for the general public.

Similar to what Natale [38] and Berger [36] emphasized regarding current scholars' behavior, people tend to find anything from information to entertainment online. This may develop the demographics of new users, where digital cultural heritage archives provided by notable institutions may reach even wider audiences of communities across the globe with an interest in heritage archives. However, people and students without background knowledge of heritage might not specifically know what they want to find and explore. At this point, university libraries may offer guidance to new users by introducing archives that encourage them to browse further. In the era of the internet, where abundant resources exist, it is important to show that libraries can adapt well to current disruptions. Hamilton and Saunderson [12] state that the ubiquity of digital materials drives institutions to be curators of archives, as they "can be published, disseminated, manipulated, shared, transferred, transformed, edited, and used in many other ways" that physical materials are not. Thus, highlighting several archives among a vast number of resources might help new users learn and further grow their interest.

Our survey also found that several institutions have already implemented this strategy by providing a group of recommended archives labeled "pick-up archives," where university libraries have promoted their distinctive special collections of digital archives. As discussed above, special collections can distinguish one library from another. These highlighted archives can be used as special labels for university libraries in the long term. Eventually, curating archives will be fruitful from the perspective of both users and libraries.

5.2 Opportunities for Internationalization

Like many other Asian countries, Japan has its own language, writing system, and characters; therefore, a language barrier exists for non-Japanese speakers to engage with the country. From the results of survey items (3), (7), (8), and (9), this study found that most universities provide access to, or at least information on, archives through their websites. Some have options to show information in English or even in multiple languages, whereas others do not, making it impossible for non-Japanese speakers to explore resources. Making them more accessible to non-Japanese speakers might attract wider international audiences, engage in more collaborative activities, and, in return, help the internationalization process and strengthen the world-class research university labels they are currently working on. Eventually, this may contribute to the preservation of global citizens' inclusive knowledge of Japanese culture.

Nowadays, many browsers provide machine translation extensions that can automatically read and translate text or content on websites from one language to another. This feature is also useful when accessing digital archives available only on Japanese websites. Although it may not provide a comprehensive idiomatic translation, it helps users access the archives and understand the information in principle, which may be the first step to discovering heritage materials. In terms of cost, it may also be beneficial for universities with limited resources because most of these features are freely available.

However, this study found that machine translation is often unable to work efficiently and is challenged by several constraints. The first issue is technical errors, which prevent the machine translation features from effectively translating webpages. The second issue this study found is that Japanese websites often use image-based designs instead of text-based designs for certain headings or information, which makes machine translation unable to detect characters or phrases and translate them.

According to Jain (cited in [18]), "presenting information about a locality in foreign languages is important when people anywhere in the world who are wired and motivated can access information on the Internet." Lee [4] argues for the need for East Asian countries to share their cultural heritage commons by referring to successful collaborative projects among European countries to develop a network for digital archiving. Therefore, creating digital archives of special collections online and providing English information might improve their discoverability and understandability for international users, which might eventually engage potential international connections and collaborations.

5.3   Open Licensing

While digital formats enable heritage surrogates, in this case digital archives, to be available online, as found in survey numbers (4) and (5), university libraries can further advance the accessibility of these digital archives by applying open licensing.

Hamilton and Saunderson [12] point out that it has been long rooted that the core value and provenance of cultural institutions' businesses is to equitably support the exchange of ideas and information through non-discriminatory access, sharing, and use between parties. The responsibilities of maximizing the potential of archives for the benefit of communities are even clearer if the institution is funded by the public. Opening archives also removes barriers to knowledge resources for "underserved populations," which reflects one of the important characteristics of a successful outreach program [36]. Many open licenses are now available, and one of the most well-known is the Creative Common license. Despite these risks, many studies have discussed the benefits of opening digital archives. Open archives have wider possibilities of being used and shared to further push new forms of creative work [12]. This implies a greater potential for engaging in collaborative research projects with diverse organizations and communities across different countries and maximizing benefits for the public.

A license also provides clear yet concise and universal information about access, reuse, and repurpose policies without having to describe them in different languages. Our findings identified several Japanese university libraries that not only provide but also promote the openness of their archives using open licensing. Implementing open licensing will accelerate the dissemination of knowledge while simultaneously preserving and promoting the heritage of countries with strong cultural roots, such as Japan.

Specifically, the implementation of open licensing may further open up the possibility of international collaboration as an agenda item for Japanese universities.

6 Conclusion

According to Tanner [39], "It is not enough to be open; it is important to be seen to be explicitly open and easily accessible." This statement highlights the importance of institutions pursuing further opportunities beyond digitizing their archives and making their digitized archives online. This study found that Japanese national universities have varying levels of openness regarding their digital archives. Regarding the goal of internationalization, much information, policies, or online instruction is often available only in Japanese. Moreover, language assistance for people who do not understand Japanese varies between universities, faculties, and departments, where one may enjoy plenty of support while others receive no support. Several technical aspects of the websites that can be improved include the problem of information gaps between the Japanese and English versions of library websites, website design issues, and the positioning of digital archive icons.

Furthermore, this study explores the opportunities for Japanese universities to improve their digital archives in terms of the presentation of the archives (improving the web-interface design and offering curated archives), internationalization (optimizing the English language option for international audiences), and open licensing.

Therefore, the results of this study are beneficial and can be used as a consideration for Japan as a country in general and for Japanese institutions aiming at internationalization. In addition, this study may serve as a reference for non-English-speaking countries and institutions seeking to improve the implementation of digital archives.

A limitation of this study is that it focused only on Japanese universities. Therefore, it is suggested that further research explore the openness of other memory institutions to obtain more comprehensive data and to further explore the challenges and opportunities that come with the implementation of open access.

Acknowledgments. This work is supported by the Japan Society for the Promotion of Science (JSPS), KAKENHI, Grant Number JP18K18508.

References

1. Sugimoto, S.: Archiving cultural and community memories in a networked information society: a Japanese perspective. **26**(1), 53 (2016). https://doi.org/10.32655/LIBRES.2016.1.4
2. UNESCO United Nations Educational, Scientific and Cultural Organization: "Heritage," in UNESCO Culture For Development Indicator: Methodology Manual, 7, place de Fontenoy, 75352 Paris 07 SP, France, pp. 131–140 (2014)
3. Anderson, R.: Can't Buy Us Love: The Declining Importance of Library Books and the Rising Importance of Special Collections (2013). https://doi.org/10.18665/sr.24613
4. Lee, H.: Collaboration in cultural heritage digitisation in East Asia. Program (London. 1966) **44**(4), 357–373 (2010). https://doi.org/10.1108/00330331011083248

5. Goto, M.: Current Movement of Digital Archives in Japan and khirin (Knowledgebase of Historical Resources in Institutes). Presented at the December 16 (2018). https://doi.org/10.23919/PNC.2018.8579461
6. Open Definition: Open Definition 2.1 (n.d.). http://opendefinition.org/od/2.1/en/
7. Tzouganatou, A.: Openness and privacy in born-digital archives: reflecting the role of AI development. **37**(3), 991–999 (2021). https://doi.org/10.1007/s00146-021-01361-3
8. Huggett, J.: Reuse remix recycle: repurposing archaeological digital data. **6**(2), 93–104 (2018). https://doi.org/10.1017/aap.2018.1
9. What is open? https://okfn.org. Accessed 04 Sep 2023
10. Conway, V., et al.: Website accessibility: a comparative analysis of Australian national and state/territory library websites. **61**(3), 170–188 (2013). https://doi.org/10.1080/00049670.2012.10736059
11. Terras, M.: Opening access to collections: the making and using of open digitised cultural content. **39**(5), 733–752 (2015). https://doi.org/10.1108/OIR-06-2015-0193
12. Hamilton, G., Saunderson, F.: Open Licensing for Cultural Heritage. Facet Publishing, UK (2017)
13. Roued-Cunliffe, H.: Open heritage data: an introduction to research, publishing and programming with open data in the heritage sector. Facet Publishing, Berlin, Heidelberg (2021)
14. Rose, H., McKinley, J.: Japan's English-medium instruction initiatives and the globalization of higher education. **75**(1), 111–129 (2017). https://doi.org/10.1007/s10734-017-0125-1
15. Yonezawa, A., Shimmi, Y.: Transformation of university governance through internationalization: challenges for top universities and government policies in Japan. **70**(2), 173–186 (2015). https://doi.org/10.1007/s10734-015-9863-0
16. Huang, F.: Challenges for higher education and research: a perspective from Japan. **39**(8), 1428–1438 (2014). https://doi.org/10.1080/03075079.2014.949535
17. Saito, K., SoungHee, K.: The internationalization of higher education in Japan: effective organization for a sustainable internationally cooperative higher education program. **9**(1), 47–63 (2019). https://doi.org/10.18870/hlrc.v9i1.441
18. Carroll, T.: Local government websites in Japan: international, multicultural, multilingual? Jpn. Stud. **30**(3), 373–392 (2010). https://doi.org/10.1080/10371397.2010.518942
19. Muta, S.: Introduction to the national archives of Japan digital archive service. In: Sugimoto, S., Hunter, J., Rauber, A., Morishima, A. (eds.) Digital Libraries: Achievements, Challenges and Opportunities. ICADL 2006. LNCS, vol. 4312, pp. 550–555. Springer, Berlin, Heidelberg (2006). https://doi.org/10.1007/11931584_72
20. Tokizane, S.: New Development of Digital Archives. Bensei Publishing, Tokyo (2023)
21. Tsukahara, Y.: The Current State of Digital Musical Materials in Japan. Cambridge University Press, England (2022). https://doi.org/10.1017/S1479409822000052
22. Miyata, K.: Issues and expectations for digital archives in museums of history: a view from a Japanese museum. In: Archiving Conference, vol. 2004, no. 1. Society for Imaging Science and Technology (2004)
23. Koga, T.: Issue-oriented strategies or extensive infrastructure for digital scholarship? The policy, practices and projects of Japanese digital archives and libraries. In: IFLA WLIC 2018. (2018). https://library.ifla.org/id/eprint/2205/1/206-koga-en.pdf
24. Inoue, T., Saheki, E., Okada, R., et al.: Web Comfortability and the Influence of Typographic Layouts for Japanese Web Sites, pp. 133–141 (2006)
25. Yeo, W., et al.: An interactive digital archive for Japanese historical architecture. In: 8th International Conference on Computer Aided Architectural Design Research in Asia (2003)

26. Marcus, A., Krishnamurthi, N.: Cross-cultural analysis of social network services in Japan, Korea, and the USA. In: Aykin, N. (eds.) Internationalization, Design and Global Development. IDGD 2009. LNCS, vol. 5623. Springer, Berlin, Heidelberg (2009). https://doi.org/10.1007/978-3-642-02767-3_7

27. Yamakawa, H.: Cross-cultural web design: a comparison between the United States and Japan. The University of Tennessee at Chattanooga (2007)

28. MEXT (Ministry of Education, Culture, Sports, Science and Technology): 1Overview. https://www.mext.go.jp/en/publication/statistics/title01/detail01/1373636.htm#01. Accessed 20 June 2023

29. Web Accessibility Initiative: Accessibility Principles. https://www.w3.org/WAI/fundamentals/accessibility-principles/. Accessed 20 June 2023

30. Wallace, A.: Open heritage data: an introduction to research, publishing and programming with open data in the heritage sector (2020). https://doi.org/10.21428/74d826b1.be9df175

31. Warrens, M.J.: Research article: new interpretations of Cohen's kappa. J. Math. (2014). https://doi.org/10.1155/2014/203907

32. Cyr, D., Trevor-Smith, H.: Localization of Web design: an empirical comparison of German, Japanese, and United States Web site characteristics. 55(13), 1199–1208 (2014). https://doi.org/10.1002/asi.20075

33. Roffia, L., et al.: Requirements on system design to increase understanding and visibility of cultural heritage, p. 26 (2011). https://doi.org/10.4018/978-1-60960-044-0.ch013

34. Petras, V., et al.: Building for success?: Evaluating digital libraries in the cultural heritage domain, p. 23 (2013). https://doi.org/10.4018/978-1-4666-2991-2.ch009

35. Harris, V.A., Weller, A.C.: Use of special collections as an opportunity for outreach in the academic library. 52(3–4), 294–303 (2012). https://doi.org/10.1080/01930826.2012.684508

36. Berger, S.E.: Rare Books and Special Collections. Facet, London (2014)

37. Haimes, P.: Zen and the art of website maintenance. 23(1), 20–21 (2016). https://doi.org/10.1145/2847596

38. Natale, E.: Digital humanities and documentary mediations in the digital age. In: Dobreva, M. (ed.), Digital Archives: Management, Use and Access, pp. 3–22. Facet Publishing, London (2018)

39. Tanner, S.: Open GLAM: the rewards (and some risks) of digital sharing for the public good. In: Wallace, A., Deazley, R. (eds.), Display At Your Own Risk (2016). http://displayatyourownrisk.org/tanner/

Scholarly Information Processing

Toward Semantic Publishing in Non-invasive Brain Stimulation: A Comprehensive Analysis of rTMS Studies

Swathi Anil[1,3] and Jennifer D'Souza[2(✉)]

[1] Department of Neuroanatomy, Institute of Anatomy and Cell Biology, Faculty of Medicine, University of Freiburg, Freiburg, Germany
swathi.anil@anat.uni-freiburg.de
[2] TIB Leibniz Information Centre for Science and Technology University Library, Hanover, Germany
Jennifer.DSouza@tib.eu
[3] Bernstein Center Freiburg, University of Freiburg, Freiburg, Germany

Abstract. Noninvasive brain stimulation (NIBS) encompasses transcranial stimulation techniques that can influence brain excitability. These techniques have the potential to treat conditions like depression, anxiety, and chronic pain, and to provide insights into brain function. However, a lack of standardized reporting practices limits its reproducibility and full clinical potential. This paper aims to foster interdisciplinarity toward adopting Computer Science Semantic reporting methods for the standardized documentation of Neuroscience NIBS studies making them explicitly Findable, Accessible, Interoperable, and Reusable (FAIR).

In a large-scale systematic review of 600 repetitive transcranial magnetic stimulation (rTMS), a subarea of NIBS, dosages, we describe key properties that allow for structured descriptions and comparisons of the studies. This paper showcases the semantic publishing of NIBS in the ecosphere of knowledge-graph-based next-generation scholarly digital libraries. Specifically, the FAIR Semantic Web resource(s)-based publishing paradigm is implemented for the 600 reviewed rTMS studies in the Open Research Knowledge Graph.

Keywords: Semantic Publishing · Digital libraries · Scholarly Publishing Infrastructure · Scholarly Publishing Workflows · FAIR data principles · Open Research Knowledge Graph · Noninvasive brain stimulation · Repetitive Transcranial Magnetic Stimulation

Supported by German BMBF project SCINEXT (ID 01lS22070), DFG NFDI4Data-Science (ID 460234259), and ERC ScienceGraph (ID 819536)
S. Anil and J. D'Souza—Both authors contributed equally to this work.

1   Introduction

Noninvasive brain stimulation (NIBS) is a rapidly evolving field in neuroscience that involves modulating neuronal activity in the brain without surgical intervention, often employing electrical currents or magnetic fields [24]. NIBS encompasses various subareas such as transcranial direct current stimulation (tDCS), transcranial alternating current stimulation (tACS), transcranial random noise stimulation (tRNS), repetitive transcranial magnetic stimulation (rTMS), among others. These techniques harness the ability of neural tissue to adapt to external stimulation by making structural, functional and molecular changes, called neural plasticity. Over the past decades, rTMS in particular has gained significant attention for its potential to enhance cognitive abilities, including attention, memory, language, and decision-making. It is also being explored as a treatment option for neuropsychiatric disorders like pharmacoresistant major depressive disorder (MDD), schizophrenia, and obsessive-compulsive disorder, as well as for stroke rehabilitation, pain management, and investigation of brain function [2,7,9,10,13,14,18,20,32,33]. The outcome of rTMS can be influenced by various stimulation parameters, highlighting the importance of dosage considerations. Stimulation parameters such as intensity, duration, frequency, and pattern play a significant role in shaping the effects of rTMS on brain activity and clinical outcomes.

An ongoing concern in the field of repetitive transcranial magnetic stimulation (rTMS) is the lack of standardized reporting for dosing parameters, which has implications for comprehensive understanding and clinical application of these techniques [38]. Currently, the reporting of rTMS dosage relies on textual descriptions, leading to varying levels of detail and specificity. This variability hampers reproducibility and the establishment of consistent protocols and effective stimulation parameters. The absence of standardized reporting practices for rTMS dosage poses challenges in comparing and replicating studies, limiting the accumulation of robust evidence and the generalizability of findings across different populations. This also poses a disadvantage in the ability to conduct meta-analyses, hindering the translation of rTMS into clinical practice in an effective manner. Therefore, efforts to establish standardized reporting guidelines for rTMS studies are warranted, aiming to enhance transparency, reproducibility, and collaboration within the field.

In this context, we recognize the opportunity for interdiciplinarity. In Computer Science, the semantic web publishing method utilizes semantic technologies and ontologies to structure and standardize data, enabling more efficient and meaningful reporting, querying, and analysis of information within the World Wide Web [5]. We thus posit the adoption of semantic web methods from Computer Science as a solution to the problem of non-standardized reporting of Neuroscience NIBS study doses. This is in keeping with the recent growing general impetus driving a change in the status quo of discourse-based scholarly communication toward Findable, Accessible, Interoperable, and Resuable (FAIR) [37] publishing as structured scholarly knowledge graphs by adopting the technologies of the semantic web [1,3,4,8,12,17,19,34]. We claim that *the adoption of FAIR reporting paradigms facilitated by semantic web technologies for NIBS dosing will mark a significant stride toward overcoming the pressing challenge of reproducibility in this field.* In turn, it will facilitate tapping into the full clinical potential of NIBS.

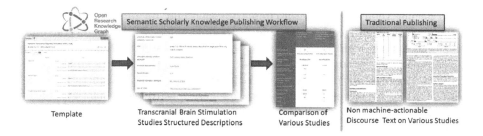

Fig. 1. Machine-actionable structured scholarly knowledge capture via semantic publishing (in red) versus traditional discourse-based non-machine-actionable publishing (in gray). (Color figure online)

Toward the semantic web publishing of NIBS dosages a few technical considerations need to be in place. These include: defining the salient entities, attributes, and relationships for the NIBS domain as standardized resources accessible on the Web via uniform resource identifiers (URIs); optionally, designing or reusing a suitable ontology that captures the concepts, relationships, and constraints of interest; and publishing NIBS doses using structured triples conforming to the RDF syntax recommended by the World Wide Web Consortium (W3C).[1] It is crucial to utilize standard ontologized vocabulary terms, incorporate appropriate metadata, and ensure data publication on the web with unique URIs for resource identification and interlinking. Fortunately, the latter required FAIR semantic web publishing functionalities are readily available within next-generation scholarly knowledge publishing digital libraries such as the Open Research Knowledge Graph (ORKG) [3,27]. The ORKG platform supports the semantic publishing [26] of scholarly knowledge as structured, machine-actionable data. Its specific functionalities include offering a robust and reliable web namespace within which to specify the vocabulary of pertinent scholarly knowledge via dereferenceable uniform resource identifiers (URIs); intuitive frontend interfaces [22] to define scholarly resources,[2] properties,[3] classes,[4] and templates[5] which via the platform's backend technologies automatically represent the growing scholarly knowledge graph in RDF syntax;[6] given the machine-actionability that semantic representations of knowledge generally entail, the ORKG supports the creation of novel comparison views over comparably structured scholarly knowledge in a similar way to comparisons of products on e-

---

[1] https://www.w3.org/TR/rdf11-concepts/.
[2] https://orkg.org/resources.
[3] https://orkg.org/properties.
[4] https://orkg.org/classes.
[5] https://orkg.org/templates.
[6] https://orkg.org/api/rdf/dump.

commerce websites [23]; and finally, SPARQL queryable interfaces[7] to further obtain customized snapshots or aggregated views of the ORKG are also supported. Figure 1 juxtaposes the semantic publishing of scholarly knowledge in the ORKG in terms of one of its workflows compared with traditional discourse-based scholarly publishing paradigm.

Returning then to the interdisciplinary vision laid out in this paper toward adopting the semantic web publishing methodology for NIBS dosages, the only remaining action items would then be to define the standardized vocabulary to represent the domain. With this goal in mind, in this paper, we showcase in practice the semantic publishing of repetitive transcranial magnetic stimulation (rTMS) – a subarea of NIBS – as a use-case toward the semantic publishing of NIBS studies, generally. rTMS is a non-invasive neuromodulation technique that applies magnetic pulses to targeted brain regions to modulate neural activity [36]. Extensive research in both humans and animals has demonstrated the therapeutic potential of rTMS in neurological and psychiatric disorders. Notably, rTMS has shown efficacy in conditions such as major depressive disorder (MDD) and obsessive-compulsive disorder (OCD). Figure 2 offers an illustrative overview of the rTMS methodology in practice. The U.S. Food and Drug

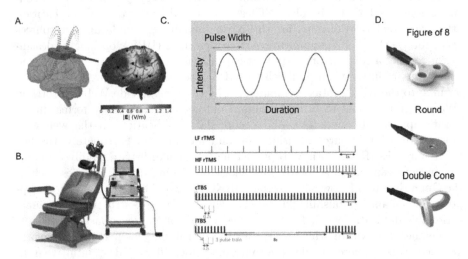

Fig. 2. Repetitive Transcranial Magnetic Stimulation (rTMS): **A.** Schematic representation of an rTMS coil positioned over a brain. The illustration shows the precise placement of the coil, adhering to the specific anatomical target, alongside corresponding computational estimation of the electric field (E-field) generated by the rTMS coil in the brain. The color gradient indicates the intensity of the electric field, highlighting the spatial distribution of the stimulation. **B.** Conventional rTMS device and experimental setup. **C.** Parameters that can influence rTMS outcome include pulse width, frequency, intensity and net protocol duration, among others. **D.** rTMS coil shapes can influence the electrical field distribution of stimulation over the brain, impacting the stimulation outcome. Courtesy: Biorender.com, SIMNIBS, Magstim.

---

[7] https://orkg.org/triplestore, https://orkg.org/sparql/.

Administration (FDA) has granted approval for the use of rTMS as a therapeutic tool, specifically for the treatment of MDD and OCD. However, due to the non-standardization of experimental protocols and data reporting of rTMS, the evidence to inform clinical application is highly inconsistent [11,29] and substantially based on trial and error. As a first step, is the discovery of standardized vocabulary to describe rTMS. An early work in this direction is the comprehensive review of rTMS studies between 1999 and 2020 by Turi et al. [30] which introduced a set of salient properties based on which over 600 rTMS studies were comparable. The standardized applicability of the properties over the large number of studies indicates their potential to be realized as a schema based on the philosophy of data-driven bottom-up ontology construction [31]. Thus, in this paper we investigate the following main research questions (**RQs**). **RQ1**: What are the properties for the structured representation of rTMS studies? This is addressed in Sect. 3. **RQ2**: How can this semantic reporting of rTMS studies specifically, and NIBS studies generally, be practically realized as a FAIR model? – addressed in Subsect. 3.1.

The primary goal of this work is to engage a broad and varied audience, especially in the field of neuroscience. We aim to foster interdisciplinary discussions to enhance understanding of the fast-evolving topic of semantic scholarly knowledge publishing, both within this paper's context and beyond. The proposed semantics-based structured recording method is a concrete first step that directly addresses the two main long-discussed problems of *transparency* and *reproducibility* of NIBS studies to facilitate clinical application [38]. Our concrete implementation of the semantic web-based technology reporting of rTMS studies serves as a demonstration use-case and a call-to-action to adopt and foster collaborations toward ORKG infrastructural extensions as a platform to support publishing of NIBS studies.

2   Background on rTMS Dosage Data Management

The management of data in rTMS studies remains a challenging task due to the varied practices in data collection, storage, and protection protocols [38]. Data is commonly collected directly from physiological signals and stored in localized databases or documentation tools. While these practices fulfil basic data storage needs, they raise significant issues concerning data interoperability, reusability, and long-term accessibility, primarily due to inconsistencies in data structures and metadata provision [38]. Moreover, data protection presents a significant challenge in this context. The sensitivity of personal data demands stringent measures to ensure security, which can further complicate data accessibility. Ensuring secure access requires a fine balance between protection and availability, often calling for robust authentication protocols and persistent identifiers [37]. Adding to the complexities is the variability in the selection of stimulation parameters, in particular the stimulation intensity, across rTMS studies, as highlighted in Turi et al.'s systematic review [30]. The lack of a standardized protocol for this crucial parameter leads to substantial inconsistencies across studies, impacting the reliability and comparability of research findings.

To refine this process, the integration of FAIR (Findable, Accessible, Inter-operable, and Reusable) principles into rTMS dosage data management presents a potential solution [37]. With the application of these principles, data could be catalogued accurately, improving findability. Accessibility could be ensured with robust authentication protocols, allowing for a more secure and open sharing of data. Interoperability, although often not prioritized in traditional rTMS studies, could be significantly enhanced through common data models and agreed-upon formats [6]. The proposed adaptations in rTMS data handling, encompassing FAIR principles and standardized intensity selection, can substantially elevate the quality of research outputs, making them more robust, reliable, and universally acceptable.

3   Supporting Semantic Technology and Semantification of rTMS Studied Doses

As a first step, for the semantic publishing of rTMS dosage, we need to define the rTMS-domain-specific resources and properties. Using the ORKG semantic scholarly knowledge publishing platform, we decide to define the rTMS resources and predicates as resources on the web with deferenceable URIs in the ORKG namespace. The use of the ORKG namespace offers: *1. Standardization and Interoperability.* It provides a framework for representing scholarly knowledge, ensuring seamless integration and data sharing across platforms. *2. Community Collaboration.* Researchers and practitioners can actively contribute to the growth and improvement of the ORKG ecosystem, refining ontology and shaping scholarly resources. *3. Enhanced Discoverability.* Adoption of the ORKG namespace improves the visibility and indexing of scholarly resources, increasing their chances of being accessed and cited. *4. Semantic Enrichment.* The comprehensive ontology of the ORKG namespace enriches scholarly resources with detailed metadata, facilitating advanced queries and analysis. *5. Community Trust and Credibility.* Utilizing the ORKG namespace adds credibility to scholarly resources through community validation, fostering trust within the scholarly community. *6. Long-term Sustainability.* The ORKG namespace, supported by an active community, ensures the maintenance and longevity of semantic web resources, giving researchers confidence in their continuity. Overall, the use of the ORKG namespace provides researchers and organizations with a standardized, collaborative, and credible framework for creating scholarly resources and predicates in the semantic web.

rTMS doses encompass multiple adjustable parameters that shape the characteristics of the stimulation [15,16,21,25,28,35]. The longitudinal review of rTMS studies between 1999 and 2020 by Turi et al. [30] characterized the rTMS dose in terms of 15 salient properties. Based on the philosophy of bottom-up discovery of standardized domain vocabulary [31], these 15 properties and their resources are defined as URIs in the ORKG namespace and then applied to document the individual rTMS doses reviewed. The 15-properties strong rTMS recording resources, detailed in Table 1, are: **1.**

Table 1. rTMS key properties and associated resources

Property	Resources
Type of rTMS	Conventional rTMS (rTMS), Intermittent theta burst stimulation (iTBS), Continuous theta burst stimulation (cTBS), Quadripulse stimulation (QPS)
Intrabust Frequency	–
Stimulation Intensity Selection Approach	Active motor threshold (AMT), Resting motor threshold (RMT), Unspecified motor threshold (MT), Functional lesion (FL), Phosphene threshold (PT), Fixed intensity (FXD), Electric field (EF)
Threshold-estimation strategies	Method of limit (ML), 5 step procedure (5STEP), Threshold hunting (TH), Maximum likelihood based threshold hunting (MLTH), Parameter estimation by sequential testing (PEST), TMS Motor Threshold Assessment Tool (MTAT)
Threshold Measurement	Electrode (E), Visual (V)
Amplitude of the Motor Evoked Potential (mV)	–
Threshold Ratio	–
Percentage or the Amplitude of the Motor Threshold Contraction	–
Percent of Stimulation Intensity	Min value, Max value
Maximum Stimulator Output	–
Stimulator Company	Cad, MedDan, MagSti, NeoNet, NeuNet, MagVen, NexSti, MagMor, Yir, BraSwa, DeyDia, YunTec, NeuSof
Stimulator Model	HS, MP, MES10, R, SR, SR2, NP, 16E05, 200, 200 2, MLR25, 200 BI, QP500, HF, MP30, MPX100, 2100CRS, MP100, R2, MPR30, NBS, PM100, CCYI, CCYIA, DMXT, NS, Sys4.3, R2P1, N-MS/D, MPC, MS/D
Coil Shape	F8, R, F8-D, D
Coil Size	–
Coil Model	MC125, MC-125, MC-B70, MCF-B70, MCF-B-65, MCF-B65, WC, AC, DC, PN9925, 992500, C-B60, FC, FC-B70, HP, Cool B65, cool-B65, Cool-DB80, Cool B56, H-ADD, H, H1, AF, DB-80, B65, MMC-140, 70BF-Cool

type of rTMS with four resource candidates, viz. conventional rTMS (rTMS), intermittent theta burst stimulation (iTBS), continuous theta burst stimulation (cTBS), and quadripulse stimulation (QPS). **2.** *intrabust frequency.* **3.**

stimulation intensity selection approach with seven resource candidates, viz. active motor threshold (AMT), resting motor threshold (RMT), unspecified motor threshold (MT), functional lesion (FL), phosphene threshold (PT), fixed intensity (FXD), and electric field (EF). **4.** *threshold-estimation strategies* with six resource candidates, viz. method of limit (ML), 5 step procedure (5STEP), threshold hunting (TH), maximum likelihood based threshold hunting (MLTH), parameter estimation by sequential testing (PEST), and TMS Motor Threshold Assessment Tool (MTAT). **5.** *threshold measurement* with two resource candidates, viz. electrode (E) and visual (V). **6.** *amplitude of the motor evoked potential in microvolts.* **7.** *threshold ratio.* **8.** *percentage or the amplitude of the motor threshold contraction.* **9.** *percent of stimulation intensity* with sub-properties 9.a. *percent of stimulation intensity (min value)* and 9.b. *percent of stimulation intensity (max value).* **10.** *maximum stimulator output.* **11.** *stimulator company* with 13 and counting resource candidates: Cad, MedDan, MagSti, NeoNet, NeuNet, MagVen, NexSti, MagMor, Yir, BraSwa, DeyDia, YunTec, and NeuSof. **12.** *stimulator model* with 31 resources: HS, MP, MES10, R, SR, SR2, NP, 16E05, 200, 200_2, MLR25, 200_BI, QP500, HF, MP30, MPX100, 2100CRS, MP100, R2, MPR30, NBS, PM100, CCYI, CCYIA, DMXT, NS, Sys4.3, R2P1, N-MS/D, MPC, and MS/D. **13.** *coil shape* with 4 resources: F8, R, F8-D, and D. **14.** *coil size.* **15.** *coil model* with 27 resources: MC125, MC-125, MC-B70, MCF-B70, MCF-B-65, MCF-B65, WC, AC, DC, PN9925, 992500, C-B60, FC, FC-B70, HP, Cool B65, cool-B65, Cool-DB80, Cool B56, H-ADD, H, H1, AF, DB-80, B65, MMC-140, and 70BF-Cool. These properties are implemented as a template https://orkg. org/template/R211955 which can be extended and reused for the explicit and standardized recording of rTMS doses. As a demonstration use-case, the 600 reviewed studies [30] were semantically published resulting in an rTMS-KG as a subgraph of the ORKG. Comparisons over the structured rTMS data were computed and published in six parts, i.e. 1, 2, 3, 4, 5, & 6, with ~100 studies compared in each part.

3.1   RTMS-KG - Findable, Accessible, Interoperable, and Reusable

rTMS-KG is an open-source machine-actionable knowledge graph of 600 rTMS doses that satisfies the FAIR publishing guidelines [37]. Each published comparison of studies in the rTMS-KG can be persistently identified with a Digital Object Identifier (DOI) ('Findable'). This resolves to a landing page, providing access to metadata, respective rTMS study data, and versioning, all of which is indexed and searchable ('Findable', 'Accessible', and 'Reusable'). rTMS-KG can be downloaded over the Web from the ORKG in RDF ('Interoperable'). The rTMS vocabulary can be mapped to existing relevant ontologies via same-as links ('Interoperable'). Finally, the ORKG provides public search interfaces to build custom views of rTMS-KG ('Accessible').

4   Conclusion

Standardization of experimental protocols and data reporting is pivotal for the advancement of the rTMS field in particular, and NIBS more broadly. Adopting consensus reporting guidelines and protocols would foster uniformity and comparability across studies, thereby facilitating a more precise evaluation of NIBS dose efficacy. Transparent reporting practices, coupled with data sharing, can bolster reproducibility, reduce publication bias, and encourage collaboration. This enhancement can be directly achieved through the semantic web publishing of scholarly knowledge, as exemplified by the ORKG. By defining a standardized vocabulary of properties and resources, and documenting upcoming studies within this predefined semantic framework, the issues of *transparency* and *reproducibility* in NIBS studies are addressed. As a result, the NIBS field can continue its trajectory of progress, delivering effective, evidence-based neuromodulation interventions for neurological and psychiatric disorders [38].

This study, for the first time, showcases the practical application of the semantic web resource-based reporting methodology for NIBS studies at large, and rTMS studies in particular. It offers transformative value by: (1) promoting standardization in the recording of NIBS enhances transparency through the explicit logging of key study properties, which in turn bolsters reproducibility, and (2) promoting the adoption of such machine-actionable documentation for NIBS studies, as evidenced by the demonstrated rTMS subarea use-case.

Acknowledgements. We thank the anonymous reviewers for their detailed and insightful comments on an earlier draft of the paper. This work was jointly supported by the German BMBF project SCINEXT (ID 01lS22070), DFG NFDI4DataScience (ID 460234259), and ERC ScienceGraph (ID 819536).

References

1. SciGraph. https://www.springernature.com/de/researchers/scigraph. Accessed 02 Nov 2021
2. Ardolino, G., Bossi, B., Barbieri, S., Priori, A.: Non-synaptic mechanisms underlie the after-effects of cathodal transcutaneous direct current stimulation of the human brain. J. Physiol. **568**(2), 653–663 (2005)
3. Auer, S., et al.: Improving access to scientific literature with knowledge graphs. Bibliothek Forschung und Praxis **44**(3), 516–529 (2020)
4. Baas, J., Schotten, M., Plume, A., Côté, G., Karimi, R.: Scopus as a curated, high-quality bibliometric data source for academic research in quantitative science studies. Quant. Sci. Stud. **1**(1), 377–386 (2020)
5. Berners-Lee, T., Hendler, J., Lassila, O.: The semantic web. Sci. Am. **284**(5), 34–43 (2001). https://www-sop.inria.fr/acacia/cours/essi2006/Scientific%20American_%20Feature%20Article_%20The%20Semantic%20Web_%20May%202001.pdf
6. Bierer, B.E., Crosas, M., Pierce, H.H.: Data authorship as an incentive to data sharing. N. Engl. J. Med. **376**(17), 1684 (2017)
7. Bikson, M., Lian, J., Hahn, P.J., Stacey, W.C., Sciortino, C., Durand, D.M.: Suppression of epileptiform activity by high frequency sinusoidal fields in rat hippocampal slices. J. Physiol. **531**(Pt 1), 181 (2001)

8. Birkle, C., Pendlebury, D., Schnell, J., Adams, J.: Web of science as a data source for research on scientific and scholarly activity. Quant. Sci. Stud. **1**(1), 363–376 (2020)

9. Durand, S., Fromy, B., Humeau, A., Sigaudo-Roussel, D., Saumet, J., Abraham, P.: Break excitation alone does not explain the delay and amplitude of anodal current-induced vasodilatation in human skin. J. Physiol. **542**(2), 549–557 (2002)

10. Elwassif, M.M., Kong, Q., Vazquez, M., Bikson, M.: Bio-heat transfer model of deep brain stimulation-induced temperature changes. J. Neural Eng. **3**(4), 306 (2006)

11. Hamada, M., Murase, N., Hasan, A., Balaratnam, M., Rothwell, J.C.: The role of interneuron networks in driving human motor cortical plasticity. Cereb. Cortex **23**(7), 1593–1605 (2013)

12. Hendricks, G., Tkaczyk, D., Lin, J., Feeney, P.: Crossref: the sustainable source of community-owned scholarly metadata. Quant. Sci. Stud. **1**(1), 414–427 (2020)

13. Karra, D., Dahm, R.: Transfection techniques for neuronal cells. J. Neurosci. **30**(18), 6171–6177 (2010)

14. Kirson, E.D., et al.: Alternating electric fields arrest cell proliferation in animal tumor models and human brain tumors. Proc. Natl. Acad. Sci. **104**(24), 10152–10157 (2007)

15. Lefaucheur, J.P., et al.: Evidence-based guidelines on the therapeutic use of repetitive transcranial magnetic stimulation (rTMS): an update (2014–2018). Clin. Neurophysiol. **131**(2), 474–528 (2020)

16. Lefaucheur, J.P., et al.: Evidence-based guidelines on the therapeutic use of repetitive transcranial magnetic stimulation (rTMS). Clin. Neurophysiol. **125**(11), 2150–2206 (2014)

17. Lewis, N., Wang, J., Poblet, M., Aryani, A.: Research graph: connecting researchers, research data, publications and grants using the graph technology. In: eResearch Australasia Conference (2016)

18. Lopez-Quintero, S., Datta, A., Amaya, R., Elwassif, M., Bikson, M., Tarbell, J.: DBS-relevant electric fields increase hydraulic conductivity of in vitro endothelial monolayers. J. Neural Eng. **7**(1), 016005 (2010)

19. Manghi, P., Manola, N., Horstmann, W., Peters, D.: An infrastructure for managing EC funded research output: the OpenAIRE project. Grey J. (TGJ) **6**(1) (2010)

20. Martiny, K., Lunde, M., Bech, P.: Transcranial low voltage pulsed electromagnetic fields in patients with treatment-resistant depression. Biol. Psychiat. **68**(2), 163–169 (2010)

21. Miranda, P.C., Lomarev, M., Hallett, M.: Modeling the current distribution during transcranial direct current stimulation. Clin. Neurophysiol. **117**(7), 1623–1629 (2006)

22. Oelen, A.: Leveraging human-computer interaction and crowdsourcing for scholarly knowledge graph creation (2022). https://doi.org/10.15488/13066. https://www.repo.uni-hannover.de/handle/123456789/13171

23. Oelen, A., Jaradeh, M.Y., Stocker, M., Auer, S.: Generate fair literature surveys with scholarly knowledge graphs. In: JCDL 2020, pp. 97–106. Association for Computing Machinery, New York (2020). https://doi.org/10.1145/3383583.3398520

24. Peterchev, A.V., et al.: Fundamentals of transcranial electric and magnetic stimulation dose: definition, selection, and reporting practices. Brain Stimul. **5**(4), 435–453 (2012)

25. Rossi, S., Hallett, M., Rossini, P.M., Pascual-Leone, A., Safety of TMS Consensus Group, et al.: Safety, ethical considerations, and application guidelines for the

use of transcranial magnetic stimulation in clinical practice and research. Clin. Neurophysiol. **120**(12), 2008–2039 (2009)

26. Shotton, D.: Semantic publishing: the coming revolution in scientific journal publishing. Learned Publishing **22**(2), 85–94 (2009)

27. Stocker, M., et al.: Fair scientific information with the open research knowledge graph. FAIR Connect **1**(1), 19–21 (2023)

28. Thielscher, A., Antunes, A., Saturnino, G.B.: Field modeling for transcranial magnetic stimulation: a useful tool to understand the physiological effects of TMS? In: 2015 37th Annual International Conference of the IEEE Engineering in Medicine and Biology Society (EMBC), pp. 222–225. IEEE (2015)

29. Thut, G., Pascual-Leone, A.: A review of combined TMS-EEG studies to characterize lasting effects of repetitive TMS and assess their usefulness in cognitive and clinical neuroscience. Brain Topogr. **22**, 219–232 (2010)

30. Turi, Z., Lenz, M., Paulus, W., Mittner, M., Vlachos, A.: Selecting stimulation intensity in repetitive transcranial magnetic stimulation studies: a systematic review between 1991 and 2020. Eur. J. Neurosci. **53**(10), 3404–3415 (2021)

31. Van Der Vet, P.E., Mars, N.J.: Bottom-up construction of ontologies. IEEE Trans. Knowl. Data Eng. **10**(4), 513–526 (1998)

32. Volkow, N.D., et al.: Effects of low-field magnetic stimulation on brain glucose metabolism. Neuroimage **51**(2), 623–628 (2010)

33. Wachter, D., et al.: Transcranial direct current stimulation induces polarity-specific changes of cortical blood perfusion in the rat. Exp. Neurol. **227**(2), 322–327 (2011)

34. Wang, K., Shen, Z., Huang, C., Wu, C.H., Dong, Y., Kanakia, A.: Microsoft academic graph: when experts are not enough. Quant. Sci. Stud. **1**(1), 396–413 (2020)

35. Wassermann, E.M.: Risk and safety of repetitive transcranial magnetic stimulation: report and suggested guidelines from the international workshop on the safety of repetitive transcranial magnetic stimulation, June 5–7, 1996. Electroencephalography Clin. Neurophysiol./Evoked Potentials Section **108**(1), 1–16 (1998)

36. Wassermann, E.M., Lisanby, S.H.: Therapeutic application of repetitive transcranial magnetic stimulation: a review. Clin. Neurophysiol. **112**(8), 1367–1377 (2001)

37. Wilkinson, M.D., et al.: The fair guiding principles for scientific data management and stewardship. Sci. Data **3**(1), 1–9 (2016)

38. Wilson, M.T., St George, L.: Repetitive transcranial magnetic stimulation: a call for better data. Front. Neural Circuits **10**, 57 (2016)

Identifying Influential References in Scholarly Papers Using Citation Contexts

Tomoki Ikoma[1](✉) ⓘ and Shigeki Matsubara[1,2](✉) ⓘ

[1] Graduate School of Informatics, Nagoya University, Nagoya, Japan
`ikoma.tomoki.d0@s.mail.nagoya-u.ac.jp`
[2] Information and Communications, Nagoya University, Nagoya, Japan
`matubara@nagoya-u.ac.jp`

Abstract. Citation count is commonly used as a straightforward metric for measuring the impact of a paper. However, since all citations are treated equally, citation count does not accurately capture the true influence of a particular cited paper on the citing paper. To accurately measure the individual impact of cited papers, it is required to identify those that have a high influence on a citing paper. This paper proposes a method to identify the influential citations using the text of citation contexts, specifically the citing sentences. Citing sentences contain the descriptions of the cited papers and the relationship between the citing paper and each cited paper. The proposed method extracts the descriptions of cited papers from the citing sentences and utilizes them to identify influential references. Experimental results have shown the benefits of using the extracted description of each cited paper.

Keywords: Scholarly document processing · Bibliometrics · Citation context classification

1 Introduction

Scientific papers cite publications for referencing, and the connections between papers are established through citations. However, while citation count is commonly used as a straightforward metric for measuring the impact of a paper, it does not accurately capture the true influence of a particular cited paper on the citing paper, as it treats all citations equally [20].

To accurately measure the individual impact of cited papers, it is required to identify those that have a high influence on a citing paper [8,9,22]. For example, a paper cited as the basis of a study can be considered more influential to the citing paper than other referenced works. By evaluating the influence of each cited work, its impact in academia can be quantitatively assessed.

This paper proposes a method to identify the influential citations using the text of citation contexts, specifically the citing sentences. Citing sentences contain the descriptions of the cited papers and the relationship between the citing

D. H. Goh et al. (Eds.): ICADL 2023, LNCS 14458, pp. 152–161, 2023.
https://doi.org/10.1007/978-981-99-8088-8_13

paper and each cited paper [19]. The proposed method extracts the descriptions of cited papers from the citing sentences and utilizes them to identify influential references. Experimental results have shown the benefits of using the extracted description of each cited paper.

2 Related Work

Valenzuela et al. [22] introduced the significant task of identifying highly influential citations. They considered a citation to be influential if a citing paper either used datasets and tools, or is directly built upon a cited paper. They proposed a method that involved a manually selected set of features, including how often a citing paper referred to a cited paper and the similarity between their abstracts. However, this method requires the time-consuming process of manually selecting keywords and phrases [18].

The Citation Context Classification (3C) Shared Task [8,9] aims to classify cited papers according to their citation purpose and influence on a citing paper. For this task, a dataset including 3,000 citation instances was provided with human-annotated labels indicating their purpose and influence. A number of methods have been proposed using this dataset. Premjith and Soman [17] identified influential citations using features extracted through Word2Vec [11]. In addition, Mishra and Mishra [12] identified influential citations using TF-IDF of words in the citing sentence as well as machine learning techniques such as Random Forest. Meanwhile, de Andrade et al. [3] identified influential citations through topic extraction using LDA [2] and the TF-IDF representation of words. Varanasi et al. [23] identified influential citations using manually selected features such as TF-IDF and sentiment of the citing sentence analyzed by VADER [6] as well as Random Forest algorithm. On the other hand, Premjith et al. [16] used a Bi-LSTM [5] model to process the citing sentence as a sequence of words for identifying influential citations. Maheshwari et al. [10], however, identified influential citations using word embeddings of the citing sentence extracted with SciBERT [1].

3 Influential References and Citation Contexts

While some cited papers are influential for a citing paper, others are less so and thus considered incidental. Influential citations include references essential for the citing paper, such as:

- datasets and tools
- applied concepts and ideas
- direct utilization of a previous work

On the other hand, incidental citations include references to papers that are not always essential for the citing paper and can be replaced by other papers, such as:

- related previous works
- documents on the social backgrounds of a work

Output: Label sequence

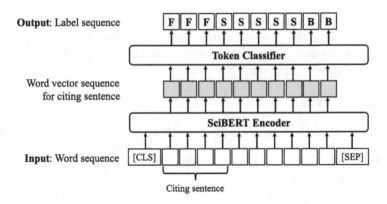

Fig. 1. Model for extracting scope of reference tag

3.1   Contents of the Citing Sentence

To evaluate the influence of cited papers, one can utilize information from citation contexts, specifically the citing sentences. They contain the following information:

– description of the content of the cited paper
– description of the relationship between the citing and multiple cited papers

The former represents what is utilized in the citing paper, while the latter represents how the cited paper contributed to the citing paper. For example, in the following citing sentence:

(3.1) *Each construct was operationalized using at least two items for measurement and analysed using* **confirmatory factor analysis** [1].

the words in bold correspond to the former while the words in italic correspond to the latter. Combining these descriptions allows to gather information of the role each cited paper had in the citing paper for evaluating citation influence.

3.2   Scope of Reference Tag

We define the scope of reference tag as the part of the citing sentence that describes the cited paper. In this paper, notations such as [1] and [2] in the example sentences indicate citation tags. For instance, in the citing sentence (3.1), the words in bold represents the scope of the reference tag. The scope of the reference tag varies from one citing sentence to another. In the citing sentence (3.1), the scope of the reference tag is the noun phrase immediately preceding the reference tag. However, in the following citing sentence:

(3.2) For example, previous studies have found that **cross institutional collaboration supports the diffusion of innovations and new ideas within a field** [2].

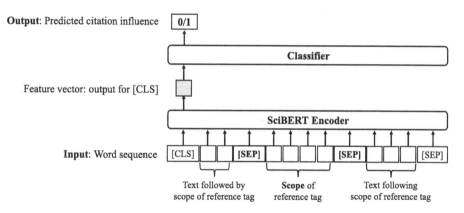

Fig. 2. Model for identifying influential citations

the clause in bold is the scope of the reference tag. In some cases, the entire citing sentence is the scope of the reference tag:

(3.3) **The NACP was formally recognized by the United States in 2002 under the mantle of the nation's overall climate change management strategy** [3].

The content of the cited paper is described in the scope of the reference tag. On the other hand, the relationship between the citing and cited paper is described in outside of the scope. Therefore, to utilize the information of the content and the contribution of a cited paper, it is crucial to distinguish the scope of the reference tag from the rest of the citing sentence.

4   Method

In this section, we propose a method to identify the influential citations based on the extracted scope of reference tag.

4.1   Extracting Scope of Reference Tag

The proposed method applies SciBERT [1] to extract the scope of the reference tag as shown in Fig. 1. The extraction model consists of an encoder and a token classifier. It takes a citing sentence as input and then extracts the scope of the reference tag through the following procedure:

1. Replace the reference tag for the cited paper with '#AUTHOR_TAG'.
2. Convert the input citing sentence into a sequence of words, as well as adding [CLS] and [SEP] at the start and end of the sentence.
3. Transform the words in the citing sentence to feature vectors with the encoder.
4. Output the list of labels that represents whether each word is included in the scope with the token classifier.

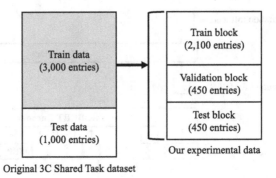

Original 3C Shared Task dataset

Fig. 3. Division of 3C Shared Task dataset

In the resulting list of labels, "F", "S", and "B" represent the front of the scope, the span of the scope, and the back of the scope, respectively. As such, the scope of reference tag is extracted as the span labeled as S. In addition, the proposed method employs the Viterbi algorithm [4] to prevent the model from generating invalid label sequences such as F after S.

4.2 Classifying Citation Influence

The citation influence is classified using a SciBERT-based model composed of the encoder and classifier as shown in Fig. 2. Based on the citing sentence, the model classifies the citation as either influential or incidental with the following procedure.

1. Insert [SEP] to the start and end of the span extracted as the scope of reference tag in the citing sentence.
2. Convert the citing sentence with [SEP] inserted into a sequence of words, as well as adding [CLS] and [SEP] at the start and end of the sentence.
3. Transform the word sequence to feature vectors with the encoder. The encoder outputs the features of the entire word sequence as embeddings of [CLS].
4. Exploiting the embeddings of [CLS], predict the citation influence with the classifier.

5   Experiments

5.1   Datasets

We trained and evaluated the proposed model on the dataset provided in the 3C Shared Task [8,9]. The 3C Shared Task dataset consists of 3,000 training and 1,000 test entries. Each entry consists of the citing sentence and the title of the citing and cited papers. Since the citation influence label is only available for the training data, the 3,000 entries of the training data were randomly split into training, validation, and test blocks as shown in Fig. 3. The training block consists of 2,100 entries while each of the validation and test blocks contain 450 entries.

In addition, we created a dataset for training and evaluating the model for extracting the scope of reference tag by annotating the scope of reference tag on the 3,000 citing sentences. A worker annotated the scope of reference tag according to the citing sentences and the corresponding titles of the citing and cited papers using the doccano [13] annotation tool. The annotation guidelines are as follows:

- The scope should include the description of the cited paper, and it should not include the descriptions of other papers.
- The reference tag itself should not be included in the scope. However, if the reference tag appears as the subject of the citing sentence, it should be included in the scope.
- If the reference tag is the subject of the citing sentence, the scope range should start with the reference tag. If not so, the scope range should end with the reference tag.

5.2 Experimental Settings

We implemented the classification model using PyTorch [14] and HuggingFace Transformers [21]. We trained the classification model with the training block, analyzed the model structure with the validation block. Then we evaluated its performance with the test block. For the evaluation metrics, we employed precision, recall and their harmonic mean F1 score. As the baseline, we trained a variant of the model that identifies influential citations based on the citing sentences, but without [SEP] inserted at the start and end of the scope of reference tag.

5.3 Experimental Result

We trained the proposed model and the baseline with the hyperparameters tuned in Sect. 5.3 then evaluated the performance of each model on the test block.

The upper part of Table 1 shows the evaluation results. The proposed model achieved an F1 score of approximately 2.3 points higher than the baseline, indicating that the information of scope of reference tag is beneficial for identifying influential citations.

In addition, we compared the performance of our model to that of the following several models proposed in the 3C Shared Task:

Scubed [12] identifies influential citations using the TF-IDF of words in the citing sentences by the Random Forest algorithm.
Paul[1] identifies influential citations with the fasttext [7] word embeddings and the similarity of the titles by applying logistic regression.

Table 1. Comparison of performance

Model	Precision (%)	Recall (%)	F1 score (%)
Proposed method	58.85	68.21	**63.18**
Baseline	54.96	68.21	60.87
Scubed [12]	59.31	62.01	60.65
Paul[1]	54.18	69.74	60.99
UFMG [3]	55.73	72.31	62.95
IREL [10]	55.84	56.41	56.12
IITP [23]	48.54	51.28	49.88

https://www.kaggle.com/code/plarmuseau/reproduce-winning-solution

Table 2. Performance of extracting descriptions of the cited papers

	Precision(%)	Recall(%)	F1 score(%)
Entire citing sentence	40.06	100.00	57.20
Proposed method	82.20	83.93	**83.06**

UFMG [3] identifies influential citations with the topics extracted using LDA [15] and the TF-IDF representation of the words.

IREL [10] identifies influential citations using word embeddings of the citing sentence extracted with SciBERT [1].

IITP [23] identifies influential citations with manually selected features such as TF-IDF and the citing sentence sentiment analyzed by VADER [6].

Table 1 shows the performance of each model. The proposed model achieved a higher F1 score than all five compared models.

6   Discussion

6.1   Evaluation of Extracting Scope of Reference Tag

We implemented the model for extracting the scope of reference tag with PyTorch [14] and Huggingface Transformers [21]. As mentioned in Sect. 5.1, we trained the extraction model with the training block, tuned the model structure and training conditions with the validation block, and evaluated the final performance with the test block. We compared the word-based precision, recall and F1 score to when the scope of the reference tag is fixed as the whole of each citing sentence.

Table 2 shows the result. The proposed method has achieved a more accurate extraction of the scope of reference tag by using SciBERT to distinguish the words referring to a cited paper.

6.2 Case Study

We analyzed citation instances that the proposed model could correctly classify.

The first example shows a citation instance that the proposed model could correctly identify as influential:

(6.1) As STS scholars have shown, **publics can be both knowledgeable about biomedicine and willing to engage in sustained debate and analysis about issues that bioethicists are grappling with** [34, #AUTHOR_TAG]; limiting participation is thus unfortunate not only for democractic reasons, but also because potentially 'useful' contributions from those outside the academy remain unheard.

In this example, the words in bold were extracted as the scope of reference tag. The extracted part describes the concept proposed in the cited paper. In addition, the subsequent part of the sentence explains the conclusion of the citing paper, which is based on the cited paper. Thus, the model correctly identified the citation as influential.

The second example shows a citation instance the proposed model could correctly identify as incidental:

(6.2) For example, **the thinning method** #AUTHOR_TAG that is used to sample ODT map occurrences will likewise be advantageous for sampling swap occurrences.

In this example, the words in bold were extracted as the scope of reference tag, which describes the method proposed in the cited paper. However, while the subsequent part mentions a possible usage of the method, it does not state that the citing paper actually utilized the cited paper. From those points, the model correctly identified the citation as not influential and thus incidental.

7   Conclusion

This paper proposed a method for identifying influential citations using the text of citation contexts, specifically focusing on the citing sentences. Citing sentences contain respective descriptions of the cited papers and the relationship between citing paper and multiple cited papers. The proposed method extracts the descriptions of cited papers from the citing sentences and utilizes them to identify influential references. Experimental results have shown the benefits of using the extracted description for each cited paper.

Acknowledgements. This work was partially supported by the Grant-in-Aid for Challenging Research (Exploratory) (No. 23K18506) of JSPS and by JST SPRING, Grant Number JPMJSP2125. The computation was carried out on supercomputer "Flow" at Information Technology Center, Nagoya University.

References

1. Beltagy, I., Lo, K., Cohan, A.: SciBERT: a pretrained language model for scientific text. In: Proceedings of the 2019 Conference on Empirical Methods in Natural Language Processing and the 9th International Joint Conference on Natural Language Processing, pp. 3615–3620 (2019)
2. Blei, D.M., Ng, A.Y., Jordan, M.I.: Latent dirichlet allocation. J. Mach. Learn. Res. 3(1), 993–1022 (2003)
3. de Andrade, C.M.V., Gonçalves, M.A.: Combining representations for effective citation classification. In: Proceedings of the 8th International Workshop on Mining Scientific Publications, pp. 54–58 (2020)
4. Forney, G.: The Viterbi algorithm. Proc. IEEE 61(3), 268–278 (1973)
5. Graves, A., Schmidhuber, J.: Framewise phoneme classification with bidirectional LSTM and other neural network architectures. Neural Netw. 18(5–6), 602–610 (2005)
6. Hutto, C., Gilbert, E.: VADER: a parsimonious rule-based model for sentiment analysis of social media text. In: Proceedings of the 8th International AAAI Conference on Web and Social Media, pp. 216–225 (2014)
7. Joulin, A., Grave, E., Bojanowski, P., Mikolov, T.: Bag of tricks for efficient text classification. In: Proceedings of the 15th Conference on European Chapter of the Association for Computational Linguistics, pp. 427–431 (2017)
8. Kunnath, S.N., Pride, D., Gyawali, B., Knoth, P.: Overview of the 2020 WOSP 3C citation context classification task. In: Proceedings of the 8th International Workshop on Mining Scientific Publications, pp. 75–83 (2020)
9. Kunnath, S.N., Pride, D., Herrmannova, D., Knoth, P.: Overview of the 2021 SDP 3C citation context classification shared task. In: Proceedings of the 2nd Workshop on Scholarly Document Processing, pp. 150–158 (2021)
10. Maheshwari, H., Singh, B., Varma, V.: SciBERT sentence representation for citation context classification. In: Proceedings of the 2nd Workshop on Scholarly Document Processing, pp. 130–133 (2021)
11. Mikolov, T., Chen, K., Corrado, G., Dean, J.: Efficient estimation of word representations in vector space. In: Workshop Track Proceedings of the 1st International Conference on Learning Representations (2013)
12. Mishra, S., Mishra, S.: Scubed at 3C task B - a simple baseline for citation context influence classification. In: Proceedings of the 8th International Workshop on Mining Scientific Publications, pp. 65–70 (2020)
13. Nakayama, H., Kubo, T., Kamura, J., Taniguchi, Y., Liang, X.: doccano: text annotation tool for human (2018). https://github.com/doccano/doccano
14. Paszke, A. et al.: PyTorch: an imperative style, high-performance deep learning library. In: Advances in Neural Information Processing Systems, vol. 32, pp. 8024–8035 (2019)
15. Pennington, J., Socher, R., Manning, C.D.: GloVe: global vectors for word representation. In: Proceedings of the 2014 Conference on Empirical Methods in Natural Language Processing, pp. 1532–1543 (2014)
16. Premjith, B., Isha, I.S., Kumar, K.S., Karthikeyan, L., Soman, K.P.: Amrita_CEN_NLP@SDP2021 task A and B. In: Proceedings of the 2nd Workshop on Scholarly Document Processing, pp. 146–149 (2021)
17. Premjith, B., Soman, K.P.: Amrita_CEN_NLP @ WOSP 3C citation context classification task. In: Proceedings of the 8th International Workshop on Mining Scientific Publications, pp. 71–74 (2020)

18. Pride, D., Knoth, P.: Incidental or influential? - Challenges in automatically detecting citation importance using publication full texts. In: Proceedings of the 21st International Conference on Theory and Practice of Digital Libraries, pp. 572–578 (2017)
19. Su, X., Prasad, A., Kan, M.Y., Sugiyama, K.: Neural multi-task learning for citation function and provenance. In: Proceedings of the 2019 ACM/IEEE Joint Conference on Digital Libraries, pp. 394–395 (2019)
20. Taşkın, Z., Al, U.: A content-based citation analysis study based on text categorization. Scientometrics **114**(1), 335–357 (2017). https://doi.org/10.1007/s11192-017-2560-2
21. Thomas, W. et al.: Transformers: state-of-the-art natural language processing. In: Proceedings of the 2020 Conference on Empirical Methods in Natural Language Processing, pp. 38–45 (2020)
22. Valenzuela, M., Ha, V.A., Etzioni, O.: Identifying meaningful citations. In: AAAI Workshop: Scholarly Big Data, pp. 21–26 (2015)
23. Varanasi, K.K., Ghosal, T., Tiwary, P., Singh, M.: IITP-CUNI@3C: supervised approaches for citation classification (task A) and citation significance detection (task B). In: Proceedings of the 2nd Workshop on Scholarly Document Processing, pp. 140–145 (2021)

Advantages of Data Reuse Based on Disciplinary Diversity and Citation Count

Emi Ishita[1]([envelope]) [ID], Yosuke Miyata[2] [ID], and Keiko Kurata[2] [ID]

[1] Kyushu University, Fukuoka 819-0395, Japan
`ishita.emi.982@m.kyushu-u.ac.jp`
[2] Keio University, Tokyo 108-8345, Japan

Abstract. The adaption of data sharing is an important process in open science. Prior studies pertaining to data sharing have focused on the data release; however, data reuse is also an important aspect. Although the advantages of data reuse have not yet been demonstrated, they have been expressed in different fields. We selected the most cited datasets in the Data Citation Index – the National Longitudinal Study of Adolescent to Adult Health (Add Health) and the Framingham Cohort – and identified articles that reused them to measure the disciplinary diversity among these articles, as well as advantage in terms of citation counts. Particularly, we identified 2,919 articles that reused the Add Health dataset published in 1,702 resources, indicating high disciplinary diversity. Articles reused that the Framingham Cohort dataset had higher citation counts than those in the journal *Circulation* from 2004 to 2010. Despite our limited analysis, these results indicate the advantages of data reuse.

Keywords: Open science · Data reuse · Data sharing · Scholarly communication

1 Introduction

The movement toward open science has become a significant focus in the field of scholarly communication. Open science aims to "increase scientific collaboration and information-sharing for the benefit of science and society" [1]. Many countries, funding agencies, and academic journal publishers aim to share research data to promote open science. The data-sharing cycle encompasses the processes of data release (publishing) and reuse. Although these processes operate in tandem, prior studies have primarily focused solely on data release [2], whereas the full impact of data sharing becomes apparent when said data are reused in subsequent studies. The reuse of data is therefore crucial in understanding data sharing in scholarly communication. Although research on data reuse has recently been conducted from multiple perspectives, it is not yet sufficient. In particular, there are few studies on the advantages of data reuse. Pasquetto et al. [3] claimed that the reuse and integrated analysis of datasets from diverse disciplines is required to solve contemporary interdisciplinary and complex problems. Some researchers also mention increased citations as a benefit of data reuse [4], but that claim still lacks empirical evidence. There remains a gap in the understanding of the characteristics and evaluation of articles that reuse data.

Hence, this study was conducted to investigate the impact of articles that reuse data. If empirical evidence can be provided to show the advantages of data reuse, data reuse will be promoted and, in turn, open science. We considered two factors to show the advantages of data reuse: the citation count of articles that reused datasets, and the diversity of the research fields that have published such articles. The effectiveness of data reuse can be supported if articles that reuse datasets are more likely to be cited than other articles published in the same journal. If articles that reuse data are published in various fields, the publishing of data may have an impact not only on the specific field that produced the data but also on other research fields. Based on this assumption, we set the following research questions (RQs).

RQ1: Are articles that reuse datasets more likely to be cited?
RQ2: What degree of disciplinary diversity of articles reuse datasets?

In terms of RQ1, we compared the average citation count of articles that reused datasets with that of all articles published in the same journal. For RQ2, we analyzed the distribution of journals and field categories across articles.

2 Related Works

Research on data reuse can be mainly categorized into the following two points of view; a) research on characteristics of articles that actually reuse data [5–8] and b) research on the process of data reuse by researchers, especially the factors that inhibit or promote data reuse [9–11].

Piwowar and Vision [5] investigated 100 datasets in the Gene Expression Omnibus data repository and analyzed the characteristics of articles that reused datasets, such as publication year, authors' affiliations, and research subjects of the articles. Sakai et al. [8] found that there are two types of data reuse: primary reuse and data integration. Yoon et al. [7] also stated that there are two types of reuse, although the subjects studied are different and the definitions of the types are also slightly different.

A typical study on data reuse is one that analyzes the positive and negative factors of data reuse by researchers. Negative factors for data reuse include concerns about data quality, uncertainty about interpretation due to lack of context for data collection, and difficulty in accessing needed data. Positive factors include satisfaction with the data reuse experience. There are many negative and positive factors involved when researchers attempt to reuse data, which illustrates some of the complexities of the phenomenon of data reuse. Thus, many studies focused on factors affecting data reuse, and the advantages of data reuse can benefit from empirical study.

3 Data Collection

3.1 Datasets Selection

We used the Data Citation Index (DCI) included in the Web of Science (WoS) platform to identify the most used datasets in articles. Note that we considered all publications that cited a dataset as an article that reused datasets. In April 2023, we obtained

15,251,389 datasets/data studies from DCI by using "2000–2023" as the publication years and "Data Set or Data Study" as content type. Each record contained fields indicating the title (TI), author (AU), publication year (PY), and the number of articles citing the dataset (Z9). The results were sorted based on the Z9 field, and the most cited dataset (Top 1) was "National Longitudinal Study of Adolescent to Adult Health (Add Health), 1994–2008 [Public Use]" (the number of articles that reused this dataset was 2,919), followed by "the Framingham Cohort" (2,153) and "RSS Optimally Interpolated Microwave and Infrared Daily Sea Surface Temperature Analysis (RSS)" (1,314). The RSS dataset is from a different field compared to the top two datasets and was cited in more than 1,000 articles; however, the dataset was published in 2018. We excluded RSS from our analysis because we also analyzed changes in how datasets were cited as they get older. Finally, Add Health (DRCI:DATA2020259020862980) and the Framingham Cohort (DRCI:DATA2020020018018704) were selected for this study.

The Add Health dataset is a longitudinal study of a nationally representative sample of over 20,000 American adolescents who were in grades 7–12 during the 1994–95 school year, and have been followed for five waves to date [12]. The Add Health includes rich demographic, social, familial, socioeconomic, behavioral, psychosocial, cognitive, and health survey data from participants and their parents; a vast array of contextual data from participants' schools, neighborhoods, and geographies of residence; and in-home physical and biological data from participants, including genetic markers, blood-based assays, anthropometric measures, and medications. The Framingham Cohort Study is a population-based, observational cohort study that was initiated by the United States Public Health Service in 1948 to prospectively investigate the epidemiology and risk factors for cardiovascular disease [13, 14]. It is a longitudinal study gathering prospective data on a wide variety of biological and lifestyle risk factors and on cardiovascular, neurological and other types of disease outcomes across three generations of participants. The Study began in 1948–50 with the recruitment of the Original cohort (5,209 participants; 2,873 women, 2,336 men; age 28–62 years, mean age 45 years) comprising two-thirds of the adult population then residing in the town of Framingham, Massachusetts, USA, and since then it had been added new data such as the Offspring cohort [13].

3.2 Selecting Articles that Reused These Datasets

Results displayed in DCI have links to publications citing these datasets. Although these publications included journal articles, proceeding papers, reports, and theses, hereafter, we call them articles. We downloaded all bibliographic records of articles citing the Add Health dataset and the Framingham Cohort. We obtained 2,919 articles that reused the Add Health, and 2,153 articles that reused the Framingham Cohort.

3.3 Obtaining Publication's Research Fields

To examine the distribution of research fields among articles, it is necessary to obtain information on the research field of each article. WoS provides field categories for records indexed on the platform, however, records downloaded from DCI do not contain WoS fields. Therefore, we obtained field category information from another index. We obtained the Fields of Research (FoR) categories [15] of each article from Dimensions, using the articles' DOIs. Note that we downloaded only article's FoRs with DOIs, and some article records obtained from DCI did not have DOIs. We downloaded FoRs for 986 of 2,919 articles from Add Health and 1,844 of 2,153 articles from the Framingham Cohort for our analysis. The FoR consists of four-digit codes, with the first two digits used for labeling. Each category was counted when multiple categories were assigned to an article.

4   Result

In this section, we show results corresponding to RQ1 and RQ2.

4.1   Average Citation Counts of Articles Reusing Data

Records downloaded from DCI indicate the number of times an article reusing data is cited. We examined the maximum, minimum, average, and standard deviation of the citation counts. The 2,919 articles that reused the Add Health were cited an average of 23.3 times (maximum of 1,164, minimum of 0, and sample standard deviation of 66.9). In contrast, the 2,153 articles that reused the Framingham Cohort were cited an average of 214.8 times (maximum of 7,058, minimum of 0, and sample standard deviation of 435.2).

We sought to investigate whether articles that reuse datasets are more likely to be cited than articles that do not reuse datasets. Our purpose was to compare the citation count of all articles that reuse a dataset with those that do not reuse a dataset. However, this comparison is difficult because the citation counts of articles are affected by many factors, such as journal reputation and publication year. In this study, we first compared articles in the same journal and in the same publication year to identify whether or not articles that reuse datasets are more likely to be cited. We considered using the impact factor of the journal for each year instead of the number of citations. However, we could not obtain the impact factors for older years, for example from 2004. We compared the average number of citations for all articles with that of articles that reuse data in a particular publication year of a specific journal. In this paper, we report the average cited count for articles that reused the Framingham Cohort, and the average citation count for of all articles in the journal *Circulation*. We only examined data from 2004 to 2010 because 10 or more articles reused the Framingham Cohort in these years (Table 1). For example, the average number of citations of all 6,093 articles published in *Circulation* in 2004 was 34.5, while the 11 articles that reused the Framingham Cohort had an average number of citations of 435.5. The number of cited articles that reused the Framingham Cohort was higher than the overall number. We also tried this for Add Health; however, there was no publication year in which 10 or more articles were reused.

4.2   Distribution of Resources and Research Fields of Articles Reusing Data

We examined the number of resources, such as journals and proceedings, containing articles that reuse data. We found that the 2,919 articles that reused the Add Health were published in 1,702 different resources, and the 2,153 that reused the Framingham

Table 1. Averaged cited number of all articles and that of articles reusing the Framingham Cohort

Year	Overall		Framingham	
	N	Citation	N	Citation
2004	6,093	34.5	11	435.5
2005	6,278	28.0	14	259.7
2006	6,051	24.9	12	490.6
2007	5,677	26.2	13	362.1
2008	6,999	16.7	11	802.8
2009	5,395	21.4	15	235.4
2010	6,675	17.0	15	237.2

Cohort were published in 382 different resources. Tables 2 and 3 show the top five resources that published articles that reused each dataset, and the number of articles published. As shown in Table 2, 9.06% of the articles that reused the Framingham Cohort were published in *Circulation*, and all the top-five-ranked journals are in the medical science field. By contrast, only 1.91% of articles citing Add Health were published in the top-ranking journal, *Journal of Adolescent Health. Social Science Research*, which is published in a field different from healthcare science, was in fourth place. Articles that reused Add Health tended to be published in journals spanning different fields than articles that reused the Framingham cohort. In addition, articles reusing Add Health were published in multiple formats, including theses or dissertations. For example, 281 articles (9.6%) included with "THESIS" in the title.

Table 2. Top five resources containing articles that reused the Framingham Cohort

Ranking	Resource Name	#articles
1	Circulation	195 (9.06%)
2	American Journal of Cardiology	116 (5.39%)
3	American Heart Journal	79 (3.67%)
4	JAMA-Journal of the American Medical Association	72 (3.34%)
5	American Journal of Epidemiology	68 (3.16%)

We also examined the FoR of articles from Dimensions and treemaps of FoR are shown in Fig. 1. 986 articles reusing Add Health were distributed across 13 fields; most were from Human Society (29.6%) and Psychology (21.0%). Similarly, 1,844 articles that reused the Framingham Cohort were distributed across 12 fields, predominantly in the fields of Biomedical and Clinical Sciences (58.9%) and Health Sciences (30.3%).

Table 3. Top five resources containing articles reused Add Health

Ranking	Resource Name	#articles
1	Journal of Adolescent Health	56 (1.91%)
2	Journal of Youth and Adolescence	31 (1.06%)
3	Journal of Marriage and Family	29 (0.99%)
4	Social Science Research	28 (0.96%)
5	Perspectives on Sexual and Reproductive Health	25 (0.86%)

Similar to the pattern for the top-five resources shown in Tables 2 and 3, many articles that reused the Framingham Cohort were published in medical science fields. Whereas articles that reused Add Health were published in a great diversity of different fields.

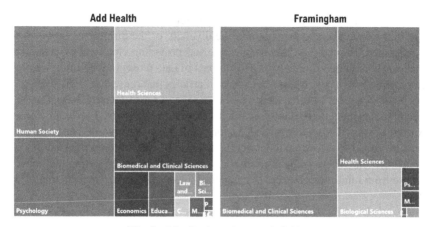

Fig. 1. Distribution of research fields

5 Discussion

We investigated the characteristics of articles that reused datasets. For articles reusing the Framingham Cohort, the average number of citations exceeded the overall average in a specific journal and period (RQ1), indicating the advantage of data reuse. Articles reusing the Add Health dataset were published in variety resources, indicating disciplinary diversity (RQ2).

We investigated whether articles that reuse datasets are more likely to be cited than articles that do not. The best approach to pursue such an analysis is to compare all articles that reused datasets and those did not reuse datasets, but this is difficult to design. In this paper, we pursued this investigation based on a specific journal and publication year. As shown in Sect. 4.1, articles that reused the Framingham Cohort dataset were cited more often than the overall average. Articles that reused Add Health could not be analyzed in the same way because there were only limited articles in a particular journal and year. The citation count of articles is affected by various factors such as the journal reputation and publication year. A method that can make more nuanced comparisons, therefore still is needed.

We investigated the diversity in the disciplines that published articles that reused datasets. The results indicated Add Health was used in a border range of research fields. We speculate that dataset may first be used in a related field and then later in other fields. For exploring that, it would be necessary to further analyze articles that reused Add Health, which has shown the potential to be extended to other fields. The Framingham Cohort, on the other hand, was used mainly in medical sciences. Therefore, we should also take into account the source fields of the datasets when we analyze disciplinary diversity.

6   Conclusion

In this study, we analyzed the advantages of data reuse in terms of the citation count of articles that reused specific datasets and the diversity of the disciplines in which they were published. Focusing on this perspective and providing empirical evidence could indicate a new direction for analyzing the impact of data reuse. In the future, we plan to develop methods to analyze a broader range of articles that reuse data. Furthermore, we plan to conduct a more detailed analysis of how articles reuse datasets. In this study, we regarded articles that cited datasets as articles that reused datasets. There can, however, be a variety of ways datasets are reused [8], for example, several datasets can be used, new data can be added to the original dataset, and datasets can be simply referred to, rather than reusing them. There is much room for further work on investigating the impact of data reuse from multiple perspectives can contribute to a deeper understanding of open science.

References

1. UNESCO, UNESCO Recommendation on Open Science. https://en.unesco.org/science-sustainable-future/open-science/recommendation. Accessed 20 Apr 2023
2. Tenopir, C., et al.: Data sharing, management, use, and reuse: practices and perceptions of scientists worldwide. PLoS ONE 15(3), e0229003 (2020). https://doi.org/10.1371/journal.pone.0229003
3. Pasquetto, I.V., Randles, B.M., Borgman, C.L.: On the reuse of scientific data. Data Sci. J. 16(8), 1–9 (2017)
4. Boté, J.J., Térmens, M.: Reusing data: technical and ethical challenges. DESIDOC J. Libr. Inf. Technol. 39(6), 329–337 (2019)
5. Piwowar, H.A., Vision, T.J.: Data reuse and the open data citation advantage. PeerJ 1, e175 (2013). https://doi.org/10.7717/peerj.175
6. Robinson-García, N., Jiménez-Contreras, E., Torres-Salinas, D.: Analyzing data citation practices using the data citation index. J. Am. Soc. Inf. Sci. 67(12), 2964–2975 (2016)
7. Yoon, J., Chung, E., Lee, J.Y., Kim, J.: How research data is cited in scholarly literature: a case study of HINTS. Learn. Publ. 32(3), 199–206 (2019)

8. Sakai, Y., Miyata, Y., Yokoi, K., Wang, Y., Kurata, K.: Initial insight into three modes of data sharing: Prevalence of primary reuse, data integration and dataset release in research articles. Learned Publishing. Early View. https://doi.org/10.1002/leap.1546
9. Curty, R.G., Crowston, K., Specht, A., Grant, B.W., Dalton, E.D.: Attitudes and norms affecting scientists' data reuse. PLoS ONE **12**(12), 1–22 (2017)
10. Winkler, C.E., Berenbon, R.F.: Validation of a survey for measuring scientists' attitudes toward data reuse. J. Am. Soc. Inf. Sci. **72**(4), 449–453 (2012)
11. Kim, Y.: A sequential route of data and document qualities, satisfaction and motivations on researchers' data reuse intentions. J. Doc. **78**(3), 709–727 (2022). https://doi.org/10.1108/JD-02-2021-0044
12. Add Health: The National Longitudinal Study of Adolescent to Adult Health. https://en.unesco.org/science-sustainable-future/open-science/recommendation. Accessed 20 June 2023
13. Framingham Heart Study: About the Framingham Heart Study. https://www.framinghamheartstudy.org/fhs-about/. Accessed 23 Sep 2023
14. Boston Medical Center: Framingham Study. https://www.bmc.org/stroke-and-cerebrovascular-center/research/framingham-study. Accessed 20 June 2023
15. Australian Bureau of Statistics. (2020). Australian and New Zealand Standard Research Classification (ANZSRC). Retrieved from https://www.abs.gov.au/statistics/classifications/australian-and-new-zealand-standard-research-classification-anzsrc/latest-release

Scholarly Knowledge Graph Construction from Published Software Packages

Muhammad Haris[1]([✉])(iD), Sören Auer[1,2](iD), and Markus Stocker[1,2](iD)

[1] L3S Research Center, Leibniz University Hannover, 30167 Hannover, Germany
haris@l3s.de, {auer,markus.stocker}@tib.eu
[2] TIB—Leibniz Information Centre for Science and Technology, Hannover, Germany

Abstract. The value of structured scholarly knowledge for research and society at large is well understood, but producing scholarly knowledge (i.e., knowledge traditionally published in articles) in structured form remains a challenge. We propose an approach for automatically extracting scholarly knowledge from published software packages by static analysis of their metadata and contents (scripts and data) and populating a scholarly knowledge graph with the extracted knowledge. Our approach is based on mining scientific software packages linked to article publications by extracting metadata and analyzing the Abstract Syntax Tree (AST) of the source code to obtain information about the used and produced data as well as operations performed on data. The resulting knowledge graph includes articles, software packages metadata, and computational techniques applied to input data utilized as materials in research work. The knowledge graph also includes the results reported as scholarly knowledge in articles. Our code is available on GitHub at the following link: https://github.com/mharis111/parse-software-scripts.

Keywords: Analyzing Software Packages · Code Analysis · Abstract Syntax Tree · Open Research Knowledge Graph · Scholarly Communication · Machine Actionability

1 Introduction

Scholarly artefacts (articles, datasets, software, etc.) are proliferating rapidly in diverse data formats on numerous repositories [3]. The inadequate machine support in data processing motivates the need to extract essential scholarly knowledge published via these artefacts and represent extracted knowledge in structured form. This enables building databases that power advanced services for scholarly knowledge discovery and reuse.

We propose an approach for populating a scholarly knowledge graph (specifically, the Open Research Knowledge Graph) with structured scholarly knowledge automatically extracted from software packages. The main purpose of the knowledge graph is to capture information about the materials and methods used in scholarly work described in research articles. Of particular interest is information about the operations performed on data, which we propose to extract by static code analysis using Abstract Syntax Tree (AST) representations of program code, as well as recomputing the scientific results mentioned in linked articles. We thus address the following research questions:

1. How can we reliably distinguish scholarly knowledge from other information?
2. How can we reliably determine and describe the (computational) activities relevant to some research work as well as data input and output in activities?

Our contribution is an approach—and its implementation in a production research infrastructure—for automated, structured scholarly knowledge extraction from software packages.

2   Related Work

Several approaches have been suggested to retrieve meta(data) from software repositories. Mao et al. [10] proposed the Software Metadata Extraction Framework (SOMEF) which utilizes natural language processing techniques to extract metadata information from software packages. The framework extracts repository name, software description, citations, reference URLs, etc. from README files and represent the metadata in structured format. SOMEF was later extended to extract additional metadata and auxiliary files (e.g., Notebooks, Dockerfiles) from software packages [6]. Moreover, the extended work also supports creating a knowledge graph of parsed metadata. Abdelaziz et al. [1] proposed CodeBreaker, a knowledge graph which contains information about more than a million Python scripts published on GitHub. The knowledge graph was integrated in an IDE to recommend code functions while writing software.

A number of machine learning-based approaches for searching [4] and summarizing [2,5] software scripts have been proposed. The Pydriller [12] and Git-Python frameworks were proposed to mine information from GitHub repositories, including source code, commits, etc. Similarly, ModelMine [11] was presented to extract and analyze models from software repositories. The tool is useful in extracting models from several repositories, thus improves software development. Vagavolu et al. [13] presented an approach that generates multiple representations (Code2vec [7], semantic graphs with Abstract Syntax Tree (AST) of source code to capture all the relevant information needed for software engineering tasks.

3   Methodology

We now describe our proposed methodology for extracting scholarly knowledge from software packages and generating a knowledge graph from the extracted meta(data). Figure 1 provides an overview of the key components. We present the implementation for each of the steps of the methodology using a running example involving the article by Mancini et al. [8] and related published software package [9].

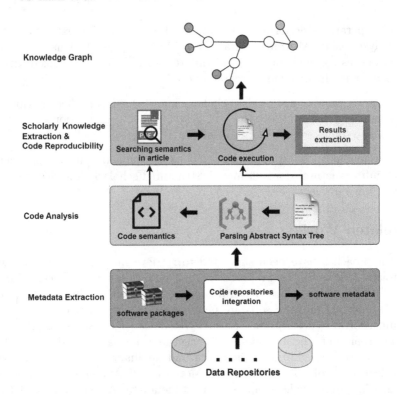

Fig. 1. Pipeline for constructing a knowledge graph of scholarly knowledge extracted from software packages: 1) Mining software packages from data repositories using APIs; 2) Extracting software metadata by analyzing the APIs results; 3) Performing static code analysis using AST representations of software to extract code semantics; 4) Constrain code semantics to scholarly knowledge by matching the extracted information with article full text; 5) Recomputing the scientific results described in articles, by executing the scripts containing scholarly knowledge; 6) Knowledge graph construction with scholarly knowledge extracted from software packages.

3.1   Mining Software Packages

We extract software packages from the Zenodo and figshare repositories by utilizing their REST APIs. The metadata of each software package is analyzed to retrieve its DOI and other associated information, specifically linked scholarly articles. Moreover, we use the Software Metadata Extraction Framework (SOMEF) to extract additional metadata from software packages, such as the software description, programming languages, and related references. Since not all software packages relate to scholarly articles explicitly in metadata, we also use SOMEF to parse the README files of software packages as an additional method to extract the DOI of linked scholarly articles.

```
1   df = pd.read_csv('../data/fmri_behavioural_new.csv') ⟶
2   dfna = df.dropna(subset=['obs_p1g2', 'obs_p2g1'])
3   dfna.head()                                                    Input dataset
4   dfm1 = dfna[['gen_p1g2', 'obs_p1g2','subject']]
5   dfm11 = dfm1.groupby(['subject'])
6
7   stats.pearsonr(dfm11['Generative p(L|H)'],dfm11['Rated p(L|H)'])
8   dfm2 = dfna[['gen_p2g1', 'obs_p2g1', 'subject']]
9   dfm22_r = dfm2.groupby('subject')
10  dfm_sj = pd.DataFrame({'P(H|H)': dfm11_r, 'P(H|L)': dfm22_r})
11  stats.ttest_1samp(dfm_sj, 0)
```

Fig. 2. Static code analysis: Exemplary Python script (shortened) included in a software package. The script lines highlighted with same color show different procedural changes that a particular variable has undergone.

3.2 Static Code Analysis

We utilize Abstract Syntax Tree (AST) representations for static analysis of Python scripts and Jupyter Notebooks included in software packages. Our developed Python-based module sequentially reads the scripts contained in software packages and generates the AST. The implemented methods and variables are represented as nodes in the tree, which facilitates the analysis of the code flow. Figure 2 shows the Python script included in the software package [9]. The script illustrates an example in which the `fmri_behavioural_new.csv` data is loaded and two statistical hypothesis tests (`pearsonr` and `t-test`) are conducted on this data, respectively. Figure 3 shows the AST of the Python script (Fig. 2) created using a suitable Python library. For simplicity, we show the AST of lines 1 and 11. We investigate the flow of variables that contain the input data, i.e., examining which operations used a particular variable as a parameter. With this analysis, we retrieve the series of operations performed on a particular variable. From our example, we conclude that `dropna`, `head`, `groupby`, `pearsonr` and `ttest_ind` operations are executed on `fmri_behavioural_new.csv` data.

3.3 Identifying Scholarly Knowledge

The information extracted via AST analysis of source code is not necessarily scholarly knowledge. In this work, scholarly knowledge is information expressed in scholarly articles. Hence, in this step we constrain the information obtained in the previous step to information mentioned in the articles linked to the analyzed software packages. We use the Unpaywall REST API[1] to retrieve the document in PDF format. To identify the scholarly knowledge, we calculate the semantic similarity between code semantics and article sentences by employing a pretrained BERT-based model to constrain words as scholarly knowledge that are

---

[1] https://api.unpaywall.org/v2/10.1101/2021.10.21.465270?email=unpaywall_01@example.com.

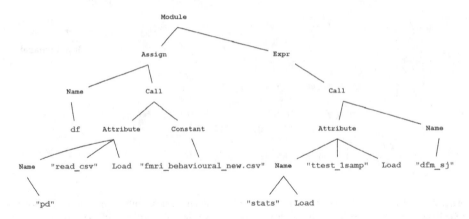

Fig. 3. Abstract Syntax Tree (AST) of the script shown in Fig. 2. For simplicity, the AST is shown only for lines 1 and 11. The child nodes of the Module node represent the operations that are performed in the respective lines of the script.

semantically similar. First, we extract the text from PDF and remove stop words. Second, we arrange the sentences in bigrams and trigrams, because computing the similarity using a sentence-based corpus could lead to inefficient search. Next, we generate embeddings of keywords extracted from article text and software packages and use cosine-similarity to find words with similar meaning. From our example (Fig. 2), the extracted terms are searched in the article and we find that `fmri`, `pearsonr` and `t test` are mentioned in the linked article (Fig. 4(a, b)). Given the match, we assume that the extracted information is scholarly knowledge.

3.4   Recompute the Research Results

For identified scholarly knowledge, we assume that the outputs of operations on data is information included in articles, and not necessarily stored as a separate dataset. In our running example, the output is a p-value and as we can see in Fig. 2, the output is merely printed to the console and presumably manually copied (and pasted into the article text). To enable rich descriptions of scholarly knowledge, we recompute the procedure outputs by executing the scripts that produce scholarly knowledge. For this, we develop a separate program to check the automatic execution of the code under consideration. If the code is not automatically executable then we introduce a human-in-the-loop step to execute the code. As different software packages may have been developed using varying versions of libraries, it is required to create a new virtual environment to execute scripts from the same package and prevent any conflicts between libraries. It is also necessary to check if the set of libraries required to execute the script are installed. If the libraries are not installed, we identify the required libraries using AST representations, and automatically install them in the virtual environment to execute the code under consideration. After successfully recomputing the code output, we assume that the computed outputs are correct and mentioned in the linked article. For our running example, we observed that the t-test returns a p-value (0.00088388), which is indeed mentioned in the paper (Fig. 4(c)).

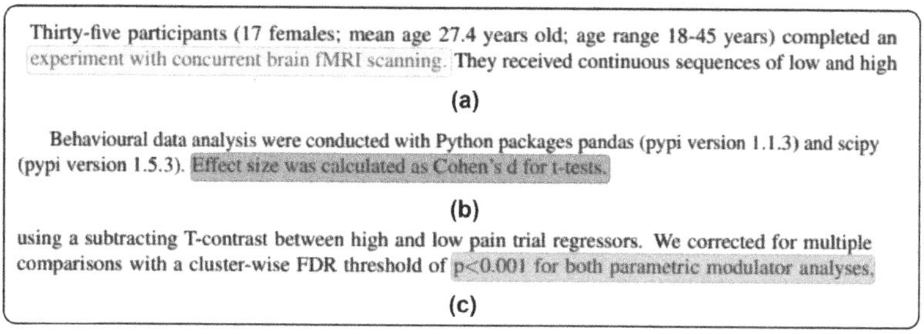

Thirty-five participants (17 females; mean age 27.4 years old; age range 18-45 years) completed an experiment with concurrent brain fMRI scanning. They received continuous sequences of low and high

(a)

Behavioural data analysis were conducted with Python packages pandas (pypi version 1.1.3) and scipy (pypi version 1.5.3). Effect size was calculated as Cohen's d for t-tests.

(b)

using a subtracting T-contrast between high and low pain trial regressors. We corrected for multiple comparisons with a cluster-wise FDR threshold of p<0.001 for both parametric modulator analyses.

(c)

Fig. 4. Snippets taken from the article (a) shows the name of the input dataset (b) & (c) shows the statistical analysis (t-test) and the produced value $p < 0.001$, respectively.

3.5 Knowledge Graph Construction

Given the extracted scholarly knowledge, we now construct the knowledge graph or, in our case, populate an the Open Research Knowledge Graph (ORKG). First the meta(data) is converted into triples that are ingested into ORKG using its REST API. This conversion is guided by ORKG templates[2], which specify the structure of information types, their properties and value ranges. Hence, templates standardize ORKG content and ensure comparable semantics. To link the extracted scholarly knowledge with templates, we search for templates by operation name. The matching template is then utilized to produce ORKG-compliant data that can be ingested. For our running example (Fig. 2), we look for an ORKG template by searching "t-test" in the ORKG interface. We obtain a reference to the ORKG Student t-test template[3], which specifies three properties, namely: has specified input, has specified output and has dependent variable. This template guides us in producing ORKG-compliant data for the scholarly knowledge extracted in the previous steps. Figure 5 shows the description of the paper in our running example in ORKG[4]. The metadata of the corresponding software package[5] can also be viewed in ORKG.

4   Validation

Since we have employed AST to extract scholarly knowledge from software packages, it is essential to demonstrate that the proposed approach reliably produces

---

[2] https://orkg.org/templates.

[3] https://orkg.org/template/R12002.

[4] https://orkg.org/paper/R601243, where readers can view the data also as a graph.

[5] https://orkg.org/content-type/Software/R601252.

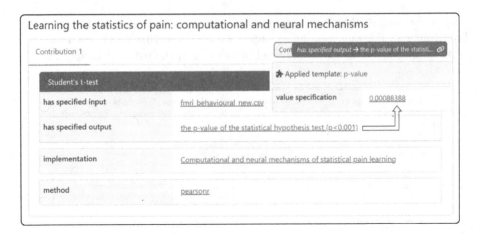

Fig. 5. ORKG Paper showing the scholarly knowledge extracted from a software package, describing key aspects (e.g., statistical method used, its input and output data) of a research contribution of the work described in the article.

the desired results. For this purpose, we compare the AST-based results with ground truth data extracted manually from software packages. To prepare the ground truth data, we have developed a Python script that iteratively reads software packages and scans each script to lookup all possible functions that load datasets (i.e., read_csv, loadtxt, genfromtxt, read_json, open). All scripts containing these functions are manually annotated for input data, operations performed on data, and output data, if any. To identify scholarly knowledge, the extracted information was searched in the full text of linked scholarly articles. Then, the manually extracted results were compared with the AST-based extracted results. The algorithmic performance is assessed using the Index of Agreement (IA) [14], a standardized measure to examine the potential agreement between results obtained using two different approaches. Its value varies between 0 and 1, indicating the potential error between the observed and predicted results. In total, we analyze 40 software packages and obtain an overall IA of 0.74. This result suggest an acceptable reliability of the proposed approach.

5   Results and Discussion

At the time of writing, more than 115,000 software packages are available on Zenodo and figshare, collectively. To expedite the execution, we consider packages of size up to 2 GB, i.e., 91,258 software packages. We analyze package metadata and the respective README files using SOMEF and find a total of 10,584 linked research articles. Our analysis focuses on Python-based software packages, of which there are 31,992. Among these, there are 5,239 Python-based implementations that are linked to 5,545 articles. We also observe that some software packages are linked to multiple articles. Table 1 summarizes the statistics. To delve further into the structural and semantic aspects of these packages, we applied the AST-based approach and discovered that 8,618 software scripts (in 1,405 software packages) contain information about input datasets and methods executed on these datasets, and, if applicable, output datasets. A total of 2,049 papers are linked to these packages. As the Open Research Knowledge Graph (ORKG) is designed purely for the publication of scholarly knowledge, we search the extracted knowledge in the full text of the linked articles (as explained in Sect. 3.3) to identify scholarly knowledge. This step requires access to the full text of linked articles, and we found that out of 2,049 articles, 665 articles are closed access. Consequently, knowledge derived from packages linked to closed-access articles cannot be constrained as scholarly knowledge. Hence, we analyze the remaining 740 packages to obtain the scholarly knowledge. We describe the metadata of 91,258 software packages and 10,941 papers in ORKG. Out of total articles, 174 articles contain rich contributions i.e., information about datasets and operations performed on these datasets. The proposed AST-based approach is an alternative route to automatically produce structured scholarly knowledge. We suggest the extraction of scholarly knowledge from software packages, and our approach addresses the limitations of NLP-based approaches.

Table 1. Statistics about the (scholarly) information extracted from software packages and added to ORKG as software descriptions, papers and their research contribution descriptions.

Entity	Total
Total software packages	115,000
Software packages of size < 2 GB	91,258 (Zenodo: 87,423; figshare: 3,835)
Python-based software packages	31,992
Software packages linked with articles	10,941, articles: 10,584
Python software packages, linked with articles	5,329, articles: 5,545
Packages containing information about datasets	1,405
Packages containing scholarly knowledge	135, (articles: 174)

6   Conclusions

We have presented a novel approach to structured scholarly knowledge production by extraction from published software packages. Based on the encouraging results, we suggest that the approach is an important contribution towards automated and scalable production of *rich* structured scholarly knowledge accessible via a scholarly knowledge graph and efficiently reusable in services supporting data science. The richness is reflected by the fact that the resulting scholarly knowledge graph holds the links between articles, data and software at the granularity of individual computational activities as well as comprehensive descriptions of the computational methods and materials used and produced in research work presented in articles.

Acknowledgment. This work was co-funded by the European Research Council for the project ScienceGRAPH (Grant agreement ID: 819536) and TIB–Leibniz Information Centre for Science and Technology.

References

1. Abdelaziz, I., Srinivas, K., Dolby, J., McCusker, J.P.: A demonstration of codebreaker: a machine interpretable knowledge graph for code. In: SEMWEB (2020)
2. Ahmad, W., Chakraborty, S., Ray, B., Chang, K.W.: A transformer-based approach for source code summarization. In: Proceedings of the 58th Annual Meeting of the Association for Computational Linguistics, pp. 4998–5007. Association for Computational Linguistics (2020). https://doi.org/10.18653/v1/2020.acl-main.449
3. Hendler, J.: Data integration for heterogenous datasets. Big Data **2**, 205–215 (2014). https://doi.org/10.1089/big.2014.0068
4. Husain, H., Wu, H.H., Gazit, T., Allamanis, M., Brockschmidt, M.: Codesearchnet challenge: evaluating the state of semantic code search (2020). https://www.microsoft.com/en-us/research/publication/codesearchnet-challenge-evaluating-the-state-of-semantic-code-search/
5. Iyer, S., Konstas, I., Cheung, A., Zettlemoyer, L.: Summarizing source code using a neural attention model. In: Proceedings of the 54th Annual Meeting of the Association for Computational Linguistics (Volume 1: Long Papers), pp. 2073–2083. Association for Computational Linguistics (2016). https://doi.org/10.18653/v1/P16-1195
6. Kelley, A., Garijo, D.: A framework for creating knowledge graphs of scientific software metadata. Quant. Sci. Stud. **2**(4), 1423–1446 (2021). https://doi.org/10.1162/qss_a_00167
7. Le, Q., Mikolov, T.: Distributed representations of sentences and documents. In: International Conference on Machine Learning, pp. 1188–1196. PMLR (2014)
8. Mancini, F., Zhang, S., Seymour, B.: Learning the statistics of pain: computational and neural mechanisms. BioRxiv 2021–10 (2021)
9. Mancini, F., Zhang, S., Seymour, B.: Computational and neural mechanisms of statistical pain learning (2022). https://doi.org/10.5281/zenodo.6997897
10. Mao, A., Garijo, D., Fakhraei, S.: SoMEF: a framework for capturing scientific software metadata from its documentation. In: 2019 IEEE International Conference on Big Data (Big Data), pp. 3032–3037 (2019). https://doi.org/10.1109/BigData47090.2019.9006447
11. Reza, S.M., Badreddin, O., Rahad, K.: ModelMine: a tool to facilitate mining models from open source repositories. In: Association for Computing Machinery, New York, NY, USA (2020). https://doi.org/10.1145/3417990.3422006
12. Spadini, D., Aniche, M., Bacchelli, A.: Pydriller: Python framework for mining software repositories. ESEC/FSE 2018, New York, NY, USA, pp. 908–911. Association for Computing Machinery (2018). https://doi.org/10.1145/3236024.3264598

13. Vagavolu, D., Swarna, K.C., Chimalakonda, S.: A mocktail of source code representations. In: 2021 36th IEEE/ACM International Conference on Automated Software Engineering (ASE), pp. 1296–1300 (2021). https://doi.org/10.1109/ASE51524.2021.9678551
14. Willmott, C.J.: On the validation of models. Phys. Geography **2**(2), 184–194 (1981). https://doi.org/10.1080/02723646.1981.10642213

Leveraging MRC Framework for Research Contribution Patterns Identification in Citation Sentences

Yang Zhao[1,2] , Zhixiong Zhang[1,2(✉)] , and Yue Xiao[3]

[1] National Science Library, Chinese Academy of Science, No. 33, Beisihuan Xilu, Beijing, China
zhangzhx@mail.las.ac.cn

[2] Department of Information Resources Management, School of Economics and Management, University of Chinese Academy of Sciences, No. 33 Beisihuan Xilu, Beijing, China

[3] School of Information Resource Management, Renmin University of China, No. 59, Zhongguancun Street, Haidian District, Beijing, China

Abstract. Research contributions convey the essence of academic papers, highlighting their novel knowledge and understanding compared to prior research. In this study, we address the challenge of identifying research contribution patterns from citation sentences by leveraging a Machine Reading Comprehension (MRC) framework. The MRC approach formulates the extraction of contribution patterns as a question-answering task, utilizing natural language queries to extract contribution patterns (CONTRIBUTION, INFLUENCE, and FIELD) from the context.

Our method outperforms the SOTA NER approach in 2022: W^2NER, achieving significant performance improvements of +23.76% and +31.92% in F1 scores for label and entity recognition, respectively. In addition, through manual validation and comparison with ChatGPT annotation results, we demonstrate that the accuracy of our approach is 21.65% higher in identifying research contribution patterns. Moreover, the MRC framework handles nested entities and resolves reference disambiguation more accurately, providing a robust solution for complex citation sentences.

Overall, our work presents an advanced approach for identifying research contribution patterns from citation sentences, showcasing its potential to enhance information retrieval and understanding within the scientific community.

Keywords: Research Contribution · MRC Framework · Contribution Pattern · Citation Sentence

1 Introduction

Research contributions, which indicate how a research paper contributes new knowledge or new understanding compared to previous research on the topic, are the most useful sort of information for researchers to comprehend the paper's primary substance [1]. Research contributions are often expressed in an academic paper's abstract, introduction,

© The Author(s), under exclusive license to Springer Nature Singapore Pte Ltd. 2023
D. H. Goh et al. (Eds.): ICADL 2023, LNCS 14458, pp. 180–193, 2023.
https://doi.org/10.1007/978-981-99-8088-8_16

or conclusion, and may also be scattered across various sections. We have explored identifying research contributions from the perspective of external citation context in our related study [2], which solves the problem of subjectivity from the author's point of view to convey the main idea of the article. Additionally, we conducted a case study to analyze the applications based on the identified contribution citation sentences. As a matter of fact, there is still a wealth of semantic knowledge embedded in contribution sentences that require further decomposition and extraction. For instance, researchers might be interested in specific contribution points, the influence of these points, the field to which they belong, and the diffusion of these contributions across various fields. These detailed contribution elements can be continuously derived from the citation content that references the paper on contribution.

To facilitate the study of application domains, scientific article focuses within a community, and the influence of article contributions, we propose extracting the following concepts from contribution sentences.

CONTRIBUTION: an article's main focus from the perspective of external evaluation.

INFLUENCE: the impact (basically positive) of the acceptable contribution in an article.

FIELD: an article's research domain.

That is to say, from a peer's perspective, what is the research work of an article, what specific domain does it contribute to, and how well is it done? For example, we identify a contribution sentence *"The identification and cloning of TRPV1 was a major landmark in stimulating a new area of research in the field of pain [11]"*, then the article [11]'s CONTRIBUTION is *the identification and cloning of TRPV1*, its INFLUENCE is *a major landmark in stimulating a new area of research in the field of pain,* and its FIELD is *in the field of pain.* Typically, we employ named entity recognition (NER) methods to identify specific patterns in contribution sentences. To be specific, the patterns to be recognized are treated as entities or phrases, then we assign BIO labels to these patterns by means of sequence labeling. A contribution pattern recognition model is then trained for extracting contribution patterns once a sufficient volume of annotated data is available. Nevertheless, there are some special characteristics in citation sentences that are different from ordinary text, that is, the citation sentence will be with a variety of citation markers, such as *"[11]", "(11)", "et al." and "person + year"*, and these citation markers are also important to help readers identify the specific citation of which article. It is difficult to identify the contribution pattern of each reference only using the NER method, this is especially true when the sentence cites several references one after another and describes the contribution of each article in turn.

Inspired by the trend of formalizing NLP problems as question-answering tasks [3–5], instead of treating the task of NER as a sequence labeling problem, our work proposes to formulate the above three category phrases extraction as a SQuAD-style [6, 7] machine reading comprehension (MRC) task (see Fig. 1 for examples). Each entity type is characterized by a natural language query, and entities are extracted by answering these queries given the contexts. For example, the task of assigning the CONTRIBUTION label to *"A new horizon in pain research was realized in 1997 when Julius and colleagues [25] identified the specific receptor responding to the hot chilli pepper active ingredient, capsaicin, in subsets of nociceptors.*" is formalized as answering the question "*What is [25] or Julius and colleagues' scientific contribution?*". This strategy naturally encodes significant prior information about the entity category to extract, which makes the MRC model the potential to disambiguate similar citation tagging classes. In addition, this framework is capable of handling both flat and nested NER [8], especially addressing the occurrence of INFLUENCE category phrases overriding FIELD category phrases, which is common in our tasks.

Based on this, we propose to leverage the MRC framework for research contribution patterns identification in citation sentences (refers specifically to the contribution sentence). This framework establishes a natural link between the question and the answer through citation markers, leading to more accurate pattern extraction. It provides a reliable solution to the problem of reference disambiguation in citation sentences and effectively handles the issue of nested entities that may arise in the NER approach.

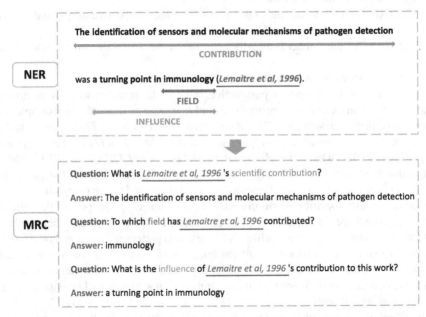

Fig. 1. Example of contribution pattern recognition based on NER vs. MRC

2   Related Work

Analysis and identification of research contributions is a novel field that has lately gained attraction. We have grouped it into two implementation paths, one of which is based on peer review, where scholars in the relevant area conduct an in-depth examination and summary of a particular paper's research contribution. For example, the Nobel Prize is judged and awarded annually by the Nobel Committee in the respective field, and the laureate's contribution to the field is summarized in the press release[1]. The other strategy

---

[1] https://www.nobelprize.org/prizes/medicine/2021/press-release/.

is to mechanically extract components or phrases of innovative contribution by using a variety of methods, these studies focus mostly on signature features that emerge in the literature. Gupta S et al. [9] present a method for characterizing a research work in terms of its focus, domain of application, and techniques used. Then they extract these characteristics by matching semantic extraction patterns, learned using bootstrapping, to the dependency trees of sentences in an article's abstract. Chen [10] extracted N-grams that reflected the innovative ideas from the abstracts of technology and engineering papers, verified the degree of innovation and searched for their existence in the Scopus database. Le et al. [11] proposed CiteOpinion, which automatically extract the main academic contribution points by means of Recognizing Categories of Moves (problems, methods, conclusions, etc.). Ferrod R et al. [12] proposed CiTelling system to capture and classify citation intent by building a fine-grained semantic representation of citations.

As for the studies of key element recognition in citation sentences, most works are still at the stage of identifying the function of citation sentences, such as citation sentiment recognition, citation intention recognition, citation content generation, and automatic citation summarization. Yousif et al. [13] performed a hybrid neural model to classify the sentiments contained in citations and achieved good results. Cohan et al. [14] propose structural scaffolds, a multitask model to incorporate structural information of scientific papers into citations for effective classification of citation intents (background information, use of methods, comparing results). In addition to textual clues present in the citation phrase, Berrebbi D et al. [15] consider the citation graph, leveraging high-level information of citation patterns, they perform a thorough experimental evaluation of graph-based models for intent prediction. Xing et al. [16] propose and train a multi-source pointer-generator network with a cross-attention mechanism for citation text generation, which aims to generate a short text to describe the cited paper B in the given context of the citing paper A. In contrast, Wu et al. [17] focus on generating multiple citations, they first build a novel generation model with the Fusion-in-Decoder approach to cope with multiple long inputs and then incorporate the predicted citation intents into training for intent control. Lahiri et al. [18] present a tool CitePrompt which uses the hitherto unexplored approach of prompt learning for citation intent classification, they get better results than previous studies with the proper choice of the pre-trained language model, the prompt template, and the prompt verbalizer. In general, the majority of investigations have been done on citation content mining by the information extraction method. By contrast, the method presented in this study tries to identify contribution patterns in the citation content from the perspective of reading comprehension, which for more precise positioning of references and better extraction.

3 Method

In this section, we explain how to extract contribution pattern phrases for each of the three categories (CONTRIBUTION, FIELD, and INFLUENCE) from contribution sentences based on the MRC framework [8].

3.1   Task Formalization

MRC models have a primary goal: to extract answer spans from a given passage, guided by a provided question. This task can be precisely defined as two multi-class classification assignments, specifically predicting the starting and ending positions of the answer spans. Consider an input sequence $X = \{x_1, x_2, ..., x_n\}$, where n signifies the sequence's length, our objective is to identify and label every phrase in X with one of three predefined tags: CONTRIBUTION, INFLUENCE, or FIELD. For each tag type y, it is associated with a natural language question $q_y = \{q_1, q_2, ..., q_m\}$, where m is the length of the query. Annotated contribution patterns expressed as $x_{start,end} = \{x_{start}, x_{start+1}, ..., x_{end-1}, x_{end}\}$ represent substrings within X that satisfy the condition 'start $\leq$ end'. Each phrase is associated with a golden label $y \in Y$. Through the generation of a natural language question q_y based on the label y, we systematically derive the triple $(q_y, x_{start,end}, X)$, which embodies the essential (QUESTION, ANSWER, CONTEXT) components that form the foundation of our task.

3.2   Model Details

To extract the text span $x_{start,end}$ of type y from X using the MRC framework, we utilize BERT [19] as our base model. In line with BERT's prerequisites, we concatenate the question q_y and the content X, resulting in the combined string $\{[CLS], q_1, q_2, ..., q_m, [SEP], x_1, x_2, ..., x_n\}$, where $[CLS]$ and $[SEP]$ are special tokens. BERT processes this combined string and outputs a context representation matrix $E \in \mathbb{R}^{n \times d}$, where d is the vector dimension of the final layer of BERT and we exclude the query representations.

We adopt the strategy for span selection for MRC, involving two binary classifiers, one to predict whether each token is the start index and the other to predict whether each token is the end index. This strategy allows us to output multiple start indexes and end indexes for a given context and a specific query, enabling the extraction of all related contribution patterns according to q_y.

Start and End Index Prediction. For the prediction of start and end indexes, given the representation matrix E from BERT, our model initially calculates the probability of each token being a start index as follows:

$$P_{start} = softmax_{each\ row}(E \cdot T_{start}) \in \mathbb{R}^{n \times 2} \tag{1}$$

Here, $T_{start} \in \mathbb{R}^{n \times 2}$ represents the learnable weights. Each row of P_{start} presents the probability distribution of each index being the starting position of a contribution pattern, given the query. The procedure for predicting the end index is analogous, except that we utilize another matrix T_{end} to obtain the probability matrix $P_{end} \in \mathbb{R}^{n \times 2}$.

Start-End Matching. In the context X, there may be multiple patterns of the same category, leading to multiple predicted start and end indexes. As these patterns could overlap, the common heuristic of matching the start index with its nearest end index becomes inadequate. Thus, the MRC model employs a method to match a predicted start index with its corresponding end index.

This matching process involves applying argmax to each row of P_{start} and P_{end}, resulting in the predicted indexes that could potentially serve as the starting or ending positions, i.e., $\hat{I}_{start}$ and $\hat{I}_{end}$:

$$\hat{I}_{start} = \{i | argmax\left(P_{start}^{(i)}\right) = 1, i = 1, \ldots, n\}$$
$$\hat{I}_{end} = \{j | argmax\left(P_{end}^{(j)}\right) = 1, i = 1, \ldots, n\} \tag{2}$$

where the superscript $^{(i)}$ denote the i-th row of a matrix. Given any start index $i_{start} \in \hat{I}_{start}$ and end index $i_{end} \in \hat{I}_{end}$, we train a binary classification model to predict the probability of them being matched:

$$P_{i_{start},j_{end}} = sigmoid\left(m \cdot concat\left(E_{i_{start}}, E_{j_{end}}\right)\right) \tag{3}$$

where $m \in \mathbb{R}^{1 \times 2d}$ represents the learnable weights.

Train and Test. During training, we pair X two label sequences Y_{start} and Y_{end} of length n representing the ground-truth label of each token x_i being the start index or end index of any pattern. We calculate two losses for start and end index predictions:

$$\mathcal{L}_{start} = CE(P_{start}, Y_{start}) \tag{4}$$

$$\mathcal{L}_{end} = CE(P_{end}, Y_{end}) \tag{5}$$

Additionally, $Y_{start,end}$ denotes the golden labels for whether each start index should be matched with each end index, where CE represents the Cross Entropy loss function. The start-end index matching loss is given as follows:

$$\mathcal{L}_{span} = CE\left(P_{start,end}, Y_{start,end}\right) \tag{6}$$

The overall training objective to be minimized is expressed as:

$$\mathcal{L} = \alpha \mathcal{L}_{start} + \beta \mathcal{L}_{end} + \gamma \mathcal{L}_{span} \tag{7}$$

$\alpha, \beta, \gamma \in [0, 1]$ are hyper-parameters governing the contributions towards the overall training objective. The three losses are jointly trained in an end-to-end fashion, with parameters shared at the BERT layer. During testing, start and end indexes are first selected separately based on $\hat{I}_{start}$ and $\hat{I}_{end}$. Then, the index matching model is used to align the extracted start indexes with the corresponding end indexes, culminating in the final extracted answers.

3.3 Dataset Construction

Since there is not yet publicly available data that can be used for our contribution pattern recognition, we need to manually construct the training dataset. In our previous related study [2], we constructed a contribution sentence dataset, and now our work is to further annotate the contribution patterns based on these contribution sentences. To be specific, we have used papers that cite the Nobel Prize in Physiology or Medicine publications, which contain rich descriptive content regarding contributions. After that, we develop a procedure to annotate the contribution patterns in each contributing sentence in turn, which could transfer the annotated data into a formal SQuAD style that matches to MRC framework. The procedure requires annotators to point out which reference the contribution belongs to, then the procedure will automatically generate a question related to the reference, and the annotator needs to draw out the corresponding answer in the original text, simultaneously, the system will automatically locate the starting position of the answer span. We list several examples in Table 1.

The formulation of questions is crucial, as they encode prior knowledge about labels and significantly influence the final results. In order to enhance the robustness of the contribution pattern identification model, it is essential to diversify the question format. We, therefore, leverage ChatGPT to help us expand question templates. We initially write a seed question for each of the three categories of patterns, and then draw support from ChatGPT to expand them into 20 identical questions of different sentence patterns each. These questions are then randomly chosen one category at a time, and the training set of questions and answers is recorded as one piece of training data. It should be noted that the citation mark in the question must be consistent with the context, for example, if the citation mark is "[6,7,8]" in the context, we must write it in the same way with the question, rather than "[6–8]", neither "[6], [7], [8]" and so on. As if we modify the formality of the citation mark, its token would be different from the ordinary mark, which leads to interference in the learning of relevant features by the model.

According to statistics, we have annotated 2,965 pairs of Q&A, which derive from 1,057 contribution sentences. It includes 2,753 items in the training set and 212 items in the test set. To ensure the reliability of annotation, we assign two annotators to perform back-to-back annotating work. Since the difficulty of annotating is not complicated after decomposing the contributions into contribution patterns, the annotators could achieve a high level of annotating agreement after training.

3.4 Experimental Setup

In order to validate the superiority of our proposed method that leveraging the MRC framework for research contribution patterns identification in citation sentences, we compare the recognition results with NER. We evaluate the recognition results using common metrics such as precision, recall, and F1-score. As for the NER comparison, we utilize the W^2NER [20] method, which presents a novel alternative by modeling the unified NER as word-word relation classification, and it has achieved the state-of-the-art level at the NER task in 2022. In addition, this approach can also solve the problems among flat, nested, and discontinuous NER, which adapt well to our task.

However, due to the complexity of reading comprehension tasks, relying solely on F1-value for evaluation may not be sufficient. We need to judge the predicted answer by understanding the core general idea of the passage. Thus, in addition to the regular evaluation metrics, we also perform manual validation. We manually proofread 212 pieces of data from the test set to analyze the consistency between predicted and annotated answers.

Table 1. Sample annotation for human-computer integration

Examples

{

  "id": "939--1--2007--10.1038/msb4100177--17202168",

  "question": "Highlight the scientific achievements that (Schwedhelm and Boger, 2003; Schlotterbeck et al , 2006) is known for.",

  "answers": {

   "text": "Detecting the unusual level of certain specific metabolites in a patient's blood or urine",

   "answer_start": 0

  },

  "context": "Detecting the unusual level of certain specific metabolites in a patient's blood or urine has long been established as an effective method to identify biomarkers for diagnosing particular diseases (Schwedhelm and Boger, 2003; Schlotterbeck et al , 2006). Recent rapid developments of advanced metabolomics technology is opening up new horizons, as hundreds or even thousands of metabolites can be measured simultaneously, providing a much more comprehensive assessment of a patient's health status (Griffin and Nicholls, 2006; Kell, 2006; Wishart et al , 2007). However, for a better and in- depth understanding of the large amounts of data generated from metabolomics, a complete and high- quality human metabolic network is essential."

}

{

  "id": "939--2--2007--10.1038/msb4100177--17202168",

  "question": "To what degree does (Schwedhelm and Boger, 2003; Schlotterbeck et al , 2006)'s contribution influence this work?",

  "answers": {

   "text": "established as an effective method to identify biomarkers for diagnosing particular diseases",

   "answer_start": 104

  },

  "context": "Same as above" }

{

  "id": "939--3--2007--10.1038/msb4100177--17202168",

  "question": "In the realm of science, what notable accomplishments can be attributed to (Griffin and Nicholls, 2006; Kell, 2006; Wishart et al , 2007)?",

  "answers": {

   "text": "hundreds or even thousands of metabolites can be measured simultaneously",

   "answer_start": 348

  },

  "context": "Same as above"

}

{

  "id": "939--4--2007--10.1038/msb4100177--17202168",

  "question": "Explain the influence of (Griffin and Nicholls, 2006; Kell, 2006; Wishart et al , 2007)'s contribution in relation to this work.",

  "answers": {

   "text": "providing a much more comprehensive assessment of a patient's health status",

   "answer_start": 422

  },

  "context": "Same as above"

}

Furthermore, we also compare our recognition results with the annotation results obtained using ChatGPT. ChatGPT[2] is a large language model based on generative pre-training Transformer 3 developed by OpenAI, known for intelligent content creation. Wei X et al. have used ChatGPT for named entity recognition and event extraction [21], confirming that its intercoder agreement exceeds both crowd-workers and trained anno-tators for all tasks [22]. Compared with other conversational AI models, ChatGPT is characterized by a rich corpus, human-like text generation, and rapid response, repre-senting one of the most advanced technologies for data annotating at present. Thus, the annotating results of ChatGPT could be a strong baseline for comparison in our study.

4　Results

This section shows the comparison of our recognition results with the results of the W^2NER method, manual checking, and ChatGPT annotation.

4.1　Results for W^2NER

Table 2 displays the experimental results of both W^2NER and our MRC framework. We observe huge performance boosts on our MRC framework over W^2NER models, which are +23.76% and +31.92% over the label and entity of W^2NER performances, respectively. It is essential to note that the substantial performance boosts do not imply that the W^2NER model is mediocre; rather, they indicate that the MRC framework is better suited for extracting contribution patterns from citation sentences in this paper.

Table 2. Results for W^2NER and MRC

Model	Precision	Recall	F1-score
W2NER-Entity	0.5492	0.3252	0.4085
W2NER-Label	0.5116	0.4729	0.4901
MRC	**0.7416**	**0.7908**	**0.7277**

4.2　Results for Manual Checking

We analyze the results of MRC model recognition in comparison with those of manual annotation. We first check the answers between predicted and annotated whether are exactly the same. If not, we will be comparing the core content of the two. For answers that are not completely predicted accurately, there are four discriminatory situations: (1) We consider a predicted answer to be correct when it is identical to the core of the annotated answer, as the first example in Table 3. (2) The predicted answer is only

---

[2] https://openai.com/blog/chatgpt/.

a portion of the annotated answer, but the important components are considered half-correct, like the second example in Table 3. (3) Predicted answers that contain more content compared to annotated answers, such as further descriptions and explanations, is also considered half-correct, as the third example in Table 3. (4) The predicted answer covers the annotated answer with a lot of irrelevant information, then the answer is incorrect, as the fourth example in Table 3.

Table 3. Judgment criteria for the correctness of predicted answers

Question	MRC model vs. Manual annotations	Judgment
Which field has McManus et al. made contributions to?	MRC: Initial models for gating of BK channels	Correct
	Manual annotation: BK channels	
What is the influence of (52)'s contribution on the development of this work?	MRC: have implications for the improvement of antiviral and antitumor vaccination ap-proaches	half-correct
	Manual annotation: not only provide novel insights into the role pDC play for the generation of cellular immune responses but also may have implications for the improvement of antiviral and antitumor vaccination approaches	
What is Rasmussen et al.'s scientific contribution	MRC: the most complete insight into the interactions between a GPCR and its cognate G protein is provided by the recent structure of the human β2 adrenergic receptor•G s protein complex	half-correct
	Manual annotation: human β2 adrenergic receptor•G s protein complex	
What is 6's scientific contribution	MRC: somatic stem cells and embryonic stem (ES) cells preceded and induced pluripotent stem cells (iPS) cells	Incorrect
	Manual annotation: iPS cells enable the use of autologous pluripotent stem cells	

Based on the above rules, out of 212 predicted answers, 166 of them are completely correct, 13 are half-correct, and 33 are incorrect. The accuracy of recognition can be up to 78.3% (+3.07% for the half-correct answers).

4.3 Results for ChatGPT Annotating

In this paper, we compare ChatGPT with the MRC-based contribution pattern identification model on the same data annotation test sets, to assess our model's performance. The evaluation criteria used in Sect. 4.2 are applied to assess the quality of ChatGPT annotation.

Results demonstrate that ChatGPT exhibits robustness in data annotation for general domains. Especially for texts with simple semantics and obvious structural features, ChatGPT can quickly identify and extract effective information with high accuracy. At the same time, ChatGPT is adept at identifying multiple citation sentences in non-standardized formats, ensuring a high recall rate. However, ChatGPT gives more random answers and poorer object identification when annotating citation sentences with unconventional sequences or non-obvious feature expressions. We, therefore, focus on the annotating results of contribution patterns in citation sentences with multiple references between the two. In 97 samples, the MRC model achieves a 71.13% accuracy (69 correct) in 97 samples, whereas the ChatGPT annotation shows a 49.48% accuracy (48 correct). Four aspects of errors in ChatGPT annotation are summarized below:

(1) Repeated citation mark identification. Although ChatGPT performs well in identifying various citation marks, it struggles to merge the same annotation objects, resulting in numerous duplicate descriptions.

(2) Misplaced extraction in citation sentences' CONTRIBUTION. ChatGPT is prone to misplacing extraction in identifying the CONTRIBUTION within citation sentences. ChatGPT identifies citations based on the probability of the occurrence position and more research is used to mark references after citations, like "*CONTRIBUTION [1]*", this model is familiar to ChatGPT. As a consequence, it is difficult for ChatGPT to accurately identify the contribution of that citation, when placing the reference mark in front of a cited sentence, as "*Author [1] CONTRIBUTION*". This error is evident in the first example in Table 4, we bold the golden answer in the context and the same below.

(3) Randomness in FIELD identification. In the case of FIELD identification, ChatGPT mainly classifies annotated objects into similar research fields by understanding their content, which leads to strong randomness and summarization and does not fully conform to the meaning of the original text. Like the second example in Table 4, ChatGPT automatically generates "immune system" as the field based on its reading comprehension, whereas this term does not appear in the original text.

(4) Challenges in identifying research contribution INFLUENCE. When identifying the influence of research contributions on complex samples, ChatGPT faces difficulties in accurately distinguishing between contribution and influence. Consequently, it encounters issues such as failing to identify the influence or extracting error answers. Particularly, when multiple citation sentences appear in succession, ChatGPT often misidentifies the contribution of the later citation sentence as the influence of the former sentence, leading to a chain of errors. Such as the third example in Table 4, the answer of ChatGPT to (43)'s INFLUENCE should be part of the (43, 44)'s CONTRIBUTION.

In general, while ChatGPT demonstrates satisfactory performance for simple and normative datasets, it struggles in complex semantic sentences and multi-reference sentences rich in domain knowledge. Its accuracy and semantic matching are weaker in such scenarios, making it less suitable for domain data annotation tasks.

Table 4. Error example of ChatGPT annotation

Contribution pattern	Context	ChatGPT Annotation
(Cox et al.'s) CONTRIBUTION	This **dual-sensing capacity of BK channels** distinguishes them from other voltage-dependent K+ channels in terms of the physiological roles they can play, allowing their voltage-sensing function to be dynamically regulated by variations in submembrane [Ca 2+]. Furthermore, as illustrated abundantly in various past articles of this journal (Cox et al., 1997; …) …	This dual-sensing capacity of BK channels distinguishes them from other voltage-dependent K+ channels in terms of the physio-logical roles they can play, allowing their volt-age-sensing function to be dynamically regulated by variations in submembrane [Ca 2+]
(21,22's) FIELD	Studies utilizing murine models of acute versus chronic infection, such as those that have used the lymphocytic choriomeningitis virus (LCMV) model system, have provided significant new insights into the potential mechanisms of **dysfunction of T-cell responses** that occur during chronic viral infection 21,22 …	immune system
(43)'s INFLUENCE	This can be considered **a critical finding** because quiescent MSCs are unable to express IDO1 (43). However, IDO1 is considered one of the key modulators of the immune tolerance mechanism (43,44) …	key modulators of the immune tolerance mechanism

5 Conclusion

This paper presents a framework for extracting detailed information from the citation sentence, such as main contributions, influence or extent of the contribution, and domain of contribution, by linking questions and answers with reference markers to achieve contribution patterns extraction based on the MRC model. Notably, this method surpasses

NER in terms of performance improvement, making it more effective for our task. What's more, the model can proficiently capture the semantic information associated with each contributing pattern category, thanks to the incorporation of supplementary cues within the questions. Simultaneously, it effectively resolves the challenge of referential disambiguation in citation sentences. Moreover, we have curated a contribution pattern dataset extracted from articles that cite Nobel Prize laureates, which will be made publicly available following further refinement.

Despite the merits of our study, certain limitations should be acknowledged. The rarity of the corpus and the complexities involved in annotation have constrained the size of our training data. To address this, we plan to expand the corpus size to enhance the model's performance. Furthermore, we intend to conduct detailed contribution analyses for specific tasks or domains, such as performing research profiling of Nobel Prize laureates. These efforts will provide deeper insights into the extracted contribution patterns and their implications in various contexts.

In conclusion, our proposed framework offers a promising approach to extracting fine-grained information from citation sentences, facilitating a deeper understanding of contributions made in academic literature. As we address the identified limitations and refine our dataset, this research can serve as a valuable resource for the scholarly community, aiding in various applications and research analyses.

Acknowledgments. This work was supported by the major project of the National Social Science Foundation of China "Big Data-driven Semantic Evaluation System of Science and Technology Literature" (Project No. 21&ZD329).

References

1. Chen, H., Nguyen, H., Alghamdi, A.: Constructing a high-quality dataset for automated creation of summaries of fundamental contributions of research articles. Scientometrics (2022). https://doi.org/10.1007/s11192-022-04380-z
2. Zhao, Y., Zhang, Z., Wang, Y., Lin, X.: Identifying research contributions based on semantic analysis of citation sentences: a case study of the 2021 Physiology or Medicine Nobel Prize laureates. In: Proceedings of the 19th International Conference on Scientometrics and Informetrics (2023)
3. Levy, O., Seo, M., Choi, E., Zettlemoyer, L.: Zero-shot relation extraction via reading comprehension. http://arxiv.org/abs/1706.04115 (2017)
4. McCann, B., Keskar, N.S., Xiong, C., Socher, R.: The natural language decathlon: multitask learning as question answering. http://arxiv.org/abs/1806.08730 (2018)
5. Li, X., et al.: Entity-relation extraction as multi-turn question answering. In: Proceedings of the 57th Annual Meeting of the Association for Computational Linguistics. Association for Computational Linguistics (2019)
6. Rajpurkar, P., Jia, R., Liang, P.: Know what you don't know: unanswerable questions for SQuAD. http://arxiv.org/abs/1806.03822 (2018)
7. Rajpurkar, P., Zhang, J., Lopyrev, K., Liang, P.: SQuAD: 100,000+ questions for machine comprehension of text. http://arxiv.org/abs/1606.05250 (2016)
8. Li, X., Feng, J., Meng, Y., Han, Q., Wu, F., Li, J.: A unified MRC framework for named entity recognition. In: Proceedings of the 58th Annual Meeting of the Association for Computational Linguistics, pp. 5849–5859 (2020)

9. Gupta, S., Manning, C.D.: Analyzing the dynamics of research by extracting key aspects of scientific papers. In: Proceedings of 5th International Joint Conference on Natural Language Processing, pp. 1–9 (2011)

10. Chen, L., Fang, H.: An automatic method for extracting innovative ideas based on the scopus® database. Knowl. Org. **46**, 171–186 (2019)

11. Le, X., et al.: CiteOpinion: evidence-based evaluation tool for academic contributions of research papers based on citing sentences. J. Data Inf. Sci. **4**, 26–41 (2019)

12. Ferrod, R., Di Caro, L., Schifanella, C.: Structured semantic modeling of scientific citation intents. In: Verborgh, R., et al. (eds.) The Semantic Web. LNCS, vol. 12731, pp. 461–476. Springer, Cham (2021). https://doi.org/10.1007/978-3-030-77385-4_27

13. Yousif, A., Niu, Z., Nyamawe, A.S., Hu, Y.: Improving citation sentiment and purpose classification using hybrid deep neural network model. In: Hassanien, A.E., Tolba, M.F., Shaalan, K., Azar, A.T. (eds.) Proceedings of the International Conference on Advanced Intelligent Systems and Informatics 2018. AISC, vol. 845, pp. 327–336. Springer, Cham (2019). https://doi.org/10.1007/978-3-319-99010-1_30

14. Cohan, A., Ammar, W., van Zuylen, M., Cady, F.: Structural scaffolds for citation intent classification in scientific publications. In: Proceedings of NAACL-HLT, pp. 3586–3596 (2019)

15. Berrebbi, D., Huynh, N., Balalau, O.: GraphCite: citation intent classification in scientific publications via graph embeddings. In: Companion Proceedings of the Web Conference 2022, pp. 779–783 (2022)

16. Xing, X., Fan, X., Wan, X.: Automatic generation of citation texts in scholarly papers: a pilot study. In: Proceedings of the 58th Annual Meeting of the Association for Computational Linguistics, pp. 6181–6190 (2020)

17. Wu, J.-Y., Shieh, A.T.-W., Hsu, S.-J., Chen, Y.-N.: Towards generating citation sentences for multiple references with intent control. http://arxiv.org/abs/2112.01332 (2021)

18. Lahiri, A., Sanyal, D.K., Mukherjee, I.: CitePrompt: using prompts to identify citation intent in scientific papers. arXiv preprint arXiv:2304.12730 (2023)

19. Devlin, J., Chang, M.W., Lee, K. and Toutanova, K.: BERT: pre-training of deep bidirectional transformers for language understanding. In: Proceedings of NAACL-HLT, pp. 4171–4186 (2019)

20. Li, J., et al.: Unified named entity recognition as word-word relation classification. In: Proceedings of the AAAI Conference on Artificial Intelligence, pp. 10965–10973 (2022)

21. Wei, X., et al.: Zero-shot information extraction via chatting with ChatGPT. http://arxiv.org/abs/2302.10205 (2023)

22. Gilardi, F., Alizadeh, M., Kubli, M.: ChatGPT outperforms crowd-workers for text-annotation tasks. http://arxiv.org/abs/2303.15056 (2023)

Cited But Not Archived: Analyzing the Status of Code References in Scholarly Articles

Emily Escamilla[1]([✉])[iD], Martin Klein[2][iD], Talya Cooper[3][iD], Vicky Rampin[3][iD], Michele C. Weigle[1][iD], and Michael L. Nelson[1][iD]

[1] Old Dominion University, Norfolk, VA, USA
evogt001@odu.edu, {mweigle,mln}@cs.odu.edu
[2] Los Alamos National Laboratory, Los Alamos, NM, USA
mklein@lanl.gov
[3] New York University, New York, NY, USA
{tc3602,vicky.rampin}@nyu.edu

Abstract. One in five arXiv articles published in 2021 contained a URI to a Git Hosting Platform (GHP), which demonstrates the growing prevalence of GHP URIs in scholarly publications. However, GHP URIs are vulnerable to the same reference rot that plagues the Web at large. The disappearance of software hosting platforms, like Gitorious and Google Code, and the source code they contain threatens research reproducibility. Archiving the source code and development history available in GHPs enables the long-term reproducibility of research. Software Heritage and Web archives contain archives of GHP URI resources. However, are the GHP URIs referenced by scholarly publications contained within the Software Heritage and Web archive collections? We analyzed a dataset of GHP URIs extracted from scholarly publications to determine (1) is the URI still publicly available on the live Web?, (2) has the URI been archived by Software Heritage?, and (3) has the URI been archived by Web archives? Of all GHP URIs, we found that 93.98% were still publicly available on the live Web, 68.39% had been archived by Software Heritage, and 81.43% had been archived by Web archives.

Keywords: Web Archiving · Digital Preservation · Open Source Software · Memento · Software Heritage

1 Introduction

A growing number of researchers reference Git Hosting Platforms (GHPs), like GitHub, GitLab, SourceForge, and Bitbucket, in scholarly publications [9]. GHPs are Web-based hosting platforms for git repositories. GHPs are commonly used by software developers, including researchers, to host software and facilitate collaboration. Researchers include GHP URIs in their publications for software products that were either used in their research or created in the course of the

D. H. Goh et al. (Eds.): ICADL 2023, LNCS 14458, pp. 194–207, 2023.
https://doi.org/10.1007/978-981-99-8088-8_17

study. However, scholarly code products hosted on the live Web with GHPs are susceptible to the reference rot that plagues the Web as a whole [12]. When navigating to a URI found in a publication, users may find a "404: Page not found" error due to either the hosting platform or the software repository being no longer available at the URI.

GHPs provide access to a repository for the lifespan of the GHP, but the long term access provided by preservation is not a priority for GHPs, as shown by the discontinuation of the GHPs Gitorious [17] and Google Code [8]. All URIs to those two platforms in scholarly publications no longer point to the content that the author originally intended, due to no fault of the author. The disappearance of these resources creates a problem for scholars interested in replicating the results as well as those interested in the context of the research findings. A reader may be able to successfully locate one of these now-defunct URIs in a Web archive, like the Internet Archive (IA), however, Web archives do not give priority to archiving software products. Therefore, there is no guarantee that any given URI will be preserved, unless a user submits a repository with IA's 'Save Page Now'[1] feature.

Software Heritage is a non-profit organization that works "to collect, preserve, and share all software that is publicly available in source code form" [19]. They utilize a 'Save Code Now' feature, as well as automated crawling, to create snapshots of origin URIs [6,7]. While Web archives typically have a large scope covering a wide variety of content types, Software Heritage is singularly focused on the archival of source code and its development history. Software Heritage announced that 202,254,500 projects have been archived as of January 17, 2023.[2] But, are the software products that scholars are referencing in their publications included in the over 202 million projects that have been captured?

In this paper, we identified the current state of scholarly code products on the live Web as well as in archives such as Software Heritage and Web archives. We analyzed GHP URIs from 2.6 million articles in the arXiv and Pub Med Central (PMC) corpora and found that 93.98% of all GHP URIs referenced were publicly available on the live Web. We also found that 68.39% of all repository URIs were captured by Software Heritage and 81.43% of all GHP URIs referenced in scholarly publications had at least one archived version in a Web archive.

2 Related Work

In a previous study [9], we studied the prevalence of GHP URIs within scholarly publications. Our corpus contained over 2.6 million publications from arXiv and PMC. We extracted 7.7 million URIs from the articles including 253,590 URIs to four GHPs: GitHub, GitLab, Bitbucket, and SourceForge. We found that, over time, a growing number of papers referenced GHP URIs, with 20% of 2021 arXiv publications containing a GitHub URI. We also found that 33.7% of publications that reference a GHP include more than one GHP URI. Scholars include URIs to

---

[1] https://web.archive.org/save/.

[2] https://twitter.com/SWHeritage/status/1615422314224701440.

resources that contributed to or impacted their research. The increasing inclusion of GHP URIs in scholarly publications points to an increased importance of the holdings of GHPs for reproducibility in research.

However, URIs to GHPs, like the Web at large, may experience reference rot. Reference rot refers to the occurrence of content drift and link rot [21]. A reference has experienced content drift when the content of the URI when it was referenced is different than the content shown to the user at present. A reference has experienced link rot when the URI is completely inaccessible on the live Web. Link rot may cause the "404: Page not found" error that most users have experienced. In a study on the use of URIs to the Web at large in the arXiv, Elsevier, and PMC corpora, Klein et al. [12] found that reference rot affects 20% of Science, Technology, and Math (STM) publications. In a study on the same corpus, Jones et al. [11] found that 75% of URI references experienced content drift, with content drift worsening over time.

Some scholars take an active role in preserving their software, a strategy known as self-archiving. Self-archiving puts the responsibility on scholars to deposit their code product into a repository that guarantees long-term preservation, like Zenodo [15] or the Open Science Framework [10]. However, a study by Milliken et al. found that only 47.2% of the academics who create software products self-archive their software [14].

Software Heritage preserves source code and its development history from the perspective that source code is itself a valuable form of knowledge that should be captured, including the unique evolution of the source code to create the code product at a given point in time [7]. Software Heritage provides a central repository containing the source code and development histories of millions of code products across programming languages, hosting platforms, and package repositories. The result is a repository that researchers can use as a more representative sample than a single hosting platform or package library to analyze source code. For instance, Pietri et al. [16] and Bhattacharjee et al. [2] leverage the scope of the Software Heritage dataset to analyze trends in software development across a more heterogeneous dataset than could be found in a single hosting platform. While studies like these have made use of the holdings of Software Heritage, they do not analyze what has or has not been preserved in Software Heritage.

3   Methodology

We used a dataset of GHP URIs from our previous study [9], where we extracted GitHub, GitLab, Bitbucket, and SourceForge URIs from a corpora of 2,641,041 arXiv and PMC articles. In total, the dataset contained 253,590 GHPs URIs that were referenced in scholarly publications. The distribution of the URIs in each GHP is shown in Table 1. For each URI in the dataset, we conducted three tests: (1) is it available on the live Web?, (2) is it available in Software Heritage?, (3) is it available in Web archives? We also analyzed the relationship between the publication date of the earliest article to reference a URI and the date of the first Software Heritage and Web archive capture of the URI[3].

Table 1. Number of URIs to each GHP and the percentage of all GHP URIs

GHP	Number of URIs	Percent of GHP URIs
GitHub	234,092	92.31%
SourceForge	12,721	5.01%
Bitbucket	3,962	1.56%
GitLab	2,815	1.11%

In this study, we adopt the terminology used by Klein et al. [12]. A URI is *publicly available* if a curl request results in a 2XX-level HTTP response code. If a URI is publicly available, we consider the URI to be **active** on the live Web. Private repositories respond to a curl request with a 404 HTTP response code. While a private repository exists and is available to the owner, it is not publicly available and accessible via the URI provided in the scholarly publication; therefore, because a URI to a private repository is not available to general users, it is not considered an active URI. Any URI that does not result in a 2XX-level HTTP response code is considered inactive, meaning that the URI is **rotten**, or is subject to link rot. In our curl requests, we opted to follow redirects and considered the resulting HTTP response code as the final status of the URI on the live Web.

We utilized the Software Heritage API [18] to determine if Software Heritage contained a snapshot of the URI. However, Software Heritage only supports searching for URIs at the repository level, whether through their browser search interface or API request. Searching for deep links to a specific file or directory will not result in a match, even if the file or directory is available within Software Heritage's snapshot of the repository. For example, https://github.com/aliasrobotics/RVD/blob/master/rvd_tools/database/schema.py is a URI that was extracted from an article in the arXiv corpus. As it is written, the Software Heritage API was not able to find a matching origin. When we truncate the URI to the repository-level (https://github.com/aliasrobotics/RVD), the Software Heritage API returned a matching origin URL. To accommodate the requirements of the Software Heritage API, we transformed all deep URIs to GitHub, GitLab, and Bitbucket to shallow, repository level URIs and requested the resulting URI from the Software Heritage API. SourceForge affords a high level of customization for hosted projects. SourceForge projects can support issue pages, documentation, wiki pages, and code repository pages. However, these pages are not required. As a results, not all SourceForge projects have publicly available source code that can be cloned via an access URL. Software Heritage

---

[3] Source code and datasets are available at https://github.com/oduwsdl/Extract-URLs.

utilizes access URLs to capture and preserve source code. As a result, Source-Forge projects that do not provide an access URL are not able to be captured by Software Heritage. In order to accurately reflect the archival rate of Source-Forge URIs in Software Heritage, we excluded SourceForge URIs to projects that did not provide an access URL. To determine if the project provided an access URL, we sent a request to the SourceForge API with the project name. From the SourceForge API response, we extracted all access URLs. Of 7,269 unique SourceForge projects, 47.08%, or 3,422 projects did not provide at least one access URL. If the project did not contain any access URLs, the project URI was excluded. Otherwise, if the project contained one or more access URLs, we requested all access URLs for the SourceForge project from the Software Heritage API. The Software Heritage API returned metadata for each snapshot includ-ing the origin (the original URI and the type of software origin), visit number, date of the snapshot, status of the snapshot, and the snapshot ID [7]. From the API response, we extracted the date of the first and last snapshot and the total number of snapshots for each URI.

We used MemGator [1], a Memento [20] aggregator that queries the hold-ings of 12 distinct Web archives, to search for the GHP URIs. The result of a Web archive crawling a live Web page, identified by a URI-R, is a *memento*, an archived version of the URI-R at a given point in time and is identified by a URI-M. After requesting the URI from each of the Web archives, MemGator compiles all of the archives' responses for the URI-R into a TimeMap that includes the URI-M of each memento and the corresponding Memento-Datetime (i.e., the date it was archived). From the resulting TimeMap, we extracted the Memento-Datetime of the first and last memento and the total number of mementos for each GHP URI-R.

McCown and Nelson [13] developed a framework for discussing the inter-section of Web archiving and the life span of a Web resource, which we have adapted to discuss the intersection of Web archiving and the life span of source code in a GHP. We define a GHP URI resource as **vulnerable** if it is publicly available on the live Web but has not been archived. If a GHP URI resource is publicly available on the live Web and has been archived, we define the GHP URI resource as **replicated**. Lastly, we define a GHP URI resource as **unre-coverable** if it is no longer publicly available on the live Web and has not been archived.

4   Results

Across all four GHPs, 93.98% of all GHP URIs referenced in scholarly publi-cations were active, as shown in Fig. 1a. However, 6.02%, or 8,882 URIs of the unique GHP URIs in scholarly publications, were rotten. GitHub had the high-est percentage of active URIs with 94.79%. Bitbucket had the lowest percentage of active URIs with 75.86% resulting in 641 rotten URIs.

As shown in Fig. 1b, 68.39% of all repository-level GHP URIs have at least one snapshot in Software Heritage. SourceForge had the highest percentage of

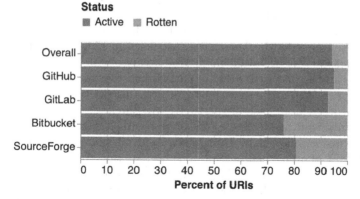

(a) Percent of active URIs

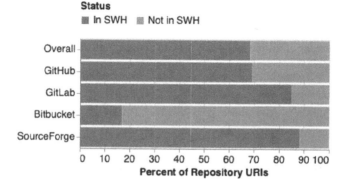

(b) Percent of repository URIs captured by Software Heritage (SWH)

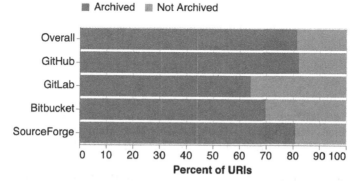

(c) Percent of URIs that had at least one memento

Fig. 1. Results of running the three tests: (1) is the URI active?, (2) has the URI been archived by Software Heritage?, and (3) has the URI been archived by Web archives?

repository URIs captured by Software Heritage with 88.34%. Bitbucket had the lowest percentage with 16.93% of repository URIs.

Across all four GHPs, 81.43% of GHP URIs have at least one memento in the Web archives queried by MemGator, as shown in Fig. 1c. GitHub had the highest percentage of URIs available in Web archives with 82.25% and Source-Forge was a close second with 81.06%. GitLab had the smallest percentages of URIs available in Web archives with 64.29%. The distribution of the percent of mementos returned from each of the twelve Web archives is shown in Table 2. Internet Archive had the largest percent of all returned mementos with 58.68%. Internet Archive is followed by Bibliotheca Alexandrina Web Archive,[4] which returned 23.29% of all mementos. However, we note that since 2022 Bibliotheca Alexandrina has functioned as a backup to the Internet Archive and provides a mirror of the Internet Archive's holdings [3]. This could explain the high percentage of GHP URIs available in both the Internet Archive and Bibliotheca Alexandrina Web archives. The remaining 18.03% of mementos are distributed across the remaining 10 Web archives.

Table 2. Percent of all mementos returned from each of the 12 Web archives

Web Archive	Percent of Mementos
Internet Archive	58.68%
Bibliotheca Alexandria Web Archive	23.29%
Archive.today	8.06%
Archive.it	3.07%
Portuguese Web Archive	2.83%
Library of Congress	2.53%
Icelandic Web Archive	0.88%
Australian Web Archive	0.35%
UK Web Archive	0.12%
Perma	0.11%
Stanford Web Archive	0.08%
BAnQ	0.0005% (1 URI-M)

Figure 2a depicts the percent of URIs archived by both Software Heritage and Web archives, only Software Heritage, only Web archives, and neither Software Heritage or Web archives. Overall, 57.21% (30,311 URIs) of all URIs were captured by both Software Heritage and Web archives and 12.99% (5,249 URIs) were not captured by either Software Heritage or the Web archives, making their resources vulnerable. Across all four GHPs, there are a higher percentage of GHP URIs that have only been archived by Web archives (26.74%) than the percentage of GHP URIs that have only been archived by Software Heritage

---

[4] https://www.bibalex.org/isis/frontend/archive/archive_web.aspx

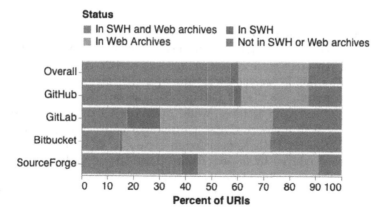

(a) Percent of repository-level URIs overall and for each GHP

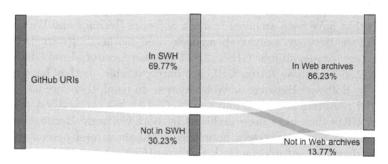

(b) Relationship between the number of GitHub URIs preserved

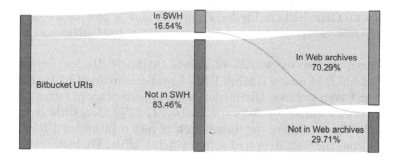

(c) Relationship between the number of Bitbucket URIs preserved

Fig. 2. Relationships between URIs that have been archived by Software Heritage (SWH) and Web archives, only Software Heritage, only Web archives, and neither Software Heritage or Web archives

(3.02%). SourceForge and Bitbucket have the highest percentage of URIs unique to the Web archives with 46.50% of SourceForge URIs and 57.15% of Bitbucket URIs only archived by Web archives. Bitbucket has the highest percentage of vulnerable URI resources with 27.15%. Figures 2b and 2c give a more detailed look at the relationship between each category for GitHub and Bitbucket URIs.

As shown in Fig. 2b, 58.43% of GitHub URIs have been archived by both Software Heritage and Web archives, while 25.76% of GitHub URIs have only been archived by Web archives. These percentages noticeably differ from the distribution of Bitbucket URIs as depicted in Figure 2c. Of all Bitbucket URIs, 14.78% have been archived by both Software Heritage and Web archives while 57.15% have only been archived by Web archives. Additionally, only 0.91% of Bitbucket URIs are archived by Software Heritage and not archived by Web archives, compared to 2.97% of GitHub URIs.

Because they have active URIs, vulnerable resources still have the opportunity to be archived by Web archives and Software Heritage. However, rotten URIs are no longer able to be preserved. Figure 3a depicts the percent of rotten URIs that have been archived by both Software Heritage and Web archives, only Software Heritage, only Web archives, and neither Software Heritage or Web archives. Across all four GHPs, 2,823 unique repository-level URIs are rotten and 32.36% of those rotten URIs are unrecoverable, as they have not been archived by Software Heritage or Web archives. In total, there are 932 unrecoverable URI resources across all four GHPs. GitLab has the smallest percentage of rotten URIs that have been archived by both Software Heritage and Web archives with 5.77%. Conversely, SourceForge has the largest percentage of rotten URIs that are captured by both Software Heritage and Web archives with 63.06%. For rotten URIs, there is a smaller percentage of URIs that have only been archived by Software Heritage (7.37%) than the percentage of URIs that have only been archived by Web archives (31.04%). This trend is similar to what we saw for all GHP URIs in Fig. 2a. Figures 3b and 3c provide a more detailed look at the relationship between each category for rotten GitHub and Bitbucket URIs.

As shown in Fig. 3b, 36.22% of rotten GitHub URIs are unrecoverable. Inversely, 23.64% of rotten GitHub URIs have been archived by both Software Heritage and Web archives. GitHub has a larger percentage of rotten URIs that have only been archived by Software Heritage (7.63%) than Bitbucket (2.14%) as shown in Fig. 3c. Again, the distribution of rotten Bitbucket URIs is distinguishable from the distribution of rotten GitHub URIs. We found that 19.70% of rotten Bitbucket URIs are unrecoverable while 50.42% of rotten Bitbucket URIs have been archived by both Software Heritage and Web archives.

For both Software Heritage and Web archives, we calculated the time between the date of the first publication to reference a URI and the date of the first capture of the URI. Software Heritage was created on June 30, 2016 [5], so we only analyzed articles that were published starting July 1, 2016. We found an average of 443 days (median of 360 days) between the first reference to the repository URI in a scholarly publication and the first capture by Software Heritage, if the

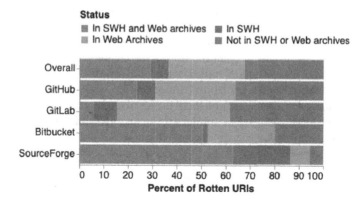

(a) Percent of rotten repository-level URIs overall and for each GHP

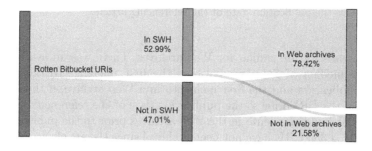

(b) Preservation of rotten GitHub URIs

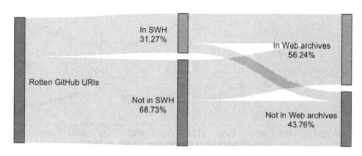

(c) Preservation of rotten Bitbucket URIs

Fig. 3. Relationships between rotten URIs that have been archived by Software Heritage (SWH) and Web archives, only Software Heritage, only Web archives, and neither Software Heritage or Web archives

repository-level URI did not have a snapshot at the time of publication. Additionally, 7,440 repository URIs that were captured before the publication date of the referencing article had not been captured since the article's publication. For these URIs, there is an average of 253 days between the last Software Heritage snapshot and the publication date of the reference article.

As shown in Fig. 4, the maximum time delta between the first reference to the repository URI in a scholarly publication and the first capture by Software Heritage has steadily decreased from 78 months for articles published in July 2016 to 9 months for articles published in April 2022. We also see that the median time delta follows a trend similar to the average time delta. The median and average time deltas have both decreased since 2021.

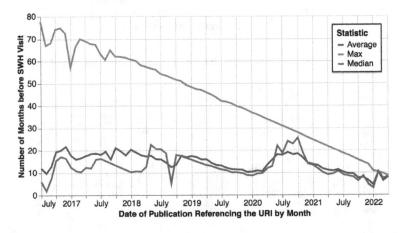

Fig. 4. Months between a publication referencing a URI and the URI being captured by Software Heritage over time. Only includes URIs not been captured by Software Heritage before the publication date of the referencing article.

These trends for are similar for Web archives. There was an average of 468 days and a median of 341 days between the first reference to the URI in a scholarly publication and the first memento in a Web archive, if there were no mementos of the URI prior to the publication date of the referencing article. Of the URIs that had a memento in the Web archives prior to the publication date of the article, 4,356 URIs have not been archived since the article was published, with an average of 201 days between the latest memento and the publication date. Figure 5 shows that the average and maximum time deltas have followed similar trends. Additionally, the maximum time delta has steadily decreased from 128 months in January 2012 to 1 month in April 2022. While the steady decline seen in maximum and average time deltas for Software Heritage and Web archives is promising, there is still a large period of time for the URI resource to move from vulnerable to unrecoverable before Software Heritage or Web archives are able to archive it.

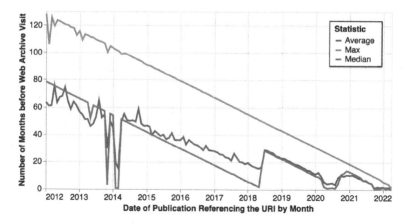

Fig. 5. Number of months between a publication referencing a URI and the URI being captured by the Web archives over time. Only includes URIs not captured by the Web archives before the publication date of the referencing article.

5 Discussion

We analyzed the GHP URIs that were extracted in a previous study from an arXiv and PMC corpora. GHP URIs from other corpora may produce a different result. For example, authors must proactively submit their paper to arXiv, which demonstrates an inclination to participate in open research. As such, authors who submit to arXiv may be more likely to submit source code projects to Software Heritage and Web archives for preservation and research reproducibility.

The smaller percentage of Bitbucket and SourceForge URIs publicly available on the live Web and preserved in Software Heritage may be correlated to the usage trends we observed in our previous study [9]. SourceForge was created in 1999, so older publications are more likely to contain a link to SourceForge than to other GHPs. Additionally, Bitbucket was referenced in scholarly publications more than GitHub from 2008 to 2014, which could also result in older publications containing a link to Bitbucket over other GHPs. As Klein et al. found, the likelihood of reference rot grows as the age of the URI increases [12], which could be reflected in the lower percentage of SourceForge and Bitbucket URIs still publicly available on the live Web. Additionally, older GHP URIs may be less likely to be preserved in Software Heritage given that Software Heritage was launched June 30, 2016. Some of the GHP URIs that are not publicly available on the live Web may have disappeared long before Software Heritage even existed to preserve them.

For the purposes of this study, we looked at the presence of an archived copy of the repository in Software Heritage and the Web archives, but did not investigate the quality of the copy. In some instances, the memento or capture may reflect that the URI is no longer available which would not be beneficial for reproducibility. In other cases, the capture may be incomplete in a way that negatively impacts reproducibility [4]. Determining that a archived copy of the repository exists is the first step in utilizing archived repositories to support reproducibility. In future work, we will investigate the quality of the mementos and captures that are currently available.

As we discussed while introducing the current software archival initiatives, the primary goal of Software Heritage is the preservation of software while Web archives work to preserve the Web at large, including a wide variety of content types. Therefore, it was interesting to find that the Web archives have archived almost 24% more scholarly GHP URIs than Software Heritage. While the repositories captured by Software Heritage are not a perfect subset of the repositories captured by Web archives, the holdings of the Web archives have a more complete coverage of scholarly repositories. A higher level of archival coverage benefits reproducibility as more scholarly software is made available to support long-term reproducibility.

With 93.98% of URIs still publicly available on the live Web, there is the opportunity to submit these URIs to be preserved. The 1.98% of URIs that are rotten and unrecoverable should serve as a warning of what could happen if the research community does not .act to preserve code products as integral research products. Researchers need to take initiative to submit code products to services like Software Heritage and Web archives to ensure the code they reference is preserved for long term access.

6   Conclusions

The inclusion of a URI to a GHP in a scholarly publication indicates the importance and impact of the repository to a scholar's research. Research reproducibility hinges on the ability of researchers to access the data and source code that contributed to a research outcome. We found that current archival efforts by Web archives and Software Heritage do not adequately preserve the GHP URIs referenced in scholarly publications. Additionally, Software Heritage, an archive solely focused on the preservation of software, contained fewer scholarly software products than the Web archives. Overall, 68.39% of the repository URIs were captured by Software Heritage while 81.43% had at least one memento in the Web archives. We also found 12.99% of the GHP URIs were not archived in Software Heritage or Web archives and 32.36% of the GHP URIs that are no longer available on the live Web and not archived in either Software Heritage or the Web archives.

References

1. Alam, S., Nelson, M.L.: MemGator - a portable concurrent Memento aggregator. In: Proceedings of the 16th ACM/IEEE-CS Joint Conference on Digital Libraries (JCDL), pp. 243–244 (2016). https://doi.org/10.1145/2910896.2925452
2. Bhattacharjee, A., et al.: An exploratory study to find motives behind cross-platform forks from software heritage dataset. In: Proceedings of the 17th International Conference on Mining Software Repositories, pp. 11–15 (2020). https://doi.org/10.1145/3379597.3387512

3. Bibliotheca Alexandrina: Internet Archive (2023). https://www.bibalex.org/en/project/details?documentid=283

4. Brunelle, J.F., Kelly, M., SalahEldeen, H., Weigle, M.C., Nelson, M.L.: Not all mementos are created equal: measuring the impact of missing resources. Int. J. Digit. Libr. **16**, 283–301 (2015)

5. Di Cosmo, R.: Software Heritage is now open, please come in! (2016). https://www.softwareheritage.org/2016/06/30/unveiling/

6. Di Cosmo, R.: Archiving and referencing source code with software heritage. In: Bigatti, A.M., Carette, J., Davenport, J.H., Joswig, M., de Wolff, T. (eds.) ICMS 2020. LNCS, vol. 12097, pp. 362–373. Springer, Cham (2020). https://doi.org/10.1007/978-3-030-52200-1_36

7. Di Cosmo, R., Zacchiroli, S.: Software heritage: why and how to preserve software source code. In: Proceedings of the 14th International Conference on Digital Preservation (iPRES), pp. 1–10 (2017). https://hal.archives-ouvertes.fr/hal-01590958

8. DiBona, C.: Bidding Farewell to Google Code (2015). https://opensource.googleblog.com/2015/03/farewell-to-google-code.html

9. Escamilla, E., Klein, M., Cooper, T., Rampin, V., Weigle, M.C., Nelson, M.L.: The rise of GitHub in scholarly publications. In: Proceedings of the International Conference on Theory and Practice of Digital Libraries (TPDL), pp. 187–200 (2022)

10. Foster, E.D., Deardorff, A.: Open science framework (OSF). J. Med. Libr. Assoc. **105**(2), 203 (2017). https://doi.org/10.5195/jmla.2017.88

11. Jones, S.M., Van de Sompel, H., Shankar, H., Klein, M., Tobin, R., Grover, C.: Scholarly context adrift: three out of four URI references lead to changed content. PLoS ONE **11**, 1–32 (2016). https://doi.org/10.1371/journal.pone.0167475

12. Klein, M., et al.: Scholarly context not found: one in five articles suffers from reference rot. PLoS ONE **9**, 1–39 (2014). https://doi.org/10.1371/journal.pone.0115253

13. McCown, F., Nelson, M.L.: A framework for describing web repositories. In: Proceedings of the 9th ACM/IEEE-CS Joint Conference on Digital Libraries (JCDL), pp. 341–344 (2009)

14. Milliken, G.: Archiving the scholarly git experience: an environmental scan. Technical report, OSF (2021). https://osf.io/ku24q/

15. Peters, I., Kraker, P., Lex, E., Gumpenberger, C., Gorraiz, J.I.: Zenodo in the spotlight of traditional and new metrics. Front. Res. Metr. Anal. **2**, 13 (2017). https://doi.org/10.3389/frma.2017.00013

16. Pietri, A., Spinellis, D., Zacchiroli, S.: The software heritage graph dataset: large-scale analysis of public software development history. In: Proceedings of the 17th International Conference on Mining Software Repositories, pp. 1–5 (2020). https://doi.org/10.1145/3379597.3387510

17. Sijbrandij, S.: GitLab acquires Gitorious to bolster its on premise code collaboration platform (2015). https://about.gitlab.com/blog/2015/03/03/gitlab-acquires-gitorious/

18. Software Heritage: Getting started with the Software Heritage API (2023). https://docs.softwareheritage.org/devel/getting-started/api.html

19. Software Heritage: Mission (2023). https://www.softwareheritage.org/mission/

20. Van de Sompel, H., Nelson, M.L., Sanderson, R.: HTTP framework for time-based access to resource states - Memento. RFC 7089 (2013)

21. Van de Sompel, H., Klein, M., Shankar, H.: Towards robust hyperlinks for web-based scholarly communication. In: Watt, S.M., Davenport, J.H., Sexton, A.P., Sojka, P., Urban, J. (eds.) CICM 2014. LNCS (LNAI), vol. 8543, pp. 12–25. Springer, Cham (2014). https://doi.org/10.1007/978-3-319-08434-3_2

Knowledge Extraction

Using Causal Threads to Explain Changes in a Dynamic System

Robert B. Allen[✉] (iD)

New York, NY, USA
rba@boballen.info

Abstract. We explore developing rich semantic models of systems. Specifically we consider structured causal explanations about state changes in those systems. Essentially, we are developing process-based dynamic knowledge graphs. As an example, we construct a model of the causal threads for geological changes proposed by the Snowball Earth theory. Further, we describe an early prototype of a graphical interface to present the explanations. Unlike statistical approaches to summarization and explanation such as Large Language Models (LLMs), our approach of direct representation can be inspected and verified directly.

Keywords: Causation · Direct Representation · Discourse · Dynamic Knowledge Graphs · Geology · Generative AI · Lexical Semantics · Multithreaded Explanations · Rules · Scientific Explanations · Semantic UML · User and Session Models · Visualization

1 Introduction

We envision interactive digital libraries that are built on knowledge bases rather than repositories of text. In this work, we focus on qualitative semantic models of systems. Systems may be defined as collections of objects that interact in stable and predictable ways over time. In (Allen, in preparation) we explore the description of systems at equilibrium. Those are systems in which none of the major states are changing (although the states of subsystems may be changing). In this companion paper, we consider qualitative descriptions of causal processes for dynamic systems with a higher-level implementation of the transitions. Our goal is to provide an explanation for users of how changes in one part of the system lead to system state changes.

In Sect. 2, we review our approach to structured descriptions and then consider discourse and causal explanations for dynamic models. In Sect. 3, we apply our approach to structured description to the Snowball Earth theory and introduce a visualization interface to support user interaction. Section 4 describes features to be explored in future work.

© The Author(s) 2023
D. H. Goh et al. (Eds.): ICADL 2023, LNCS 14458, pp. 211–219, 2023.
https://doi.org/10.1007/978-981-99-8088-8_18

2 Semantic Models

2.1 Structured Descriptions

In an approach we call direct representation, we propose that unambiguous rich semantic descriptions of systems can be developed with well-defined, standardized vocabularies. We focus on the description of relatively well-defined scenarios, rather than attempt to work with unrestricted natural language (also see Allen, in preparation). We build on ontologies (e.g., SUMO; Pease 2011) and other linguistic resources such as FrameNet (Ruppenhofer et al. 2016) and VerbNet, which we use to develop descriptions of systems using sequences of transitions. Our models are implemented as object-oriented programs which take advantage of features such as inheritance and concurrency. Indeed, we have proposed an ontology-based semantic UML. There are many advantages to this approach, but challenges remain such as handling granularity and incorporating other constraints.

Ontologies typically provide a hierarchical classification of terms and some of their associated properties. Beyond their specification in ontologies, we need to consider objects in the context of systems. However, many ontologies have limited coverage of processes and the description of the ways that objects typically interact. Unlike objects that fit neatly into hierarchical classification systems, processes have distinct footprints (Ruppenhofer et al. 2016). The details of processes depend on the objects to which they are applied (compositionality). For instance, the process of opening a door is different from opening a can or opening a restaurant. To handle such differences, and to add tighter constraints in the model, we develop descriptions of object-transition pairs that include the conditions under which the transition will trigger. Object-transition pairs can readily be extended into full propositions with semantic roles as arguments. Each step adds constraints and still more detail can be added with modifiers for the objects. In addition to expected states, models may include constraints, be broken, or incorporate ambiguous or missing data. A complete corpus of object-transition pairs would be many times larger than current dictionaries but could be developed with semi-automated tools.

Our approach is an alternative to Large Language Models (LLMs). LLMs reportedly often fabricate or "hallucinate" assertions. By comparison, our approach of direct representation provides inspectable and verifiable representations. It supports explainable AI (Mueller et al. 2021).

2.2 Discourse

Even if we have found "natural lines of fracture" for a system, there is leeway in how models are presented. In linguistics, discourse is the study of the intended effects of statements. Typically, discourse refers to interactive communication and includes discourse schemas (McKeown 1987), discourse macro-structures (Swales 1990, VanDijk 1981), and discourse planning (Hovy 1988). Several types of discourse are usually distinguished: Description, explanation, narrative, negotiation, and argumentation.

Description (or exposition) is subtly distinct from and interlocks with explanation. Explanations are often more didactic. For instance, an explanation might have a fore-warning such as "Remember this event, it's important in a later sequence of events". Some aspects are shared across the different types of discourse. Our distinction between description and explanation is related to the distinction between fabula and syuzhet in traditional story-narrative theory. The fabula is the raw events that form the story while syuzhet is the presentation.

There are several accounts of explanation (den Boef & van Woudenberg 2023; Pitt 1998). Causation is central in many of them, especially scientific explanations. To distinguish between explanation and narrative it is helpful to consider different senses of narration. In a broad sense, a narrative is any description of connected events, as in narrative history. However, a story narrative is sometimes seen as a distinct type of discourse. An important goal of a story narrative is to manage and manipulate the interest of the reader. For instance, to maintain drama, the outcome of the story is typically undisclosed until the end, whereas in explanation the goal is usually known, even emphasized, from the beginning.

Galileo famously described inertial motion by ignoring friction. The approach of ignoring minor factors has come to be known as Galilean modeling (Thagard 1999; Weisberg 2013). In our approach, the causal schema leaves out many details but could allow the user to view them by drilling down. This can be considered an interactive extension of Galilean models.

2.3 Causation

In Allen et al. (2005) we defined causation as a change of state that leads to another change of state. For instance, we say that "sunset causes the temperature to drop". This is a version of the common definition in which a cause is an event *without which* another event would not occur. Causal rules (generalizations or abstractions) also implicitly suggest a comparison to a normative (equilibrium) state. For instance, the assertion smoking causes cancer implies a comparison to the alternative of not smoking. Assertions of causation are often used as a shortcut for presenting a detailed mechanism. However, the assertion does not necessarily imply a detailed understanding of the underlying mechanism (Thagard 1999). For instance, we may believe that smoking causes cancer without understanding the intermediate steps. There may also be unsubstantiated or only partially confirmed claims of causation but these need to be treated as discourse claims. We can describe sequences of transitions in an equilibrium system, but we do not consider them as causal relationships because, by the definition of an equilibrium system, there are not any system-level state changes. Thus, we can claim that one event is a necessary condition for another event but not that it is a cause (cf., INUS conditions, Mackie 1974).

3 Snowball Earth Example

3.1 Overview of Snowball Earth Theory

The Snowball Earth model (Hoffman and Schrag 2000) is an account of proposed geological processes associated with the development of low-latitude glaciers that froze the surface of the Earth completely. Geologic evidence suggests this happened about 650 million years ago, and possibly a few other times. According to the theory, only when volcanic CO_2 in the atmosphere created extreme greenhouse warming did the surface thaw.

3.2 Semantic Model of the Snowball Earth Theory

In Allen (in preparation), we developed a small, detailed, state transition description graph for the equilibrium (before any freezing) for part of the theory. One major issue for that was a multilevel representation of streams (collections) of photons. The individual photons had interactions that resulted in collection-level transitions. Here, we consider using chains of state transitions to describe causal relationships. Objects are associated with Dimensions which are properties or processes. Most of those Dimensions are subdivided into States. For the model, states were defined that best illustrated the effects of the transitions; these states could be described more rigorously if needed.

3.3 User-Guided Graphical Interaction

We implemented a prototype graphical interface to support causal explanations. It is written in Python with the Tkinter graphics package. The current version is constructed to illustrate and explore key features rather than implement a fully usable service. The curved links are generated with splines but are positioned manually.

Decisions about how to segment and present the model are aspects of discourse. We broke the description of the events into three Episodes (cf., vanDjik 1981) which are roughly analogous to the chapters in a book. Each episode was composed of an Equilibrium phase that is later disrupted by a Causal (Process) phase: (a) Initial Equilibrium followed by Freezing, (b) Frozen Equilibrium followed by Thaw, and (c) Initial Equilibrium followed by heavy Sedimentation. Note that there are several different types of Sedimentation processes (calcium, iron, magnesium); we will address differentiating these in future work.

3.4 System at Equilibrium

Figure 1 shows a screenshot of the interface. At the top right is a widget to select episodes. The control panel is at the lower right. The left (main) panel shows system entities, their dimensions, states, and interaction links between them. It is divided according to sub-regions of the earth. In the upper part of the panel are entities and their dimensions that apply generally across the earth, such as temperature. In the lower portion are transition dimensions associated specifically with the Atmosphere, the Oceans, and the Land.

In Fig. 1, one of the Freeze Equilibrium processes is shown. Specifically, it shows first that photons from the sun are absorbed into the surface of the earth. The extent of that absorption determines the temperature of the surface, which, in turn, controls the extent of the ice cap. The temperature equilibrium is maintained because an equal amount of heat (Infrared photons) is radiated out from the surface of the earth. This is described in text for the user upon selecting the Episode Overview control panel option. The distinction between visible light photons and IR photons is nuanced. In future work, system-level annotations such as this should be fully structured and incorporated into the knowledge base and graphical presentation.

3.5 Causal Processes

Following the Snowball Earth Theory, the system state of primary interest is the ice coverage of the earth's surface. Figure 2 shows the interface for viewing the cause and mechanism associated with that extensive freezing over of the earth's surface (bold green

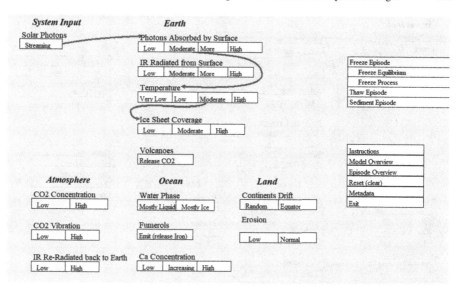

Fig. 1. Prototype interface with one of the Initial Equilibrium processes in red. (Color figure online)

arrows). According to the theory, continental drift affected the reflection of photons so much that the earth cooled and freezing was triggered. Specifically, it suggests that the drifting continents aligned near the equator, which increased the albedo, reduced the number of photons absorbed, reduced the temperature, and, thus, increased the ice coverage. As shown in the figure, the equilibrium process (red) is disrupted by the change in reflected light (green) by reducing the number of photons absorbed at the earth's surface.

The continental drift transition is shown in the lower center of the figure. The alignment of the continents at the equator is indicated as the change from the light yellow "Random" state to the darker yellow "Equator" state. The causal path (green), leads from there to the photons-absorbed dimension (top). Again, there is a state change with the previous state in light yellow and the later state in yellow. The path continues, resulting in changes in temperature and ice sheet coverage. However, the equilibrium (red) line is terminated since the state of the system has changed. Because the change in the absorption of photons and subsequent changes are due to the alignment of the continents at the equator, we can say that it is the cause of the Snowball freeze.

The final leg of the (green) Freeze Process suggests that the increased ice coverage causes more photons to be reflected (and fewer absorbed) which further reduces the temperature. In other words, there is a positive feedback loop. However, at some point, the supply of liquid water to form the ice will be exhausted and there will be no further increase in the size of the ice cap. In our approach, both the low-level descriptive model and the process threads are sequences of state changes implemented by a program. Potentially the feedback loop could be considered a design pattern.

The change in temperature due to continental drift had other effects and in some cases, the representations overlapped but we do not show those in this view. To avoid

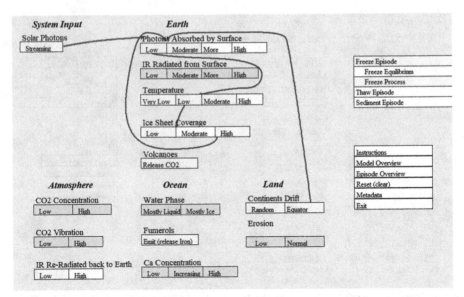

Fig. 2. As proposed by the theory, the change in the continents' positions disrupts the equilibrium process and causes the earth to freeze over. This image shows the equilibrium process as a red arrow (upper left) and the effect of the drift (green arrows) in the continents' positions on reflected energy, temperature, and ultimately ice cover. (Color figure online)

ambiguity, most states not associated with the highlighted transitions are grayed out for the presentation of this causal process although they are included in other Episodes.

4   Future Work

4.1   Incorporating Additional Details

The causal schemas present a relatively high-level overview of the events, based on the underlying structured descriptions (Sect. 2; Allen, in preparation). Because the schema is abbreviated, users may want to get a deeper understanding by drilling down into the details. For instance, in the schema shown in Fig. 1, the reflection of photons by the atmosphere is not mentioned.

Each dimension is associated with an information box that can be accessed by clicking on the label of that dimension (Fig. 3). Potentially, the user could step through the sequence and the descriptions could be presented sequentially. As described in the note, the overall Earth temperature overlaps with the Ocean and Land temperatures. There is a sort of inheritance from the broad earth system to the subsystems (subregions).

4.2   Concurrency, Time, and Timelines

Our model would benefit from a richer representation of time and concurrency. For instance, we noted that the explanation of the Sedimentation processes includes events from both the Freeze and Thaw episodes. The understanding of temporal relationships can be facilitated with graphical timelines (Allen 2005, 2011).

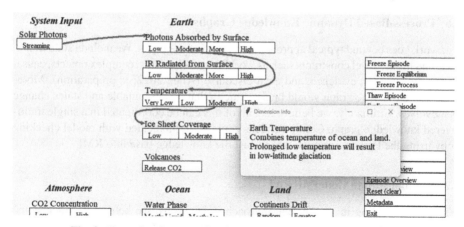

Fig. 3. Example of a popup for richer descriptions of the dimensions.

4.3 Multithreaded Narratives

Dynamic systems typically have states and facets that interact in complex, concurrent ways. The situation is analogous to the presentation of a multi-threaded story narrative (e.g., Aronson 2010). Moreover, many discourses are interactive (e.g., conversations). Maintaining coherence and planning presentations are needed across different types of discourse (e.g., Hovy 1998).

4.4 Verbal Narrative Explanations and User Models

The interface could present an audio narrative (e.g., Allen and Nallaru 2009) for each of the schemas. Current narratives were simple recountings of the schema transitions. Potentially, they could be much richer and include a range of well-defined discourse moves such as the implications of a given state change for other parts of the system and they could be integrated with the Overview (Sect. 3) options. Further, the narratives could adapt to the knowledge and interests of the users; adaptive hypertext (Brusilovsky 1998) and tutoring systems do this. We could also record the propositions the user has viewed and use the record to structure later presentations for that user.

4.5 Graphical Animation

User interaction with these system descriptions may be compared to a gamer's interaction with a video game. Techniques for planning for user interaction might be adapted from video games such as Goal Oriented Action Planner (GOAP) and partial order planning (Hartsook et al. 2011). Perhaps even richer animations could be generated to resemble sequences of scenes analogous to comic strips and full animation could be implemented with graphics engines such as Blender (upbge.org).

4.6 Process-Based Dynamic Knowledge Graphs

Our work goes beyond typical approaches to knowledge graphs. We include state transitions and higher-level constructs such as workflow mechanisms, complex objects, causal claims, hypotheses, evidence, and even discourse (Allen 2022; in preparation). Moreover, our knowledge graph would be dynamic in that it is executable and states change as it evolves. Ultimately, we believe that all of this can be coordinated in a single multi-layered knowledge graph. Conflict checks could be implemented with model checking or by using the Python Element Tree to cast the knowledge base into XML.

4.7 Relationship to Generative AI

While the modeling in the current approach is laborious, we believe it will become simpler as more tools are developed and the semantic resources are refined. If this work can be scaled, it provides an alternative to the current generation of LLMs. A ChatGPT summary of the Snowball Earth theory we generated is particularly shallow, apparently reflecting the limitations of the current generation of LLM. Nonetheless, LLMs might be useful for generating and refining the knowledge base.

5 Discussion

In previous work (Allen 2022), we explored developing highly structured scientific research reports. This work is related to that because rich, structured descriptions of systems are central to science. We focus on science because scientific presentations are relatively unambiguous, of inherent interest, and have well-developed models. While our earlier work focused on experimental research paradigms, geology is dominated by observation and modeling.

The approach developed here can be extended to incorporate and allow exploration of the evidence for the original Snowball Earth model as well as recent debates about it. Potentially, these rich models could also be extended to describe explanatory coherence and abduction (Thagard 1992). Morevoer, related approaches could be used to develop synthetic languages and models of communities for digital humanities (Allen and Chu 2021).

References

Allen, R.B.: A focus-context browser for browsing historical newspapers. JCDL 260–261 (2005). https://doi.org/10.1145/1065385.1065445

Allen, R.B.: Visualization, causation, and history, iConference (2011). https://doi.org/10.1145/1940761.1940835

Allen, R.B.: Implementation issues for a highly structured research report. In: Silvello, G., et al. (eds.) TPDL 2022. LNCS, vol. 13541, pp. 320–327. Springer, Cham (2022). https://doi.org/10.1007/978-3-031-16802-4_28

Allen, R.B.: Structured qualitative descriptions of physical systems at equilibrium, (extended version of a paper at International System Dynamics Conference), in preparation

Allen, R.B., Chu, Y.M.: Semantic Modeling of Pottery Making, Pacific Neighborhood Consortium (PNC) (2021). https://doi.org/10.23919/PNC53575.2021.9672253

Allen, R.B., Nallaru, S.: Exploring history with narrative timelines. HCII (2009). https://doi.org/10.1007/978-3-642-02556-3_38

Allen, R.B., Wu, Y., Luo, J.: Interactive causal schematics for qualitative scientific explanations. In: Fox, E.A., Neuhold, E.J., Premsmit, P., Wuwongse, V. (eds.) ICADL 2005. LNCS, vol. 3815, pp. 411–415. Springer, Heidelberg (2005). https://doi.org/10.1007/11599517_50

Aronson, L.: The 21st Century Screenplay. Silman-James Press (2010)

Brusilovsky, P.: Methods and techniques of adaptive hypermedia. In: Brusilovsky, P., Kobsa, A., Vassileva, J. (eds.) Adaptive Hypertext and Hypermedia, pp. 1–43. Springer, Dordrecht (1998). https://doi.org/10.1007/978-94-017-0617-9_1

den Boef, R., van Woudenberg, R.: Non-causal explanations in the humanities: some examples. Found. Sci. https://doi.org/10.1007/s10699-023-09910-3

Hartsook, K., Zook, A., Das, S., Riedl, M.O.: Toward supporting stories with procedurally generated game worlds, computational intelligence and games (CIG) (2011). https://doi.org/10.1109/CIG.2011.6032020

Hoffman, P.F., Schrag, D.P.: Snowball Earth, 2000. Sci. Am. **282**(1), 68–75 (2000). https://doi.org/10.1038/scientificamerican0100-68

Hovy, E.: Planning coherent multisentential text, ACL (1988). ACL: aclanthology.org/P88-1020/

Mackie, J.L.: The Cement of the Universe: A Study of Causation. Oxford University Press, London (1974)

McKeown, K.: Text Generation. Cambridge University Press (1985)

Mueller, S.T., et al.: Principles of explanation in human-AI Systems, AAAI Workshop (2021). arXiv:2102.04972

Pease, A.: Ontology: A Practical Guide, Articulate (2011)

Pitt, J.C: Theories of Explanation. Oxford University Press (1988)

Ruppenhofer, J., Ellsworth, M., Schwarzer-Petruck, M., Johnson, C.R.: FrameNet II: extended theory and practice. International Computer Science Institute (2016). https://framenet2.icsi.berkeley.edu/docs/r1.7/book.pdf

Swales, J.: Genre Analysis: English in Academic and Research Settings. Cambridge University Press (1990)

Thagard, P.: Conceptual Revolutions. Princeton University Press (1992)

Thagard, P.: How Scientists Explain Disease. Princeton University Press (1999)

van Dijk, T.A.: Episodes as units of discourse analysis, 1982, Analyzing discourse: text and talk. In: Tannen, D. (ed.), Analyzing Discourse: Text and Talkpp. 171–195. Georgetown University Press (1981)

Weisberg, M.: Simulation and Similarity: Using Models to Understand the World. Oxford (2013)

Increasing Reproducibility in Science by Interlinking Semantic Artifact Descriptions in a Knowledge Graph

Hassan Hussein[1]([✉])(iD), Kheir Eddine Farfar[1](iD), Allard Oelen[1](iD),
Oliver Karras[1](iD), and Sören Auer[1,2](iD)

[1] TIB Leibniz Information Centre for Science and Technology, Hannover, Germany
{hassan.hussein,kheir.farfar,allard.oelen,oliver.karras,
soeren.auer}@tib.eu
[2] L3S Research Center, Leibniz University of Hannover, Hannover, Germany

Abstract. One of the pillars of the scientific method is reproducibility –
the ability to replicate the results of a prior study if the same procedures
are followed. A lack of reproducibility can lead to wasted resources, false
conclusions, and a loss of public trust in science. Ensuring reproducibility is challenging due to the heterogeneity of the methods used in different fields of science. In this article, we present an approach for increasing the reproducibility of research results, by semantically describing and interlinking relevant artifacts such as data, software scripts or simulations in a knowledge graph. In order to ensure the flexibility to adapt the approach to different fields of science, we devise a template model, which allows defining typical descriptions required to increase reproducibility of a certain type of study. We provide a scoring model for gradually assessing the reproducibility of a certain study based on the templates and provide a knowledge graph infrastructure for curating reproducibility descriptions along with semantic research contribution descriptions. We demonstrate the feasibility of our approach with an example in data science.

Keywords: Reproducibility Assessment · Scholarly Knowledge
Graph · FAIR Data Principles

1 Introduction

One of the guiding principles for scientific work is to guarantee the reproducibility of research findings as long as the researcher employs the same methodology as the original study. Reproducibility is a major concept in which we distinguish and describe access to scientific resources and their completeness to the extent necessary to efficiently and successfully engage with scientific research [8]. Due to the variety of methodologies used across different research fields, ensuring reproducibility is a challenging issue. Employing subjective processes, such as visual interpretation or data analysis, can result in diverse outcomes even when the exact methods are used, thus deepening the problem. Reproducibility issues can result in erroneous results, and a decline in public confidence in science. To assess the validity and reliability of results, it is crucial to be able to reproduce a study's results using the same methodology. So, guaranteeing reproducibility in scientific research can be challenging and complex. The FAIR data principles by Wilkinson et al. [27] are one of the most widely used guidelines for increasing machines' ability to automatically reuse data (i.e., machine actionability). The FAIR principles provided a conceptual model for outlining our novel approach, which increases the reproducibility of research results by semantically denoting and connecting all relevant artifacts, such as data, or software scripts via a knowledge graph. In this work, we address the following research questions: *What are the requirements for creating a general reproducibility assessment for various scientific fields?*, and *How to foster collaboration and knowledge exchange in scientific communities?* In this study, we leverage the Open Research Knowledge Graph (ORKG[1]) infrastructure to select some use case and to implement our reproducibility score. For answering the research questions, we design a semantic template model for knowledge graphs that enables the construction of standard descriptions needed to increase the reproducibility in different disciplines. Additionally, we develop a scoring model to gradually assess the reproducibility of a study based on templates. Based on our case study, we are confident that semantic templates will help researchers describe research artifacts relevant to improve the reproducibility of their work. The article is structured as follows. In Sect. 2, we discuss related work. In Sect. 3, we present our proposed scoring pillars. In Sect. 4, we explain how we implemented the templates and the scoring models. In Sect. 5, we present a use case based on our approach. Finally, in Sect. 6, we conclude and discuss potential future work.

2   Related Work

Recent studies have shown that reproducibility is a significant issue in the scientific community. According to a survey conducted by the journal Nature, more than 70% of researchers have tried and failed to reproduce another scientist's experiments, and more than 50% have failed to reproduce their own experiments [1]. This lack of reproducibility can lead to wasted resources, and false conclusions. Reproducibility faces some major issues, including setting up the proper technological infrastructure [6], the need to encourage and motivate researchers to publish and disclose their work publicly [1,7], and promoting the best approaches among researchers [2,13]. Howison et al. [12] emphasized that the challenges of sharing code and gaining academic credit for open-source collaborations have not yet been adequately addressed. There are some convincing proofs that much scientific research has not been able to be replicated [11]. In our literature review, we could find some common problems that hinder the research reproducibility as follow:

– **The unavailability of the replication data:** Reproducibility   is   a
  tribulation in both the natural and social sciences [10,18,21]. Two-thirds of

---

[1] https://orkg.org/.

all political science publications disclosed in the American Political Science Review (APSR) between 2013 and 2014 did not furnish replication materials, according to Key [15]. In genetics [20], medicine [24], economics [3,5,17], and sociology [19] is still the same problem. As per Vines et al. [26], the availability of research data declined dramatically over time following publication, by 17% annually in 516 studies with article ages ranging from 2 to 22 years.

- **The data accessibility:** Data accessibility is a crucial aspect of scientific research that can have a significant impact on the reproducibility of studies [22]. Furthermore, a comparison on ORKG[2] shows absolutely inadequate percentage of data accessibility in various research domains (e.g., agricultural science.., etc) across different geographical regions ranging from 3.26% to 39.26%.
- **The data completeness:** Chen et al. [4] argue that just concentrating on the data is insufficient. They stress that the data must be accompanied by software, workflows, and explanations. These elements must all be documented throughout the typical iterative and completed research lifecycle to be prepared for a timely open release of the results.
- **License:** Feger and Wozniak [8] state that external variables such as licensing limitations and expiration periods may impact sharing.

Another comparison on the ORKG[3] demonstrates various approaches for computational reproducibility. The comparison originated from work [9] that discusses most of the reproducibility approaches, specifically sharing data and code, etc. The work also presented some of the tools used in each approach (e.g., the TIER Protocol, Do-Files, etc.). After reviewing some of these approaches and tools to comprehend the issues underlying each one of them. We can conclude that most of these approaches are time-consuming to implement, have a steep learning curve for new users, have compatibility issues with some software or systems, and user interface problems.

3   FAIR-Based Reproducibility

Our model will foucs on the four pillars: availability, accessibility, linkability, and license. These pillars directly impact the reproducibility of artifacts in any study. We now discuss each of the pillars and what they mean in detail.

- **Availability:** We define availability as the willingness of researchers to make their artifacts, such as data, resources, and methods, voluntarily available to other scientists.
- **Accessibility:** In our earlier study [14] we set the accessibility measures on a top maturity level when assessing the accessibility of a knowledge graph (KG). In addition, article 06.1 in data access and research transparency (DART)[4] states that "researchers making evidence-based knowledge claims should

---

[2] https://orkg.org/comparison/R589387/.

[3] https://orkg.org/comparison/R589371/.

[4] https://www.dartstatement.org/2012-apsa-ethics-guide-changes.

reference the data they used to make those claims". The guide further declares that "if these are data [the researchers] themselves generated or collected, researchers should provide access to those data or explain why they cannot."

- **Linkability:** We suggest that using ontologies to link scientific data with other sources is crucial for facilitating the reproducibility of scientific findings. The World Wide Web Consortium (W3C)[5] has been working to develop standards for linked data[6] to facilitate the integration of data from different sources.
- **License:** A valid license makes it feasible for researchers to comprehend the responsibilities and constraints associated with using the artifact, ensuring that they can use, and modify the artifact legally as required. Reproducibility was found to be negatively correlated with the lack of a license [23].

4   Implementation

The ORKG infrastructure implements best practices, such as the FAIR principles, offers a wide range of services to make it easier to curate, share, and use FAIR scientific information [25]. Because of these features, the ORKG is an ideal infrastructure to implement our approach. In this section, we explain what the reproducibility score is and how it works. In addition, we present the ORKG template engine and how it supports implementing the reproducibility score.

4.1   Reproducibility Score

The reproducibility score is a method aiming to evaluate some of the fundamental requirements (e.g., availability) for making the scientific contribution or experiment reproducible. As illustrated in Fig. 1, the first stage is allowing the user to add their paper's metadata. Secondly, the user picks the appropriate template for their research contribution or constructs a template if needed. (Figure 2 illustrates a template). We propose to add a checkbox to mark a certain property in a template as reproducibility description property, thus distinguishing between conventional templates and templates that users can employ specifically for reproducibility. Thirdly, the user describes the research contribution guided by the chosen template. Finally, the system automatically computes the reproducibility score for the given contribution.

Given a reproducibility score, the user can review the full report as shown in Fig. 3. By availability we mean that the contribution curator utilized the resource by a value. The accessibility attribute represents a resource of type URL(ORKG has different data types including resource, URL...etc) and has an HTTP response code of 200, which denotes that the related artifact is reachable. The system considers this resource unsuitable for this test if it is not of type URL. Linkability indicates that the data curator linked the resources to a reliable ontology. Finally, a URL-based resource that is available under an open license,

---

[5] https://www.w3.org/.

[6] https://www.w3.org/standards/semanticweb/data.

such as the MIT License, is considered to have a favorable License, allowing for reuse and redistribution. Figure 3.

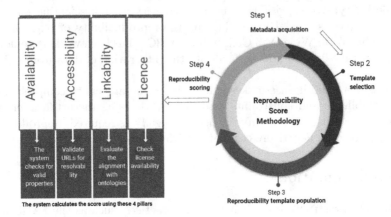

Fig. 1. Workflow illustrating the architecture and components of the reproducibility score, showcasing the systematic process for assessing reproducibility in scientific research.

4.2 Score Calculation

The score calculation assesses the four pillars, namely the availability, accessibility, linkability, and licenses of artifacts automatically once the end user adds their contribution. A higher reproducibility score implies a higher degree of allowing other researchers to repeat the given experiment. The artifacts linked in the reproducibility template are categorized into one of three cases:

- **Valid:** the artifact meets the criteria for being complete, accurate, and relevant to the problem at hand.
- **Inapplicable:** an artifact cannot be used in a specific context or for a specific purpose due to its limitations or characteristics. For example, if the data is not of type URL, it cannot be checked for accessibility.
- **Not Valid:** data is incomplete, inaccurate, or does not fulfill the standards for quality and reliability. For example, if data is not linked with a trusted ontology when its type is a resource then it is not valid.

The score for the four pillars is the trimmed mean for set of properties for a given contribution of a matrix with 4 columns(pillars) and n rows(properties values), while excluding the highest and lowest values to avoid outliers is calculated as follows:

$$\overline{X}tr = \frac{1}{n-2} \sum i = 2^{n-1} \operatorname{trim}(x_i, 0.5) \tag{1}$$

where $\operatorname{trim}(x_i, 0.5)$ represents the trimming of x_i by 0.5 (i.e., removing the highest and lowest 50% of values) to avoid outliers.

To calculate the trimmed mean of each row, you can apply this equation to each row of the matrix separately. To calculate the trimmed mean of each column, you can transpose the matrix and apply the equation to each row (which corresponds to each column of the original matrix).

$$\overline{X}_{tr,1} = \frac{0 + 100}{2} = 50 \tag{2}$$

We repeat this process for each of the other rows, and obtain the following trimmed means. The system continuously allows the user to improve their contribution's reproducibility score. As the user can preserve editing their contribution and add the missing artifacts as needed.

4.3 ORKG Templates

The ORKG provides a template system that empowers domain experts to define the structure of contributions. Templates automatically generate user-friendly input forms to assist researchers in providing the necessary data. The system enables the definition of constraints on properties, such as data types and cardinality of values, to generate appropriate input forms and perform data validation. It implements a subset of the Shapes Constraint Language (SHACL) [16] which proportionately enables the interoperability with existing SHACL-based systems and ensures uniformity in the verification and management of data. The template system serves as a controller, supervising what data should be collected based on the research field and problem. Furthermore, it aligns with the FAIR data principles. By utilizing external ontologies and linking data to them, researchers are able to increase the discoverability, accessibility, and reusability

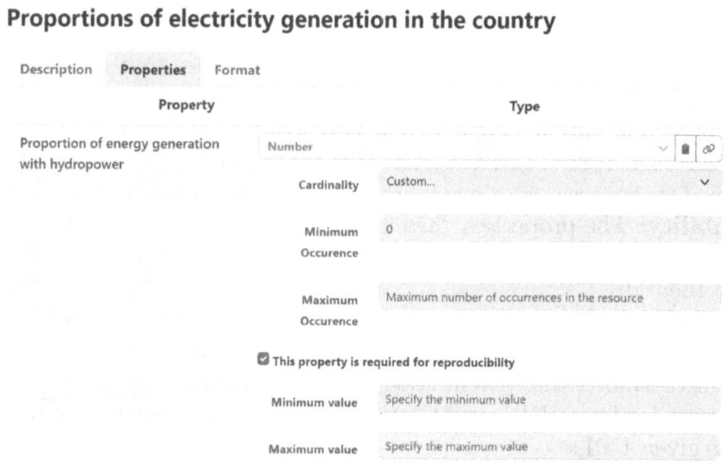

Fig. 2. A screenshot of the ORKG template system, depicting a property, property type, and cardinality.

of their contributions. By using a template system, researchers can compare their work with others and establish a common language (i.e., standardized vocabulary). In addition, to further promote and incentivize reproducibility within the ORKG platform, we propose the implementation of a new feature: a "required for reproducibility" checkbox. When the template designer selects this checkbox, it implies that the associated property is considered a crucial element in determining the overall reproducibility score of a given artifact.

5 Reproducibility Score Use Cases

In this section, we demonstrate a use case for the proposed reproducibility score in data science. As shown in Fig. 3, the horizontal axis of the report shows the average reproducibility score for a given property, while the vertical axis represents the unique score for each of the four pillars of reproducibility.

5.1 Papers with Code

The Papers With Code (PWC)[7] system aims to promote information sharing about the evolution of machine learning research. A subset of this data is fed to ORKG by modeling the different aspects covered by the data in a structured way. This includes the algorithms used, their evaluation on specified benchmark datasets, and the metrics used to measure performance (e.g., precision, recall, f-measure). An ORKG template named Leaderboard[8] is created to guide users in adding more data to the graph, adhering to the established model. We chose one of the papers[9] imported into ORKG as an example to demonstrate the score concept (Fig. 3). We used this paper because it shows some properties that use URLs. Next we explain what this report means:

- **Availability:** All data is available so that the vertically-aggregated score is 100%.
- **Accessibility:** The score is 100% for some properties that are of type URL (e.g., source code). The system also checks to see if the specified URL can be reached with an HTTP response code of 200. In addition, all the other resources that are not of type URL (e.g., has model) were identified as inapplicable for this test. As a result, the vertically-aggregated score is 100%.
- **Linkability:** The properties "has model" and "research problem" are of the type resource but not associated with ontologies. For this reason, the system scored them 0%.
- **License:** The system assigned a score of 100% to properties "has benchmark" and "has model" because they are not of type URL and is inapplicable for this test. Furthermore, the system allocated a 0% score for the property "source code" as it is of type URL and the system could not correlate a proper license for the given URLs.

---

[7] https://paperswithcode.com/about.

[8] https://orkg.org/template/R107801.

[9] https://orkg.org/paper/R478126.

has benchmark	Benchmark WikiText-2	✓	—	✗	—	100%
has model	Inan et al 2016 - variational lstm tied h 650	✓	—	✗	—	100%
source code	github.com	✓	✓	—	✗	100%
	github.com	✓	✓	—	✗	100%
	github.com	✓	✓	—	✗	100%
	github.com	✓	✓	—	✗	100%
	github.com	✓	✓	—	✗	100%
research problem	Language Modelling	✓	—	✗	—	100%
Final Score		**100%**	**100%**	**0%**	**100%**	

Fig. 3. A view of how the reproducibility score computed for the PWC use case.

6 Conclusion and Future Work

The approach focuses only on measuring the four pillars: availability, accessibility, linkability, and license, to provide a thorough assessment of the dependability and robustness of a study's findings. Our use of ORKG templates in this score implementation permits an effective and automated calculation of the score. To show the adaptability and effectiveness of this approach in different domains we presented, a use case in data science. In future work, we plan to implement the reproducibility score as an open assessment tool. Publishers (e.g., Springer) can integrate it into their services. We also intend to do a qualitative assessment for the reproducibility score.

Supplemental Material Statement: Source code is available on Github[10].

References

1. Estimating the reproducibility of psychological science. Science **349**(6251), aac4716 (2015). https://doi.org/10.1126/science.aac4716, https://www.science.org/doi/abs/10.1126/science.aac4716
2. Buys, C.M., Shaw, P.L.: Data management practices across an institution: survey and report. **3**(2), 1225 (2015). https://doi.org/10.7710/2162-3309.1225
3. Chang, A.C., Li, P.: Is economics research replicable? Sixty published papers from thirteen journals say "usually not" (2015). https://shorturl.at/jlpxQ
4. Chen, X.: Open is not enough. Nat. Phys. **15**, 7 (2019)

---

[10] https://gitlab.com/TIBHannover/orkg/orkg-frontend/-/merge_requests/1015.

5. Dewald, W.G., Thursby, J.G., Anderson, R.G.: Replication in empirical economics: the journal of money, credit and banking project. **76**(4), 587–603 (1986). https://www.jstor.org/stable/1806061
6. Feger, S.S., Dallmeier-Tiessen, S., Woźniak, P.W., Schmidt, A.: The role of HCI in reproducible science: understanding, supporting and motivating core practices. In: Extended Abstracts of the 2019 CHI Conference on Human Factors in Computing Systems, CHI EA 2019, pp. 1–6. Association for Computing Machinery, New York (2019). https://doi.org/10.1145/3290607.3312905
7. Feger, S.S.: Interactive tools for reproducible science - understanding, supporting, and motivating reproducible science practices, p. 221 (2020)
8. Feger, S.S., Woźniak, P.W.: Reproducibility: a researcher-centered definition. **6**(2), 17 (2022). https://doi.org/10.3390/mti6020017, https://www.mdpi.com/2414-4088/6/2/17
9. Figueiredo Filho, D., Lins, R., Domingos, A., Janz, N., Silva, L.: Seven reasons why: a user's guide to transparency and reproducibility. **13**(2), e0001 (2019). https://doi.org/10.1590/1981-3821201900020001, http://www.scielo.br/scielo.php?script=sci_arttext&pid=S1981-38212019000200400&tlng=en
10. Freese, J., Peterson, D.: Replication in social science. Annu. Rev. Sociol. **43**(1), 147–165 (2017). https://doi.org/10.1146/annurev-soc-060116-053450
11. Goodman, S.N., Fanelli, D., Ioannidis, J.P.A.: What does research reproducibility mean? Sci. Transl. Med. **8**(341), 341ps12–341ps12 (2016). https://doi.org/10.1126/scitranslmed.aaf5027, https://www.science.org/doi/abs/10.1126/scitranslmed.aaf5027
12. Howison, J., Herbsleb, J.D.: Scientific software production: incentives and collaboration. In: Proceedings of the ACM 2011 Conference on Computer Supported Cooperative Work, CSCW 2011, pp. 513–522. Association for Computing Machinery, New York (2011). https://doi.org/10.1145/1958824.1958904
13. Hoy, M.B.: Big data: an introduction for librarians. Med. Reference Serv. Q. **33**(3), 320–326 (2014). https://doi.org/10.1080/02763869.2014.925709. pMID: 25023020
14. Hussein, H., Oelen, A., Karras, O., Auer, S.: KGMM - a maturity model for scholarly knowledge graphs based on intertwined human-machine collaboration. In: Tseng, Y.H., Katsurai, M., Nguyen, H.N. (eds.) ICADL 2022. LNCS, vol. 13636, pp. 253–269. Springer, Cham (2022). https://doi.org/10.1007/978-3-031-21756-2_21
15. Key, E.M.: How are we doing? Data access and replication in political science. PS: Polit. Sci. Polit. **49**(2), 268–272 (2016). https://doi.org/10.1017/S1049096516000184
16. Knublauch, H., Kontokostas, D.: Shapes constraint language (SHACL). W3C Candidate Recommendation **11**(8) (2017)
17. Krawczyk, M., Reuben, E.: (Un)available upon request: field experiment on researchers' willingness to share supplementary materials. **19**(3), 175–186 (2012). https://doi.org/10.1080/08989621.2012.678688
18. Leek, J.T., Peng, R.D.: Reproducible research can still be wrong: adopting a prevention approach. Proc. Natl. Acad. Sci. **112**(6), 1645–1646 (2015). https://doi.org/10.1073/pnas.1421412111, https://www.pnas.org/doi/abs/10.1073/pnas.1421412111
19. Lucas, J.W., Morrell, K., Posard, M.: Considerations on the 'replication problem' in sociology. **44**(2), 217–232 (2013). https://doi.org/10.1007/s12108-013-9176-7
20. Markowetz, F.: Five selfish reasons to work reproducibly. **16**(1), 274 (2015). https://doi.org/10.1186/s13059-015-0850-7
21. Munafò, M.R., et al.: A manifesto for reproducible science. **1**, 0021 (2017). https://doi.org/10.1038/s41562-016-0021

22. Nosek, B.A., et al.: Promoting an open research culture. Science **348**(6242), 1422–1425 (2015). https://doi.org/10.1126/science.aab2374, https://www.science.org/doi/abs/10.1126/science.aab2374

23. Peng, R.D.: Reproducible research in computational science. **334**(6060), 1226–1227 (2011). https://doi.org/10.1126/science.1213847

24. Savage, C.J., Vickers, A.J.: Empirical study of data sharing by authors publishing in PLoS journals. **4**(9) (2009). https://doi.org/10.1371/journal.pone.0007078, https://journals.plos.org/plosone/article?id=10.1371/journal.pone.0007078

25. Stocker, M., et al.: FAIR scientific information with the open research knowledge graph. **1**(1), 19–21 (2023). https://doi.org/10.3233/FC-221513, https://content.iospress.com/articles/fair-connect/fc221513

26. Vines, T.H., et al.: The availability of research data declines rapidly with article age. **24**(1), 94–97 (2014). https://doi.org/10.1016/j.cub.2013.11.014, https://www.cell.com/current-biology/abstract/S0960-9822(13)01400-0, publisher: Elsevier

27. Wilkinson, M.D., et al.: The FAIR guiding principles for scientific data management and stewardship. Sci. Data **3**, 1–9 (2016). https://doi.org/10.1038/sdata.2016.18

An End-to-End Table Structure Analysis Method Using Graph Attention Networks

Manabu Ohta[1]($\boxtimes$) , Hiroyuki Aoyagi[1], Fumito Uwano[1] ,
Teruhito Kanazawa[2] , and Atsuhiro Takasu[2]

[1] Okayama University, Okayama, Japan
{ohta,uwano}@okayama-u.ac.jp, ao2516@s.okayama-u.ac.jp
[2] National Institute of Informatics, Tokyo, Japan
{tkana,takasu}@nii.ac.jp

Abstract. This paper proposes an end-to-end table structure analysis method using graph attention networks (GATs) that includes table detection. The proposed method initially identifies tables within documents, estimates whether horizontally adjacent tokens within the table belong to the same cell using GATs, subsequently estimates implicitly ruled lines required for cell separation but not actually drawn, and finally merges the remaining tokens to estimate cells, again using GATs. We have also collected 800 new tables and annotated them with structural information to augment the training data for the proposed method. Evaluation experiments showed that the proposed method achieved an F-measure of 0.984, outperforming other methods including the commercial ABBYY FineReader PDF in accuracy of table structure analysis with table detection. This paper also showed that the 800 newly annotated tables enhanced the proposed method's accuracy.

Keywords: Table structure analysis · Document analysis · Graph attention network

1 Introduction

Academic papers are readily available on digital libraries such as Google Scholar and DBLP[1]. The user experience in digital libraries [8], however, could be greatly improved with enhanced support for online paper browsing. This involves transforming the content of papers for better understanding and ensuring proper linkage between digital libraries and web resources. In this paper, we focus on tables, which are commonly used in a wide range of documents. Particularly in academic papers, tables are frequently employed to summarize data statistics and experimental results. However, graphs, which are more visually appealing than tables, are better for understanding and comparing numeric values at a glance. Therefore, automatic graph generation from a table has been studied [14]. Because of diverse table writing styles, accurate table structure analysis is crucial.

---

[1] https://dblp.org.

© The Author(s), under exclusive license to Springer Nature Singapore Pte Ltd. 2023
D. H. Goh et al. (Eds.): ICADL 2023, LNCS 14458, pp. 230–239, 2023.
https://doi.org/10.1007/978-981-99-8088-8_20

Chi et al. proposed a graph neural network (GNN) model for recognizing the structure of tables in PDF files, called GraphTSR [3]. Zheng et al. proposed the Global Table Extractor (GTE) [15], a vision-guided systematic framework for joint table detection and cell structure recognition, which consists of several vision-based neural networks (NNs). We also proposed a table structure analysis method [1] and analyzed the structure of tables using four NN modules: horizontal merge, vertical merge and cell generation to merge adjacent tokens in a table, and implicitly ruled line (IRL) estimation to estimate IRLs that are necessary to separate cells but not actually drawn. In ICDAR 2013 table dataset experiments, the method from [1] outperformed the top performer [5] by 2.6 points, achieving an F-measure of 0.972 for cell adjacency reproducibility.

In this paper, we propose an end-to-end table structure analysis method. The main contributions of this paper are summarized as follows. First, we integrated CascadeTabNet [12] into [1] to add table detection functionality in documents, thereby enabling us to perform the complete pipeline of table recognition from PDF to table structure. Second, we proposed an improved NN model for token merging by incorporating graph attention networks (GATs) [13]. We demonstrated that this approach achieved higher accuracy compared to both the commercial ABBYY FineReader PDF[2] and the method proposed in [1]. Third, we manually annotated 800 tables with structural information to enhance training.

2   End-to-End Table Structure Analysis Method

Figure 1 illustrates the processing flow of the end-to-end table structure analysis method proposed in this paper. The blue rectangles are NN modules and we introduced GATs into the horizontal merging and cell generation modules. In the proposed method, an input PDF document is first converted to an image and CascadeTabNet is used to detect tables from the document image. The PDF document is also converted to an XML file using pdfalto[3]. The detected table region and the XML file are then used as input for the table structure analysis. In the preprocessing, the tokens in the table are extracted from the table region in the XML file and the ruled lines are also detected using PDFMiner[4] and OpenCV[5]. In the postprocessing, the final table structure is determined using the same approach as in [11]. We use the same NN module for the IRL estimation as in [1]. The details of the other NN modules are described below.

2.1   Table Detection with CascadeTabNet

CascadeTabNet [12] is an end-to-end table structure analysis method that uses Cascade R-CNN to detect tables in document images and the cells in the tables. The evaluation experiments in [12] used the ICDAR 2013 table dataset, the

---

[2] https://pdf.abbyy.com.
[3] https://github.com/kermitt2/pdfalto.
[4] https://github.com/pdfminer/pdfminer.six.
[5] https://opencv.org.

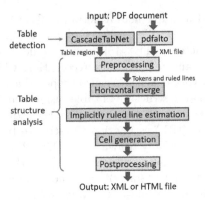

Fig. 1. Processing flow of the proposed end-to-end table structure analysis method.

ICDAR 2019 table dataset [4] and the TableBank dataset [9]. As a result, the F-measure, which indicates the reproducibility of table detection, was 1.0 and 0.943 for the ICDAR 2013 table dataset and TableBank, respectively (both ranked first). We use the CascadeTabNet, which is publicly available on GitHub[6], only for table detection and not for cell detection.

2.2 Horizontal Merge

Horizontal merge repeatedly merges two horizontally adjacent tokens until there are no more adjacent tokens to merge. First, an undirected graph is created where the tokens are nodes and the adjacencies of the tokens are edges. Next, the merger estimates whether two horizontally adjacent tokens are in the same cell or not, and if so, merges them. The top two tables in Fig. 2 show an example of the horizontal merge. Note that the ICDAR 2013 table dataset [5] is used for the table in this figure. An undirected graph is generated based on the adjacency of the tokens, as shown in Fig. 2.

Figure 3 shows the model for the horizontal merge and the cell generation. In the figure, n is the number of all tokens and e is the number of all adjacent token pairs. The model shown in Fig. 3 incorporates GATs [13] using PyTorch Geometric[7]. The dimensions of 2), 3), 4), and 5) are 42, 11, 84, and 11, respectively. To obtain distributed representations of the token text, we use glove-wiki-gigaword-100[8] as the pre-trained model of Word2vec [10]. Binary cross entropy is used as the loss function and Adam [7] as the optimization function.

Table 1 summarizes the input token features of 2) and 4) in Fig. 3 and Table 2 summarizes the adjacency features of adjacent token pairs of 3) and 5) in Fig. 3. In Table 1, the part of speech (POS) of a token is represented as a 12-dimensional one-hot vector obtained using the Natural Language Toolkit

---

[6] https://github.com/DevashishPrasad/CascadeTabNet.

[7] https://github.com/pyg-team/pytorch_geometric.

[8] https://nlp.stanford.edu/projects/glove.

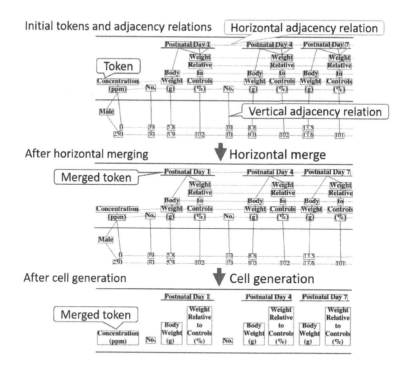

Fig. 2. Example of horizontal merge and cell generation.

(NLTK)[9]. In Table 2, the text similarity between adjacent tokens is computed using a Python library called difflib.

2.3 Cell Generation

After the IRL estimation, two vertically or horizontally adjacent tokens are alternately merged to form a cell using the model in Fig. 3. This cell generation is performed iteratively until there are no more adjacent tokens to merge. In Fig. 2, many vertically adjacent tokens in the middle table are merged after the cell generation, as seen in the bottom table.

The cell generation and horizontal merge models are identical, with the cell generator merging both horizontally and vertically adjacent tokens. Furthermore, the cell generator employs augmented token features and augmented adjacency features of token pairs, resulting in higher-dimensional input feature vectors compared to the horizontal merger. For example, in addition to Table 1, we incorporate token features such as the word count within a token and the token count within the associated column or row. Consequently, the dimensions of 2), 3), 4), and 5) in Fig. 3 are 57, 19, 114, and 19, respectively.

---

[9] https://www.nltk.org.

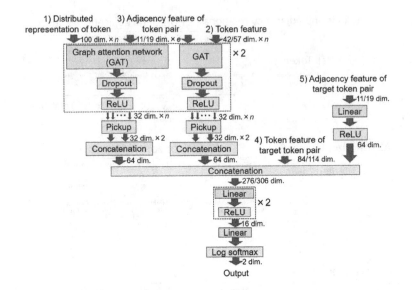

Fig. 3. Model for horizontal merge and cell generation.

3   Experiments

3.1   Experimental Setup

The 209 tables from [1] and 800 newly annotated tables train the NN modules for horizontal merging, IRL estimation, and cell generation in the proposed method. The 800 tables were collected from the PDF documents published from January 2022 to October 2022 on the websites of public organizations in Japan and the US. Subsequently, Aoyagi annotated them with table structural information, including cell positions and text within the cells. To evaluate the accuracy of table structure analysis, we use the ICDAR 2013 table competition test dataset [5] as in the experiments in [1]. This table dataset consists of 156 tables collected from documents published by the EU and US governments, including PDF documents containing these tables and XML files with the annotated table structure.

The accuracy of the table structure analysis is evaluated using the metrics based on the reproducibility of cell adjacency relations defined by Göbel et al. [6] and a Tree-Edit-Distance-based Similarity (TEDS) defined by Zhong et al. [16].

3.2   Experimental Results

Table Structure Analysis Accuracy. The accuracy of end-to-end table structure analysis including table detection is in Table 3, while Table 4 covers table structure analysis without table detection. The table regions are specified manually when analyzing tables without table detection. 209 tables trained the

Table 1. Token features used for horizontal merge.

Feature	Dimension
Token size (width and height)	2
Coordinate coincidence with other tokens	6
Whether the token is numeric or not	1
Part of speech (POS) of the token	12
Possibility of a subheading	1
Whether the first letter of the token is uppercase or not	1
Whether the token is within parentheses	1
Whether the token is a symbol* or not	1
Whether or not the token starts with a symbol*	1
Whether or not the token ends with a symbol*	1
Surrounding tokens' feature	15
Total	42

symbol: "-", "", "#", "/", "%", "&", "$", "+", "(", ")", dagger, double dagger

Table 2. Adjacency features of two adjacent tokens used for horizontal merge.

Feature	Dimension
Distance between adjacent tokens	1
Same font or not	1
Same style or not	1
Coordinate match between adjacent tokens (centroid)	1
Coordinate match between adjacent tokens (upper left corner)	1
Coordinate match between adjacent tokens (upper right corner)	1
Textual similarity between adjacent tokens	1
Existence of a ruled line between adjacent tokens	1
Merging position	2
Adjacency direction ("horizontal" for the horizontal merge)	1
Total	11

ICPRAM 2022 method [1], while 1,009 tables, including 800 newly annotated ones, trained the proposed method. We discuss the difference in the number of the tables used for training in Sect. 3.3. Note that the commercial software ABBYY FineReader PDF works with document images and does not utilize PDF-related information, such as the text within the documents. Therefore, we also calculate the evaluation metrics while disregarding OCR errors in the analyzed result, represented as "ABBYY FineReader with OCR correction" in Table 3, to ensure a fairer comparison.

Table 3. Accuracy of end-to-end table structure analysis with table detection.

Input	Method	Adjacency (micro avg.)			Adjacency (macro avg.)			TEDS
		Recall	Precision	F	Recall	Precision	F	
PDF	Proposed	0.984	0.985	0.984	0.976	0.972	0.974	0.969
	ICPRAM 2022 [1]	0.954	0.970	0.962	0.943	0.951	0.947	0.948
Image	ABBYY FineReader	0.950	0.971	0.960	0.943	0.951	0.947	0.958
	ABBYY FineReader with OCR correction	0.965	0.986	0.975	0.958	0.964	0.961	0.965
	GTE [15]	–	–	–	0.927	0.944	0.935	–

Table 4. Accuracy of table structure analysis without table detection.

Input	Method	Adjacency (micro avg.)			Adjacency (macro avg.)			TEDS
		Recall	Precision	F	Recall	Precision	F	
PDF	Proposed	0.986	0.986	0.986	0.978	0.977	0.977	0.982
	ICPRAM 2022 [1]	0.967	0.977	0.972	0.955	0.968	0.961	0.969
	GraphTSR [3]	0.860	0.885	0.872	0.855	0.819	0.837	–
Image	GTE [15]	–	–	–	0.958	0.968	0.962	–

The accuracy of the proposed method with table detection was 2.2 and 2.7 points higher than the accuracy of the ICPRAM 2022 method [1] in terms of micro-average and macro-average F-measures of cell adjacency reproducibility, respectively, and the TEDS was 2.1 points higher. Compared to the commercial software ABBYY FineReader PDF with corrected OCR errors, the F-measures of cell adjacency reproducibility were 0.9 (micro-average) and 1.3 (macro-average) points higher, respectively, and the TEDS was 0.4 points higher. Without table detection, the F-measures of cell adjacency reproducibility of the proposed method were 1.4 (micro-average) and 1.6 (macro-average) points higher and the TEDS was 1.3 points higher than those of [1], respectively, as shown in Table 4.

Accuracy of Three NN Modules. The results of the horizontal merging are shown in Table 5(a). There were 6 token pairs that should have been merged but were not, and 17 that should not have been merged but were. Note that "GT" and "NM" in Table 5 stand for "Ground Truth" and "Not Merged," respectively. Thus, the horizontal merge successfully merged 99.8% of the 3,039 token pairs that should have been merged, while mistakenly merging 20.2% of the 84 token pairs that should not have been merged.

The results of the IRL estimation are shown in Table 5(b). In the training data, there were 83,776 IRLs and 38,217 non-IRLs. Because of this imbalance, the same number of IRLs and non-IRLs generated by SMOTEENN [2] were used to train the IRL estimator. As shown in Table 5(b), the percentage of IRLs mistakenly estimated as non-IRL was 3.0%, and conversely, the percentage of non-IRLs mistakenly estimated as IRL was 11.7%.

The results of the cell generation are shown in Table 5(c), with 179 token pairs that should have been merged but were not, and 7 token pairs that should

Table 5. Results: (a) Horizontal merging, (b) IRL estimation, and (c) Cell generation.

	(a)	Predicted			(b)	Predicted			(c)	Predicted	
		Merged	NM			IRL	Non-IRL			Merged	NM
GT	Merged	3,033	6	GT	IRL	13,423	412	GT	Merged	493	179
	NM	17	67		Non-IRL	482	3,630		NM	7	25,127

not have been merged but were. The cell generator failed to merge 26.6% of the token pairs that should have been merged, but erroneously merged only 0.03% of the token pairs that should not have been merged.

3.3 Effectiveness of the Created Table Dataset

In the evaluation of the proposed method without table detection, the micro- and macro-averages of the F-measure and TEDS were 0.982, 0.970, and 0.977, respectively, when trained with only the 209 tables [1]. However, when trained with all the 1,009 tables (adding 800 tables), they improved by 0.4, 0.7, and 0.5 points, respectively, as shown in Table 4.

The number of erroneously merged and erroneously non-merged token pairs in the horizontal merge was 17 and 4, respectively, when trained with the 209 tables. When trained with the 1,009 tables, they were 17 and 6, respectively, as shown in Table 5(a). Hence, token pairs can be horizontally merged with relatively high accuracy, even when trained with the 209 tables. The false positives and false negatives of IRLs in the IRL estimation were 881 and 595, respectively, when trained with the 209 tables. When trained with the 1,009 tables, these errors were 482 and 412, respectively, as shown in Table 5(b), and the errors were reduced by 399 and 183, respectively. Thus, the 800 tables improved IRL estimation accuracy. The number of erroneously merged and erroneously non-merged token pairs in the cell generation was 11 and 270, respectively, when trained with the 209 tables. When trained with the 1,009 tables, these errors were 7 and 179, respectively, as shown in Table 5(c), and the errors were reduced by 4 and 91, respectively. Thus, the 800 tables improved cell generation accuracy.

4 Conclusion

In this paper, we proposed an end-to-end table structure analysis method using GATs. In addition to the CascadeTabNet for table detection, our method includes three NN modules: horizontal merging, IRL estimation, and cell generation. The GATs are employed to merge adjacent tokens in tables during the horizontal merging and cell generation. The evaluation experiments showed that the micro-average F-measure for cell adjacency reproducibility in the end-to-end table structure analysis with table detection was 0.984, surpassing the commercial ABBYY FineReader PDF by 0.9 points when disregarding the OCR errors and by 2.4 points for the original results. The micro-average F-measure for cell adjacency reproducibility without table detection was 0.986, surpassing that of [1] by 1.4 points. Furthermore, the accuracy of the IRL estimation and cell generation modules, as well as the overall table structure analysis, improved by incorporating 800 newly annotated tables into the training data.

We have two main future goals: i) Evaluating the proposed method on datasets other than the ICDAR 2013 dataset to broaden its applicability to table images, ii) Developing an automatic graph generation application to visualize table data analyzed by our method, enhancing the user experience in digital libraries.

Acknowledgements. This work was supported by JSPS KAKENHI Grant Number JP22H03904 and ROIS NII Open Collaborative Research 2023 (23FC02).

References

1. Aoyagi, H., Kanazawa, T., Takasu, A., Uwano, F., Ohta, M.: Table-structure recognition method consisting of plural neural network modules. In: Proceedings of the 11th International Conference on Pattern Recognition Applications and Methods - Volume 1: ICPRAM, pp. 542–549 (2022)
2. Batista, G.E.A.P.A., Prati, R.C., Monard, M.C.: A study of the behavior of several methods for balancing machine learning training data. SIGKDD Explor. Newsl. **6**(1), 20–29 (2004)
3. Chi, Z., Huang, H., Xu, H.D., Yu, H., Yin, W., Mao, X.L.: Complicated table structure recognition. arXiv:1908.04729 (2019)
4. Gao, L., et al.: ICDAR 2019 competition on table detection and recognition (cTDaR). In: Proceedings of the 2019 International Conference on Document Analysis and Recognition (ICDAR), pp. 1510–1515 (2019)
5. Göbel, M., Hassan, T., Oro, E., Orsi, G.: ICDAR 2013 table competition. In: Proceedings of the 12th International Conference on Document Analysis and Recognition (ICDAR), pp. 1449–1453 (2013)
6. Göbel, M., Hassan, T., Oro, E., Orsi, G.: A methodology for evaluating algorithms for table understanding in pdf documents. In: Proceedings of the 2012 ACM Symposium on Document Engineering, pp. 45–48 (2012)
7. Kingma, D.P., Ba, J.: Adam: a method for stochastic optimization. In: Proceedings of the 3rd International Conference on Learning Representations (ICLR) (2015)
8. Kuhar, M., Merčun, T.: Exploring user experience in digital libraries through questionnaire and eye-tracking data. Libr. Inf. Sci. Res. **44**(3), 101175 (2022)
9. Li, M., Cui, L., Huang, S., Wei, F., Zhou, M., Li, Z.: TableBank: table benchmark for image-based table detection and recognition. In: Proceedings of the Twelfth Language Resources and Evaluation Conference, pp. 1918–1925 (2020)
10. Mikolov, T., Chen, K., Corrado, G.S., Dean, J.: Efficient estimation of word representations in vector space. arXiv:1301.3781 (2013)
11. Ohta, M., Yamada, R., Kanazawa, T., Takasu, A.: Table-structure recognition method using neural networks for implicit ruled line estimation and cell estimation. In: Proceedings of the 21st ACM Symposium on Document Engineering (2021)

12. Prasad, D., Gadpal, A., Kapadni, K., Visave, M., Sultanpure, K.: CascadeTabNet: an approach for end to end table detection and structure recognition from image-based documents. In: Proceedings of 2020 IEEE/CVF Conference on Computer Vision and Pattern Recognition Workshops (CVPRW), pp. 2439–2447 (2020)

13. Veličković, P., Cucurull, G., Casanova, A., Romero, A., Liò, P., Bengio, Y.: Graph attention networks. In: Proceedings of International Conference on Learning Representations (2018)

14. Yamada, R., Ohta, M., Takasu, A.: An automatic graph generation method for scholarly papers based on table structure analysis. In: Proceedings of the 10th International Conference on Management of Digital EcoSystems, pp. 132–140 (2018)

15. Zheng, X., Burdick, D., Popa, L., Zhong, X., Wang, N.X.R.: Global table extractor (GTE): a framework for joint table identification and cell structure recognition using visual context. In: Proceedings of 2021 IEEE Winter Conference on Applications of Computer Vision (WACV), pp. 697–706 (2021)

16. Zhong, X., ShafieiBavani, E., Jimeno Yepes, A.: Image-based table recognition: data, model, and evaluation. In: Vedaldi, A., Bischof, H., Brox, T., Frahm, J.-M. (eds.) ECCV 2020. LNCS, vol. 12366, pp. 564–580. Springer, Cham (2020). https://doi.org/10.1007/978-3-030-58589-1_34

Co-attention-Based Pairwise Learning for Author Name Disambiguation

Shenghui Wang[1(✉)] , Qiuke Li[1], and Rob Koopman[2]

[1] University of Twente, Drienerlolaan 5, 7522 NB Enschede, The Netherlands
shenghui.wang@utwente.nl
[2] OCLC, Schipholweg 99, 2316 XA Leiden, The Netherlands
rob.koopman@oclc.org

Abstract. Digital libraries face a pressing issue of author name ambiguity. This paper proposes a novel pairwise learning model for author name disambiguation, utilizing self-attention and co-attention mechanisms. The model integrates textual, discrete, and co-author attributes, amongst others, to capture comprehensive information from bibliographic records. It incorporates an optional random projection-based dimension reduction technique for efficiency to handle large datasets. The attention weight visualizations provide explanations for the model's predictions. Our experiments on a substantial bibliographic catalogue repository validate the model's effectiveness using accuracy, F1, and ROC AUC scores.

Keywords: Author name disambiguation · Attention mechanisms · Explainable machine learning · Feature Integration

1 Introduction

Managing digital libraries demands precise author publication retrieval. Yet, the surge in publications has led to a challenge: authors sharing identical names, especially with just initials, hampers retrieval accuracy. This issue obstructs access to specific authors' works and hinders author-level bibliometric analysis. Efforts to assign unique author identifiers [8,26], face slow adoption due to workload and author reluctance. Thus, automatic authorship identification is crucial to address this ambiguity [5,25].

In the field of author name disambiguation (AND), prior research explores machine-learning-based (ML-based) and non-machine-learning-based (non-ML-based) approaches [10]. Non-ML-based methods involve graph network analysis techniques [22,24,30] and heuristic-based approaches [17,27,28]. ML-based techniques utilize labeled training data and are categorised into supervised [9,12,20], unsupervised [19,23,29], and semi-supervised methods [14,32,34]. In recent years, deep neural networks have been introduced to address author name ambiguity problems [3,16,31]. Although these models achieve high performance due to neural networks' pattern recognition abilities, they often lack interpretability, raising practical and ethical concerns [7].

© The Author(s), under exclusive license to Springer Nature Singapore Pte Ltd. 2023
D. H. Goh et al. (Eds.): ICADL 2023, LNCS 14458, pp. 240–249, 2023.
https://doi.org/10.1007/978-981-99-8088-8_21

While these methods hold promise, most existing AND approaches rely on a single schema, either graphs [13,18] or text analysis techniques [3,15,31], often overlooking latent information from various bibliographic record attributes, including textual, discrete, and co-author attributes. Moreover, many studies primarily focus on scientific papers [21], whereas books in digital libraries pose additional challenges, making authorship identification among books more challenging compared to scientific papers.

To tackle these issues, we propose a novel pairwise learning model employing self-attention and co-attention mechanisms for author name disambiguation. This model integrates diverse feature categories, including text, discrete data, and co-author information, capturing comprehensive latent details from bibliographic records. We incorporate an optional dimension reduction technique based on random projection. This ensures both efficiency and model effectiveness. Additionally, we visualise attention weights to provide insights into its predictions. We conducted experiments on a substantial bibliographic repository comprising around 2 million records and 500,000 author names. Our empirical evaluation establishes the model's effectiveness, assessed through accuracy, F1 score, and ROC AUC scores.

2   Related Work

We categorising previous approaches in AND into three groups: feature aggregation, sub-model combination, and a combination of both methods.

Feature Aggregation. Integrating diverse information types often involves aggregating features directly. For instance, Levin et al. [14] combined author and subject features with citation data using product conjunctions, enhancing feature precision. Qiao et al. [19] introduced a heterogeneous graph convolutional network embedding method for low-dimensional representations, facilitating hierarchical agglomerative clustering.

Sub-model Combination. Sub-models are commonly employed to process distinct features in AND. Müller et al. [16] proposed a binary classifier with three auxiliary models-semantic title, surface title, and simple co-author models. These models focus on different aspects of the classification problem and are combined using a multi-layer neural network. Pooja et al. [18] presented an unsupervised framework that leverages relational and non-relational aspects by using variational graph autoencoders for document embedding, followed by hierarchical agglomerative clustering.

Mixed Method: Zhou et al. [33] adopted a mixed approach, combining feature aggregation and sub-model combination. They fused raw document features and built similarity graphs, followed by a fusion encoder. This encoder integrated the graphs and passed the information to a multi-layer perceptron for binary classification in AND.

3 Methodology

We begin with the following definitions:

- Author name: A string s_k containing only family names and first initial, for example, "R. Smith." Here, k represents the k-th author name.
- Author ID: A unique identity code a_i, representing a real-world author.
- Record: A bibliographic record r_j, with a set of attributes.
- Name block: A record cluster $\mathbf{B}_k = \{\langle a_1^k, r_1^k \rangle, \ldots, \langle a_i^k, r_j^k \rangle, \ldots, \langle a_m^k, r_n^k \rangle\}$, where m is the number of distinct authors that share the same author name (i.e., the same surname and the first initial), and n is the number of records that are associated with the same author name.

Our goal is to determine whether two records in a given name block, (r_i^k, r_j^k), are authored by the same real-world author.

3.1 Co-attention-Based Model Architecture

Our co-attention-based AND model (Fig. 1) predicts whether pairs of records, each from the same name block, share the same author. These records have three attribute types that undergo distinct processing steps. Firstly, textual features, which encapsulate the primary topic and a concise content summary, are converted into embeddings using a pretrained multilingual BERT model [4]. For efficiency and increased training data utilization, we offer an optional random projection method [2] to map high-dimensional BERT embeddings (768) to a lower-dimensional subspace (128). Secondly, discrete attributes like languages, publication years, country codes, and publisher names are processed through a linear embedding layer, aligning their dimensions with those of the textual features' context vectors. Thirdly, we capture co-authorship information within an undirected network, with each node representing a unique author name and edges connecting authors who have co-authored one or more papers. We compute embeddings for each node using the Node2Vec graph embedding algorithm [6]. These embeddings are then concatenated into a hidden context matrix and normalized using batch normalization [11] for efficient training.

Let d represent the dimension of hidden vectors after the batch normalization layer, l denote the maximum length of title tokens for each record, m indicate the number of metadata columns for each record, and n stand for the maximum number of co-authors for each record. We use $\mathbf{X}^A \in \mathbb{R}^{l \times d}$ to represent a matrix of hidden vectors $\{\mathbf{h}_{\mathbf{x}_1^A}, \mathbf{h}_{\mathbf{x}_2^A}, \ldots, \mathbf{h}_{\mathbf{x}_l^A}\}$ produced by BERT for the first record's title tokens. Similarly, $\mathbf{X}^B \in \mathbb{R}^{l \times d}$ is the matrix containing $\{\mathbf{h}_{\mathbf{x}_1^B}, \mathbf{h}_{\mathbf{x}_2^B}, \ldots, \mathbf{h}_{\mathbf{x}_l^B}\}$, generated by BERT for the second record's title tokens. The hidden matrix of metadata columns is $\mathbf{Y}^A \in \mathbb{R}^{m \times d}$ for the first record and $\mathbf{Y}^B \in \mathbb{R}^{m \times d}$ for the second record. Similarly, the hidden matrix of co-authors is $\mathbf{Z}^A \in \mathbb{R}^{n \times d}$ for the first record and $\mathbf{Z}^B \in \mathbb{R}^{n \times d}$ for the second record.

To simplify, we represent all hidden context vectors of each record as $\mathbf{H}^A \in \mathbb{R}^{N \times d}$, comprising $\{\mathbf{h}_1^A, \mathbf{h}_2^A, \ldots, \mathbf{h}_N^A\}$, and $\mathbf{H}^B \in \mathbb{R}^{N \times d}$, comprising $\{\mathbf{h}_1^B, \mathbf{h}_2^B, \ldots,$

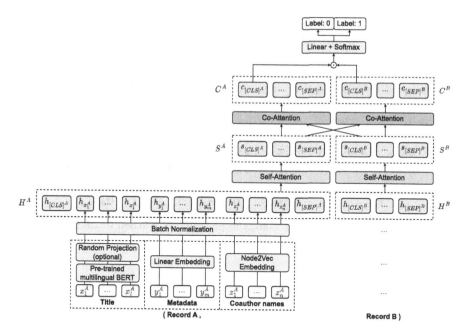

Fig. 1. The structure of the co-attention-based AND model.

$\mathbf{h}_N^B\}$, where $N = l + m + n + 2$. These matrices are constructed by concatenating the above embeddings, as follows:

$$\mathbf{H}^A = \begin{bmatrix} \mathbf{h}_{[\text{CLS}]^A} \\ \mathbf{X}^A \\ \mathbf{Y}^A \\ \mathbf{Z}^A \\ \mathbf{h}_{[\text{SEP}]^A} \end{bmatrix}, \ \mathbf{H}^B = \begin{bmatrix} \mathbf{h}_{[\text{CLS}]^B} \\ \mathbf{X}^B \\ \mathbf{Y}^B \\ \mathbf{Z}^B \\ \mathbf{h}_{[\text{SEP}]^B} \end{bmatrix},$$

where $\mathbf{h}_{[\text{CLS}]^A}$, $\mathbf{h}_{[\text{SEP}]^A}$, $\mathbf{h}_{[\text{CLS}]^B}$, and $\mathbf{h}_{[\text{SEP}]^B}$ are vectors with dimension d, generated by a distinct linear embedding layer, converting tokens $\{[\text{CLS}]^A, [\text{SEP}]^A, [\text{CLS}]^B, [\text{SEP}]^B\}$ into $\{\mathbf{h}_{[\text{CLS}]^A}, \mathbf{h}_{[\text{SEP}]^A}, \mathbf{h}_{[\text{CLS}]^B}, \mathbf{h}_{[\text{SEP}]^B}\}$. A [CLS] token summarizes sequence information and is used for prediction, while [SEP] tokens mark the end of sequences.

To determine the importance of each vector in the hidden matrices $\mathbf{H}^A$ and $\mathbf{H}^B$, we employ self-attention and co-attention modules. Self-attention is designed to capture interactive connections among all the features within a record:

$$\mathbf{S}^A = \text{SelfAttn}(\mathbf{H}^A), \ \mathbf{S}^B = \text{SelfAttn}(\mathbf{H}^B),$$

where $\mathbf{S}^A \in \mathbb{R}^{N \times d}$ and $\mathbf{S}^B \in \mathbb{R}^{N \times d}$ are matrices representing each record's features. For capturing inter-record connections, we utilize co-attention modules:

$$\mathbf{C}^A = \text{CoAttn}(\mathbf{H}^A, \mathbf{H}^B), \ \mathbf{C}^B = \text{CoAttn}(\mathbf{H}^B, \mathbf{H}^A).$$

We utilize the outputs $\mathbf{c}[CLS]^A \in \mathbb{R}^d$ and $\mathbf{c}[CLS]^B \in \mathbb{R}^d$ from $\mathbf{C}^A$ and $\mathbf{C}^B$ as comprehensive representations of the two records. To derive the overall representation $\mathbf{r} \in \mathbb{R}^d$ for the record pair, we compute the element-wise product of $\mathbf{h}[CLS]^A$ and $\mathbf{h}[CLS]^B$. This result is then processed through a fully connected layer followed by a softmax layer to determine the probability of whether the record pair shares the same or different authors. The probability, represented as a vector $\mathbf{o} \in \mathbb{R}^{d_o}$, where d_o equals 2 for pairwise AND tasks, contains two values. The first value indicates the probability of the two records having the same author, while the second represents the probability of different authors. The sum of these probabilities equals 1. The linear and softmax layers are defined as follows:

$$\mathbf{r} = \mathbf{c}_{[CLS]^A} \odot \mathbf{c}_{[CLS]^B}, \quad \mathbf{o} = \text{softmax}(\mathbf{W}_o{}^T \mathbf{r} + \mathbf{b}_o),$$

where $\mathbf{W}_o \in \mathbb{R}^{d \times d_o}$ and $\mathbf{b}_o \in \mathbb{R}^{d_o}$ are the parameters learned during training.

4   Dataset

In our study, we assessed our model using the Dutch Central Catalogue, a repository of over 90 million bibliographic records managed by OCLC. A significant portion of these records lacks comprehensive textual data like abstracts or summaries. Following OCLC's metadata guidance, we retained specific attributes for each record, including title, co-author(s), language code, country code, publication year, and publisher name.

Approximately 64 million of these records contain at least one Author ID (e.g., ORCID [8] ISNI [1]), which have been verified by library cataloguers or publishers. Consequently, they serve as our ground truth for training and testing purposes. We organized them into clusters known as name blocks. After filtering out name blocks with just one record, we retained 6 million records distributed across 893k name blocks. We randomly selected 1k name blocks for testing and another 1k for validation. To assess the model's performance, we constructed four distinct training sets of varying sizes, as detailed in Table 1. We created all possible record pairs by pairing up each two records within each name block and under-sample negative pairs to match the number of positive pairs.

5   Experiment and Results

5.1   Experiment Setup

We compare our co-attention-based AND model with four baseline models.

Mean-based AND incorporates all context vectors after the batch normalisation layer in the same way as the proposed model. It then calculates their mean to derive the final representation of the record pair.

Linear-based AND is similar to the mean-based model, but instead of the mean calculation, it employs a fully connected layer.

Table 1. Statistical information of different training sets

Set	#Blocks	#Records	#Authors	#Pairs	#Pos.	#Neg.
Test	1,000	53,162	12,829	515,586	257,793	257,793
Validation	1,000	51,819	12,479	520,716	260,358	260,358
Small.Train	100	4,786	1,187	45,994	22,997	22,997
Medium.Train	1,000	50,143	12,228	486,732	243,366	243,366
Large.Train	10,000	437,731	107,273	4,377,174	2,188,587	2,188,587
X-Large.Train	100,000	2,074,432	505,122	22,997,808	11,498,904	11,498,904

Title-based AND concatenates the titles of two records in a pair and jointly processes them using BERT. It then applies a random projection calculation on the context vector of the [CLS] token to produce the final representation.

Full-text AND connects all features of the two records, encodes them using BERT and random projection to produce the final representation.

Each of these baseline models uses fully connected and softmax layers to make predictions. We evaluated their performance using standard metrics, including accuracy (Acc), F1 score, and ROC AUC (Area Under the ROC Curve).

5.2   Impact of Random Projection

To assess the impact of random projection, we compared the baseline title-only model with and without random projection, focusing on accuracy, F1 score, and ROC AUC scores. We observed a slight decline in the model's performance, with an approximate decrease of 1–2% across all training datasets when using random projection. On the other hand, despite the initial cost of 8 min and 15 s for generating and caching BERT embeddings, we experienced a significant reduction in training time per epoch, from 15 min and 52 s to a mere 18 s. This substantial time-saving justified our choice to adopt random projection consistently in all subsequent experiments.

5.3   Model Comparison

Here we compare the classification results of the proposed co-attention-based model and the four baseline models. As depicted in Fig. 2, the Mean-based AND model consistently performs the poorest among all five models across various training set sizes. The impact of training set size on the Title-based and Full-text models is limited, with only around a 1% improvement when using the largest dataset compared to the smallest.

Conversely, the co-attention-based and linear-based models exhibit substantial performance gains with larger training sets, eventually surpassing the two simple text-based baselines when utilizing Large and X-Large training sets, with

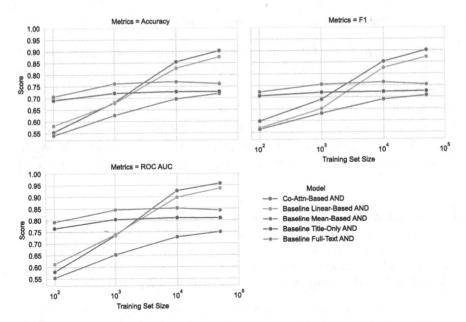

Fig. 2. The comparison between our Co-Attn-based model and the baselines

performance still improving. This suggests that complex correlations among different feature types become increasingly important in authorship detection with ample training data. The co-attention-based model excels in capturing these correlations, consistently achieving 3–5% higher accuracy, F1 scores, and ROC AUC scores when trained on the two largest datasets.

5.4   Effect of Self and Co-attentions

To assess the impact of self- and co-attention mechanisms on authorship prediction, we investigate the suitability of self-attention and co-attention mechanisms in highlighting essential components that influence prediction. We rescale attention weights to a fixed range of (0, 1). Elements with an attention weight of 1 are depicted in the darkest color, while those with 0 appear in white.

The first example in Fig. 3a showcases two records from different authors, distinguished by varying titles, publication years, languages, countries, and publishers. Self-attention primarily focuses on the publication years "1750" and "2013" and the publisher name "Ohio State University Press." It also extends attention to languages, country codes, and title words such as "handlung," "evidence," and "community." In the second and third examples, self-attention centers on publication years and publisher names, giving less weight to titles. In contrast, co-attention weights (in Fig. 3b) distribute their focus across various attributes, attending to languages, countries, co-authors, and select title words.

Upon analyzing co-attention weights for different attributes, titles emerge as the most significant attribute for the co-attention mechanism, with a mean

Index	Label	Prediction	Title	Pub. Year	Lang.	Co.	Pub. Name	Coauthors
1	Diff.: 0	Diff.: 0.000001	grif handlung den ebrechen	1750	dui	de	NA	
			s evidence : inq literature , and community in the late Middle Ages	2013	eng	us	Ohio State University Press	
2	Same: 1	Same: 1.000000	De leer van het wijs afzaken volgens het ch disch	1876	ned	id	Van Dorp & Co	
			is de origine et natura	1887	lat	nl	NA	Kaiser, F.
3	Diff.: 0	Diff.: 0.000000	Visions of quality : how luators , understand and represent program quality	2001	eng	nl	JAI	Hinn, D.
			30	1908	eng	gb	Murray	Victoria, Esher, V.

(a) Self-attention weights

Index	Label	Prediction	Title	Pub. Year	Lang.	Co.	Pub. Name	Coauthors
1	Diff.: 0	Diff.: 0.000001	grif handlung den ebrechen	1750	dui	de	NA	
			s evidence : inq literature , and community in the late Middle Ages	2013	eng	us	Ohio State University Press	
2	Same: 1	Same: 1.000000	De leer van het wiis afzaken volgens het ch disch	1876	ned	id	Van Dorp & Co	
			is de origine et natura	1857	lat	nl	NA	Kaiser, F.
3	Diff.: 0	Diff.: 0.000000	Visions of quality : how luators , understand and represent program quality	2001	eng	nl	JAI	Hinn, D.
			30	1908	eng	gb	Murray	Victoria, Esher, V.

(b) Co-attention weights

Fig. 3. Attention weights for correctly classified examples from the Large training set. Each pair is indexed with its true and predicted label.

weight of 0.3402. For the self-attention mechanism, titles and publication years take precedence over other attributes, with mean weights of 0.1697 and 0.1161, respectively. While it remains challenging to explicitly explain individual pairwise classifications based on these attention weights, they offer valuable insights into the process.

6   Conclusion

Our research presents a novel approach for pairwise author name disambiguation within the Dutch Central Catalogue, primarily comprising books with limited textual data. Our experiments highlight the advantages of incorporating additional attributes, which boost performance in AND tasks. The inclusion of self- and co-attention mechanisms enhances the model's ability to capture hidden data patterns, leading to more accurate predictions. Efficiently handling large-scale datasets, we introduce a random project-based dimension reduction stop, ensuring both processing efficiency and model effectiveness with extensive data. We also provide attention weight visualizations, offering partial insights into the model's decision-making process, although further research is needed to enhance explainability.

References

1. ISNI - FAQs. https://isni.org/page/faqs/. Accessed September 2023
2. Achlioptas, D.: Database-friendly random projections: Johnson-lindenstrauss with binary coins. J. Comput. Syst. Sci. **66**(4), 671–687 (2003)
3. Boukhers, Z., Asundi, N.B.: Whois? Deep author name disambiguation using bibliographic data. In: Silvello, G., et al. (eds.) TPDL 2022. LNCS, vol. 13541, pp. 201–215. Springer, Cham (2022). https://doi.org/10.1007/978-3-031-16802-4_16
4. Devlin, J., Chang, M.W., Lee, K., Toutanova, K.: BERT: pre-training of deep bidirectional transformers for language understanding. In: North American Chapter of the Association for Computational Linguistics (2019). https://api.semanticscholar.org/CorpusID:52967399
5. Ferreira, A.A., Gonçalves, M.A., Laender, A.H.: A brief survey of automatic methods for author name disambiguation. ACM SIGMOD Rec. **41**(2), 15–26 (2012)
6. Grover, A., Leskovec, J.: Node2vec: scalable feature learning for networks. In: Proceedings of the 22nd ACM SIGKDD International Conference on Knowledge Discovery and Data Mining, pp. 855–864. KDD 2016. Association for Computing Machinery, New York (2016). https://doi.org/10.1145/2939672.2939754
7. Guidotti, R., Monreale, A., Ruggieri, S., Turini, F., Giannotti, F., Pedreschi, D.: A survey of methods for explaining black box models. ACM Comput. Surv. (CSUR) **51**(5), 1–42 (2018)
8. Haak, L.L., Fenner, M., Paglione, L., Pentz, E., Ratner, H.: ORCID: a system to uniquely identify researchers. Learn. Publ. **25**(4), 259–264 (2012)
9. Han, D., Liu, S., Hu, Y., Wang, B., Sun, Y.: Elm-based name disambiguation in bibliography. World Wide Web **18**(2), 253–263 (2015)
10. Hussain, I., Asghar, S.: A survey of author name disambiguation techniques: 2010–2016. Knowl. Eng. Rev. **32** (2017)
11. Ioffe, S., Szegedy, C.: Batch normalization: accelerating deep network training by reducing internal covariate shift. In: International Conference on Machine Learning, pp. 448–456. PMLR (2015)
12. Kim, K., Sefid, A., Weinberg, B.A., Giles, C.L.: A web service for author name disambiguation in scholarly databases. In: 2018 IEEE International Conference on Web Services (ICWS), pp. 265–273. IEEE (2018)
13. Km, P., Mondal, S., Chandra, J.: A graph combination with edge pruning-based approach for author name disambiguation. J. Am. Soc. Inf. Sci. **71**(1), 69–83 (2020)
14. Levin, M., Krawczyk, S., Bethard, S., Jurafsky, D.: Citation-based bootstrapping for large-scale author disambiguation. J. Am. Soc. Inform. Sci. Technol. **63**(5), 1030–1047 (2012)
15. Liu, W., et al.: Author name disambiguation for PubMed. J. Am. Soc. Inf. Sci. **65**(4), 765–781 (2014)
16. Müller, M.-C.: Semantic author name disambiguation with word embeddings. In: Kamps, J., Tsakonas, G., Manolopoulos, Y., Iliadis, L., Karydis, I. (eds.) TPDL 2017. LNCS, vol. 10450, pp. 300–311. Springer, Cham (2017). https://doi.org/10.1007/978-3-319-67008-9_24
17. Pooja, K., Mondal, S., Chandra, J.: An unsupervised heuristic based approach for author name disambiguation. In: 2018 10th International Conference on Communication Systems & Networks (COMSNETS), pp. 540–542. IEEE (2018)
18. Pooja, K.M., Mondal, S., Chandra, J.: Exploiting similarities across multiple dimensions for author name disambiguation. Scientometrics **126**(9), 7525–7560 (2021). https://doi.org/10.1007/s11192-021-04101-y

19. Qiao, Z., Du, Y., Fu, Y., Wang, P., Zhou, Y.: Unsupervised author disambiguation using heterogeneous graph convolutional network embedding. In: 2019 IEEE International Conference on Big Data (Big Data), pp. 910–919. IEEE (2019)
20. Rehs, A.: A supervised machine learning approach to author disambiguation in the web of science. J. Informet. **15**(3), 101166 (2021)
21. Sanyal, D.K., Bhowmick, P.K., Das, P.P.: A review of author name disambiguation techniques for the PubMed bibliographic database. J. Inf. Sci. **47**(2), 227–254 (2021)
22. Shin, D., Kim, T., Choi, J., Kim, J.: Author name disambiguation using a graph model with node splitting and merging based on bibliographic information. Scientometrics **100**(1), 15–50 (2014). https://doi.org/10.1007/s11192-014-1289-4
23. Tang, J., Fong, A.C., Wang, B., Zhang, J.: A unified probabilistic framework for name disambiguation in digital library. IEEE Trans. Knowl. Data Eng. **24**(6), 975–987 (2011)
24. Tang, L., Walsh, J.: Bibliometric fingerprints: name disambiguation based on approximate structure equivalence of cognitive maps. Scientometrics **84**(3), 763–784 (2010)
25. Tekles, A., Bornmann, L.: Author name disambiguation of bibliometric data: a comparison of several unsupervised approaches. Quantit. Sci. Stud. **1**(4), 1510–1528 (2020)
26. Torres-Salinas, D., Arroyo-Machado, W., Thelwall, M.: Exploring WorldCat identities as an altmetric information source: a library catalog analysis experiment in the field of scientometrics. Scientometrics **126**(2), 1725–1743 (2021)
27. Varadharajalu, A., Liu, W., Wong, W.: Author name disambiguation for ranking and clustering PubMed data using NetClus. In: Wang, D., Reynolds, M. (eds.) AI 2011. LNCS (LNAI), vol. 7106, pp. 152–161. Springer, Heidelberg (2011). https://doi.org/10.1007/978-3-642-25832-9_16
28. Waqas, H., Qadir, M.A.: Multilayer heuristics based clustering framework (MHCF) for author name disambiguation. Scientometrics **126**(9), 7637–7678 (2021)
29. Wu, H., Li, B., Pei, Y., He, J.: Unsupervised author disambiguation using Dempster-Shafer theory. Scientometrics **101**(3), 1955–1972 (2014)
30. Xu, J., Shen, S., Li, D., Fu, Y.: A network-embedding based method for author disambiguation. In: Proceedings of the 27th ACM International Conference on Information and Knowledge Management, pp. 1735–1738 (2018)
31. Yamani, Z., Nurmaini, S., Sari, W.K., et al.: Author matching using string similarities and deep neural networks. In: Sriwijaya International Conference on Information Technology and Its Applications (SICONIAN 2019), pp. 474–479. Atlantis Press (2020)
32. Zhao, J., Wang, P., Huang, K.: A semi-supervised approach for author disambiguation in KDD CUP 2013. In: Proceedings of the 2013 KDD CUP 2013 Workshop, pp. 1–8 (2013)
33. Zhou, Q., Chen, W., Wang, W., Xu, J., Zhao, L.: Multiple features driven author name disambiguation. In: 2021 IEEE International Conference on Web Services (ICWS), pp. 506–515. IEEE (2021)
34. Zhu, Y., Li, Q.: Enhancing object distinction utilizing probabilistic topic model. In: 2013 International Conference on Cloud Computing and Big Data, pp. 177–182. IEEE (2013)

MuP-SciDocSum: Leveraging Multi-perspective Peer Review Summaries for Scientific Document Summarization

Sandeep Kumar[1], Guneet Singh Kohli[2], Tirthankar Ghosal[3(✉)], and Asif Ekbal[1]

[1] Department of Computer Science and Engineering,
Indian Institute of Technology Patna, Patna, India
{sandeep_2121cs29,asif}@iitp.ac.in
[2] Department of Computer Science and Engineering, Thapar Institute of Engineering and Technology, Patiala, India
[3] National Center for Computational Sciences, Oak Ridge National Laboratory,
Oak Ridge, USA
ghosalt@ornl.gov

Abstract. Scientific article summarization poses a challenge because the interpretability of the article depends on the objective, experience of the reader. Editors/Chairs assign experts in the domain as peer reviewers. These experts often write a summary of the article at the beginning of their reviews which offers a summarized view of their understanding (perspectives) on the given paper. Multiperspective summaries can provide multiple related but distinct perspectives of the reviewers rather than being influenced by a single summary. Here in this work, we propose a method to produce abstractive multiperspective summaries of scientific articles leveraging peer reviews. Our proposed method includes performing extractive summarization to identify the essential parts of the paper by extracting contributing sentences. In the subsequent step, we utilize the extracted pertinent information to condition a transformer-based language model comprising of a single encoder followed by multiple decoders that share weights. Our goal is to train the decoder to not only learn from a single reference summary but also to take into account multiple perspectives when generating the summary during the inference stage. Experimental results show that our approach achieves the best average ROUGE F1 Score, ROUGE-2 F1 Score, and ROUGE-L F1 Score with respect to the comparing systems. We make our code public (https://github.com/sandeep82945/Muti-percepective-summarization) for further research.

Keywords: Peer Reviews · Summarization · Deep Learning · Scholarly document

D. H. Goh et al. (Eds.): ICADL 2023, LNCS 14458, pp. 250–267, 2023.
https://doi.org/10.1007/978-981-99-8088-8_22

1   Introduction

Rapid increases in the number of publications in scientific fields motivates the development of automatic summarization tools for scientific articles. A summary of a scientific article is crucial as it provides a condensed overview of the main points and contributions of the research. It enables readers to quickly grasp the key findings and arguments presented in the paper, thus helping them decide whether they want to invest time in reading the full paper. Additionally, it serves as a reference for future research and discussions and aids editors and reviewers in understanding the paper and making an informed decision on its acceptance or rejection. Furthermore, it is useful for other researchers who wish to cite the paper and need to comprehend the content of the paper.

Summarizing scientific articles is challenging as it requires understanding complex language and technical terms, condensing lengthy and detailed articles and having subject expertise to properly grasp and comprehend them [1,27]. Also, it involves condensing multiple perspectives and findings on the same research, which may require subject expertise and critical evaluation skills. The standard approach for evaluating automated summary systems is to compare their output with human-written summaries. However, creating large annotated datasets of human-written summaries for scientific articles is challenging due to the time, effort, and expertise required in summarizing such complex and technical content.

A common, yet underutilized, source of manuscript summaries lies within the peer review process. Peer reviewers, often experts in the field, provide detailed comments and summaries on the manuscripts they review. Each reviewer has a unique interpretation of the manuscript, bringing to light different aspects of the paper and offering a unique perspective. These multiple summaries of a single manuscript not only demonstrate to the editor how each reviewer has interpreted the manuscript, but also reveal significant differences in perspectives among the reviewers. This offers a rich set of data that can be utilized for generating summaries of scientific articles. This paper proposes a method that capitalizes on these multiple perspectives to create more comprehensive and inclusive summaries of scientific articles. The objective of multiperspective scientific summarization is not to be swayed by a single summary, but to incorporate multiple related but distinct perspectives of the reviewers.

However, a limitation of previous research in this area has been the assumption that each document has only a single optimal, reference summary referred to as a "gold summary". Different readers can have different perspectives when summarizing the same document, which can result in variations among human-written summaries [19]. The accuracy of evaluating summarization systems using automated metrics is hindered by the use of only one reference or "gold" summary [19,44]. The use of only one reference summary, particularly for longer and complex documents, may prevent the model from effectively capturing important information and different perspectives during training [21].

Our approach consists of two main stages. First, we employ an extractive summarization process to identify the essential parts of the paper by extracting contributing sentences. This step allows us to capture the most important information and perspectives from the paper based on the reviewers' comments and interpretations. In the second stage, we use this extracted information to condition a transformer-based language model. Our model architecture includes a single encoder followed by multiple decoders that share weights. This design allows us to train the decoder to not only learn from a single reference summary, but to consider multiple perspectives when generating the summary. The goal is to produce abstractive summaries of scientific documents that capture a holistic view of the manuscript as understood by multiple expert reviewers. By leveraging the insights of multiple experts, we aim to produce summaries that offer a comprehensive understanding of the paper, and allow readers to gain a multi-faceted view of the work. This method provides a promising approach for improving the quality and diversity of automatic scientific article summarization, addressing the challenges posed by the complexity and technicality of scientific content, and harnessing the power of multiple perspectives offered by expert peer reviewers.

We summarize our contributions below:

- We present a novel two-stage method for multi-perspective summarization. The first stage performs extractive summarization to identify the essential parts of the paper, while the second stage employs an abstractive approach to generate comprehensive summaries.
- We introduce a transformer-based model that uses a single encoder and multiple decoders, enabling the generation of summaries from different perspectives.
- We leverage the wealth of peer review data as a source of multiple expert-written summaries, which have been previously under-utilized in scientific summarization tasks.
- Our experimental results show that our proposed method outperforms other state-of-the-art systems, achieving the highest average ROUGE-1, ROUGE-2, and ROUGE-L F1 scores.

The rest of this paper is organized as follows: Sect. 2 describes the related works of contributing sentence classification, types of summarization, and the scientific paper summarization task, and how our work is different from them. In Sect. 3, we describe our proposed methodology. In Sect. 4, we provide detailed information about the experimental setup, including the methodology, results, and human evaluation and analysis. Finally, in Sect. 5, we conclude the paper and discuss future directions.

2   Related Works

In this section, we discuss the contributing sentences and the work related to their classification task. We then turn our attention to the topic of automatic text summarization before narrowing our focus to scientific paper summarization. Finally, we delineate how our work differs from previous studies in the field.

2.1   Contributing Sentence Classification

In the context of classifying contributing sentences in scholarly NLP contributions, a task featured in SemEval-2021, several strategies were observed [12].

The objective of identifying the contribution sentences from articles has typically been approached via two strategies: a binary classification or a multi-class classification. The binary classification approach designated sentences as either contributing or not. For instance, Teams YNU-HPCC [29] and INNOVATORS [2] both leveraged BERT as a binary classifier. The KnowGraph@IITK [37] team employed a SciBERT + BiLSTM architecture, while UIUC_BioNLP [26] used BERT, also enhancing it with features related to sentence context. Alternatively, some teams employed a multi-class classification strategy, categorizing sentences into one of the 12 IUs or as non-contributing. Team DULUTH [30] used deBERTa [3] for this task, and ECNUICA [25] deployed an ensemble of RoBERTa, SciBERT, and BERT [30]. They incorporated context features such as surrounding sentences and paragraph sub-titles. Team ITNLP [45] also used BERT for multi-class classification, adding sentence context and paragraph headings as features.

These sentences contribute to the overall understanding of the main ideas, key points, and important details contained within the original source. So, we use contributing sentences to support and enhance the performance of our approach.

2.2 Automatic Text Summarization

Automatic text summarization can be categorized into two main strategies: extractive and abstractive. Extractive summarization focuses on selecting crucial segments from the text and presenting them as they appear in the original document. This is typically done by assessing each sentence's importance in a document and subsequently selecting the sentences to be included in the summary (Erkan and Radev, 2004 [15]; Parveen, Ramsl, and Strube, 2015 [34]). Neural network-based techniques have shown effectiveness in summarizing news articles (Cao et al., 2015 [5]; Cheng and Lapata, 2016 [7]). On the other hand, abstractive summarization aims to rephrase the important information in a new and condensed form. Abstractive summarization is computationally more complex than extractive summarization and requires a deeper understanding of the original content. However, abstractive methods can generate more concise summaries, even shorter than any sentence in the source document [4]. In Nallapati et al. [33], the authors adapt a bidirectional GRU-RNN [8] as the encoder and an uni-directional GRU-RNN with the same hidden layer size as the decoder. Transformer introduced by Vaswani et al. [41], the Transformer model for abstractive text summarization replaced the recurrent layers with self-attention layers. Instead of processing the input sequentially, the Transformer uses a multi-head self-attention mechanism, which allows it to handle long-range dependencies effectively. It significantly outperformed the RNN/CNN-based models for various tasks, including summarization, due to its superior ability to capture the context and semantics of the input text. This study generates abstractive summary of scientific papers.

2.3   Scientific Paper Summarization

Scientific paper summarization refers to the method of extracting and condensing the key elements from a scholarly research article into a brief, concise overview. This enables the significant information of the research, often complex and extensive, to be communicated in a more digestible and accessible format. Scientific paper summarization is a fast-evolving research field. Extractive models perform sentence selection to create summaries [35]; Cohan and Goharian [11], while hybrid models identify salient text and summarize it [39]. Cohan et al. [9] proposed the first model for abstractive summarization of single, longer-form documents like research papers.

Citation-based summarization leverages inter-paper reference relationships to formulate summaries, concentrating on the citation context and associated texts. This approach uses a paper's references from other works to generate summaries, providing a significant understanding of the paper's scientific contribution. Citation-based summarization has been an active area of research with the aim of summarizing the contribution of a target paper. Several studies have been conducted in this area [13,22,28,32], which proposed methods for extracting a set of sentences from the citation sentences to summarize the contribution of the target paper. The generated summaries may not fully capture all important aspects of the target paper. To address this issue, Yasunaga et al. [43] proposed the integration of both the target paper's abstract and its citation sentences. However, citation summarization helps improve a paper's summary quality but doesn't aid authors in drafting the summary while writing the paper.

IBM Science Summarizer [14] is a system for retrieval and summarization of scientific articles in computer science. It summarizing each section of the relevant paper obtained by search and filtering process independently. Lloret et al. [28] suggested two approaches for generating research article abstracts, one is extractive, and the other is based on extractive and abstractive technique.

LaySumm 2020 shared task [6] introduced a task of summarizing a technical or scientific document in simple, non-technical language that is comprehensible to a lay person (non-expert). Several teams contributed unique strategies for lay summarization in the competition. Gidiotis et al. [17] and Kim [23] used fine-tuned versions of the PEGASUS model, with Kim also incorporating a BERT-based extractive model. Reddy et al. [36] used an extractive sentence classification method. Roy et al. [16] leveraged the BART encoder in their systems, while Mishra et al. [31] utilized a standard encoder-decoder framework.

Our approach is novel in its utilization of multiperspective review summaries written by expert reviewers as the basis for scientific article summarization. This method differs from previous works that rely on a single reference summary, as it leverages the power of multiple reference summaries for training. Unlike previous studies on citation-based summarization, our approach extracts the contributing sentences of the scientific document and uses them directly to generate the summary. The lack of annotated datasets for training models to produce abstractive, multiperspective scientific paper summaries presents a major challenge in the field. To address this issue, we make use of the summaries present in peer review texts. Reviewers in various scientific fields often provide an introductory summary of the main points and key contributions of a paper, and each paper typically receives multiple reviews. Our proposed solution is an end-to-end extractive and abstractive architecture that generates a summary from the input scientific paper. During the training of the abstractive model, multiple golden summaries are used to teach the model how to generate multi-perspective summaries.

3   Methodology

Figure 1 shows the overall proposed architecture of our approach. The abstract and extracted contributing sentences from the full text are used to train the Multi-Perspective Framework. We explain each component of the architecture as follows:-

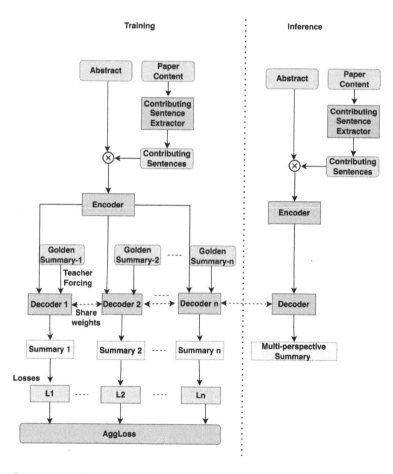

Fig. 1. Our proposed architecture. Here, Input (Abstract and the Paper content) at the top; (a) Training Pipeline (Left); (b) Inference Pipeline (Right);

3.1   Contributing Sentence Extraction

The main difficulty in summarizing scientific papers is their length and complexity. In this part of our architecture, our goal is to assist the next abstractive model by selecting only the salient enriching part of the full text of the paper. We extract the contributing sentences from the full textual document of the paper using an attention-based deep neural model named ContriSci [18]. ContriSci is a deep neural architecture that leverages multi-task learning to identify statements from a given research article that mention a contribution of the study.

3.2   Multi Perspective Framework

Training: Given a set of extractively selected salient sentences, denoted as C, we initially transform them into a sequence of hidden representations, denoted as M, using a consistent encoder for each target summary. To cater to the task of multi-reference summarization, multiple decoder frameworks are utilized to uncover various possible golden summaries. For a single instance of M, there could be multiple, say k, golden summaries. The decoder functions at the word level to predict these summaries, denoted as Y.

$$h_t^{(k)} = Decoder(M, y_{t-1}) \tag{1}$$

Here, k represents the k_{th} decoder for k_{th} golden summary. We implement the teacher forcing method on each decoder with each reference summary to train the decoder.

$$P(y_t|y_{<t,C})^{(k)} = softmax(W_d h_t + b_d) \tag{2}$$

where h_t is the hidden representation of y_t (the t-th word in the target summary).

We maximize the conditional log likelihood for a given N observation $(C^{(i)}, Y^{(i)})_{i=1}^N$

$$L_{MLE}^{(k)} = -\sum_{i=1}^{i=N}\sum_{t=1}^{t=T} logP(y_t^{(i)}|y_{<t}^{(i)}C^{(i)}) \tag{3}$$

We aggregated the losses using objective function f

$$L_{MuliMLE} = Min(L_{MLE}^{(1)}, L_{MLE}^{(2)}, .., L_{MLE}^{(k)}) \tag{4}$$

$$MultiRouge = f_{mean}(Rouge^{(1)}, Rouge^{(2)}, .., Rouge^{(k)}) \tag{5}$$

We define our proposed two different aggregation objectives:- First among the losses from the multiple reference summary, we choose the minimum loss for training. In particular, the model was trained using the generated summary that had the smallest loss compared to the reference summary. We refer our proposed architecture with this training objective as $Multi_{best}$.

$$AggLoss = L_{MuliMLE} \qquad (6)$$

Next, we took the weighted mean of the losses between the k generated summaries and the k reference summaries to generalize the shared weights of the decoders.

$$f_{mean} = \sum_{t=1}^{t=k} \beta_i(V^t) \qquad (7)$$

$$\beta_i = \frac{V^i}{\sum_{t=1}^{t=k} V^t} \qquad (8)$$

Here, V^i represents the loss associated with the t-th generated summary.

$$AggLoss = \alpha_1 L_{MuliMLE} - \alpha_2 MultiRouge \qquad (9)$$

We refer to our proposed architecture with this training objective as $Multi_{mean}$. Here, Rouge refers to the Rougue-1 F1 score between the predicted summary and the reference (or golden) summary. The objective during training is to minimize $L_{MultiMLE}$ and maximize the $MultiRouge$ score[1]. In particular, we combine the loss from each reference summary while training the models. Hence the prediction model is capable of generating predictions considering the multiple editor's perspective learned during training. However, if one of the summaries of a paper deviates significantly from highlighting the overall contribution of the paper and that reference is used during training, the predictions are expected to be less accurate and is one of the main reasons for exploring a multi-perspective approach. For the two different objective functions f_{best} and f_{mean} we name the corresponding architecture as $Multi_{best}$ and $Multi_{mean}$ respectively. We call the final loss after aggregation of the multiple losses as AggLoss.

Inference: During training, the decoder's weights are shared, so the final weights after training have learned to take into account different perspectives. During inference we initialize a decoder with the weights to generate a single output summary as shown in Fig. 1(b). Given the extractively selected salient sentences C, the encoder first transforms C into a sequence of hidden representations M. After that, the decoder predicts Y at the word level for M.

$$h_t = Decoder(M, y_{t-1}) \qquad (10)$$

---

[1] We set the value of α_1: 1 and α_2: 100 empirically, weighing the importance and normalizing the two losses given their different scales.

$$P(y_t|y_{<t,C})^{(k)} = softmax(W_d h_t + b_d) \qquad (11)$$

where h_t is the hidden representation of y_t (the t-th word in the target summary).

4   Experiments

In this section, we discuss the results of our proposed model and compare it with other state-of-the-art systems. We aim to demonstrate that using multiple references for summary, rather than just one, can improve the performance compared to traditional abstractive and extractive methods. Additionally, we examine the effect of utilizing extractive summarization techniques, specifically the identification of contribution sentences, prior to the application of the abstractive summarization method. We use the BART autoencoder for pre-training sequence-to-sequence models for the encoder and decoder. The encoder part is a bidirectional encoder that corresponds to the structure of BERT [42], and the decoder part is an auto-regressive decoder following the settings of GPT. During the pre-training process, BART receives the corrupted document as input and predicts the original uncorrupted document. In this way, BART can effectively learn contextual representations. When fine-tuned for the summarization task, the bidirectional encoder part encodes the original document, and the decoder part predicts the reference summary. BART obtains excellent performance on the summarization task.

We gave the input to BART as follows:

Input text: Abstract [SEP] Contributing sentences

Here, the input to the BART model is Abstract, and the contributing sentences separated by a token [SEP].

4.1   Dataset

We use the dataset collected from OpenReview by the MuP 2022 shared task for our task. This has been used for training while the hidden test set[2] is used for final evaluation. The number of papers used for training, validation, and testing in this experiment are 18,934, 3,604, and 4,610 respectively. The brief description of the dataset can be found in [10].

4.2   Experimental Settings

To train the ContriSci, we use the default hyperparameters with which ContriSci is trained. We use the BART large fine-tuned on CNN/DailyMail dataset [20] to initialize both our encoder and decoder from the hugging face library[3]. We use a dynamic learning rate, warm up 1000 iterations, and decay afterwards. We train the model for 10 epochs with the batch size of 4. We train all the models on a single GPU (NVIDIA A100 80 GB).

---

[2] https://github.com/allenai/mup.

[3] https://huggingface.co/.

4.3   Result and Analysis

Automatic Evaluation: Table 1 shows that our method $Multi_{mean}$ outperforms all the other systems for comparison. To evaluate the performance of our system during inference, we employ the same method used by other comparable systems. Specifically, we calculate the ROUGE score between the generated summary and each reference summary in the paper, then take the average of these scores. GATS describes an extractive summarization approach using GATs to rank sentences in discourse facets of a paper, creating a graph for each article. Our proposed method $Multi_{mean}$ is abstractive and outperforms GATS by an average ROUGE score of 8.4. The LTRC system divides a paper into sections such as the abstract, introduction, and conclusion. They found that the best results were achieved when training the model on only the introduction of the paper. GUIR implemented a two-step summarization process. The first step involved extracting the most salient sentences from the document by training a classifier. In the second step, these sentences were used to write an abstractive summary. However, $Multi_{mean}$ extracts the most important contributing sentences from each section of the paper to train our model, and it outperforms both LTRC and GUIR by 2.2 and 2.0 average ROUGE score, respectively. The AINLPML system uses a two-stage approach for the task, first an extractive summarization step with a contributing sentence identification model, and then a BART model is fine-tuned on the extracted summary generated from the previous step. They, along with other systems, used only one reference summary for training. However, we used multiple references for training and utilized multiple decoders to generate a multi-perspective summary. Our proposed $Multi_{mean}$ outperforms AINLPML by 1.6 points.

Table 1. Our result compared to other comparison systems. Here R represents the ROUGE F1 metric; Compared to other systems, our system shows superior performance in terms of the ROUGE F1 metric (R), with a paired t-test revealing a statistically significant difference ($p < 0.05$).

	R-1	R-2	R-L	Avg
GATS [1]	33.7	7.4	17.7	19.6
LTRC [40]	40.7	12.5	25.0	26.0
GUIR [38]	41.4	12.5	24.8	26.2
AINLPML [24]	41.1	13.3	25.4	26.6
Our proposed $Multi_{mean}$	**42.91**	**14.92**	**26.84**	**28.2**

Ablation Study: We analyze the effectiveness of our model by performing an ablation study in Table 2. First, we trained the model on a single reference summary by randomly choosing one of the golden summaries from all available golden summaries. In the case of utilizing the abstract and full text of

Table 2. Ablation study of our proposed architecture; *Contri* refers to Contributing sentences

Experiments	ROUGE 1_F	ROUGE2_F	ROUGEL_F	Avg ROUGE_F
Bart (Full Text)	40.73	12.28	24.38	25.79
Bart (Abstract + *Contri*)	40.96	13.17	25.36	26.50
Our proposed $Multi_{best}$	41.11	13.21	25.39	26.57
Our proposed $Multi_{mean}$	42.91	14.92	26.84	28.20

Table 3. Human evaluation (on a Likert scale 1–5)

	Faithfulness	Readability	Coverage	P-Coverage
LTRC	4.5	4.7	3.5	2
GATS	5.0	2.6	2.3	2
GUIR	4.0	4.3	3.8	2.5
AINLPML	4.5	4.6	3.9	2.5
Our method	4.5	**4.8**	**4.1**	**3.6**

the paper as input text, our proposed approach achieved 25.79 avg. ROUGE F score. Next, we took the abstract of the paper, along with a collection of contribution sentences from the remaining portion of the paper. Our proposed approach achieved 26.50 ROUGE F score. The improvement of 0.29 points in ROUGE F score between the previous architecture and this one clearly shows the significance of the contributing sentences in generating these summaries.

Next, to understand the effectiveness of the multi-perspective training, we trained the previous architecture in the multi-objective training fashion, i.e., $Multi_{best}$. The slight improvement observed may be attributed to the method's similarity to a single reference summary, but with the added benefit of utilizing a best reference summary dynamic rather than a random one. However, we observed a surprising improvement of 1.63 points in the ROUGE F score in our $Multi_{mean}$ architecture. This may be because the training objective of this architecture is not biased towards any particular reference summary, but rather aims to generalize the model towards all of the reference summaries. As a result, the model learns from each reference summary, taking into account the perspective of each reviewer.

Human Evaluation: In order to conduct our study, we asked four domain experts in NLP (experts with 5+ years of experience in the field) to annotate a set of 150 randomly selected papers, along with their results. We provided the experts with access to the paper PDFs and the ground-truth reviews. The randomly selected papers were from the validation set because the ground-truth review for the test set is private and we do not have access to it. We reimplemented the comparison systems and evaluated the set on them. Following [10], we asked experts to rate the generated summaries according to three characteristics: faithfulness, readability, and coverage, on a Likert scale (1–5). To evaluate the multi-perceptiveness of our proposed architecture, we also defined a characteristic called P-Coverage. We asked experts to rate whether the generated summary captures the key points from each of the reference summaries. The results of the human evaluation can be found in Table 3. Consistent with the automated evaluation results, our approach outperforms the rest of the systems in terms of readability and coverage, and is very close to leading in terms of faithfulness. GATS achieves a better faithfulness score than our proposed method since it is an extractive approach. Additionally, a higher P-Coverage compared to other systems indicates that our proposed system effectively captures a diverse range of perspectives.

Table 4. Output summary generated through single-reference and multi-perspective training

> **Single Perspective:** *This paper proposes a new learning rule that constrains the distance a network can travel through L-space in any one update. The proposed rule penalizes each step of SGD to reduce the magnitude of the resulting step in L2-space. This learning rule thus changes the course of learning to track a shorter path in function space. The paper shows that the L/' ratio decreases throughout optimization*
>
> **Multi-perspective:** *This paper studies the relationship between parameter and function distances in a Hilbert space. The authors show that the two distances are nontrivial related and that the L/' ratio decreases throughout optimization, reaching a steady value around when test error plateaus. They then propose a new learning rule that constrains the distance a network can travel through L-space in any one update. This allows new examples to be learned in a way that minimally interferes with what has previously been learned. Finally, they show how the L distance could be applied directly to optimization*

Case Study: The following case study helps us understand the efficacy of multiperspective settings compared to a traditional single one. Table 4 shows a comparison of the generated summary using a single reference ($Multi_{best}$) and a multiperspective summary ($Multi_{mean}$). Our proposed multi-perspective framework captures various details from multiple target summaries, which are lacking when trained on only a single reference summary. We make the following two observations:

1) Relationship between parameter and function distances in a Hilbert space: The proposed model summary explains the nontrivial relationship and how it affects optimization, while the other does not mention the relationship between the two distances.

2) Direct application of L distance to optimization: The single setting summary does not mention how the L distance can be applied directly to optimization, while the multiperspective provides this information.

One reviewer mentioned (1) in their summary, and the other mentioned (2), due to which both got included in our output. Now in the single reference setting, the model is trained against a single summary, and since it did not include (1) or (2) perspective, it never got included in the final summary. The multiperspective summary gives a more technical overview of the paper's methods and results, allowing the reader to gain a deeper understanding of the content and make a more informed evaluation. The use of technical terms and definitions also helps readers who need to become familiar with the field. The proposed Multi-Perspective Framework can provide context for different interpretations of summaries and determine what various reviewers consider important in the final summary. We also performed an error analysis to analyze where our model fails. We discovered that in the case of highly technical papers abundant with mathematical symbols, the model tends to generate somewhat incoherent summaries. Additionally, we found that if the paper's text, formatted using an automatic PDF parser, is not properly structured (e.g., disjointed sentences, unconnected words), the resultant summary tends to lack coherence.

5   Conclusion and Future Work

We addressed an interesting problem of multiperspective summarization of scientific papers by proposing an end-to-end extractive and abstractive architecture. Our results, based on automated and human evaluations, suggest that this architecture performs better than other comparable systems in addressing this task. We found that the extractive summarization technique, which extracts the paper's contributions, assists in this task. The results of the experiment and analysis indicate that considering the reviewers' multiperspective views enhances the summary's quality and results in improved performance compared to utilizing just one perspective. In the future, we plan to identify other features (such as section information) apart from the paper's contribution to improving the performance.

Acknowledgment. Sandeep Kumar acknowledges the Prime Minister Research Fellowship (PMRF) program of the Govt of India for its support. Asif Ekbal acknowledges the Young Faculty Research Fellowship (YFRF), supported by Visvesvaraya PhD scheme for Electronics and IT, Ministry of Electronics and Information Technology (MeitY), Government of India, being implemented by Digital India Corporation (formerly Media Lab Asia).

References

1. Akkasi, A.: Multi perspective scientific document summarization with graph attention networks (GATS). In: Proceedings of the Third Workshop on Scholarly Document Processing, pp. 268–272. Association for Computational Linguistics, Gyeongju (2022). https://aclanthology.org/2022.sdp-1.33

2. Arora, H., Ghosal, T., Kumar, S., Patwal, S., Gooch, P.: INNOVATORS at SemEval-2021 task-11: a dependency parsing and bert-based model for extracting contribution knowledge from scientific papers. In: Palmer, A., Schneider, N., Schluter, N., Emerson, G., Herbelot, A., Zhu, X. (eds.) Proceedings of the 15th International Workshop on Semantic Evaluation, SemEval@ACL/IJCNLP 2021, Virtual Event / Bangkok, Thailand, 5–6 August 2021, pp. 502–510. Association for Computational Linguistics (2021). https://doi.org/10.18653/v1/2021.semeval-1.61

3. Auer, S., et al.: Improving access to scientific literature with knowledge graphs. Bibliothek Forschung Praxis **44**(3), 516–529 (2020). https://doi.org/10.1515/bfp-2020-2042

4. Cao, M.: A survey on neural abstractive summarization methods and factual consistency of summarization. CoRR abs/2204.09519 (2022). https://doi.org/10.48550/arXiv.2204.09519

5. Cao, Z., Wei, F., Li, S., Li, W., Zhou, M., Wang, H.: Learning summary prior representation for extractive summarization. In: Proceedings of the 53rd Annual Meeting of the Association for Computational Linguistics and the 7th International Joint Conference on Natural Language Processing (Volume 2: Short Papers), pp. 829–833. Association for Computational Linguistics, Beijing (2015). https://doi.org/10.3115/v1/P15-2136, https://aclanthology.org/P15-2136

6. Chandrasekaran, M.K., Feigenblat, G., Hovy, E.H., Ravichander, A., Shmueli-Scheuer, M., de Waard, A.: Overview and insights from the shared tasks at scholarly document processing 2020: CL-SciSumm, LaySumm and LongSumm. In: Chandrasekaran, M.K., et al. (eds.) Proceedings of the First Workshop on Scholarly Document Processing, SDP@EMNLP 2020, Online, 19 November 2020, pp. 214–224. Association for Computational Linguistics (2020). https://doi.org/10.18653/v1/2020.sdp-1.24

7. Cheng, J., Lapata, M.: Neural summarization by extracting sentences and words. In: Proceedings of the 54th Annual Meeting of the Association for Computational Linguistics (Volume 1: Long Papers), pp. 484–494. Association for Computational Linguistics, Berlin (2016). https://doi.org/10.18653/v1/P16-1046, https://aclanthology.org/P16-1046

8. Chung, J., Gülçehre, Ç., Cho, K., Bengio, Y.: Empirical evaluation of gated recurrent neural networks on sequence modeling. CoRR abs/1412.3555 (2014). http://arxiv.org/abs/1412.3555

9. Cohan, A., et al.: A discourse-aware attention model for abstractive summarization of long documents. In: Walker, M.A., Ji, H., Stent, A. (eds.) Proceedings of the 2018 Conference of the North American Chapter of the Association for Computational Linguistics: Human Language Technologies, NAACL-HLT, New Orleans, Louisiana, USA, 1–6 June 2018, Volume 2 (Short Papers), pp. 615–621. Association for Computational Linguistics (2018). https://doi.org/10.18653/v1/n18-2097

10. Cohan, A., Feigenblat, G., Ghosal, T., Shmueli-Scheuer, M.: Overview of the first shared task on multi perspective scientific document summarization (MuP). In: Cohan, A., et al. (eds.) Proceedings of the Third Workshop on Scholarly Document Processing, SDP@COLING 2022, Gyeongju, Republic of Korea, 12–17 October 2022, pp. 263–267. Association for Computational Linguistics (2022). https:// aclanthology.org/2022.sdp-1.32

11. Cohan, A., Goharian, N.: Scientific document summarization via citation contextualization and scientific discourse. Int. J. Digit. Libr. **19**(2–3), 287–303 (2018). https://doi.org/10.1007/s00799-017-0216-8

12. D'Souza, J., Auer, S., Pedersen, T.: SemEval-2021 task 11: NLPContribution-Graph - structuring scholarly NLP contributions for a research knowledge graph. In: Proceedings of the 15th International Workshop on Semantic Evaluation (SemEval-2021), pp. 364–376. Association for Computational Linguistics, Online (2021). https://doi.org/10.18653/v1/2021.semeval-1.44, https://aclanthology.org/2021.semeval-1.44

13. Elkiss, A., Shen, S., Fader, A., Erkan, G., States, D.J., Radev, D.R.: Blind men and elephants: what do citation summaries tell us about a research article? J. Assoc. Inf. Sci. Technol. **59**(1), 51–62 (2008). https://doi.org/10.1002/asi.20707

14. Erera, S., et al.: A summarization system for scientific documents. In: Padó, S., Huang, R. (eds.) Proceedings of the 2019 Conference on Empirical Methods in Natural Language Processing and the 9th International Joint Conference on Natural Language Processing, EMNLP-IJCNLP 2019, Hong Kong, China, 3–7 November 2019 - System Demonstrations, pp. 211–216. Association for Computational Linguistics (2019). https://doi.org/10.18653/v1/D19-3036

15. Erkan, G., Radev, D.R.: LexRank: graph-based lexical centrality as salience in text summarization. CoRR abs/1109.2128 (2011). http://arxiv.org/abs/1109.2128

16. Ghosh Roy, S., Pinnaparaju, N., Jain, R., Gupta, M., Varma, V.: Summaformers @ LaySumm 20, LongSumm 20. In: Proceedings of the First Workshop on Scholarly Document Processing, pp. 336–343. Association for Computational Linguistics, Online (2020). https://doi.org/10.18653/v1/2020.sdp-1.39, https://aclanthology.org/2020.sdp-1.39

17. Gidiotis, A., Stefanidis, S., Tsoumakas, G.: AUTH @ CLSciSumm 20, LaySumm 20, LongSumm 20. In: Proceedings of the First Workshop on Scholarly Document Processing, pp. 251–260. Association for Computational Linguistics, Online (2020). https://doi.org/10.18653/v1/2020.sdp-1.28, https://aclanthology.org/2020.sdp-1.28

18. Gupta, K., Ahmad, A., Ghosal, T., Ekbal, A.: ContriSci: a BERT-based multitasking deep neural architecture to identify contribution statements from research papers. In: Ke, H.-R., Lee, C.S., Sugiyama, K. (eds.) ICADL 2021. LNCS, vol. 13133, pp. 436–452. Springer, Cham (2021). https://doi.org/10.1007/978-3-030-91669-5_34

19. Harman, D., Over, P.: The effects of human variation in DUC summarization evaluation. In: Text Summarization Branches Out, pp. 10–17. Association for Computational Linguistics, Barcelona (2004). https://aclanthology.org/W04-1003

20. Hermann, K.M., et al.: Teaching machines to read and comprehend. CoRR abs/1506.03340 (2015). http://arxiv.org/abs/1506.03340

21. Hirsch, E., et al.: iFacetSum: coreference-based interactive faceted summarization for multi-document exploration. In: Adel, H., Shi, S. (eds.) Proceedings of the 2021 Conference on Empirical Methods in Natural Language Processing: System Demonstrations, EMNLP 2021, Online and Punta Cana, Dominican Republic, 7–11 November 2021, pp. 283–297. Association for Computational Linguistics (2021). https://doi.org/10.18653/v1/2021.emnlp-demo.33

22. Jaidka, K., Kumar Chandrasekaran, M., Rustagi, S., Kan, M.Y.: Overview of the CL-SciSumm 2016 shared task. In: Proceedings of the Joint Workshop on Bibliometric-enhanced Information Retrieval and Natural Language Processing for Digital Libraries (BIRNDL), pp. 93–102 (2016). https://aclanthology.org/W16-1511

23. Kim, S.: Using pre-trained transformer for better lay summarization. In: Proceedings of the First Workshop on Scholarly Document Processing, pp. 328–335. Association for Computational Linguistics, Online (2020). https://doi.org/10.18653/v1/2020.sdp-1.38, https://aclanthology.org/2020.sdp-1.38

24. Kumar, S., Kohli, G.S., Shinde, K., Ekbal, A.: Team AINLPML @ MuP in SDP 2021: scientific document summarization by end-to-end extractive and abstractive approach. In: Proceedings of the Third Workshop on Scholarly Document Processing, pp. 285–290. Association for Computational Linguistics, Gyeongju (2022). https://aclanthology.org/2022.sdp-1.36

25. Lin, J., Ling, J., Wang, Z., Liu, J., Chen, Q., He, L.: ECNUICA at SemEval-2021 task 11: rule based information extraction pipeline. In: Proceedings of the 15th International Workshop on Semantic Evaluation (SemEval-2021), pp. 1295–1302. Association for Computational Linguistics, Online (2021). https://doi.org/10.18653/v1/2021.semeval-1.185, https://aclanthology.org/2021.semeval-1.185

26. Liu, H., Sarol, M.J., Kilicoglu, H.: UIUC_BioNLP at SemEval-2021 task 11: a cascade of neural models for structuring scholarly NLP contributions. In: Palmer, A., Schneider, N., Schluter, N., Emerson, G., Herbelot, A., Zhu, X. (eds.) Proceedings of the 15th International Workshop on Semantic Evaluation, SemEval@ACL/IJCNLP 2021, Virtual Event/Bangkok, Thailand, 5–6 August 2021, pp. 377–386. Association for Computational Linguistics (2021). https://doi.org/10.18653/v1/2021.semeval-1.45

27. Liu, Y., Ni, A., Nan, L., Deb, B., Zhu, C., Awadallah, A.H., Radev, D.R.: Leveraging locality in abstractive text summarization. CoRR abs/2205.12476 (2022). https://doi.org/10.48550/arXiv.2205.12476

28. Lloret, E., Romá-Ferri, M.T., Palomar, M.: COMPENDIUM: a text summarization system for generating abstracts of research papers. Data Knowl. Eng. **88**, 164–175 (2013). https://doi.org/10.1016/j.datak.2013.08.005

29. Ma, X., Wang, J., Zhang, X.: YNU-HPCC at SemEval-2021 task 11: using a BERT model to extract contributions from NLP scholarly articles. In: Palmer, A., Schneider, N., Schluter, N., Emerson, G., Herbelot, A., Zhu, X. (eds.) Proceedings of the 15th International Workshop on Semantic Evaluation, SemEval@ACL/IJCNLP 2021, Virtual Event/Bangkok, Thailand, 5–6 August 2021, pp. 478–484. Association for Computational Linguistics (2021). https://doi.org/10.18653/v1/2021.semeval-1.58

30. Martin, A., Pedersen, T.: Duluth at SemEval-2021 task 11: applying deBERTa to contributing sentence selection and dependency parsing for entity extraction. In: Palmer, A., Schneider, N., Schluter, N., Emerson, G., Herbelot, A., Zhu, X. (eds.) Proceedings of the 15th International Workshop on Semantic Evaluation, SemEval@ACL/IJCNLP 2021, Virtual Event/Bangkok, Thailand, 5–6 August 2021, pp. 490–501. Association for Computational Linguistics (2021). https://doi.org/10.18653/v1/2021.semeval-1.60

31. Mishra, S.K., Kundarapu, H., Saini, N., Saha, S., Bhattacharyya, P.: IITP-AI-NLP-ML@ CL-SciSumm 2020, CL-LaySumm 2020, LongSumm 2020. In: Proceedings of the First Workshop on Scholarly Document Processing, pp. 270–276. Association for Computational Linguistics, Online (2020). https://doi.org/10.18653/v1/2020.sdp-1.30, https://aclanthology.org/2020.sdp-1.30

32. Nakov, P., Schwartz, A.S., Hearst, M.A.: Citances: citation sentences for semantic analysis of bioscience text (2004)

33. Nallapati, R., Zhou, B., dos Santos, C.N., Gülçehre, Ç., Xiang, B.: Abstractive text summarization using sequence-to-sequence RNNs and beyond. In: Goldberg, Y., Riezler, S. (eds.) Proceedings of the 20th SIGNLL Conference on Computational Natural Language Learning, CoNLL 2016, Berlin, Germany, 11–12 August 2016, pp. 280–290. ACL (2016). https://doi.org/10.18653/v1/k16-1028

34. Parveen, D., Ramsl, H.M., Strube, M.: Topical coherence for graph-based extractive summarization. In: Proceedings of the 2015 Conference on Empirical Methods in Natural Language Processing, pp. 1949–1954. Association for Computational Linguistics, Lisbon (2015). https://doi.org/10.18653/v1/D15-1226, https://aclanthology.org/D15-1226

35. Qazvinian, V., et al.: Generating extractive summaries of scientific paradigms. CoRR abs/1402.0556 (2014). http://arxiv.org/abs/1402.0556

36. Reddy, S., Saini, N., Saha, S., Bhattacharyya, P.: IIITBH-IITP@CL-SciSumm20, CL-LaySumm20, LongSumm20. In: Proceedings of the First Workshop on Scholarly Document Processing, pp. 242–250. Association for Computational Linguistics, Online (2020). https://doi.org/10.18653/v1/2020.sdp-1.27, https://aclanthology.org/2020.sdp-1.27

37. Shailabh, S., Chaurasia, S., Modi, A.: KnowGraph@IITK at SemEval-2021 task 11: building knowledge graph for NLP research. In: Palmer, A., Schneider, N., Schluter, N., Emerson, G., Herbelot, A., Zhu, X. (eds.) Proceedings of the 15th International Workshop on Semantic Evaluation, SemEval@ACL/IJCNLP 2021, Virtual Event/Bangkok, Thailand, 5–6 August 2021, pp. 467–477. Association for Computational Linguistics (2021). https://doi.org/10.18653/v1/2021.semeval-1.57

38. Sotudeh, S., Goharian, N.: GUIR @ MuP 2022: towards generating topic-aware multi-perspective summaries for scientific documents. In: Proceedings of the Third Workshop on Scholarly Document Processing, pp. 273–278. Association for Computational Linguistics, Gyeongju (2022). https://aclanthology.org/2022.sdp-1.34

39. Subramanian, S., Li, R., Pilault, J., Pal, C.J.: On extractive and abstractive neural document summarization with transformer language models. CoRR abs/1909.03186 (2019). http://arxiv.org/abs/1909.03186

40. Urlana, A., Surange, N., Shrivastava, M.: LTRC @MuP 2022: multi-perspective scientific document summarization using pre-trained generation models. In: Proceedings of the Third Workshop on Scholarly Document Processing, pp. 279–284. Association for Computational Linguistics, Gyeongju (2022). https://aclanthology.org/2022.sdp-1.35

41. Vaswani, A., et al.: Attention is all you need. In: Guyon, I., et al. (eds.) Advances in Neural Information Processing Systems 30: Annual Conference on Neural Information Processing Systems 2017, 4–9 December 2017, Long Beach, CA, USA, pp. 5998–6008 (2017). https://proceedings.neurips.cc/paper/2017/hash/3f5ee243547dee91fbd053c1c4a845aa-Abstract.html

42. Vaswani, A., et al.: Attention is all you need. CoRR abs/1706.03762 (2017). http://arxiv.org/abs/1706.03762

43. Yasunaga, M., et al.: ScisummNet: a large annotated corpus and content-impact models for scientific paper summarization with citation networks. In: Proceedings of AAAI 2019 (2019)

44. Zechner, K.: Fast generation of abstracts from general domain text corpora by extracting relevant sentences. In: 16th International Conference on Computational Linguistics, Proceedings of the Conference, COLING 1996, Center for Sprogteknologi, Copenhagen, Denmark, 5–9 August 1996, pp. 986–989 (1996). https://aclanthology.org/C96-2166/

45. Zhang, G., Su, Y., He, C., Lin, L., Sun, C., Shan, L.: ITNLP at SemEval-2021 task 11: boosting BERT with sampling and adversarial training for knowledge extraction. In: Proceedings of the 15th International Workshop on Semantic Evaluation (SemEval-2021), pp. 485–489. Association for Computational Linguistics, Online (2021). https://doi.org/10.18653/v1/2021.semeval-1.59, https://aclanthology.org/2021.semeval-1.59

Author Index

Printed in the United States
by Baker & Taylor Publisher Services